THE RHETORIC OF
CULTURAL DIALOGUE

PETER R. LI

PETER R. ERSPAMER

Cultural Memory
in
the
Present

Mieke Bal and Hent de Vries, Editors

THE RHETORIC OF
CULTURAL DIALOGUE

*Jews and Germans from Moses Mendelssohn
to Richard Wagner and Beyond*

Jeffrey S. Librett

STANFORD UNIVERSITY PRESS

STANFORD, CALIFORNIA

Stanford University Press
Stanford, California
© 2000 by the Board of Trustees of the
Leland Stanford Junior University

Printed in the United States of America

Library of Congress Cataloging-in-Publication Data
Librett, Jeffrey S.
    The rhetoric of cultural dialogue : Jews and Germans from Moses
Mendelssohn to Richard Wagner and beyond / Jeffrey S. Librett.
        p.   cm.—(Cultural memory in the present)
    Includes bibliographical references (p.) and index.
    ISBN 0-8047-3622-7 (alk. paper)—ISBN 0-8047-3931-5 (pbk. : alk. paper)
    1. Jews—Germany—History—1800–1933.   2. Jews—Germany—Intellectual
life—18th century.   3. Jews—Germany—Intellectual life—19th century.
4. Germany—Civilization—Jewish influences.   5. Germany—Ethnic relations.
6. Judaism—Relations—Christianity.   7. Christianity and other religions—
Judaism.   8. Jews—Cultural assimiliation—Germany.   I. Title.   II. Series.
DS135.G32 L53   2000
943'.004924—dc21   00-055707

Original printing 2000

Last figure below indicates year of this printing:
09 08 07 06 05 04 03 02 01 00

Typeset by BookMatters in 11/13.5 Adobe Garamond

For Dawn and Malachi and Sasha

Acknowledgments

Chapter 6 appeared in a much shorter, and quite different, form as "Writing (as) the Perverse Body in Friedrich Schlegel's *Lucinde*," in Juliet Flower MacCannell and Laura Zakarin, eds., *Thinking Bodies* (Stanford, Calif.: Stanford University Press, 1994), 132–40.

I would thank Peter U. Hohendahl, Werner Hamacher, Winfried Menninghaus, and Götz Braun for introducing me, once upon a time, to the questions posed today by the literature and philosophy of the German Enlightenment and Romantic epochs. I am grateful to Loyola University Chicago for supporting the initial research for this book in the form of a research leave in 1992–1993, for granting me a summer research award in 1996 in order to continue work on the manuscript, and for supporting the inclusion of images through a subvention award. I am indebted more specifically to my colleagues in the Department of Modern Languages and Literatures, as well as in the Departments of English Literature and Philosophy, who have warmly supported my work on this project and patiently awaited its results. Without such support and patience, life would have been a good bit more difficult than it has been. I am grateful further to the following individuals, who have read and responded to various chapters in the manuscript or otherwise discussed this work with me along the way: Willy Apollon, Hartmut Böhme, Edward Breuer, Anne Callahan, Andrew Cutrofello, Wiley Feinstein, Nikolai Hormers, Juliet F. MacCannell, David Martyn, Andrew McKenna (whose help on proposal and chapter drafts was invaluable), Janice Mouton, David Posner, Mark Redfield, Tom Reinert, the members of the Chicago German Studies Circle (notably, Peter D. Fenves, Sander L. Gilman, Helmut Müller-Sievers, and Géza von Molnár), John Stopford, Robert Stockhammer, and

Liliane Weissberg. Thanks for research assistance go to Aaron Bunch, Matt Longo, and David Williams. Much appreciation is also due to Helen Tartar and Kate Warne of Stanford University Press for the sensitivity, intelligence, and patience they have brought to the publication process. Finally, more thanks than are sayable are due to Dawn Marlan for her constant support of this project, her critical responses to the work, and so much more, and to Malachi and Sasha for serving as constant reminders of what is important.

J.S.L.

Contents

Illustrations

Preface: What This Book Is About

I deny that there has ever been . . . a German-Jewish dialogue in any genuine sense whatsoever, i.e., *as a historical phenomenon*. It takes two to have a dialogue, who listen to each other, who are prepared to perceive the other as what he is and represents, and to respond to him. Nothing can be more misleading than to apply such a concept to the discussions between Germans and Jews during the last 200 years. This dialogue died at its very start and never took place. It died when the successors of Moses Mendelssohn—who still argued from the perspective of some kind of Jewish totality, even though the latter was determined by the concepts of the Enlightenment—acquiesced in abandoning this wholeness in order to salvage an existence for pitiful pieces of it, whose recently popular designation as German-Jewish symbiosis reveals its whole ambiguity. To be sure, the Jews attempted a dialogue with the Germans, starting from all possible points of view and situations, demandingly, imploringly, and entreatingly, servile and defiant, with a dignity employing all manner of tones and a godforsaken lack of dignity, and today, when the symphony is over, the time may be ripe for studying their motifs and for attempting a critique of their tones. No one, not even one who always grasped the hopelessness of this cry into the void, will belittle the latter's passionate intensity and the tones of hope and grief that were in resonance with it. The attempt of the Jews to explain themselves to the Germans and to put their own creativity at their disposal, even to the point of complete self-abandonment [*Selbstaufgabe*], is a significant phenomenon, the analysis of which in adequate categories is yet to be accomplished and will perhaps become possible only now that it is at an end. In all this I am unable to perceive anything of a dialogue. . . . Where Germans ventured on a discussion with Jews in a humane spirit, such a discussion, from Wilhelm von Humboldt to Stefan George, was always based on the expressed or unexpressed self-abandonment [*Selbstaufgabe*] of the Jews.   —Gershom Scholem[1]

The Church Fathers often justify the figural interpretation on the basis of certain passages in early Christian writings, mostly from the Pauline Epistles. . . . Those

passages in the Pauline Epistles which contain figural interpretations were almost all written in the course of Paul's bitter struggle in behalf of his mission among the Gentiles; many are answers to the attacks and persecutions of the Judaeo-Christians; nearly all are intended to strip the Old Testament of its normative character and show that *it is merely a shadow of things to come*. His whole figural interpretation was subordinated to the basic Pauline theme of grace versus law, faith versus works: the old law is *annulled*; it is *shadow* and *typos*; observance of it has become useless and even harmful since Christ made his sacrifice; a Christian is justified not by works in observance of the law, but by faith; and in its Jewish and Judaistic sense *the Old Testament is the letter that kills, while the new Christians are servants of the new covenant, of the spirit that gives life*. This was Paul's doctrine, and the former Pharisee and disciple of Gamaliel looked eagerly in the Old Testament for passages in support of it. As a whole it ceased for him to be a book of the law and history of Israel and became from beginning to end a promise and prefiguration of Christ, in which there is no definitive meaning [*endgültige Bedeutung*], but only a prophetic meaning [*Vorbedeutung*] which has now been fulfilled, in which everything is written "for our sakes." (I Cor. 9:10, cf. Rom. 15:4). . . . It was not until very late, probably not until after the Reformation, that Europeans began to regard the Old Testament as Jewish history and Jewish law.
—Erich Auerbach[2]

This book takes as its historical topic the problematic relationship, or "dialogue," between Jews and Christian—Protestant and Catholic—Germans in the period of the so-called *emancipation*. The period of emancipation is generally seen as extending from the beginning of the discussion of the possible "civic improvement" of the Jews around 1781, when Christian Wilhelm Dohm's treatise *Über die bürgerliche Verbesserung der Juden* (*On the Civic Improvement of the Jews*) was published, to 1871, when civil rights were finally (if only for a short while) granted to all Jews within Bismarck's Second Empire. In this study, I represent and attempt to render in a new way at least translucent, if not—for reasons of principle that will emerge in what follows—absolutely transparent, the position strikingly stated by Gershom Scholem in the famous passage cited above: despite certain appearances, there never was a dialogue between Jews and Germans.

How is one to "understand," beyond the limits of Scholem's important but still explicitly provisional analysis, this failure of any Jewish-German dialogue to have materialized, despite the German Jews' active participation in, and increasingly radical assimilation into, German culture from the late eighteenth century on? First of all, in my view one must, by an apparent paradox, situate this failure within a world in which *all* dialogue remains marked by a certain impossibility. (The phrase "the rhetoric of dialogue" in my title refers on one level, accordingly, to the *mere* "rhetoric" of dialogue, in the sense of false or sophistical claims to the achievement of a dialogue one has not achieved and cannot achieve.) A few words, then, on dialogue and its impossibility before moving forward. By "dialogue" I understand here what I take to be the commonsense notion of dialogue, which is also that for which the hermeneutic tradition (from Friedrich Schleiermacher to Wilhelm Dilthey to Martin Buber to Hans-Georg Gadamer and Paul Ricoeur) attempts to provide one or another type of philosophical foundation: the symmetrical exchange of expressions of intention between dyadic partners, to the end of mutual and nonviolent understanding.[3] According to our most common conceptions of such exchange, which are deeply embedded in the history of Western metaphysics, the symmetry of a reciprocal relationship between equal partners guarantees both the nonviolence of this relationship and the possibility of true, mutual understanding. Violence—the exercise of force or power prior to the determination of truth—would prevent understanding; conversely nonunderstanding would entail at least the virtual violence implied by the disfiguration of the other's intentions. Therefore, nonviolence and true understanding must be simultaneously secured. The proponents of hermeneutic dialogue accordingly assume that, through the symmetry of reciprocal exchange, power is harmonized with truth insofar as truth takes on the powerless power that results from its legitimate and nonviolent triumph over nontruth (or misunderstanding). What, then, is the "impossibility" by which I consider such dialogue—whether it takes place between individuals or between cultures viewed as, or represented by, individuals—to remain forever marked?

Most briefly and thetically, there is no understanding that does not pass by way of violence, the violence of the reduction of the other to the self, the reduction of the different to the self-same, which is always an effect of force. Hence, as writers such as Emmanuel Levinas, Jacques Lacan, Jacques Derrida, and Paul de Man have argued in various ways, there is no understanding that is not misunderstanding. The reciprocal exchange of hermeneutic dialogue will always simply redouble and perpetuate the violence of the misunderstanding of the other. The resultant mutual violence may be that of counterbalancing forces, a violence which holds itself in check or fails to appear as such, and it may seem or be, in a given instance, a violence of extremely small proportions producing negligible effects, but it is not less a matter of violence merely because it can appear in micrological or minimal ways. This violence, which is always overlooked or denegated by the representatives of hermeneutics (and regardless of whether hermeneutics explicitly presents itself in a commonsensical, philological-methodological, or mystical guise), affects the project of nonviolent dialogue with a certain impossibility. Further, the impossibility of nonviolent dialogue applies not only to individual exchange but also to the cultural exchange with which it is interdependent. The rhetoric of intercultural dialogue, too, infinitely postpones and prevents the nonviolent dialogue whose accomplishment it means to serve. Or, to adapt for a moment the Lacanian dictum on the binary opposition of the sexes to the question of intercultural relationships: there is no cultural relation. Less one-sidedly and more precisely, the cultural relation is a relation without relation. I would affirm the humanistic goal of intercultural "understanding" to the degree that identity politics risks repeating the violent embarrassments of revealed religion (illegitimate universalization and absolutization of this or that cultural particularity and relativity). One of the main polemical/theoretical implications of this study, however, is that the attainment of this goal requires not so much the emphatic defense, but rather the radical transformative critique—the affirmation of the relentless self-interruption—of dialogical rhetoric and of the notion of "understanding" with which it is allied.

If dialogue is always impossible, or doubly violent, then what distinguishes the absence of Jewish-German dialogue from the absence of dialogue in general? Doesn't the claim that there is no nonviolent cultural dialogue tend to legitimate, in the most untenable manner to say the least, precisely the kinds of violent exclusion of which the Holocaust is perhaps the most extreme example in human history? Obviously, I think not. Indeed the following pages are based on the hypothesis or wager that the only way to grasp the specificity of the historical nondialogue between Jews and Germans is by placing it within the endless context of the general nondialogicity of which this singular nondialogue is at once a particularization and a particularly massive denegation. The difference between the Jewish-German nonrelation (or dialogue) specifically and nonrelation in general is that the Jewish-German nonrelation is established and maintained by German Christianity (on the levels of both theology and its attendant institutional-discursive structures) as a legitimate *asymmetry*—

indeed, a divinely sanctioned one—making up only half of the dialogical nonrelation. That is, there is no direct *reciprocality* of the violence of interpretation in this case. For Christianity has always viewed itself as the ultimate meaning or speech of the silent or dumb utterance that is Judaism. As I consider in more detail in the Introduction with reference to Erich Auerbach's "Figura," Jews have been associated, since at least St. Paul, with the prefigural, dead letter of the law, while German Christianity has associated German Christians with the literal, living spirit of faith that realizes this law. The Jews have represented the uncannily mechanical body of language (and so also the mechanical language of the body), while Christians have played the role of the sole organic animation of that mechanical, dead language-body (or body-language). In short, Jews have been denied, by the very structure of the Jewish-Christian relation since St. Paul, the right to interpret the speech of Christians, and Christians have reserved for themselves alone the right to speak the truth of Jewish writing. Therefore, the only position for the Jew within Christian discourse is that of having always already been comprehended by that discourse; the Jew can never be recognized as one capable of comprehending the Christian in turn. By the same token, Christians have been obliged to construct Christian speech on the foundations of, and precisely as a response to, Jewish writing. In this sense, the right of Christendom to a monopoly on the violence of interpretation within the Judaeo-Christian framework has always been limited— undermined—from within by the necessity under which Christendom stands of exercising this violence. Christendom is dependent upon its slave for its sovereignty; thus, it is ruled by that slave in turn. This is a situation from which Christendom can only attempt to free itself anew by continually imposing itself, with ever-renewed violence, on its slave, Jewish discourse, which represents here the materiality of discourse as such. German Christian anti-Semitism consists therefore above all in the anxious desire to rid itself—either by absorption or by expulsion or by extermination—of the material figurality of language, the rhetoric or sophistry of non-self-comprehending speech that is associated with the Jew. In order to develop this thesis somewhat further before launching into the readings of texts from the epoch of emancipation that make up the body of this book, I undertake in the Introduction an explication of the implicit rhetorical and ontological presuppositions that structure (non)dialogue in general. (These presuppositions make up the second sense in which the phrase the "rhetoric of dialogue" in my title is to be understood.) On this basis, I am able to indicate—in terms, but also beyond the limits, of both Scholem and Auerbach—the precise rhetorical and ontological shape of Jewish-German (non)dialogue specifically, first in its medieval form and then in its Reformation, Enlightenment, and Romantic forms.

Before sketching briefly the trajectory of the readings that follow in the body of the text, however, a word should be said about the period on which the study focuses. If Jewish-German dialogue is impossible from the start, then why have I concentrated on the historical period of the so-called emancipation? The epoch of emancipation extends from the first public deliberations (in the late eighteenth century) concerning the possibility of granting full civilian status to the Jews in the German principalities to the granting of these rights under Bismarck.[4] This period in the history of Jewish-German (non)relations was called into existence by the rise of Enlightenment humanism and universalism in combination with the absolutist state, and it continued up to the period of (anti)decadent post-Romanticism and the age of capital in the late nineteenth century. It is generally taken to represent a kind of "high point" in the relations between Jews and Christians in Germany. Prior to this period there was relatively little intimate contact between the Jewish and Christian worlds in Germany. Afterward anti-Semitism in its modern and ultimately racialist form became particularly virulent. But at the beginning of this period, the manifold pressures toward the theological and/or political unification of the faiths induced some of the more advanced philosophical and literary minds in the German principalities (such as Lessing and Mendelssohn) to raise questions on two related levels. First, in favor of natural theology or rational metaphysics, they questioned in new ways the specificities of positive religions and so the limits of the Jewish-Christian relation. Second, and consequently, they were compelled to place in question the constellation of ontological and rhetorical concepts of (Jewish-Christian) dialogue that underlied that relation. For these reasons, it is particularly illuminating to read texts from the epoch of emancipation if one wishes to gain a glimpse of the rhetorical-ontological structures of both dialogue in general and Jewish-German dialogue in particular. The moment of greatest optimism concerning the *possibilities* for a modern Jewish-Christian dialogue in the German context—the moment from the Enlightenment through the early Romantic salon culture—provides, through an only apparent paradox, the clearest view through to the *impossibilities* from which those (on both sides) who attempted to achieve this dialogue were never able to free themselves.[5]

Having originally chosen for these reasons to focus on the epoch of emancipation, I have been compelled, of course, to investigate within this epoch the displacements of the rhetoric of Jewish-German dialogue in the passage from the Enlightenment (Part I) to the Romantic period (Part II) to the mid-nineteenth-century post-Romantic period (Part III). Within the period of the Enlightenment, first of all, it has been necessary further to distinguish between the forms taken by Jewish-German dialogue in the context of rationalist presuppositions, on the one hand (Chapter 1), and of irrationalist, *Sturm und Drang* presuppositions, on the other (Chapter 2). In the case of the passage from the Enlightenment/counter-Enlightenment period to the Romantic one, having expected to find only that the Enlightenment and Romanticism approached "the Jewish question" from two slightly different points of view, I was surprised to find something in fact much more significant: the turn from Enlightenment to Romanticism, the very genesis of the German Romantic discourse, is articulated to a great extent in terms of the rhetoric of Jewish-Christian dialogue as overdetermined by the rhetoric of the Catholic-Protestant dialogue it prefigures. And this has by no means been adequately clarified heretofore in the literature on the subject. The theory and practice—both aesthetic and social— of early German Romanticism have their genesis, I argue, in the confrontation of Jewish letter with Protestant spirit that the German Enlightenment prepares (Chapters 3 through 5). Further, the turn from early to late Romanticism, especially in its Neo-Catholic variant, is motivated, I suggest, by the continuing attempt to solve the problem of the Jewish-Protestant relation (Chapter 6). Having traced within Romanticism the passage from early to late, I describe the undoing of the emancipatory version of the rhetoric of Jewish-German dialogue in (anti)decadent post-Romantic discourses of the mid-nineteenth century (Chapters 7 and 8).

Thus, Part I traverses the tension between rationalism and irrationalism, while Part II traces the passage from aesthetic pantheism to its ostensible transcendence by Neo-Catholicism, as two versions of a synthesis of Jew with Christian qua feminine with masculine. Pursuing this development further, Part III concerns itself with the phantasms of the post-Romantic discourse of the mid-nineteenth century, the theopolitical horizon of which I characterize in terms of a renewal of Protestantism that is at once a renewal of paganism. Within this theopolitical horizon, Part III focuses on the common ideological ground shared by both left and right cultural-political programs for what I call the *reversal* of emancipation, that is, the emancipation of Germanic Europe from what appear, to a paranoid perspective, to be Europe's Jewish taskmasters.

In each of these sections, the book takes the form of a series of close readings of important texts by more or less canonical—if not all equally "major"—authors. The study limits itself to a small selection of authors who represent the most advanced or influential thinking on and around the question of the Jewish-Christian relationship in the epoch under consideration, and each chapter focuses on one or two principal texts. In this way, the book provides a synecdochic historiography of the discourse of Jewish-German emancipation. What is being partially graphed here is not simply the history of a *reality*, but the history of a relatively autonomous *discourse*, the discourse of Jewish-German emancipation, whose ontological modality is complex and uncertain, mixed of the fictional or merely possible and the real, the phantasmatic and the material, the necessary and the impossible, as we shall have ample opportunity to reconsider in the chapters that follow.

But let me telegraph somewhat further here the trajectory of this series of readings. Under the rubric of Enlightenment, I undertake detailed readings of two major philosophical texts by Moses Mendelssohn from the last phase of his career, texts that illustrate the manner in which he responds to the two principal countercurrents to his brand of Enlightened natural theology, namely, the rationalist and irrationalist variants of militant Protestantism (Chapters 1 and 2). I omit almost all discussion of the very complex case of Kant here, for reasons I spell out in the Introduction. For the period of Romanticism, I interpret five texts by Friedrich Schlegel of various sorts: literary-critical, philosophical, theological, and literary. Through these readings, I retrace and explain the development from his early Protestant and aestheticist-pantheist phase to his later Neo-Catholic phase (Chapters 3, 4, and 6). On my account, this development crystallizes around Schlegel's two successive interpretations of Lessing in 1797 and 1804, respectively, treatments of which open and close Part II. Further, I analyze in Part II a novel by Dorothea Mendelssohn-Veit-Schlegel (Chapter 5), which shows how she positions herself with respect to, and also contributes to, this gradual "Neo-Catholicizing" development. It is of some importance to these analyses in Part II, of course, that Dorothea is Moses Mendelssohn's daughter and becomes the wife of Friedrich Schlegel. Schlegel himself therefore must be understood in turn as having *chosen*— for discursive reasons that I try to clarify—to become the son-in-law of Moses Mendelssohn (a kind of Jewish double of Gotthold Ephraim Lessing), if some years after Mendelssohn's death. It is moreover not merely by chance that, in the course of her relationship with Schlegel, Dorothea converts first to Protestantism and then to Catholicism. These biographical constellations, too, I argue, must be retraced in terms of the illogical logic, or the philosophical rhetoric, of Jewish-German dialogue. Finally, to demarcate the (frighteningly proleptic) end of the emancipatory discourse on both left and right in the post-Romantic period, I analyze in Part III the essays on the Jews by Karl Marx and Richard Wagner (Chapters 7 and 8). In the Postscript, I sketch briefly the fate of the rhetoric of Judaeo-Christian dialogue in modernism, beyond the end of the emancipatory prospect, and close with a word on some current debates concerning Holocaust memory.

THE RHETORIC OF
CULTURAL DIALOGUE

Introduction

In the Preface, I quickly sketched out this book's topic, principal con-
tentions, and historical, authorial, and textual scope. Here, before launching into the detailed readings that comprise the book, I provide further theoretical and historical background by addressing the following questions.
First, what exactly is the rhetorical structure of hermeneutic dialogue, in
general, as commonly and commonsensically conceived? Second, what are
the ontological-modal dimensions of such dialogue and its component elements, and precisely how is the dimension of the impossibility of dialogue
situated with respect to its other ontological dimensions? Third, how is the
early Christian and medieval determination of the Jewish-Christian relation
to be understood in terms of our analysis of the rhetoric of dialogue? How
does the application of this analysis to the tradition of medieval "figural
interpretation" help us begin to grasp the ultimate failure of any Jewish-
German dialogue to occur? Fourth, so as to make the transition to the epoch
of emancipation, how and why is this Jewish-Christian relation displaced in
the passage from the medieval context, by way of the Lutheran Reformation, to the contexts of the German Enlightenment? Fifth, in what sense
and for what reasons does the Catholicizing German Romantic discourse
return—albeit in an irrevocably post-Enlightenment manner—to the
medieval form of the Jewish-Christian relation? Finally, and more briefly, in
what way does the overturning of Neo-Catholic Romanticism issue in the
reversal of the discourse of Jewish-German emancipation?

The Rhetoric of Dialogue

Let us take as our point of departure the text cited as the Preface's epigram, where in striking terms—indeed, in the most precise and courageously honest five pages I have ever read on the subject of Jewish-German relations—Scholem not only emphatically denies that there has ever been a Jewish-German dialogue but also has the wherewithal to acknowledge that he does not possess conceptual tools adequate to the comprehension of this phenomenon. In spite of his acknowledgment that the phenomenon of Jewish-German nondialogue remains to be understood, however, Scholem does provide here what seems on the face of it a perfectly reasonable, commonsensical definition of dialogue. I can therefore think of no better way of introducing the notion of dialogical rhetoric that I will pursue in the following chapters than by analyzing Scholem's definition of dialogue with a view to the rhetorical—and also the ontological—dimensions it presupposes, or of which it can be taken to be a figure.

Before beginning this analysis, I should say a brief word about the main sources on which it draws. The principal oppositions that guide the analysis—those between rhetoric and philosophy, figural and literal uses of language, figural transformation and persuasive power, material writing and spiritual speech—have comprised the extended focus of the work of Jacques Derrida and Paul de Man.[1] In the process of radicalizing and marginally exceeding the achievements of the phenomenological and structuralist traditions, Derrida, de Man, and students of their work have clarified at once the *centrality* of these binary oppositions to the history of Western philosophical and literary discourses and their extreme *instability*, the nonsituability of the borders between their binary poles. In a way that attempts to be accessible to readers with little or no familiarity with Derrida and de Man, I extend this work of clarification here by rendering even more explicit than they have anywhere done the ontorhetorical structure of hermeneutic dialogue and by broaching, as they certainly nowhere have even attempted, a historiography of Jewish-Christian (non)relations in ontorhetorical terms.[2]

For Scholem, then, dialogue is a matter of "two . . . who listen to each other, who are prepared to perceive the other as what he is and represents and to respond to him."[3] Let us assume for the sake of argument that Scholem is not reducing hermeneutics to a theory of sensuous perception and that therefore to "perceive" the other here is to understand the other, to *take on* the other in his or her own subjectively experienced *truth* (*wahrnehmen* is Scholem's word). Beyond this understanding, in order to dialogue with the other, I must "respond to" him or her ("erwidern") in some way. Thus, dialogue for Scholem is comprised of the mutual *understanding* (or recognition) and *response* of two independent subjects. This combination of understanding and response combines passive and active dimensions so as to give rise to a dialogical relationship of mutuality in which neither term does violence to the other, even if no transcendence of duality and separateness in an immediate unity is envisioned here, as in the mystical dialogical theory of Martin Buber, for example, which Scholem explicitly criticizes on more than one occasion.[4] According to Scholem's conception, in order to enter into dialogue with you, I must first strive to understand you, to take you as you give yourself. In this sense I must passively mould myself to your self-presentation. Secondly, however, I must also respond to you, and in this sense I must behave actively toward you. If I only strove to understand you, if I only took you for what you claim to be, if I let you establish unilaterally the terms of our transaction, then I would be allowing you to do violence to me, whereas if I responded to you prior to having understood you, then I would necessarily do violence to you, putting my own views inappropriately in the place of yours. In either case, monological violence would be the order of the day. And the same goes for your relationship to me. This, then, is the notion of ideal dialogue with which we begin.

What are the implicit rhetorical presuppositions—or what is the rhetorical correlate—of such a notion of dialogue? How can we translate the building blocks of this notion—self, other, understanding, and response—into rhetorical concepts? First, let us recall the most basic concepts with which rhetoric is concerned.

Insofar as rhetoric is concerned with the persuasive power of figural language, the fundamental distinction around which it turns is always some version of the distinction between literal and figural uses of language, proper and improper expressions, original or derivative meanings of verbal forms. In other words, the fundamental distinction around which rhetoric turns is nothing other than the distinction between itself and its opposite, philosophy, the distinction between the language of persuasion and that of proof, unjustified and justified linguistic-conceptual power, and therefore also nondialogical and dialogical communication. Rhetoric in this way paradoxically includes its opposite, philosophy, constitutively within itself.

Upon minimal reflexion, it is easy to see what role the distinction between figural and literal at the elliptical center of rhetoric implicitly plays in a commonsensical definition of dialogue such as the one Scholem provides (Figure 1). To take the other on the other's terms—or to "put myself in the other's place" (admittedly, an ambiguous formulation, but that will be part of my point here)—is to reduce my way of seeing things to his or hers: it is to make myself into a figural expression of the literal truth or literal expression represented by the other. Conversely, to respond to the other, to tell the other how I see things, to tell the other specifically how I view what the other views differently, is to make myself into the literal expression of the figural expression for which the other now stands. The commonsense notion of dialogue, then, stated in rhetorical terms, would be this: in dialogue, each partner functions both as the literality of the figurality of the other and as the figurality of the literality of the other. Dialogue is the interplay of two double translations: two interlocutors each regard themselves as translating both the other's figures into their own literal expressions and their own figures into the literal expressions of the other. Rhetorical concepts, in short, determine the status of self and other in the two substitutive relationships between self and other (viz. understanding and response) that together comprise the dialogical relation. Moreover, because dialogue is made up not only of what functions as literal language but also of what functions as figural language, dialogue is the dialogue of dialogue (or literal, philosophical, nonviolent language) with nondialogue (or figural, rhetorical, violent language). As rhetoric includes philosophy within itself, so dialogue (or philosophy) includes its binary opposite, nondialogue (or rhetoric), within itself.

The Ontological Status of (Rhetorically Mediated) Dialogue: Impossible, Unreal Necessity

Assuming that this is a "proper" rhetorical translation of the commonsensical notion of hermeneutic dialogue that, in terms of Scholem's formulation, we are taking as our point of departure, it is now necessary to ask ourselves the following (partially rhetorical) question: To what extent does such a notion of dialogue make sense? That is, to what extent is such

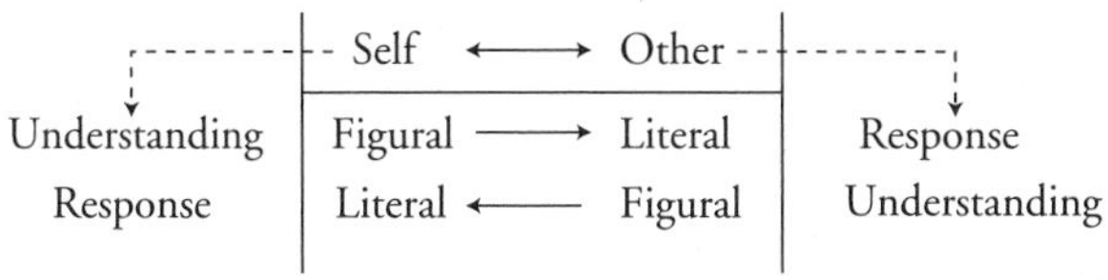

```
                    ┌── Self ◄──────► Other ──┐
         ┌──────────┘                          └──────────┐
         ▼          ┌──────────────────────────┐          ▼
Understanding       │ Figural ──────► Literal   │       Response
   Response         │ Literal ◄────── Figural   │    Understanding
                    └──────────────────────────┘
```

FIGURE 1. Dialogical Rhetoric

dialogue possible? Or more broadly and more to the point: On what modal-ontological register does dialogue take place? By what modal structures or concepts is it overdetermined?

To consider the question first in Scholem's hermeneutical terms, that is, in the terms of my interlocutor here: clearly, on the one hand, in order to perceive the other as "what he is and represents," I have to perceive the other to some extent in terms of what *I* perceive him to be. I cannot *understand* or recognize the other without to some extent already *responding* to the other, contributing something of my own to the mere perception of that other. Response therefore anticipates understanding and interferes with it. Response *prevents* and always already *interrupts* understanding, and it thus introduces violence into the claim to have understood.[5] On the other hand, of course, I cannot merely *respond* to the other without having my response appear to be already entangled in some kind of (however inadequate) *understanding* of the other even as it begins to take shape. I cannot tell the other how I view what he or she views differently without speaking to some kind of presupposed understanding of what he or she views differently and how he or she views it. Understanding *anticipates*, *interferes with*, and thus does violence to response. Therefore, the passivity of understanding the other never quite occurs because it is always interruptively infected by the activity of response; and the activity of response never quite occurs either, because it is always dragged down by the passive, receptive understanding of what it responds to. Dialogue is not simply the complementary, additive conjunction of understanding and response, passivity and activity, but it is this conjunction conjoined with the constitutive mutual interruption and violent undoing of the terms conjoined.[6] Dialogue consists neither of understanding nor of response and paradoxically both.

Before drawing the consequences of these considerations for the modal status of dialogue, let me restate them in "my own" rhetorical terms. On the one hand, in the movement of understanding, whenever I reduce myself to a figure of the other's literality, I unwittingly make my own figuration of that literality into the literal truth with respect to which that literality functions as a mere figure. That is, I unwittingly make the other into a mere figure for me, for my comprehensive understanding of the other. And on the other hand, in the movement of response, insofar as I attempt to reduce the other to a figure of my own literal truth, I cannot but function implicitly also as the mere derivative and approximative figure of the other's figure, which thereby confronts me as a literal expression or truth. The translation from figural to literal or from literal to figural, then, whichever way it is going (and whether it is going from me to you or from you to me), is constitutively interrupted by its supplementary reversal. The rhetoric of dialogue operates as its own continual disfiguration and de-literalization. Dialogue occurs not as the synthetic totalization of monological elements, but as the self-interrupting movement through which one monological substitution or translation is undermined by its converse, which is in the process of being undermined in turn. Dialogue is the violently self-undermining translation of literal into figural and of figural into literal, a process that extends, in principle, into infinity.

The implications of this analysis for the question of the possibility or impossibility of (rhetorical) dialogue—or more generally and precisely for the question of its ontological modality—are as follows. On the one hand, dialogue is *impossible* because each of its monological building blocks, the translative movements of understanding and response, without whose conjunction or synthesis dialogue cannot take place, is undone insofar as it occurs. Yet on the other hand, dialogue is *necessary* for the same reason, precisely because each of these monological movements is always interrupted, or dialogically undermined by its reversal, even as it occurs.[7] (And it occurs whenever we use language, even silently, since my language is always originally the language of an anonymous other with whom I must come to some sort of responsive understanding.) Being impossible, of course, dialogue is also unreal (for reality presupposes possibility), yet being necessary, it must be not only possible but also real. Dialogue, then, is neither possible nor impossible, and both, neither real nor unreal, and both, along the infinitely thin line of the necessity that measures the self-effacing distance between possibility and reality.[8]

Having adumbrated the sense in which dialogue is both impossible and necessary, taking place continually by means of its own interruption,

before concluding this discussion of modality and dialogue it is necessary
to consider briefly the ontological-modal statuses of the figural and literal
terms between which dialogue moves and of which it is unstably composed. To do so is necessary not only for the sake of situating this impossible necessity of dialogue more precisely but beyond this in order to lay the
"groundwork" for the discussion of Jewish-German dialogue in what follows. What, then, are the *modal concepts* that are attached to the *figural* and
the *literal* elements of the translations that (fail to) make up dialogue?
While continuing to explicate the implicit assumptions of the commonsensical notion of dialogue to which Scholem makes reference—to reveal,
as it were, the literal truth behind his figuration of dialogue—we can establish the following schematic coordinates. Depending on the orientation we
adopt at any given moment, we are forced, by the pre-Kantian metaphysics
in terms of which we still operate in so many ways, to assume either that
the real or that the possible constitutes the figural dimension (whether we
situate it in our own speech or in that of the other). Indeed, if figures of
speech are different from literal expressions, which we take to—transpar-
ently—convey their conceptual contents, either it is in the sense that figures
are more material, more heavy with the reality of imagery and feeling than
plain speech (or than the languages of philosophy or science), which materiality or weight we may or may not consider to be a good thing; or it is
because figures are more airy and ideal, more unreal, virtual, anticipatory,
or reminiscent than the literal, a "fact" which once again we may evaluate
positively or negatively. If we view the real (the materially existent) as the
figural, and the possible (the ideal or essential) as the literal, then we are
behaving ontorhetorically as idealists, rationalists, or essentialists, a behavior we register in such expressions as: "So your *meaning*, I take it, in *essence*,
is the following. . . ." In this case, we are granting a privilege to the purity
of essential possibility as the literal center and origin of things. If, to the
contrary, we view the possible as the figural, while determining the real as
the literal, then we are adopting the ontorhetorical position of realism,
empiricism, existentialism, or historicism, as we make evident by saying
things like: "So what you're *really* saying, in *effect*, is this . . . ," or "What
you're *actually referring* to is this. . . ."[9] Here, we take the "hard core" of
reality as our literal point of departure. The rhetoric of dialogue is always
further determined by these two different ontorhetorical configurations,
one of which defines at any given moment every one of the monological

substitutions of literal for figural or figural for literal by means of which the impossible necessity of dialogue plays itself out.[10]

But to take this reflexion one step further: if the rhetorical terms of figural and literal are always linked with the ontological terms of possible and real, respectively (or the reverse), then what are the ontological significations of figural and literal per se? Have they no ontological meaning already, even before being associated with the possible or the real? Do not "the figural" and "the literal" seem to carry ontological connotations of their own, prior to their correlation one way or another with "the possible" and "the real"? At least from the standpoint of nonpoetic discourses (that is, of all those discourses that privilege the literal), the figural is marked from the outset, whether it is subsequently overdetermined as possible or as real, by one or another kind of negativity or absence, by a lack of being, a nonbeing, a fictionality, an ornamental nonreality, and finally an incapacity to be: the figural is thus the *impossible*, that which cannot be (either possible or real), that which is incapable of (literal) being. The literal, in turn, again whether as possible or real, as ideal essence or material existence, enjoys the elevated status of positivity, presence, fullness of being, of that which is ultimately unavoidable, and so, it would seem, of the *necessary*, that which—literally—cannot *not* be (both possible and real).[11] Hence, when two interlocutors, neither of whom is merely either possible or real, either figural or literal, encounter one another hermeneutically in terms of the commonsensical concept of dialogue, the paradoxical mixture of necessity and impossibility characteristic of the dialogical relation comes to be, first of all, separated off from itself. Secondly, necessity and impossibility thus separated are then distributed, ideologically, in every instant of the dialogue, and in each of the interlocutors' discourses (or minds), one onto each of the interlocutors between whom the dialogue takes place. The *necessary presence* of dialogue can thereby appear to be secured, anchored, and purified, even if always fleetingly, in one of those interlocutors (whichever one is being implicitly designated as the *literal* at any given moment), while the *impossible absence* (the impossibility as the absence) of dialogue is sacrificially cast off onto, and along with, the other of the two interlocutors (that is, the one who is then functioning as the *figural*). In this way, the presence or more precisely the *necessity* of dialogue is always (ideologically, or if one prefers, rhetorically) identified with whatever subject is functioning as *literal* within it (a term which is always in principle shifting and open to the negotiation of power and meaning that is the dialogical process). And in its turn, the absence or rather the *impossibility* of dialogue is always (equally ideologically or figurally) identified with whatever subject is functioning there as the *figural*, whether this subject be me or you.

The Rhetoric of Jewish-Christian Dialogue

Now that we have examined the rhetorical components of hermeneutic dialogue and then adumbrated the ontological status of such dialogue as well as that of each of its rhetorical components, we are in a position to return to the more specific question of Jewish-German dialogue, beginning with Scholem's at once surprising and obvious verdict: this dialogue never took place. How must we understand what Scholem tells us about the failure of Jewish-German dialogue in particular, against the backdrop of the rhetoric of dialogue in its universal necessity-impossibility? Let us focus on Scholem's very simple main point in this text, which he elaborates in the two closely related texts published with it in the second volume of *Judaica*.[12] The Jews "attempted a dialogue with the Germans," Scholem writes, even to the point of self-abandonment (*Selbstaufgabe*), but the Germans did not attempt a dialogue in turn with the Jews. Rather, all of their attempts to deal with the Jews presupposed that Jews abandon themselves as Jews, that they commit a kind of cultural suicide. Now, in terms of our reading of Scholem's notion of dialogue so far, for the German Jews to attempt a dialogue with the (Christian) Germans to the point of self-abandonment is for them simply to devote themselves to the *understanding* of their interlocutor, to make themselves into the figure of their interlocutor's literal truth, without *responding* to him in turn by making themselves into the literal truth of that interlocutor's figure. For the Germans to demand the self-abandonment of the Jews as the condition of any "dialogue" is in turn (again in Scholem's terms) for them to refuse to do anything but *respond* to the Jews, without attempting to *understand* them in the first place. In our rhetorical translation, it is for the (Christian) Germans to posit themselves unilaterally as the literal truth of the Jews' figure, without entertaining the possibility that the Jews might be also the literal truth of what they, the (Christian) Germans, merely figurally represent.

While Scholem's presentation of the asymmetrical shape of Jewish-German (non)dialogue is to a great extent persuasive, adumbrating the *main contours* of the story, it does not quite tell the *whole* story. First of all, it is not possible, as the preceding analysis of the impossible necessity of dialogue makes clear, for the Jews simply to play figure to the Germans' literal truth. On the one hand, the Jews of Germany cannot avoid, to some extent, offering a novel reading of the German culture, responding to it, that is, reducing it to their own conception, which is influenced by their different cultural "origins," and also expecting some understanding in return (an expectation implied by their response itself). Those who emphasize the active dimension of the Jewish appropriation of, or response to, German culture, therefore, are not completely wrong. Indeed, painfully strange as it is to note, the Germans were in a certain sense right to distrust the Jewish assimilation, and not merely, as Scholem remarks, because they found such a self-abandonment spineless or lacking in principles, but also because they must have intermittently felt the self-subordination to be disingenuous, even if in most cases the more appropriate term, rather than *disingenuous*, would probably be simply *naïve*.[13] The extraordinary creativity and frequent brilliance of German Jewish contributions to a variety of cultural domains from the late eighteenth century on—from Moses Mendelssohn to Felix Mendelssohn, from Heinrich Heine to Karl Marx, from Karl Kraus to Franz Kafka, from Arnold Schönberg to Theodor Adorno, from Sigmund Freud to Walter Benjamin, from Alfred Einstein to Hannah Arendt, and on and on—bear ample witness to the fact that the Jewish self-assimilatory understanding and assumption of German culture comprised also a strong response. Nonetheless, that this response was either not capable of conceiving itself as such, or, where it was, not in a position in terms of social power to acknowledge this self-conception, and that this response was never or almost never received as such, except with hostility, gave this participation the character of a continuous disaster, as Scholem rightly insists, and not of some happily creative conjunction to be celebrated as "German-Jewish symbiosis."

Secondly, and conversely, we know that the Germans did not manage and could not have managed to be completely comfortable in the knowledge that they were the literal truth to which the Jewish figures were always already reduced. The simple reason for this is that, as we have shown above, any translation of a figure into its ostensibly literal meaning makes the literal meaning, the interpretation, appear also as a mere figure of the original figure it interprets, which henceforth takes on a literal coloration. Isn't all "secondary" literature, for example, a mere figure that pales by comparison to the literal presence of the works it treats, even though that secondary literature supposes itself to accomplish the restoration of the literal truth—be it as content or form, as historical reference or eternal meaning—of the figured "primary" works?[14] (As we shall reconsider in a moment, the New Testament defines itself in Paul as a kind of "secondary literature" on the Old.) Clearly, not all in Christian Germany can have been insensitive to this dialectic, even if they were not by and large consciously aware of it as such. Consequently, Christian Germany constituted a *passive* (mis)*understanding* of (and not only an *active response* to) Judaism, but disavowed whatever knowledge it had of this situation. Hence, the paranoid aggression Germany visited upon its Jews—and the more intensively the further assimilation progressed—in order to defend against all odds the belief that Christian Germany was the literal, but spiritual truth of which the Jews were, at an infinite and absolute distance, the mere figural anticipation. In terms of the privilege granted to spirit as active, subjective will over matter conceived as passive object by even the most modern metaphysics, to become passive is to become material, to become dead. And nobody likes to be dead, to imagine that they are dead.

But on what basis are the Christian Germans in the emancipatory epoch so certain, apart from unconsciously nagging self-doubts, that they are and have the right to play the role of the literal truth with respect to the figural nontruth of the Jews—a belief so apparently strong that even the Jews in modern Germany are in part tempted to share it? The answer is usefully condensed in the extremely important, even if at times somewhat confused essay by Erich Auerbach entitled "Figura," first published in 1939.[15] As Auerbach shows (although his explicit interest is not Jewish-German relations per se), and as is broadly known yet still rarely reflected upon, the reason why modern Germans feel they can play literal truth to the Jews' figures, and even feel they owe it to themselves and the world to do so is above all this: eighteen hundred years of Christendom are backing them up in the form of what is known as the figural interpretation of the scriptures. According to so-called figural interpretation (to which I shall refer here also as the prefiguration-fulfillment model), a practice of scriptural interpretation which begins with Paul and is developed further by the early church fathers, as Auerbach indicates, "the persons and events of the Old Testament [are] prefigurations of the New Testament and its history of salvation" (30), while the New Testament has the status of "fulfillment" (30) and "truth" (34 passim). As a result of the institutionalization of figural interpretation in the Christianized Roman Empire, Christians generally consider Jews, like the Old Testament, mere prefigurations, and themselves, like the New Testament, the literal fulfillment or truth of their prefigurative Jewish elders.[16] From the point of view of the Christian discourse, then, the Jews are figures, the Christians the literal truth.[17]

In spite of its formidable persuasive power and pervasive influence through our own day, however, this prefiguration-fulfillment model of Jewish-Christian relations is from the start marked by an extreme structural fragility that requires of those who would uphold this model an unerring commitment to the violent denegation of this very fragility.[18] As we have seen above, the passage from figural to literal is always reversible: the literal can always come to seem the mere figure of what figures it, which is henceforth rendered literal (or in any case, in a less narrowly dialogical structure, it can always come to seem the figure of something else, one knows not what).[19] In order to prepare for the chapters that follow, let us retrace the outlines of Auerbach's argument, attempting to track how this reversibility, this ineluctable recidivism of the literal into the fault of its immanent/ imminent figurality, repeatedly enters into Auerbach's analysis of figural interpretation, cutting against the grain of Auerbach's explicit thesis about *figura* in the Christian age. In this way, we will be enabled to glimpse the peculiar combination of persuasive power and hopelessness that characterizes the prefiguration-fulfillment model. While retracing Auerbach's steps, we will have to keep in mind the ontological analysis of the rhetoric of dialogue sketched above.[20]

Due to his realist prejudice, the dogmatic preference for concretion over abstraction, which as we shall see is also a symbolist prejudice, Auerbach looks unfavorably upon allegorical or spiritualist traditions.[21] Accordingly, he treats figural interpretation as the opposite of allegory, as if figuralism were realism, literalism, or symbolism:

Figura is something real and historical [*etwas Wirkliches, Geschichtliches*] which announces something else that is also real and historical. . . . Tertullian expressly denied that the literal and historical validity [*wörtliche und geschichtliche Geltung*] of the Old Testament was diminished by the figural interpretation [*Figuraldeutung*]. He was definitely hostile to spiritualism and refused to consider the Old Testament as mere allegory; according to him, it had real, literal meaning [*wörtlichen Wirklichkeitssinn*] throughout, and even where there was figural prophecy, the figure had just as much historical reality as what it prophesied. The prophetic figure, he believed, is a concrete historical fact [*sinnlich-geschichtliche Tatsache*], and it is fulfilled by concrete historical facts.[22]

And a bit further on, contrasting Tertullian with Origen, who is more allegorical than Tertullian, even though he is "far from being as abstractly allegorical as, for example, Philo" (36), Auerbach writes:

The difference between Tertullian's more historical and realistic interpretation and Origen's ethical, allegorical approach reflects a current conflict, known to us from other early Christian sources: one party strove to transform the events of the New and still more of the Old Testament into purely spiritual happenings, to "spirit away" their historical character—the other wished to preserve the full historicity of the Scriptures along with the deeper meaning. In the West the latter tendency was victorious, although the spiritualists always maintained a certain influence, as may be seen from the progress of the doctrine of the different meanings of Scripture; for while the adherents of this doctrine recognize the literal or historical sense, they sever its connection with the equally real prefiguration by setting up other, purely abstract interpretations beside or in place of the prefigural interpretation. St. Augustine played a leading part in the compromise between the two doctrines. On the whole he favored a living, figural interpretation, for his thinking was far too concrete and historical to content itself with pure abstract allegory. (36–37; 68–69)

Thus, figural interpretation is opposed to allegorical as concretion to abstraction, or as the living to the dead. What makes figural interpretation better than allegorical for Auerbach is that in the former, neither the figural nor the literal, neither the prefiguration nor its fulfillment, loses its reality. Indeed, Auerbach allows himself to go so far as to say (although he admits that he knows better) that the only place in figural interpretation for spirituality or ideality—that is, for pure possibility—is in the interpretation that binds together the reality of prefiguration with the reality of its fulfillment.[23] Moreover, Auerbach's desire to oppose figural interpretation to allegorical modes is so insistent that toward the end of the essay—despite the fact that, as we shall see, he has encountered along the way serious resistance to this model in the very empirical-historical "facts" of the tradition of figural interpretation—he still tries to uphold the opposition between figural and allegorical interpretation. This time he characterizes it in terms of an opposition between Christian and pagan:[24]

We may say roughly that the figural method in Europe goes back to Christian influences, while the allegorical method derives from ancient pagan sources, and also that the one is applied primarily to Christian, the other to ancient material. . . . But such observations are too general and imprecise, for the many phenomena that reflect an intermingling of different cultures over a thousand years do not admit of such simple classifications. (63; 84)

Despite this insistence on the realist, antiallegorical character of figural interpretation, however, Auerbach's essay also contains an entirely different model of figural interpretation (53–60; 77–82), in which figural interpretation is no longer *opposed* to allegory, as if figural interpretation were an instance of symbol, but rather situated quite explicitly *between* allegory and symbol. According to this model, figural interpretation combines the mutually opposed traits of allegory and symbol, but it also remains split between the two. It does not replace (pagan, or more to the point, Jewish) allegory with (Christian) symbol, but instead hovers between the two modes, forever reducing each to the other. Before considering this second model more closely, however, it is important for us first to see how the historical "phenomenon" of figural interpretation resists the initial realist/symbolist model within Auerbach's own account.

The historical "facts" of figural interpretation resist Auerbach's realist (or symbolist) model first of all because there exists a traditional distinction between the prefigurative and the literal functions of any given piece of Old Testament text.

Beside the opposition between *figura* and fulfillment or truth, there appears another, between *figura* and *historia*; *historia* or *littera* is the literal sense or the event related; *figura* is the same literal meaning or event in reference to the fulfillment cloaked in it, and this fulfillment itself is *veritas*, so that *figura* becomes a middle term between *littera-historia* and *veritas*. (47; 73)

In short, the prefiguration is split into *three terms*. The prefiguration in the narrower sense—as *figura* per se—is not literal in the sense of real nor is it literal in the sense of possible, essential, or true. Indeed, as we will consider further below in terms of its consequences for the history of religion, we may further infer that the literal only functions as literal (or, in a realist vision, as reality) *on the one hand* insofar as it is separated off from its prefigural function, but separated off in such a way that it prefigures that prefigural function in turn, and *on the other hand* insofar as it simultaneously appears as what is prefigured (even if in a delayed manner) by its (ideal or possible) fulfillment. For if *veritas* fulfills *historia* or *littera* (by way of *figura*), then it also points toward, represents, or figures *historia* or *littera* in turn as its own origin. Here, the end is also the beginning and the beginning is also the end. In other words, *littera* prefigures *figura* which prefigures *veritas* which prefigures *littera*. Each term in this triangular relay is neither real nor possible, and neither literal nor figural, and yet somehow both ("a middle term"). Auerbach's claim that figural interpretation preserves the literal reality of figures thus already needs to be qualified by the observation that literalness and figurality are as incompatible as they are simultaneously present in each term of the prefiguration-fulfillment relation.

A second example of the resistance of the tradition of figural interpretation to the realist/symbolist model Auerbach somewhat credulously wishes to apply to it—"credulously" because it is in these terms that this tradition wants to understand itself—arises in Auerbach's discussion of Paul. (I refer the reader to the passage I have quoted above, along with the passage from Scholem, as epigram.) Since the tradition *begins* with Paul, moreover, this is not just any example, but rather *the* exemplary example: if Paul's text does not substantiate the notion that figural interpretation is an achieved imaginative realism, then this notion is subject to serious doubt. And indeed, according to Paul, the prefiguration is precisely not to be respected in its integral reality, at least not without further ado. Rather, from the standpoint of the (Christian) fulfillment, the (Jewish) prefiguration is, on the one hand, not real, not yet self-realized (otherwise it would require no fulfillment), and on the other hand, all too real, all too material. More dialectically and precisely, from the standpoint of the fulfillment, the prefiguration is not real enough because it is too real, and it is still too real because it is not yet real. Because the prefiguration is too real—dead letter—it must be made real—living spirit—by being made unreal, that is, negated, killed off, rendered merely possible or ghostly.[25] Thus, with reference to Paul himself, at the "origin" of the tradition of figural interpretation, an "origin" that remains—despite our own quotation marks—authoritatively influential, it would be extremely difficult to characterize figural interpretation either as realism or as a symmetrical balance between prefiguration and fulfillment. But Auerbach characterizes it in both of these ways insofar as he defines *figura* in the Christian world, at the beginning of his discussion, as "something real and historical which announces something else that is also real and historical."[26]

Finally, it is not only the reality of the *prefiguration* that comes to seem questionable as Auerbach's analysis proceeds but also the reality and self-sufficiency—the achieved literality—of the *fulfillment*. And it is on this level in particular that not merely Auerbach's realist/symbolist interpretation of figural interpretation but the very goal of figural interpretation itself—the rhetorical establishment of Christianity as literal fulfillment—becomes threatened. For as Auerbach writes in his discussion of Augustine:

> . . . the "heavenly" fulfillment is not complete, and consequently, as in earlier writers but more definitely in Augustine, the confrontation of the two poles, figure and fulfillment, is sometimes replaced by a development in three stages: the Law or history of the Jews as a prophetic *figura* for the appearance of Christ; the incarnation as fulfillment of this *figura* and at the same time as a new promise of the end of the world and the Last Judgment; and finally, the future occurrence of these events as ultimate fulfillment. . . . Augustine has in mind two promises, one concealed and seemingly temporal in the Old Testament, the other clearly expressed and supra-temporal in the Gospel. (41–42; 70–71)

When the fulfillment comes to seem prefiguration—that is, when it becomes clear that the reading still remains to be read, that the spirit gives rise to, or is identifiable as, a dead letter in its turn—one denies, or illusorily overcomes, the prefigural character of the fulfillment by making reference to the end of the world. At that—eternal or eternalizing—moment, the world (or temporality as prefiguration) and its end (or eternity as fulfillment) will one day have been condensed into a signifying-signified, letter-spirit unity no longer in need of any reading whatsoever. Apocalypse becomes the answer that Pauline Christianity provides—Nazi Germany fantasized it as total war—to the threatening possibility of its own inevitably still-prefigural and incomplete character (or, if one prefers, to the temporality of being).

Thus, the movement from prefiguration to fulfillment is not simply a movement from reality to reality, because both terms are marked by a certain nonreality or figurality, nor is it simply a movement from figural to literal, because both terms are divided between their figurality and their literality. How, then, does Auerbach reformulate his model of figural interpretation when, in the latter part of the third section of his essay, devoted to the "Origin and Analysis of Figural Interpretation," he turns "to define figural interpretation more sharply and to distinguish it from other, related forms of interpretation" (53; 77)? Let us attempt to state this new

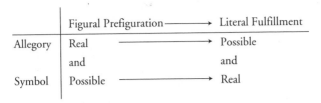

	Figural Prefiguration	⟶	Literal Fulfillment
Allegory	Real	⟶	Possible
	and		and
Symbol	Possible	⟶	Real

FIGURE 2A. Figural Interpretation as Totalization of the Literal

Figural-Literal Prefiguration → Figural-Literal Fulfillment

Allegory/Symbol   Allegory/Symbol

Figural/Literal	⟶	Literal/Figural
(Real)		(Possible)
and		and
Literal/Figural	⟶	Figural/Literal
(Possible)		(Real)

FIGURE 2B. Figural Interpretation as Repetition of the Figural-Literal Split

model as succinctly as possible in terms of the ontorhetorical configurations sketched above. (See Figures 2a and 2b.)

As I have already indicated, Auerbach here compares and contrasts figural interpretation with both allegory and symbol, arguing that it is midway between the two (53–60; 77–82).[27] If figural interpretation is between allegory and symbol, if as the border between the two it also combines the two, this means—in terms of the ontorhetorical configurations sketched above—that it is an intermediate combination of the rationalist-idealist and the empiricist-realist ontorhetorical configurations. For if allegory places a concrete figure in a subservient signifying relation to a magisterial abstraction, then we can say that for *allegory, the real* (or the material image, the personification, the transient existence, and so forth) *is the figural*, whereas *the possible* (the immaterial idea, the eternal essence, and so on) *is the literal*. Conversely, if in *symbolic* modes of representation concretion is privileged over abstraction, then in symbol *the possible* (the abstract, essential, ideal, and so on) *is the figural* whereas *the real* (the concrete, existential, material, and so forth) *is the literal*. If the prefiguration-fulfillment model splits the middle between allegory and symbol, then it must somehow chiasmically combine these two ontorhetorical configurations, the idealist or rationalist position characteristic of allegory and the realist or empiricist one suited to symbol. And indeed it does so, as follows. The prefiguration is a real event (figure) that points beyond itself to a (literal) meaning, but it is also a mere (figural) possibility or anticipation that will finally become (literally) real when it punctually arrives in its truth. The figural prefiguration is a real event pregnant with unrealized possibilities, and the fulfillment is the essential meaning of that real event, but this meaning presents itself precisely as another event. We still seem to have moved from the figural to the literal in an unambiguously, chiasmically totalizing way.[28] The prefiguration is, in the end, not real enough because it is too real, whereas the fulfillment is perfectly real because it has the character of the unreal—the radically spiritual. The prefiguration-fulfillment model seems, in this form, to be formidably stable (see Figure 2a).

But things are not as harmoniously simple as they seem. Since the prefiguration is doubly figural, namely, as reality and as possibility, it is also doubly literal: where reality is figural, possibility is literal, and conversely, where possibility is figural, reality is literal. Likewise, the fulfillment does not combine within itself merely two kinds of literalness—reality and possibility—but two kinds of figurality as well, for reasons analogous to those just stated with respect to the prefiguration. The result is that *the passage from prefiguration to fulfillment is not merely the passage from figural to literal, but rather the passage from one doubled and self-reversing figural-literal pair to another*, the reiteration of the inwardly differentiated structure of that pair rather than its overcoming (see Figure 2b). It is the passage from the figural to the literal and *thereby* the reduction of the literal to a figure of the originally figural term. The fulfillment is just as prefigural as the prefiguration, and it awaits in turn its own fulfillment, its own absorption of its figurality into literalness: its own absorption of the *difference* between figurality and literalness—a difference which *is* figurality—into the *identity* of figurality and literalness—which would be literalness *itself*.[29] The combination of allegory and symbol, or the happy medium between the two as which Auerbach would like to interpret figural interpretation, is split within itself, divided against itself, all along the line, into its figural, i.e., prefigural dimension, and its literal, i.e., fulfilled one. And insofar as the Christian fulfillment here remains prefigurative, while prefigurativity is what this fulfillment posits as the essential trait of Judaism, Christianity is always under pressure to denegate its identity with Judaism (that is, with the principle of difference), an identity which Christianity has ostensibly overcome.

From Medieval Figuralism to the German Enlightenment

The fragility of these rhetorical foundations of medieval Christianity renders Luther's Reformation structurally inevitable in its most general rhetorical outlines, if not in innumerable concrete specifics, including when and where it will occur. Although it is not possible to argue in any historically detailed way for this here, my working hypothesis, which seems to me as if it must be self-evident to anyone who has some acquaintance with both Luther's discourse and the instability of the literal-figural distinction, is as follows: from the standpoint of the rhetoric of Jewish-Christian dialogue, what happens in Luther's Reform is that one half of Christianity's uncannily doubled, literal-figural, fulfilled-prefigurative structure denounces its other half for having become a mere figure. To provide just one example of how this structure is made explicit in Luther's own text, in *Von der Freiheit eines Christenmenschen* (*The Freedom of a Christian*) Luther argues—in a letter to none other than the Pope himself—that the church has come to take the place of God all too literally.

See how dissimilar are Christ and his place-holders [*statthalter*: his figural representatives, those who literally hold his place, or who put themselves in his place or take his place], although they all want to hold his place and I fear indeed that they have become all too truly the ones who hold his place [*ßo sie doch alle wollen seyne statthalter seyn/und ich furwar furcht/sie seyen alßu warhafftig seyne statthalter*]. For a place-holder is a place-holder in the absence of his lord [*ym abweßen synes herrn*]. If a Pope rules in the absence of Christ, who does not live in his heart, is the same not all too truly the one who holds Christ's place? But what can such a crowd be then other than a gathering without Christ? But what can such a Pope be then other than an Anti-Christ or an idolator? How much better the Apostles did, who called themselves, and had themselves called, only the servants of Christ, living in him, not the place-holders of the absent one.[30]

What Luther is saying, through this nearly untranslatable play on the word "statthalter," is that the figure—the "statthalter"—has become (or come to replace, or in Derridian terms, to supplement) the literal fulfillment—Christ himself—and that the literal fulfillment has regressed or been degraded to the status of a mere figure. Christianity and along with it the Christian god—the fulfillment—have become a second Judaism—a mere material prefiguration: the church has become a dead letter. As the above analysis of figural interpretation suggests, however, this turn of events, this splitting of the church into its Judaism and its Christianity, its dead letter and its living spirit, was inevitable—though of unpredictable time, place, and concrete shape—insofar as the becoming-mere-prefiguration of the fulfillment is structurally immanent to the position of the fulfillment as such. Sooner or later, here or there within the Christian realms, something like the Reformation had to get started, for the church only prefigured itself from the start, endlessly contained and failed to contain its own Judaism within itself.

Needless to say, this splitting of Christianity into its (Catholic) Judaism and its (Protestant) Christianity has far-reaching consequences for the subsequent history and structure of Jewish-Christian dialogue, especially in the German principalities, divided between these two halves of Christianity as they are.[31] I shall accordingly say here a few schematic words about these consequences and the displaced repetitions of this splitting, in particular those that occur in the transitions from the (post-)Reformation period (by which I mean broadly the sixteenth and seventeenth centuries) to the Enlightenment and from the Enlightenment to Romanticism. I will begin by tracing a path from the medieval version of the prefiguration-fulfillment model to its Lutheran-Reformation correlate and I will proceed from there to characterize the theological and philosophical garb in which this model appears during the German Enlightenment and then in German Romanticism.

In order to grasp in terms of the rhetoric of *figura* the passage from the medieval to the postmedieval situation, it is necessary to recall and to elaborate briefly upon the *triangular structure* of Jewish-Christian dialogue in the medieval context, for clearly once the Reformation occurs, we have to do with a triangular situation in which the points of the triangle are occupied by Jews, Catholics, and Protestants (see Figure 3). This triangularity itself, of course, is not new in the Reformation. As we have seen, the properly "prefigural" function of the Old Testament was an intermediate term between its materially "literal," pre-prefigural (or postfulfillment) function and its spiritually literal "fulfillment" (and the delayed prefiguration of the pre-prefiguration in turn) in the New Testament: *littera* or *historia* became *figura*, which led to *veritas*, which led back, in a manner that was subject to denegation, to *littera* or *historia*.[32]

Now, if we consider this structure further with respect to the religio-historical traditions of the Christian context, then it appears that, in the medieval Jewish-Christian, prefiguration-fulfillment relation, the Jews are

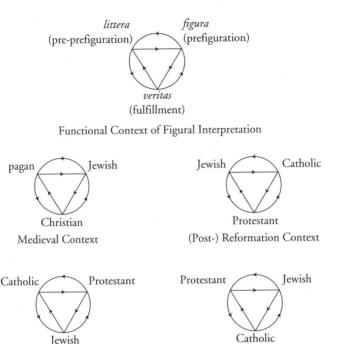

Functional Context of Figural Interpretation

Medieval Context

(Post-) Reformation Context

Enlightenment Context

Romantic Context

FIGURE 3. Triangulations of Dialogical Rhetoric in the Judaeo-Christian Field (or, the Rhetorical Wheel of Judaeo-Christian [Mis]Fortune)

clearly already the second step in a three-step sequence: the (as it were utterly material) pagans are overcome by (and thus prefigure in their own way) Judaism (viewed as a material anticipation of the spiritual), which is overcome by (and prefigures) Christianity in its turn (as the utterly spiritual fulfillment).[33] The Jewish overcoming of the pagans is regarded at this point, of course, as still having been a residually pagan overcoming of the pagans, so to speak, a mere anticipation of the real overcoming of the pagans, which occurred then with the arrival of Christianity.[34] Moreover, by a strange dialectics that will be important especially in Parts II and III below, the Christian overcoming (or fulfillment) can be seen as more complete than the Jewish one precisely by virtue of including more of the pagan element within itself. It escapes the fate of reproducing its opposite by taking that opposite into itself. Because it is less strictly monotheistic and anti-idolatrous than Judaism, Christianity is more so. By a further turn of the screw, however, the fact that *veritas* depends on *littera* entails that *littera* is the literal truth of *veritas* (qua figure). That is, rationalist ontorhetoric is supplemented by empiricist ontorhetoric in figural interpretation, which completes the progressive triangulation and makes it double as an implicitly regressive one (this regressive movement is represented in Figure 3 as a circle). The fact that *littera* fulfills *veritas* and that, as a result, there is a constant, implicit displacement of each of the terms of the triangle in a backward or counterclockwise direction (turning the religio-historical clock back even as the West tries repeatedly to turn it ahead) is what each historical concretization of the triangle has to deny in order to prevent being relieved immediately by the next concretization in turn.

Now, in the (post-)Reformation context, from the standpoint of Lutheranism, this triangular structure is repeated and displaced, the result being that it overdetermines itself in a vexed manner. In this instance, Judaism occupies the position the Middle Ages had reserved for the pagans (that is, the position of *littera* or *historia*, the initial pre-prefiguration and, as we shall see, the fulfillment of the fulfillment).[35] Sooner or later, Judaism is destined by the medieval structure to find itself in this position, of course, for even in the medieval structure, it functions as a kind of fulfillment of paganism's prefiguration: it is *figura* as fulfillment of *littera*, and so it is the very self of *littera* itself.[36] In turn, once the Reformation has begun, the Catholic Church occupies the position it had reserved in the medieval context for Judaism (the position of *figura*, the initial pre-fulfillment or the prefiguration of *veritas* as fulfillment).[37] The (Lutheran) Protestant Church, finally, occupies the position formerly occupied by the Catholic Church (that of *veritas*, the ultimate fulfillment of the prefiguration, and so in turn—in a way that unsettles Protestant discourse—the delayed prefiguration of the literal pre-prefiguration). On the one hand, that is, Protestantism is now the true overcoming of (henceforth pagan) Judaism, an overcoming only prefigured by the (henceforth Jewish) medieval Catholic Church. This overcoming is achieved, again paradoxically (or dialectically), by virtue of the fact that ("truly" Christian) Protestantism takes into itself more of Judaism than did Catholicism (namely, the placement of the text into the hands of the individual), and therefore less (for these hands are now the letterless hands of faithful supplication). Protestantism now fulfills the prefiguration of the fulfillment of Christianity, just as Catholicism once was taken to fulfill the prefiguration of the monotheistic overcoming of polytheistic idolatry.

On the other hand, Protestantism (here, *veritas*) prefigures Judaism (*littera*) in a delayed manner, insofar as Judaism appears in the guise of the origin on which Protestantism depends, the origin it merely represents or figures. The structure of the relation between *veritas* and *littera*, as of that between final and efficient causality in conscious production, is that the end is the beginning of the beginning, and the beginning is the end of the end.[38] From this perspective, Protestantism is even more pagan than the Judaism it prefigures, and indeed, when measured in terms of the *elements* of the medieval pagan-Judaeo-Christian triangle, Protestantism appears to have stepped into the position of the pagans.

Before pursuing the turning of the tropological wheel beyond the end of the (post-)Reformation period, however, it is important to insert a brief clarifying remark on the aspect of *history* I take the turns of the wheel to represent and what kind of *necessity* is involved here. First of all, the axis around which the wheel turns, or the motor that drives it, and so that to which it refers throughout, is no doubt the fear of the impossible absence mentioned above. In more human terms it is the fear of death, the anxiety about mortality, and more specifically the desire to imagine the community to which one belongs as purified of death. At least in the West this tends to mean purified of time and so also of the (decaying) body, including the body of language.[39] Building on ancient Greco-Roman and Hebrew foundations, early Christian figuralism constitutes itself as a guarantee or demonstration that such a purification has been achieved within the community of Christ. Further, even at the far end of the Middle Ages, Western religious culture still attempts to overcome the opposition between material letter and spirit, or (quasi-synonymously) multiplicity and unity, difference and identity, repetitive deferral and pure origination, death and life, in terms of dialectical triads established between very large positive-religious cultural communities. Moreover, beyond the onset of the Reformation, this attempt still takes the form of the desire to establish a one-to-one correspondence between the two triadic schemas of pagan/Jewish/Christian, on the one hand, and *littera/figural/veritas*, on the other hand. Due to this dialectical structure of postmedieval Judaeo-Christian desire, modern *Geistesgeschichte*, as the history of the major (sometimes pseudosecular) religio-historical, literary, and philosophical periods and movements within the Judaeo-Christian West since the Middle Ages, comes to appear quite predictable and even necessary in its broadest outlines, as determined by rhetorical concepts. Once the Protestant Church has occupied the position of paganism in a Christian mode, it is not at all surprising that the entire cycle (the passage from pagan to Jewish to Christian) should repeat itself. Indeed, it appears as if it could hardly have been avoided. In the next phase, some form of Neo-Judaic cultural movement will gain a certain, if only momentary and fleeting, hegemony. And in the *next* phase, a Neo-Catholic movement will, again, perhaps only fleetingly, have to assert itself. Of course, innumerable determinations of these quasi-inevitable Neo-Judaic and Neo-Catholic movements or moments (which we will be considering below) as also of the Reformation Protestantism whose position in the rhetorical history of Judaeo-Christianity we have just sketched will *not* have been predictable by reference to the rhetoric wheel of Judaeo-Christian (mis)fortune. Such determinations include time and place of origin, as well as political, scientifico-technological, and socioeconomic aspects, resulting from forces that are relatively independent of the religio-cultural discourses. Moreover, if we abstract from historical inertia, it even seems as if it would have been possible for the history of Judaeo-Christianity suddenly, and entirely, to take its distance from typological dialectics, as well as from positive religion, at the very least during the eighteenth century, if not already in the Reformation. The fact that it did not, however, testifies precisely to the inevitability of one or another manifestation of such inertia, to the tendency toward meaningless and ("ideally") unnecessary institutional-discursive repetition (and self-prescription). That is, it testifies to the power of historicity itself, which is finally nothing other than this self-repetitive and self-anticipatory power of the letter. Beyond the end of the medieval period, the turning of the rhetorical wheel of Judaeo-Christian (mis)fortune testifies to the inertial self-repetition (and self-anticipation) of the power of the letter of Western positive religio-philosophical traditions, which is just the letter of the ideological-metaphysical desire to overcome the letter itself, to overcome mechanical repetition and anticipation by purifying life or presence of the death, that is, the absence (as pastness or futurity), on which it sustains itself.

To return to "our story": the Enlightenment overcoming of Lutheran Protestantism, the next shift in the self-displacing circling of the triangle, will pose (or be exposed to) the threat of a *reemergence of Judaism as the privileged religio-cultural figure of literal, spiritual fulfillment.* For just as medieval Christianity fell back into the prefigural, previously (pagan) Jewish position because, as fulfillment (*veritas*) of the Jewish prefiguration (*figura*), it was also the (Jewish) prefiguration of the (pagan) literalness (*littera*) that prefigured that prefiguration, thus precisely fulfilling or realizing Jewish (pre)figurality *as* (pre)figurality—this is what we call the onset of the Reformation; so Protestantism now falls back into the prefigural, previously (Judaeo-)Catholic position precisely because this same Protestantism prefigures the (Jewish) literalness that prefigured the Catholic prefiguration—and this is what we call the transition to the Enlightenment.[40]

Indeed, historically, Lutheran Protestantism does not take long to become a material, institutional presence, with its own (quasi-Catholic) orthodoxy and its own protesting dissidents. The ostensibly regressive replacement of the spiritually literal truth of pure (Lutheran) inwardness by the outward, merely prefigurative figures of that truth occurs almost without delay, but with special intensity in the second half of the seventeenth century, after the Peace of Westphalia.[41] This development gives rise to various attempts to fulfill the Reformation prefiguration or promise, from seventeenth-century Pietism on, culminating in the Enlightenment turn—more or less radically self-consistent, depending on the case—away from all revealed religion toward rational, natural religion.[42] Through this turn, the most radical representatives of German Enlightenment hope to achieve a complete liberation of the literal, universal, spiritual truth from any figural, particular letter, any trace of material, historical, revealed *littera* whatsoever.[43] The very notion of such a complete liberation from the letter, however, is so utterly entangled with the tradition of positive religion in the West, and so also with the rhetoric of figural interpretation, that the Enlighteners cannot help but turn—in their search for a discourse that would fulfill the desire to overcome prefigurality—to (pagan) Judaism, which henceforth represents the literal fulfillment of the Reformation itself. Thus, in light of the reflexions we have been advancing on the rhetorical structure of the history of Judaeo-Christianity, it is not by chance that one of the exemplary figures of this turn is the Jewish defender of natural religion, Moses Mendelssohn. The relative marginalization of Mendelssohn in the history of the reception of Enlightenment as a mere "Popular-philosoph" must be taken therefore as a denegation of his very centrality. But before outlining the reading of Mendelssohn that comprises Part I below, let me briefly illustrate this passage from the Reformation to the Enlightenment triangulations of Judaeo-Christianity by reference to some of the major writer-thinkers and groups of writer-thinkers who make up Mendelssohn's context.

How, then, do the more important figures of the Enlightenment context propose (or find themselves exposed to) the promise (or threat) of the passage from a quasi-pagan Protestantism to a quasi-pagan Judaism as rational essence of spirit?[44] Let us begin with those forms of thought that appear most clearly as attempts to *prevent* or *evade* this turn from Protestantism toward Judaism as its essence. We can then proceed to those forms of thought that *bring about* (or at least *go along with*) this formally inevitable next turn of the rhetorical wheel of Judaeo-Christian (mis)fortune.

The first group of those who evade the Enlightenment turn from Protestantism to what must appear as its Jewish essence are the English and French deists. Even though these deists operate outside of a strictly Lutheran context, the tendency of their work illustrates clearly the transition from the early (post-)Reformation period to the Enlightenment in the terms I've spelled out. With the possible exception of Toland, who (at least according to some interpreters) blames on pagan *rather than* Jewish influences the corruption of Christianity that occurs in Catholicism, other English deists, such as William Whiston, Matthew Tindal, Thomas Morgan, Anthony Collins, T. Wollston, Peter Annet, and Lord Henry Bolingbroke, all attempt to perfect (post-)Reformation Christianity qua natural religion by ridding it of the (quasi-pagan) Jewish elements that undermine it from within.[45] This sudden and vehement turn, on the part of so many serious theological thinkers, against the threat of the Judaization of Protestant Christianity can be accounted for by the fact that, just as medieval Catholicism had (for reasons of its rhetorical underpinnings) fallen back into Judaism by falling forward into paganism, so Protestantism was about to fall back into Catholicism by falling forward into Judaism. In order to prevent the dialectics of figural interpretation from undermining the privilege of purified Christianity as model for natural religion, the deists in England preferred to undo the tradition of figural interpretation itself, emphasizing what had always been the negative aspect of the prefiguration understood as radical materiality.[46]

If in England the tendency of deism was to make Christianity safe for rational universality by ridding it of its Judaeo-pagan material particularity, denying its prefigurative roots in the Old Testament, then in France the principal deistic trend, exemplified by Voltaire, was to undermine institutional Christianity, which in any case was still closely connected to Rome, by emphasizing its fatal rootedness in (pagan) Judaism. The atheistic Holbachians, although even more radical in their opposition to religion, took a similar tack: the affirmation of the prefiguration-fulfillment model of the Jewish-Christian relation in order to reduce all of Christianity to its (pagan-)Jewish origins. If the position of Protestantism as literal fulfillment of Catholicism implies that the literal fulfillment of Protestantism in turn is Judaism, then the French deists and atheists can be seen to be drawing the inference that all of Christianity must go in order to prevent this eventuality: ultimately, even being an atheist is apparently more desirable than ending up a Jew.[47]

To turn now to the German context, those who, working within the period of the Enlightenment (but not necessarily in an Enlightenment vein), more or less manifestly defend themselves against the structurally prescribed threat of the becoming Jewish of Lutheran Protestantism are dispersed across a surprisingly broad and heterogeneous philosophical spectrum.[48] In Lutheran orthodoxy, not only the defense but also its hopelessness are manifest, as Luther's opposition to the Judaeo-Catholic letter rigidifies itself by taking itself *à la lettre*. Perhaps the most glaring—even (unwittingly) self-parodic—example of this discourse is the position represented by Lessing's orthodox opponent, the Pastor Goeze, whose very name means "idol" (!), to whom we will return in a moment. But more subtly, too, among the Enlightenment-tinged Lutherans, the prodigious efforts of J. D. Michaelis, the prominent Orientalist, to contain and master ancient Hebrew culture precisely by reducing it to the viewpoint of the Protestant rational spirit while polemically denying the significance of (Rabbinic) Judaism, read as one more denegational acknowledgment of the threat of the becoming Jewish *littera* or *historia* of Protestant *veritas*. Moving still further in the direction of Enlightenment rationality and further away from Lutheran orthodoxy, the neological school of Semler, Sack, Spalding, and Jerusalem follows in these matters, despite other differences, approximately the pattern of English deism: the repudiation of figural interpretation in the service of the rationalization of revelation. The radical deism of Hermann Samuel Reimarus, in turn, follows what in our context amounts to substantially the same pattern as French deism. Nature and reason replace the Judaeo-Christian God and his revelation, while Christianity is reduced to its Judaic essence in order to be rejected on the basis of the inessentiality of this essence.

Strikingly, however, even when we move to the irrationalist opposite extreme—the *Sturm und Drang* counter-Enlightenment—very much the same phenomenon of a defense against a Judaization of Protestantism emerges. In the case of the Lutheran Pastor Herder's writings on the Old Testament, for example, this defense takes the misleading form of an exaltation of the Old Testament, but it is an exaltation that reduces the Old Testament first of all to folk poetry, a kind of natural aesthetic phenomenon, and then to the "spirit" of that poetry, a spirit which, as such, is to be understood as belonging ultimately to the supernatural nature of its Protestant fulfillment. The diasporic Jews are for Herder in no way intimately connected to the sublime tradition of the ancient Hebrews, a tradition which lives on rather in the Protestant spirit it will have become long since.[49] Similarly, Friedrich Heinrich Jacobi, the irrationalist-empiricist opponent of Lessing and Mendelssohn, of whom more below (especially in Chapter 2), explicitly associates Enlightenment with Judaic—and also with Catholic—forms of thought. As paranoid and unrealistic as that may seem (especially the linkage of Enlightenment with Catholicism), the above presentation of the triangulations of the rhetoric of Judaeo-Christian dialogue explains why he was not completely wrong to draw these inferences. For he was thus grasping, if in a somewhat benighted fashion, a crucial dimension of the history of religious ideology. He was mistaken, however, to think that he could escape the operations of such ideology and enter the realm of truth (or of "the true" [*das Wahre*], as he tends to say) merely by attempting belatedly to arrest the circulation and self-displacement of the triangle in what I have called its (post-)Reformation form (or letter).[50]

So much, then, for the various forms of relatively explicit *resistance* to the Enlightenment (self-)Judaization of Protestantism. In what kinds of writer-thinkers does the rhetorically prescribed movement of this Judaization become manifest in a more *affirmative* mode? It is the most advanced representatives of the German Enlightenment who, it seems to me, need to be mentioned here. This is the case not, of course, because Judaism is actually the essence of Protestantism but because, in the moment of the German Enlightenment, the fulfillment of Protestantism had to be envisioned—insofar as Enlightenment thought could not halt the inertial self-perpetuation of positive religion in its Judaeo-Christian typological structure—in terms of a Judaization. I shall consider briefly only two such representatives, in addition to Mendelssohn himself.

First, there is the complicated example of Lessing, who realizes Protestantism by taking a step toward its Judaization. (I examine Lessing's position in much greater detail in Chapters 3 and 6, in the context of the discussion of Friedrich Schlegel's Lessing reception.) In his infamous debate with Lutheran orthodoxy as represented by Pastor Goeze, for example, Lessing opposes Goeze's paradoxically spiritualizing literalism—"the letter is the spirit, and the Bible is religion," Goeze insists—with the separation of letter and spirit. The Protestant absorption of letter into spirit, and hence of Jew into Christian, which Goeze still upholds, is countered by Lessing, then, with a defense of the separation of letter from spirit. Lessing's gesture here must be read in two ways that, taken together, add up to Judaizing Protestantism. On the one hand, since Goeze's unification of letter and spirit presents itself here as Christian, their separation by Lessing appears quasi-Jewish. On the other hand, of course, to let spirit inhere in letter as does Goeze is to open oneself to the accusation that one is a Jewish, spiritless fetishist of the letter, whereas to say that the Bible contains a spirit that is distinct from its letter as does Lessing is to perform a Christian gesture par excellence. In light of this consideration, Lessing's gesture comprises a hyper-Protestant critique of Protestant orthodoxy. The question remains as to what spirit is when it has become the spirit (and no longer the letter) of the Protestant absorption of letter into spirit. What does it mean to take only the spirit of the word or letter, "spirit," to take "spirit" spiritually, or figuratively, refusing to respect the letter of its distinction from the letter? Lutheran Protestant spirit goes beyond itself here and moves dangerously close—especially for the paranoid yet somnambulistically savvy opponents of Lessing's hyper-Protestant reflexion—to an assimilation of itself to the letter of Judaism. Moreover, in the ring parable of *Nathan der Weise*, the conclusion of the controversy with Goeze, Lessing comes very close to arguing explicitly that this spirit of Protestantism consists essentially in its Judaism. For the parable ultimately situates spirituality nowhere else but in the good ethical *works* to which it gives rise, in precisely those ethical works with the condemnation of which as *dead letter* Luther's Reformation (and Pauline Christianity more generally) had begun.[51] Thus, Lessing is not only a "friend" of the Jews but, beyond this, he is perilously close to losing his German spirit to Jewish materiality itself.

Second, there is the vexed question of the Jewish or non-Jewish character of Kant's philosophy. The affinity of his formalistic legalism with the Jewish "letter" has been noted, of course, from his first critics onward, playing an important role (for example) in Hegelianisms of all sorts ever since. This affinity has also been assumed by Jewish-German (and not only German) Kant disciples for two hundred years, always in highly problematic ways.[52] And in fact, the ethico-theological privilege Kant grants to the law of practical reason does tend to situate spirit back in the law of works and the works of law, as did Lessing in his ring parable. Still, Kant's anti-Semitic moments are well known, and these taken together with the denial of the status of a religion to Judaism in *Religion within the Limits of Mere Reason* make it clear that Kant wishes to supplant Mosaic Judaism rather than to participate in it.[53] Indeed, the ambition of his philosophy is everywhere to establish some kind of ultimately spiritual articulation of letter with spirit, as can be verified with reference to various levels of his architectonic. For example, not only does he characterize the relationship between politics and morality as one between the letter and the spirit of the law, but also the center of his critical system, the aesthetico-teleological reflexive judgment as outlined in the *Kritik der Urteilskraft*, is charged with the task of establishing a mediation between the understanding and reason, the faculties of the laws of nature and freedom, or (passive) heteronomy and (active) autonomy, which is to say the "faculties" (or "capacities"—"Vermögen") of letter and spirit, respectively. Kant's philosophy thus appears to be one continuous attempt to achieve the Judaeo-Christian dialogue in a decidedly legislative—quasi-Judaic—and yet also decidedly spiritual manner. Finally, however, the complexity of Kant's at once extremely intimate, subtly hostile, and from today's perspective astonishingly rivalrous relationships with Mendelssohn in particular and with Judaism in general is such that I have decided to exclude it almost entirely from the present study.[54] To have engaged Kant in any serious way here would have meant not only running the risk of having Kant—as "fulfillment"—take over a book in which Mendelssohn was meant to play more than a subordinate—or merely "prefigurative"—role but also leaving out the extensive readings in Romanticism and post-Romantic thought that make up a significant part of the book.[55]

Now that I have determined the "appropriate" context of Mendelssohn's work to be the Enlightenment discourse understood as a tendentially (self-)Judaizing Lutheranism, I am in a position to situate in this context the readings of Mendelssohn I carry out in Part I. How does Moses Mendelssohn's work actually fit into the Enlightenment context of these religio-cultural and ideological tendencies? Is he a progressive "Judaizer" of Protestant rationality or a regressive "Protestantizer" of the Jewish letter?[56] In Part I, I trace Mendelssohn's own ambivalences about this alternative by reading two texts closely, both from the last few years of his career, in which he addresses the rationalist and irrationalist critics of his own vexed Jewish natural theology.

These readings show how Mendelssohn's ambivalence gains expression when, in the face of his Protestant rationalist foes, he reluctantly allows himself to posit Judaism as the exemplary overcoming of Protestantism (i.e., as the fulfillment of the Protestant anticipation of natural religion) and then backs away to some extent from this Jewish particularism in favor of a discourse on natural religion that emphasizes solely its indifference to all positive, revealed religion. As I have argued elsewhere by means of a reading of Mendelssohn's *Letters on Sentiments* from 1755, in some of his earliest works in German, those focusing on psychological and aesthetic themes in particular, Mendelssohn attempts to demonstrate by example and argument only that Judaism is *compatible* with rational spirit, always without any manifest suggestion that Judaism would have any *privileged* relation to such rational spirit.[57] From the standpoint of the assumptions of the Lutheran Enlightenment, however, when Mendelssohn presents himself as a spiritual Jew, it looks as if he were in principle committing himself to conversion, for what could a spiritual Jew be, if not a Christian? Mendelssohn, for his part, foresees from the beginning the danger of this response to his work, a danger he registers in *Letters on Sentiments*, for example, by raising indirectly the question of whether or not he is committing cultural suicide by attempting to participate in would-be secular rational discourse. And indeed, the danger is soon realized. Mendelssohn's most outspoken opponents within the heyday of Enlightenment discourse (such as Lavater and Cranz, even if their commitments to rationality are not always ingenuous) boldly reassert what is, in (post-)Reformation terms, the quasi-self-evident proposition that rationality is Protestant (that Protestantism is the most rational religion). They therefore also publicly suggest that Mendelssohn, merely by presenting himself as an ostensibly rational man, even if he is still outwardly a Jew (i.e., outwardly outward), has already in principle declared his readiness to convert to Protestantism, to turn himself (outside) in. He should accordingly either convert to Protestantism, they suggest, or publicly prove its irrationality as well as the superior rationality of Judaism.

In the face of these provocations, Mendelssohn is ultimately pushed, as I show in Chapter 1, to the point of arguing in *Jerusalem, or on Religious Power and Judaism*, even if reluctantly and in a rather indirect way, that Judaism is in fact more compatible with rationality than either Protestantism or Catholicism. Here, according to my narrative, Mendelssohn moves from arguing (as he had implicitly in earlier texts such as *Letters on Sentiments*) that *Jews can be rational* (that they can have rational feelings) to arguing that *rationality is Jewish*, in the sense that Judaism is more compatible with rationality than either Protestantism or Catholicism. And as we shall see, Mendelssohn presents Judaism here as being more compatible with rationality precisely because it synthesizes the medieval, Catholic *fusion* of church and state (in the name of the church) with the Protestant leaning toward their *separation* (in the name of a privileged state).

At the opposite end of the spectrum, in the final polemical exchanges of Mendelssohn's career, his (and Lessing's) most outspoken enemies within the *Sturm und Drang* counter-Enlightenment—led and represented by Jacobi—take the rear-guard position that, since rationality is material (Jewish), the (Protestant) spirit is to be defended in the name of irrationality. I examine this polemic in Chapter 2, focusing on *Morning Hours, or Lectures on the Existence of God*, where Mendelssohn makes his last effort to establish natural religion beyond all positive religions. Here, Mendelssohn argues that (Jewish) *rationality is truly religious*, by showing the compatibility of Spinozist pantheism seen as a (Jewish) rationality with Leibnizian theism, as a figure of (Christian) religion.

But there is a further dimension of the German Enlightenment context that is of crucial relevance to this study, a methodological one, which it is necessary to sketch out here before going on to discuss the Catholicizing Judaism of German Romanticism which follows quasi-inexorably upon the Judaizing Protestantism of the Enlightenment. In terms of Judaeo-Christian denominations, as I have tried to indicate thus far, the Enlightenment tries alternately to resist and to carry out the passage from Protestantizing Catholicism (or simply Protestantism) to Judaizing Protestantism (or simply Judaism). In terms of philosophical methodology, however, it tries to ground knowledge alternately in rationalist and empiricist ontorhetorical configurations. In the middle and late periods of the German Enlightenment, especially, the very question of how to approach philosophy in general is in critical condition: rationalism and empiricism divide the field. Further, the terms of this question of true philosophical method echo the terms of the Jewish-Christian (i.e., Jewish-Protestant) "dialogue," the question of the true positive religion, in surprising—and yet also surprisingly obvious—ways.

As we have seen, rationalism coincides ontorhetorically with the allegorical dimension of figural interpretation, while empiricism overlaps ontorhetorically with its symbolic dimension. Since the allegorico-symbolic relation of figural interpretation constitutes (from the Christian standpoint) the Jewish-Christian *relation*, existing *between* the two, it cannot be determined whether allegory or symbol is essentially Jewish, or consequently which of these representational modes is essentially Christian. And yet, because the relation consists of these two terms—allegory and symbol—and conjoins these other two terms—Jewish and Christian—it is difficult to resist *attempting* to make this latter determination. Hence, one finds oneself confronted with the following apparent undecidability. Allegory seems Jewish because its abstract character coincides with the abstraction with which Judaism is identified insofar as Judaism is seen as a radically anti-idolatrous monotheism. Accordingly, symbol seems Christian because, just as symbolic art privileges concretion, so does Christianity (in the forms of the embodiment of God in humanity, the Eucharist, the iconic traditions, and so forth). On the other hand, allegory seems Christian because it, like Christianity, is radically spiritual; and symbol thus seems Jewish because of the worldly materiality and even literal realism it shares with the ostensibly Jewish fetishism of the legalistic letter.[58] Thus, since rationalism and empiricism are the modern philosophico-methodological names for the same ontorhetorical configurations that define the exegetical-aesthetic categories of allegory and symbol, respectively, both rationalism and empiricism can be aligned with both Jewish and Christian. But because the Enlightenment finds itself compelled to choose both between rationalism and empiricism *and* between Judaism and (Protestant) Christianity, it can hardly avoid attempting to align, in any given instance, one method with one positive religion. We will be concerned, in Part I, largely with the entanglements of Mendelssohn's Jewish public persona and personal-imaginary self-identity with his philosophical options, and we will continue to deal with the religio-political implications of the rationalist-empiricist dilemma and its post-Kantian avatars in Parts II and III below. It is therefore important that we review here the structure of these alignments of methods with religious groups by detailing briefly the Enlightenment options for the determination of the philosophical-methodological identity of Judaism.

First of all, in the German Enlightenment it seems quite "logical" for Judaism to be *identified* with rationalism and *opposed* to empiricism. The spirit of radical abstraction that so strongly characterizes Jewish monotheism is, after all, a trait it obviously shares with rationalist idealism. To this extent both discourses—Judaism and rationalism—can be placed in opposition to the strewn, heterogeneous, quasi-idolatrous concreteness of the natural given on which empiricism is founded. Moreover, the blank-slate metaphor of empiricism can be read as implying the radical negation of the "letter." Empiricism requires that the "dead letter" of rationalism be cleared away, and thereby implies that rationalism is to empiricism as Judaism is to Christianity, namely, its fallen rise, its preliminary aftermath or degradation. Thus, both as "monotheistic" abstraction and as "dead" letter, both as excessive spirituality and as excessive materiality, rationalism and Judaism can be seen as representing kindred principles to which empiricism and Christianity would be radically opposed by virtue of both their quasi-"polytheistic" concreteness and their "lively" openness to natural presence.

This analogical, phantasmatic, and ideological possibility, however, can be easily reversed. For rationalism is clearly the opposite of Judaism insofar as rationalism's radical intellectuality or spirituality is opposed to that which, especially from the standpoint of Lutheran Protestantism, renders Judaism associable with materiality, namely, its exacerbated concern with the "law," ritual, works, the "dead" letter, and so forth. The non-philosophical, nonsystematic, non-"rational" character of Judaism even at its most textually and interpretively acute (for example, in Talmudic interpretation) appears, from this point of view, to be situated at the furthest possible remove from the self-thinking thought of rationalism since Descartes. Finally, even the blank-slate metaphor of Locke points both to the empiricists' desire to be open to a certain kind of materiality that they construe as a writing, albeit a writing of that which is given in nature, and to their cultivation of a certain kind of abstraction, the abstraction from concrete particularity in the ascending movement of the mind toward the laws of nature. In these two ways, the fundamental metaphor of the empiricist model advertises its affinities with the abstract materiality of Judaic textualism (as conventionally posited within Christianity), and thereby confirms the opposition of rationalism to Judaism.[59]

Thus, in the discursive context into which Mendelssohn enters at the beginning of his career, the *religio-cultural* opposition between Jewish and Lutheran (or in more national terms, Jewish and German) is doubled, over-determined, but in an undecidable or reversible way (a way that, in turn, reflects the undecidability inherent in the rhetorical structure of this opposition), by the *methodological* opposition between rationalism and empiricism. Further, the opposition between rationalism and empiricism itself is becoming particularly unstable, as I've suggested, just as Mendelssohn enters philosophical discourse. Across the length of his career, the Leibnizian-Wolffian tradition of rationalist metaphysics, which had formerly been firmly entrenched in German university discourse, comes increasingly under fire from empiricist and materialist philosophies of English and French provenance, leading—notably by way of Mendelssohn—to the Kantian "overcoming" of the rationalist-empiricist opposition through the transcendental-critical turn.[60] Faced with the choice between rationalism and empiricism, a choice which must confront him—both for epistemological and for cultural-identity-political reasons—as utterly impossible, Mendelssohn constantly insists, in each of his works, and despite his (no doubt oddly) pronounced preference for the rationalist mode, upon the necessity of reconciling the claims of rationalism with those of empiricism. Despite the discreetly aggressive gesture in *Jerusalem* through which he accords Judaism a superior rationality, he always attempts to determine the middle ground on which the two major epistemological methods of his day, as well as their religio-cultural equivalents, could come to an understanding whereby the excesses and failings of each would be corrected.

From Early Romanticism to Late Romanticism and Beyond

The discourse of German Romanticism begins with an attempt to assimilate the Enlightenment legacy, which in terms of the rhetorical wheel of Judaeo-Christian (mis)fortune consists—despite a massive effort of denegation—in the tendency to pass from a prefigurative Protestantism to its Neo-Judaic realization. I retrace this attempted assimilation in Chapters

3 to 5, using Friedrich Schlegel and Dorothea Mendelssohn-Veit-Schlegel to represent by synecdoche the inauguration of German Romanticism in general. The Judaizing Protestantism of the German Enlightenment is condensed, for the early Romantics, in the intertwined testimonies of Kant (whom I largely ignore here), Lessing, and Mendelssohn (the combined significance of the latter two for the genesis of Romanticism having been generally underestimated, as I show). As I illustrate in Chapter 6, the Catholicizing Romantics ultimately "resolve" (and so avoid) the (irresolvable) problem these late Enlightenment figures pose—the undecidability of the relation between letter and spirit—by absorbing the spirit of the (Jewish) letter and the letter of (Lutheran Protestant) spirit into what appears as the higher unity of a *Catholic*, quasi-pre-Reformation Christianity (see Figure 3 above). Through this solution, Friedrich and Dorothea Schlegel—along with Novalis, who precedes them, and other Catholicizing Romantics, who for the most part follow them—negate any possibility of Jewish-Christian dialogue by "achieving" it, rendering it henceforth superfluous, in the form of the letter-spirit unity that Catholicism would provide.[61] Judaism and Protestant Christianity have now been reconciled and synthesized, since the principle of the Neo-Judaic letter has absorbed into itself, or fallen back into unity with, the Lutheran Protestant spirit it fulfilled in the Enlightenment, in order to give rise now to the stabilized institutional spirituality of the Neo-Catholic Church, the "crossing" between the two extremes. The Enlightenment's Jewish fulfillment of Protestantism thus prefigures, and is fulfilled in turn by, a Catholic fulfillment that fuses excessive letter with excessive spirit.

While Schlegel and his lover and then wife Dorothea Mendelssohn-Veit-Schlegel, that "exemplary" Romantic couple, only gradually discover this Neo-Catholic solution in the years extending from 1797 to 1808, in Part II I show that Schlegel articulates both his early Romantic aesthetic pantheism and his later Neo-Catholic political theology in terms of extended readings of Lessing (Chapters 3 and 6), each time positioning his own views as the logical conclusion of Lessing's intervention in the Lutheran tradition. As for the early Friedrich Schlegel of the "Athenäum" period, attention to Schlegel's readings of Lessing from 1797 and 1801 (Chapter 3) reveals a local genesis of Schlegel's early aesthetics of generic hybridization (i.e., the famous Romantic "Mischung") that has been severely underemphasized in the literature on Schlegel. The early Romantic conception of the infinitely varied and fragmentary work of art, from which Schlegel will take his distance once he has replaced it with his Neo-Catholic ideology, is at least in large part *derived from* and *authorized by* Lessing's quasi-Judaizing attempt, in his theological and dramatic texts, to overcome the literalism of orthodox Lutheran spirit.

And this goes also for the form of early Romantic sociality, i.e., the salon culture around the turn of the century. In Chapter 4, I look at two important early Schlegel texts in order to demonstrate this rootedness of Romantic sociality in Jewish-Christian dialogue. In Schlegel's public letter to Dorothea, "On Philosophy," of 1798 and in his novel about her, *Lucinde*, of 1799, desire to sublate the opposition between the spirit of (Judaic) letter and the letter of (Christian) spirit in evidence in "On Lessing" expands itself into an androgynous gender theory that attempts to sublate the opposition between feminine and masculine. The homology between the gender relation and the Jewish-Christian relation is established in these texts not only by the fact that the exemplary erotic and sentimental couple there consists of Dorothea, the Jewess, and Schlegel himself, the Protestant, but also by the specific ways in which Schlegel presents this relationship in "On Philosophy" and *Lucinde*. What the development of this homology suggests, further, is that the unheard-of poetico-philosophical mixing of Jews and Christians as of women and men—and hence especially of Jewish women with Christian men—which characterizes Romantic sociality is not, as is generally supposed, a mere example or epiphenomenon of a typically Romantic openness to mixing that would have had its origin else-where (namely, in the aesthetic theories of the German postclassical spirit pure and simple, or in other more specifically political-social forces).[62] Rather, this Romantic openness to mixing is itself from the beginning formulated as a response to, and an understanding of, the inextricably semiological and religio-historical problem of Jewish-Christian dialogue as figural interpretation, a problem Schlegel encounters in a critical way in Lessing's text.

Mere mixing does not, of course, produce a compound, and Schlegel is not, at this stage, able to formulate the sublations he desires except in terms of the privilege of Protestant spirit qua masculinity over its opposite. Therefore, although Dorothea illuminates this problematic asymmetry by registering some reservations in her own novel, *Florentin*, of 1801 (Chapter 5), it is only with their common discovery of the Neo-Catholic solution

(Chapter 6) that the Schlegels manage to avoid the undecidable alternative between Judaic letter and Protestant spirit, an alternative which appears to them as both philosophically and personally intolerable.

If this logic of the Schlegels' development has tended to be over-looked or de-emphasized in the criticism, this is no doubt for at least two reasons. First, a largely German or German-dominated, and in its self-conception often either vaguely Christian or vaguely pagan, scholarly community has evidently been habitually disinclined to grant Judaism and the problem of the (Jewish) letter such a large role either in the Enlightenment or in Schlegel's thinking. Thus, it has privileged the pagan, classical, "poetic" Goethe over the friend-of-the-Jews and "critic" Lessing as a crucial German forerunner of Schlegel. It has tended—not wrongly, yet one-sidedly, and in what reads today as something of a repression not only of the "Jewish" question but also (and more fundamentally) of the questions of the materiality of language and of the temporality of being—to speak of Schlegel as having to resolve the tensions between nature and spirit or pagan and Christian, rather than letter and spirit or Jewish and Christian.[63] (What lends further tension to this situation is that, as we've seen, heathens and Jews, as well as heathens and Protestants, find themselves in an overdetermined and problematic unity once Luther's Reformation has been institutionally secured.)

Secondly, the notion of Catholicism as a synthesis or an achieved balance of Jewish and Protestant tendencies, as a dialectical overcoming of the Jewish synthesis of Protestantism with medieval Catholicism, no doubt seems illogical and so unthinkable on two counts. Protestantism comes of course *after* Catholicism and so it superficially seems that, if there is to have been any synthesis, it will have been Protestantism that synthesized Catholicism with Judaism in order to produce a truly spiritual spirit. This point of view is one version of the reasoning of Lutheran Protestantism as well as of the—in this sense, regressively—Protestantizing Enlighteners and counter-Enlighteners we have considered above.[64]

But according to the illogical logic of typological rhetoric at the end of Enlightenment, Neo-Catholicism appears to fulfill the Judaizing Protestantism of the Enlightenment by mediating between the Lutheran emphasis on the inwardness of conviction (that is, of a pure spirituality into which the materiality of the letter of the law would be totally dissolved) and the opposed Jewish emphasis on traditions of interpretation and on the appropriate form of works (in the sense of Mitzvot).[65] Of course, by no means do I wish to establish here that Catholicism is, in fact, or should properly be construed as, the sublative synthesis of Jewish letter and Protestant spirit, but merely to suggest what seem to have been Schlegel's—phantasmatic or ideological—reasons for imagining that it might comprise such a synthesis. For only the appreciation of these reasons can enable us to "understand" how Schlegel passes from the extreme aesthetic sophistication of his work around the turn of the century to the equally extreme and apparently willful theological naïveté of his later self-subordination to the authority of an opaque revelation.

But if the path of Romanticism leads from an early aesthetic absolute to a later theological one, from the cultivation of the fragmentary work within the context of a pantheistically inflected post-Protestantism to the awestruck capitulation before an old-fashioned Catholic revelation, what is the *philosophical correlative* of the Catholic solution? What corresponds, that is, to the rationalist-empiricist correlative of the Jewish-Protestant opposition about which the Enlightenment felt the (unsatisfiable) need to decide? Since Schlegel operates in a post-Kantian philosophical universe, the rationalist-empiricist disjunction takes for him the form of a transcendental disjunction between practical reason (*Vernunft*) and the understanding (*Verstand*), a disjunction which takes on also the proper names of various philosophers. In Chapter 6, I examine one example of the allegorical use of a pair of proper names for these Kantian faculties that, when crossed, engender the aesthetic dimension. Here, Fichte occupies the systematic philosopher's position par excellence, the rationalist-idealist position of purely self-positing "reason," and Lessing, the poet and critic, occupies the empiricist-materialist position of the "understanding," while Schlegel posits himself as the sublation of this opposition, the philosopher-poet who goes beyond both philosophy and poetry by sacrificing both on the altar of a revealed, Catholic truth.

Finally, if the epoch of emancipation already in one sense ends, as I suggest, in the ideology of Catholicizing German Romanticism, then this end attains its end—that is, the fulfillment of a prefigured impossibility fulfills itself—toward the middle of the nineteenth century, even before Jews have attained civil rights in all German lands. From the Neo-Catholic moment, we move on (in Part III) to a return simultaneously, and in an only apparently paradoxical manner, to Protestantism and to paganism. Neo-Catholicism inevitably recognizes itself as prefigurative in turn, and what it prefigures then appears anew as Protestantism, but as a Protestantism that goes beyond God for the second time. This Neo-Protestant neopaganism regards itself as trapped between a Neo-Catholicism that appears as a Judaized Christianity, on the one hand, and Judaism pure and simple, on the other hand. It therefore necessarily articulates itself as a desperate need to emancipate itself from Judaism. Further, this post-Romantic *reversal of emancipation* takes on a whole range of political guises, the extreme forms of which I retrace by considering both right-wing and left-wing versions. In the work of Karl Marx (Chapter 7) and Richard Wagner (Chapter 8), the projected *emancipation of the Jews from the Germans*—and thus also into, or for, their own (the Jews') potential Germanness—is explicitly reversed. It becomes the projected *emancipation of the Germans from the Jews*. Hence, again both surprisingly and not at all surprisingly, and in a way to which both Marx and Wagner are completely blind, it becomes the projected emancipation of the Germans *from* their Germanness and *into* or *for* their potential Jewishness. But I will reserve until Part III further comment on this somewhat strange turn of discursive events, before concluding, in the Postscript, with a sketch of the fate of typological theopolitics through the modernist moment and then again today.

PART I

ENLIGHTENMENT

1

Judaism Between Power and Knowledge

THE UNDECIDABILITY OF THE LAW IN MOSES
MENDELSSOHN'S 'JERUSALEM, OR ON RELIGIOUS
POWER AND JUDAISM' (1783)

By attempting a career as a German-language writer in the Berlin Enlightenment, Moses Mendelssohn undertakes the perilous task of moving, as a Jew, from the outside to the inside of a (more or less) secular philosophical and aesthetic discourse that is still profoundly indebted to Lutheran Protestant presuppositions and patterns of thought and experience. In blatant contradiction to one of the more tenacious of these presuppositions, Mendelssohn must demonstrate by his argumentative performance—and in writing—that a Jew can exemplify the concrete, literally fulfilled spirituality of the "rational" Word and not merely the abstract, (pre)figural materiality of the "irrationally" corporeal dead letter. He must show, in short, that, like a Christian, when a Jew writes, he is actually speaking. Mendelssohn must establish the spiritual "voice," as we still blithely say, of the Jewish writer (as non-Jewish writer, i.e., as nonwriter). Indeed, one can readily discern in Mendelssohn's early texts a sustained attempt to speak, although he is a Jew, as "spirit," as substantial inwardness. In *Letters on Sentiments* (1755), for example, as I have shown in detail elsewhere, Mendelssohn not only proposes a theory of sentiments or feelings (*Empfindungen*) in the form of an epistolary philosophical dialogue (where the epistolary-dialogical form itself already displaces writing in the direction of speech) but also attempts to demonstrate by his example that a Jew can have and know feelings in the emphatic sense.[1] He shows therefore in terms of the "aesthetic," where poetic feelings become the touchstone of the voice of spirit, that Judaism does not necessarily exclude—hence, need not be excluded from—the concrete inwardness and spirituality of which the orthodox Christianity of Mendelssohn's day still considers itself the exclusive possessor. Further, Mendelssohn extends this project (or gesture) and renders it even more explicit both in *Phädon* (1767) and in his Hebrew text, "On the Soul." As is well known, in these texts he expounds a rational psychology developed along Leibnizian-Wolffian lines, insisting on the immortality of the soul, a doctrine whose ostensible absence from ancient Hebrew texts is one of the traditional Christian bases for the reduction of the Old Testament revelation to the status of mere "prefiguration."[2]

But Mendelssohn's gesture does not just blithely present the Jews to the eighteenth-century society of bourgeois Christian intellectuals as being more spiritual, more rationally soulful, and (thus) more alive than this society likes to think they are. Rather, as is indicated already by the uncannily haunting motif of suicide in *Letters on Sentiments* and *Phädon*, Mendelssohn is worried about the degree to which his intervention may expose the Jews to the threat of cultural suicide in the form of an ultimately total assimilation, by implicit or explicit conversion, into the Christian German society and culture that surrounds them.[3] The fact that Mendelssohn is translating Leibnizian philosophy into Hebrew for the Jewish community testifies to the danger of assimilation from within, as well as from without. Moreover, several "outward" signs indicate that, at the time, this threat is very real in the rapidly modernizing Berlin Jewish community of Mendelssohn's day. From the 1760s on, the Jewish economic and intellectual elite increasingly adopt the language (German, rather than Yiddish) and clothing (including headdress) of their Christian environment. They also begin to teach the secular educational subjects and to appropriate the cultural practices (such as theater attendance) of their surroundings while becoming increasingly neglectful of Jewish law. More gravely, from about 1770 until 1830, an "epidemic" of conversions occurs whose highest rate of increase is situated during the period from 1770–1805 and whose felt proportions in and around that period are suggested by the statistic that, between 1759 and 1812, in 20 to 25 percent of Jewish families in Berlin at least one person had converted. Finally, and in intimate connection with these aspects of the assimilatory and conversionary tendency, starting at about the time when Mendelssohn writes *Jerusalem* and extending until the death-knell of Jewish-German salon culture (the French occupation of Berlin in 1806), the Berlin Jewish community is marked by previously unheard-of rates of divorce, extra- and premarital interreligious love affairs, and illegitimate children born to interreligious couples.[4] Thus, if Mendelssohn argues in *Jerusalem* both that orthodox Judaism is utterly compatible with rationality and that Jews should not have the right to excommunicate other Jews, then he is clearly countering tendencies toward assimilation and conversion from within, that is, on the basis of the Jews' free renunciation of Judaism, as well as from without.

Concerning the latter tendency or danger, which in turn evidently conditions the danger from within, Mendelssohn's realistic worry is that (insensitive yet) "hopeful" Christians may respond to Mendelssohn's exemplary demonstration of Jewish rationality or spirit by imagining that, if Judaism is *not* radically opposed, as pure prefigural letter, to the fulfilling spirit and is perhaps even prepared to acknowledge itself to be *essentially* reducible to that spirit, then nothing remains to separate Judaism from Christianity except the merely inessential, exterior accessory of the letter. Because Lutheran Protestant Christianity is inaugurated as the ambition to contain less materiality or letter than any other positive religion, i.e., to contain only that letter which cancels itself and raises itself up without residue into spirit itself, conversion of the Jews to Lutheran Protestant Christianity will be the logical, rational, enlightened next step.[5] As is well known, on the basis of Mendelssohn's consistent commitment to reason qua spirit, certain of his Christian readers infer that Mendelssohn is on the brink of, or has effectively broached, conversion. They therefore enjoin him publicly—the first and most prominent instance of this is Johann Caspar Lavater in his open letter to Mendelssohn of 1769, and the second major instance is August Friedrich Cranz in his (anonymously) published text of 1782—either to convert or to explain openly why Judaism appears, by the light of reason (as they think is unlikely), more persuasively spiritual than Christianity. Mendelssohn largely evades Lavater's provocation, while he accepts Cranz's invitation somewhat more fully insofar as he elaborates, in *Jerusalem, oder über religiöse Macht und Judentum*, a theory of how Judaism compares to Christianity with respect to both state violence and religious dogma (or simply power and knowledge).[6] I will therefore look into this exchange with Cranz in some detail. I will show quickly that Cranz's provocation of Mendelssohn is explicitly based on: (1) Cranz's understanding of the Jewish-Christian relation as one between prefigural letter and fulfilling spirit; and (2) his misunderstanding of Mendelssohn as having argued, in the Preface to the German translation of Manasseh Ben Israel's "Salvation of the Jews" (on which a bit more in a moment), that Judaism is essentially reducible to its own spirit. At somewhat greater length, I will show that, contrary to Cranz's misunderstanding, in the Preface to Ben Israel's text Mendelssohn does not actually argue for the ultimate reducibility of Judaism to spirit. Rather, he complicates—and in this sense undermines—the simple, hierarchical, binary opposition between letter and spirit, figural and literal, Jew and Christian. Finally, and in greater detail, I will show how, in his answer to Cranz in *Jerusalem*, Mendelssohn persistently carries out this reversal and displacement of the opposition constitutive of the rhetoric of Jewish-German dialogue. As we will see, the main gesture of *Jerusalem* is the argument that Christianity, not Judaism, is the religion of the "letter" insofar as Christianity tries to control spirit by means of revealed doctrine.[7] In contrast, Judaism is the religion of the "spirit" insofar as it does not prescribe dogma but only specific ceremonial actions.[8] Here, Mendelssohn (reluctantly) broaches the passage from the (post-)Reformation to the Enlightenment discourse I have characterized in the Introduction as a passage from Protestantism as prefiguration to its Judaizing fulfillment. But again, it is not so much the simple reversal of the relationship between Judaism and Christianity that is Mendelssohn's point. Instead, he undertakes the unsettlement of the reified opposition between letter and spirit. The "spirituality" of which it is (literally) a "matter" here is the "spirituality" that lies beyond the opposition between (literal) spirit and (prefigural) matter.

The Context of the Publication of 'Jerusalem': Cranz's Misreading of Mendelssohn's Preface to "Salvation of the Jews"

The discussion that occasions the composition of *Jerusalem* can be taken to begin with Mendelssohn's publication in 1782 of a Preface to the German translation of Manasseh Ben Israel's "The Salvation of the Jews."[9] (The translator is Mendelssohn's disciple, younger colleague, friend, and doctor, Markus Herz, at whose wife's salon Mendelssohn's daughter, Dorothea, will meet Friedrich Schlegel fifteen years hence, thereby initiating a translation-project of a rather different sort.) Manasseh Ben Israel, a prominent Dutch Jew and also one of the teachers of Spinoza, had addressed the "Salvation of the Jews" in 1656 to the English authorities in order to argue before them for the readmittance of Jews into England, from where they had been expelled in 1290. Mendelssohn organizes the German translation and republication of Ben Israel's text in 1782 in order to argue for the amelioration of the civic condition of the Jews in Prussia (and so also to help create a situation that would no longer encourage apostasy). In the wake of the publication of the Enlightenment text, *On the Civic Improvement of the Jews* (September 1781), by Christian Wilhelm Dohm (a councilor in the Prussian War Ministry), as well as the proclamation of the Edict of Tolerance by the Emperor Joseph II, which substantially improves the civic condition of the Jews in Bohemia (October 1781) and then in Austria (January 1782), Mendelssohn feels called upon to enhance the tendency toward tolerance by making available knowledge of the English precedent from a century before.[10] But the aspect of the German publication of the "Salvation of the Jews" that turns out to give rise to the most animated and extensive debate is Mendelssohn's decision to take the composition of his Preface in part as an occasion to controvert one of the arguments made by Dohm in *On the Civic Improvement of the Jews*. A proponent of the integration of the Jews into German civic life, Dohm had argued, as is well known, that if and when the Jewish communities were integrated into the German states around them they ought to retain, like the Christian churches, the right to excommunicate their members at their own discretion. Somewhat surprisingly, and yet evidently (in part) in order to prevent the weakening of the Jewish community from within by bitter struggles between the *Maskilim* (Enlighteners) and the traditionalists, Mendelssohn argues in his Preface that, because church and state should be separate entities, no religion has any legitimate right of excommunication, and that therefore the Jews should no more be granted this right than the Christians. This argument is, at least manifestly, the argument around which all of the others turn in the debate we are considering here.

In response to Mendelssohn's Preface to "Salvation of the Jews," August Friedrich Cranz anonymously publishes a provocation entitled "The Search for Light and Law," in which he suggests that, with the suspension of the political authority of Judaism to excommunicate its wayward children—which he takes to be a suspension of the legalistic and political dimension of Judaism, a suspension of its anchoring in, and identification with, the letter—Mendelssohn has taken the first half of the step toward conversion.[11] Cranz challenges Mendelssohn therefore either to complete this step, renouncing Judaism altogether, or to clarify what distinguishes Judaism from Christianity and why, although a rational theologian, he nonetheless prefers to remain a Jew. Mendelssohn's answer to this challenge comprises *Jerusalem*, in which, after restating his argument on the necessary separation of church and state, Mendelssohn declines Cranz's gracious invitation to conversion. He argues, on the one hand, that Orthodox Jewish law remains binding on Jews even if they should one day become, as he hopes, citizens of the German states. On the other hand, Jewish law is neither a political law, and so does not legitimately include the possibility of excommunication, nor a system of belief, and so leaves reason free to explore the domain of knowledge at its will.

But before examining these arguments in more detail, it is necessary to look more closely at the terms of Cranz's objection in "The Search for Light and Law" and to compare them with Mendelssohn's text in the Preface. For Cranz not only invites Mendelssohn either to convert or to prove the superiority of Judaism over Christianity but he also (in the same breath, so to speak) asks him to use language in a new way:

The lawgiver of the Jews and of the Christian Church which emerged out of that oldest of faiths, Moses, spoke to his people with his face hidden because, as the tradition indicates, the children of Israel could not endure the brilliance of his face. In the epoch of the so-called new covenant the Christians boasted that they saw Moses with his face uncovered. This imagistic mode of representation [*bildliche Vorstellungsart*] evidently means nothing other than that there was a time where the eyes of still-unenlightened nations [*unaufgeklärter Nationen*] could not yet endure the full pure truth, and that there came another time, where people dared to look more sharply into the bright sun, and believed themselves sufficiently strong to come out with language more purely, to throw off the covering, and to teach unmasked that which was otherwise dressed in hieroglyphs and more than half hidden in figural modes of representation [*figürlichen Vorstellungsarten*].[12]

With these words Cranz distinguishes between Jews and Christians as between those who can experience or express the truth only in a mediated, figural, material, improper form and those who can experience or express it in an unmediated or immediate, literal, spiritual, proper form. In so doing he identifies with the term *enlightened* what he takes to be the specifically Christian capacity for immediacy.[13] Cranz's challenge to Mendelssohn is accordingly not only a challenge to come clean and complete his conversion but simultaneously and *indistinguishably* a challenge to get proper and complete his overcoming of, or his emergence from, (pre)figurality, which means also his overcoming of the disfigurative performativity inherent in the figural, his emergence as a whole (literal) figure from disfiguration.[14] Cranz grants that Lavater's earlier challenge was inappropriate because it made public use of private knowledge, and that Mendelssohn was therefore justified, in his response, to "cover his face" and to answer from behind a curtain like the original Moses. But Cranz goes on to argue that Mendelssohn has finally provided a public occasion for the demand of further explication by publicly rejecting the right of excommunication and therefore beginning to cast aside the legalistic and political aspect of Judaism, which alone distinguishes it from Christianity. According to Cranz, one can now justly demand of Mendelssohn his total self-revelation, his total annihilation of any figurality that would continue to veil his speech. This annihilation, I am suggesting, is here synonymous with conversion:

You yourself emerged from behind the curtain for a moment unmasked with a brilliant glimpse of truth; you have aroused the expectations of the public in search of truth; to see you in your entirety—this must not be an appearance allowed to disappear again immediately like a fleeting meteor. . . . Now, my dear Herr Mendelssohn, now that you have begun to take the first step freely, now you must not fail to take the second step you owe us, to show yourself complete(ly) [*sich ganz zu zeigen, nicht schuldig bleiben*]. You granted us a Preface, which traversed the darkness like a lightning-bolt; let us now read a complete Postface by you and therewith let the dawn of truth break forth into a beautiful day, in order to enhance the journeys in the light of those who are friends of light and who wish to take certain steps led by the hand of truth. (76)

In this rather confused way, Cranz, who is himself speaking from behind a mask of anonymity, nonetheless reveals that what is at stake in this debate is not merely or even principally state and religion or Judaism and Christianity, but rather the status of language in its figural and nonfigural dimensions.[15] That is, he reveals that the determinations of the relations between state and religion and between Jewish and Christian are here entangled with, and dependent upon, the clarification of the relations between figural and literal uses of language. The notion of the inassimilability of the Jews into the German states as into secular Christian reason functions, in this exemplary expression of German anti-Semitism, as a mask or figure for the inassimilability of figurality into the literal language of truth.

Mendelssohn's Preface to "Salvation of the Jews": Contesting the Figural-Literal Opposition

Cranz's invocation of the opposition between prefigural letter and fulfilling spirit as a model for the relationship between Jews and Christians strikingly bears witness to the power of ideologies to control reading, for in order to continue to operate without further ado in terms of this model, Cranz manages to ignore the main argument Mendelssohn repeatedly makes in his Preface to Manasseh Ben Israel's text. Mendelssohn does not in fact argue that the essence of the (Jewish) letter is the (Christian) spirit *except insofar as he also argues the converse*, that the essence of the (Christian) spirit is the (Jewish) letter. To make both of these arguments at once is entirely different from making one of them alone. Since Mendelssohn repeats his objections to the right of excommunication in greater detail in *Jerusalem*, we will postpone discussion of the grounds and implications of these objections until we consider *Jerusalem* itself. For the moment, it is necessary to show that, even in the introductory developments of the Preface, the considerations to which Cranz does not explicitly respond, and which have never to my knowledge come into focus in the literature on Mendelssohn, Mendelssohn's main gesture is to complicate and disrupt the letter-spirit distinction.[16] We will consider two avatars or quasi-synonymous transformations of this distinction: the distinction between rhetorical (or false) and philosophical (or true) language, and that between nonproductive and productive activity.

Mendelssohn unsettles the former distinction through his discussion of the anti-Semitic legends about the Jews:

More than one legend has maintained itself since those days because it has not yet occurred to anyone to place them in doubt. Some have been supported by such weighty authorities that no one has dared to take them for legend and slander. Others have maintained themselves on the level of their consequences although they themselves have not been believed for a long time. In general, slander is so poisonous that it always leaves behind a certain effect in the mind [*von so giftiger*

Art, daß sie immer einige Wirkung in den Gemüthern zurückläßt] even when its untruth has been discovered and commonly recognized.[17]

While the medieval gentiles slandered the Jews, among other things accusing them of poisoning the wells of the Christians (6, 7), the gentiles, through this slander, have poisoned themselves and each other, not to mention the Jews. The result: even when the falsity of the slander is proven, it continues to appear to be true. Like sophistical rhetoric, the poisonous slander of anti-Semitic legends produces the effects of persuasiveness in the absence of truth. Moreover, since the "poisonous" character of the Jews has always been bound up with their prefigural and thus rhetorical function within—and yet of necessity outside of—Christianity, the "poisonous" character of the gentiles' anti-Jewish slander in Mendelssohn's text fairly directly corresponds to what, on his account, that slander projects onto the Jews.[18] The "poison" of Jewish "rhetoric," then, resides according to Mendelssohn nowhere else but in the Christian "rhetoric" about Jewish "poison."

But Mendelssohn pushes his reversal of the hierarchical binary opposition of Jewish letter and Christian spirit one step further here, makes it one step more explicit, by arguing that the persistence of Christian slander and of the barbarous violence it generates is based not merely on the historical tenacity of legends but also on the excessive adherence to the *letter of the law* on the part of the Christian authorities in their persecutions of the Jews. In order to illustrate the way these anti-Semitic legends have functioned, Mendelssohn recounts the false story that Elector Joachim II was poisoned by his physician, a Jew named Lippold, in an act that led to the expulsion of the Jews from the land. He then contrasts this story with the facts of the case as recently ascertained through the historical researches of an eighteenth-century physician named Möhsen. Quoting Möhsen, Mendelssohn writes that Möhsen is right to remark, on behalf of the rulers of the time, "'The Princes in those days took themselves to be secure in the adequate carrying out of their duties as rulers when they passed accusations and investigations on to their advisory councils who were responsible for legal matters, and these believed that they had proceeded according to law when they fulfilled the letter of the law [*die Buchstaben des Gesetzes erfüllten*]'" (8).

But Mendelssohn goes on to suggest, in a mildly antinomian gesture, that this excuse is none: "In this way of course barbaric laws are much more destructive than no laws at all" (8). Further, not only is following the letter of the law worse than following no law at all when the laws are barbaric but also the formal lawfulness of trials can often blind one to the injustice and untruth of the claims these trials supposedly substantiate. Referring to Christians of his acquaintance, especially those from Catholic lands, Mendelssohn argues that they are often strengthened in their adherence to prejudices by the "lawful form [*gesetzmäßige Form*]" (9) of the trials in which Jews are convicted of crimes they have not committed. Finally, at the end of his discussion of vestigial medieval prejudices against the Jews, Mendelssohn summarizes:

> For one cannot emphasize too strongly the important truth that barbaric laws have more terrible consequences the more lawful the trials are and the more strictly the judges make their judgments in accordance with the letter [*nach dem Buchstaben urtheilen*]. Unwise laws can only be corrected by divergences, just as mistakes in calculation can only be compensated for by other mistakes. (10)

Thus, Mendelssohn not only attributes both the "poison" and the "rhetoric" of the Jews to Christian anti-Semitism as the "poison" of "slander," thereby returning the "gift" of that "poison" to its malevolent giver, but in addition he argues that the excessive fixation on the letter of the law, with which the Jews continue to be identified even in Enlightenment Germany, has been the Christian institutional and discursive basis of the barbarisms (*Barbarey* [7]) of medieval-style Christian anti-Semitism. Mendelssohn reverses the traditional alignments, then, taking the side of spirit in his own name as a Jew, while suggesting that it is the involvement of Christian society with the rhetorical materiality of the legalistic letter that causes it to project that very materiality onto the Judaism from which it must violently differentiate itself in order to come ideologically into being.

Mendelssohn's disruption here of the Jew-as-letter, Christian-as-spirit model of Jewish-Christian relations takes not only the form of the analysis of the poisonously rhetorical legalism of anti-Semitic Christianity but also that of the redefinition of the relations between nonproductive and productive labor.[19] Having treated the topic of the backward persistence of medieval Christian paranoia, Mendelssohn turns to address a contemporary fear: because the Jews, being excluded from farming and handwork, are largely involved in commerce, they are essentially parasites, whose labor is nonproductive, and so their increasing prosperity will create an impossible burden for the rest of the society.

In some recent writings one finds the criticism repeated that 'the Jews produce nothing. They are in their current constitution neither farmers nor artisans nor handworkers, and hence they do not help nature in its production, nor do they give to its products any new form; but rather they merely carry and transport the raw or improved products of the lands from one place to another. They are thus just consumers, who must become a burden on the producers.' Indeed, a great and otherwise insightful mind recently complained out loud over the abusiveness of the situation wherein the producer has so many middlemen to take care of, so many useless snouts to feed! (12)

If the Jews' numbers increase without any alteration in the kind of work they are allowed to do, so the argument continues, as nonproductive consumers they will place an intolerable burden on the state. But if, on the other hand, they are allowed to practice farming and handwork, then they will provide vexatious competition for the Christians who traditionally and currently practice these professions. In order to counter these arguments, which threaten to stall the emancipation of the Jews before it even gets underway, Mendelssohn takes two steps.

First, he argues that, if only farming and handwork count as productive labor, then even most of the work done by *Christians* under current social conditions is nonproductive labor. Those involved in education, intellectual work, and the army do not produce physical products per se, and even the food industry (*Nehrstande*) consists largely of people who buy, sell, and transport food products and the implements necessary to their production and consumption, while those who own land, as well as the masters of guilds, rarely get their hands literally dirty in the real production of real goods (13). Merely mediating work is by no means exclusively the property of the Jews.

Second, Mendelssohn argues that this so-called nonproductive labor is in fact a kind of productivity.

Not merely making, but also doing means producing [*Nicht bloß Machen; sondern auch Thun heißt hervorbringen*]. Not only those who work with their hands, but altogether those who merely do, further, occasion, or simplify [*thut, befördert, veranlasset, erleichert*] something that can serve the use or pleasure of other human beings deserve the name of producers [*Hervorbringers*] and they deserve this name sometimes all the more, the less movement one can perceive in their extremities. . . . To the happiness of the state as of the individual human being various sensuous and supersensuous things belong, physical and spiritual goods, and whoever contributes in any way, more or less distantly, mediately or immediately [*auf irgend*

eine mehr, oder minder entfernte, mittelbare oder unmittelbare Weise], to their production or completion, is not to be called merely a consumer. He does not eat his
bread for free but has produced in order to earn it. (13–14)

Mendelssohn relativizes the absolute, qualitative distinction between nonproductive and productive labor here by reducing it to a quantitative distinction between a "more or less" distant contribution to production. He
thus not only includes "mediated" as well as "immediate" productivity
within productivity as such but also implies that *all* productive labor is to
one or another degree "mediated," because its contribution to actual production is to one or another degree "distant" from the goods that result
from such production.

How, then, does this unsettling—or "mediation"—of the distinction
between nonproductive and productive labor amount to a version of the
unsettling of the distinction between ostensibly Jewish, (pre)figurally self-
differential letter and ostensibly Christian, punctually literal or self-same
spirit? In other words, if one prefers, what is the unstated analogical structure that makes the social and theological levels of the medieval (and also,
residually, the modern) system of Jewish-Christian relations so tightly
coherent that we almost never explicitly thematize the basis of this coherence? Clearly, in the set of ideological correspondences that still comprise
the Western metaphysical milieu, letter is to spirit as mediation (or absolute
distance) is to immediacy (qua absolute proximity). The figure, we often
assume, does not truly add meaning to the utterance but merely at best
serves as a useless ornament. As the etymology of "metaphor" suggests, it
"transports" a signifier toward a signified that does not belong to it and vice
versa, thereby introducing an element of dispropriation, just as the nonproductive labor of transportive middlemen introduces dispropriation
both in that they move goods from one place to another where these goods
do not belong and in that they eat the food which, "properly" speaking,
does not belong to them (since they have not "earned" it). The figural
expression "produces" a meaning that is none, that is not properly a meaning, whereas the literal expression "produces" a meaning onto which one
can get one's hands or into which one can readily sink one's teeth. The
"work" produced by the figure is a "work" that lacks meaning, a "work" in
the absence of spirit, a "work" that is actually none except in the denigrat-
ing sense that, for example, Luther gives the term. But the "work" produced by the literal expression is the "work" of meaning itself, the "work"

that is the direct and immediate translation of its spiritual essence, "work" (in the sense of labor) that is ultimately pure manifestation of faith. In all these senses, then, the nonproductive-productive labor distinction appears to be merely another version of, a synonym for, the letter-spirit distinction. Accordingly, when Mendelssohn shows that the "nonproductive" resides at the heart of Christian society and then argues that the "nonproductive," in general, is so intimately a part of the "productive" that the "productive," in general, could well be seen as a mere variant of the "nonproductive," he is suggesting that the "Jewish" letter is essential to the "Christian" spirit. Indeed, it is so essential that this spirit can be regarded as a mere *variant* and dependent derivative of the letter from which it wishes to distinguish itself in order to appear to come into autonomous being. Spirit is a mere figure or ghost, in other words, of the oddly animated letter that is its most literal expression or truth.[20]

Given these opening arguments against the simplicity of the opposition between letter and spirit, it is a rather stunning testimony to the power of ideology (in the guise of both Western metaphysics and Western anti-Semitism) that Cranz could have taken Mendelssohn's rejection of the right of excommunication to comprise simply a half-veiled move from the prefigurative legalism of Judaism to the fulfilling spirituality of Christianity. In order to see more closely what Mendelssohn's rejection of excommunication *does* involve, we now turn to its most full-blown elaboration in *Jerusalem*.

Church and State as Knowledge and Power in 'Jerusalem'

Like his discussions of both the medieval slander against the Jews and the modern prejudice against the "nonproductive" character of Jewish work, Mendelssohn's discussion of the question of excommunication—the question of religious power—first in the Preface to Ben Israel's text and then more expansively in *Jerusalem* reverses and complicates the polarities with which Cranz and more generally the discourse of anti-Jewish Christianity operate.[21] We shall see below that he aligns religion, as the (essentially spiritual) religion of reason, not with the literal but with the figural, indeed the endlessly (pre)figural, while he aligns the state, as political and legislative power, not with the figural but with the literal, in the sense of the materially performative or effective.[22] Moreover, he transforms the relation between these two terms from one of linear, historical progress—the progress from state to religion, from Jewish to Christian— into one of nonlinear, nonhistorical, inscriptive undecidability.[23] On this basis, he proceeds first to argue for the separation of state and religion and then to argue that the affirmation of this separation is perfectly compatible with Judaism.[24] But in order to be able to appreciate the systematic complexity of Mendelssohn's argument in favor of the proper separation of state and religion, and his way of situating Judaism with respect to this division, we have to see how Mendelssohn understands *what is at stake in the question* of these relations at the very outset of *Jerusalem*, as well as how he positions Catholicism and Protestantism with respect to these stakes.

Two things are at stake for Mendelssohn in the solution of the problem of the relations between state and religion, or power and reason (or, as we might say today, knowledge).[25] One of these things is sacrificed with each possible solution to the problem. If state and religion are at odds, "then the human race is sacrificed to their discord,"[26] torn asunder, divided between a thought (or a spirit) that refuses and tends to undermine all force, on the one hand, and a force (or letter) constantly attempting to control that thought, on the other hand. But if state and religion are in a harmonious unity, one loses "the most noble treasure of human happiness, for they seldom get along except in order to banish from their realm a third moral being, *the freedom of conscience*, which knows how to derive some advantage from their disunity" (33; 103). When power and thought are one, thought has no room in which to maneuver, lacks the distance from power it needs in order to be the thought it is. Power tends to prevail. Hence, even if Mendelssohn argues in *Jerusalem* for the division of church and state, the separation of thought from power, his larger task is to find some way of formulating and reconciling with itself a *simultaneous presence and absence of the unity of church and state*.[27]

In order to comprehend how he addresses this larger task in Section II of *Jerusalem*, where Judaism comes into view (and where he answers Cranz's impertinent suggestion that, in abandoning the division between church and state, Mendelssohn has abandoned Judaism for Protestantism), it is necessary to keep in mind the way in which, at the outset, Mendelssohn positions the two main Christian religions (or the two main historical formations within the Christian religion) with respect to this question of the unity or disunity of state and religion. The answer is quite simple. Catholicism represents the *unity* of state and religion, and so the gain of humanity at the price of the loss of freedom of conscience, while Protestantism represents the *division* of state and religion, and so the gain of freedom of conscience at the cost of the loss of humanity qua wholeness. In Catholicism, letter and spirit are one under the domination of the letter; in Protestantism, letter and spirit are two under the domination of the spirit.

> Despotism has the advantage of being consistent. However burdensome its demands may be to the healthy human understanding, they are, nevertheless, coherent and systematic. It has a definite answer to every question. . . . The same holds true for ecclesiastical government according to Roman Catholic principles. . . . Your structure is completely built, and perfect calm reigns in all its parts. To be sure, only that dreadful calm which, as Montesquieu says, prevails during the evening in a fortress which is to be taken by storm during the night. Yet he who considers tranquillity in doctrine and life to be happiness will find it nowhere better secured to him than under a Roman Catholic despot; or rather, since even in this case power is still too much divided, under the despotic rule of the church itself.
>
> But as soon as freedom dares to move anything in this systematic structure, ruin immediately threatens on all sides; and in the end, one no longer knows what will remain standing. Hence the extraordinary confusion, the civil as well as ecclesiastical disturbances, during the early years of the Reformation, and the striking embarrassment on the part of the teachers and reformers themselves whenever they had occasion to settle the question of "how far?" in matters of right. . . . Even now, in our more enlightened times, the textbooks of ecclesiastical law have not been able to be freed of this indeterminacy. (34; 103–4)

Of course, it should be noted that in these passages the Catholic unity of state and church is not perfect and does not manage to consolidate itself without giving way to the Protestant division of state and church, while in turn the Protestant tendency to divide the two does not lead to an abandonment of some attempt to link them.[28] Thus, if, in view of the desirability of the preservation of both humanity and freedom of conscience, what one *ought to have* is some sort of synthesis of the unity and division of church and state, the historical fact is that one *always has* in some sense both unity and division of church and state, but never in any kind of synthesis.[29] Rather, one always has neither a unity nor a division of church and state, and both, yet in such a way that this unity and division remain at odds with each other. In short, the relationship between church and state is *undecidable*, and yet this situation is not a happy one, for Mendelssohn, because it has the structure of a paradoxical and even violent tension. In Section II, Mendelssohn argues that Judaism is a revealed law in which power (or state) and knowledge (or church) are unified, and yet that Judaism is utterly compatible with both complete freedom of thought (or natural religion) and the modern, secular state, in other words, compatible with the situation in which state and religion are separate. Here, Mendelssohn construes Judaism as the ideal synthesis of Catholicism and Protestantism, the ideal synthesis of the despotic reign of the *unity* of letter and spirit and the chaotic misrule of their *disunity*. In order to retrace Mendelssohn's path to the formulation of this solution, let us begin by seeing how he argues his relative preference for the (typically Protestant) division between state and religion over their (typically Catholic) unification.

Mendelssohn begins by setting up state and religion so that they are de facto distinct and opposed. Once a human being has realized that in solitude he can do neither his duty to himself and to his God nor his duty to his fellow humans, Mendelssohn argues, duties the fulfillment of which is necessary to his happiness, he or she must enter into society and work there to promote the common good. The fulfillment of these duties, the promotion of this common good, has two components: act (*Handlung*) and thought (*Gesinnung*). The former comprises the performance of what the duty demands, while the latter ensures that this occurrence comes "from the true source . . . i.e., from genuine motives" (*aus ächten Bewegungsgründen*),[30] motives identical with what ensures their causal relation to action.

A society attempts to assure the presence of these two components of the fulfillment of duty in two different ways: through government (*Regierung*) or the state it attempts to control behavior, while through education (*Erziehung*) or religion it attempts to control thought. These two social institutions both operate by means of reasons or grounds (*Gründe*), but by means of grounds of two different sorts, government operating through "motives" or, in a more literal translation of the German, "grounds of movement" (*Bewegungsgründe*), while education operates through "true reasons" or "grounds of truth" (*Wahrheitsgründe*). Mendelssohn further associates "the grounds of movement" or motives (*Bewegungsgründe*) with the exercise of force (*zwingen*), with seduction (*locken*), with the external (*äußere Bewegungsgründe*), with punishment (*bestrafen*), with discipline (*züchtigen*), and with the manipulation of the emotions of fear and hope (44; 113). He associates the "grounds of truth" (*Wahrheitsgründe*), in contrast, with knowledge, the grounds of the faculty of Reason, and conviction (*Erkenntnis, Vernunftgründe, Überzeugung*) to be brought forth by instruction (*lehren*) and preaching (*predigen*), and also, in a word fitting this schema particularly poorly, with persuasion (*Überredung* [45; 114]). Despite the slippage implied by this latter term, however, we can see that Mendelssohn is defining state and religion as being in fact separate entities and that he is doing so by opposing in a very traditional way the "rhetoric" or the "letter" of the state to the "philosophy" or the "spirit" of religion. In other words, as we might say by invoking the terms of speech-act theory, he is trying to set up the violent *performativity* of the state in opposition to the nonviolent *constativity* of religion.

In order to appreciate fully the sense of Mendelssohn's construal of the state-religion version of the letter-spirit opposition, however, it is necessary to understand that he diverges in one—absolutely decisive—respect here from the most pervasive, traditional Christian schematization of this opposition. He associates the nonviolent spirituality of religion with *figural* language, while he associates the violent materiality of the state and its laws not with the figural but with the *literal*. That is, here the letter is the literal, whereas for Christianity, in its traditional denigration of Judaism, the letter is the figural. Somewhat further on, Mendelssohn makes quite explicit this position of figures on the side of religion or thought, in a passage it behooves us to consider. The passage arises in the context of an argument against one version of the invasion of religion by the state (or of their undesirable and violent unification), namely, the requirement that civil officials swear oaths of faith concerning objects of the "inner sense" (*den inneren Sinn* [66; 133]), i.e., questions of belief, conviction, or persuasion ("Glaubst du? Bist du überführt? überredet? dünkt es dir?" [66; 133]). For Mendelssohn, such oaths amount to a "cruel torture" (*grausame Folter* [66; 133]) of the conscience:

The perceptions of the inner sense are in and for themselves seldom so graspable that the spirit could hold them fast with certainty and repeat them as often as demanded. They escape it sometimes, when it believes itself to be grasping them. Over that of which I now believe myself to be certain, a little doubt slips or steals in the next moment, and waits hiding in a fold of my soul without my awareness. (66; 134)

Objects of the inner sense are—paradoxically—so immediately present to us that they can be grasped only mediately and across a process of deferral; they are so internal to us that they escape internalization. They are so properly what we mean, they are no longer properly our own. This is because they are accessible to us only as figures:

Many assertions for which today I would be happy to become a martyr appear to me tomorrow perhaps as problematic. If I am to go so far as to repeat or express these inner perceptions through words and signs [*Worte und Zeichen*] or swear upon words and signs which others have laid before me, the uncertainty becomes even greater. My neighbor and I cannot possibly connect the same inner feelings [*innern Empfindungen*] with the same words, for we cannot juxtapose, compare, and correct these feelings except through still more words. We cannot explain the words with reference to things [*Sachen*], but rather we must again take refuge in signs and words and in the final analysis in metaphors, because, by means of this artifice we can, as it were, lead the conception of the inner sense back to external sense perceptions [*am Ende zu Metaphern, weil wir, durch Hülfe dieses Kunstgriffs, die Begriffe des innern Sinnes auf äussere sinnliche Wahrnehmungen gleichsam zurückführen*]. But what confusion and unclarity must remain behind, in this way, in the meaning of words, and how extremely must the ideas differ which different people in different times and centuries connect with the same external signs and words? (66; 134)

In questions of the "inner sense," the signified is always a signifier, the literal always again the figure of a figure, because the only way I can have access to my own truth is through words that are not originally my own. Religion, as the discourse of knowledge and persuasion, is thus a discourse that is figural at its (lost) foundations, a discourse of knowledge in which knowledge as such—as inner sense—does not actually appear.

Indeed, the fact that we do not control our beliefs, that they are not subject to our will, not properly our own, is at once the reason why the state has no right to demand specific beliefs of its citizens and the reason why the church may not behave like a state in demanding that we hold certain beliefs in order to belong to its community (and so has no legitimate right to excommunication).[31] According to the contract theory to which Mendelssohn adheres, upon becoming a member of any state or other form of community, we agree to give certain things in order to obtain certain things in return.[32] These things can include objects and behaviors or actions, but not thoughts or other inward states or experiences. We contract to behave in certain ways or to give up certain possessions in order to receive certain forms of behavior or objects in turn. But since our beliefs are not subject to our wills in the way behaviors are, we could never contract to give them away, could never contract, in joining the state or any religious group, to let the state or religious group dispose of them as it wishes. Thus, the de jure rejection of both the unity of church and state and the right to excommunication on the part of religious communities within the state (which are therefore not contractual communities insofar as they are communities of belief) has for one of its necessary conditions the figural, originally improper status of our beliefs, thoughts, and spirit in general, the fact that our spirit is so intimately our own (or that we are so intimately *its* own) that we do not control it except in a most indirect, mediated, figural manner.[33]

The reason for both the de facto and the de jure separation of church and state, then, is that knowledge of matters of the inner sense is figural, only mediately present, whereas power is literal, immediately present, while in a certain sense the figural simply does not allow of, and therefore should not be forced to claim to allow of, translation into the literal. Still, Mendelssohn is not only aware that state and religion *tend* to be (or *are*) impossible to separate insofar as power interferes with knowledge and belief affects behavior but also, in another sense, that they *should* not be separated, because powerless knowledge cannot affect or improve the world in any way, as it should, and conversely power bereft of knowledge is without any real (i.e., spiritual or rational) value. Accordingly, while the main contours of Mendelssohn's argument support the separation of church and state, there remain certain gestures by which he suggests that there both will inevitably be and should indeed be a unity of church and state.

As far as the de jure necessity of the unification of knowledge and power is concerned, in the dual sense that knowledge should become powerful and that power should absorb knowledge into itself in order to become the power of the justice knowledge imparts, Mendelssohn makes this more than explicit a number of times.

Blessed be the state which succeeds in governing the nation by education [*Erziehung*] itself; that is, by infusing it with such morals and convictions [*Sitten und Gesinnungen*] as will of themselves tend to produce actions conducive to the

common weal, and need not be constantly urged on by the spur of the law. . . .
Under all circumstances and conditions, however, I consider the infallible measure
of the goodness [*Güte*] of a form of government to lie in the degree to which it
achieves its purposes by morals and convictions; in the degree, therefore, to which
government is by education itself. . . . Hence, one of the state's principal efforts
must be to govern men through morals and convictions. (41–43; 110–12)

The state should become religion, the literal should become the figural,
what *is* should disappear into what *ought* to be, for the meaning of the
state, the literal sphere of what *is*, is violence, whereas the meaning of religion, the figural realm of what merely *ought* to or might be, the pure possibility of rational truth, is nonviolence.

As for the de facto necessity of the unification of power and knowledge, this necessity also has two senses. First, it can be understood as the
action of knowledge on power, or the becoming powerful of knowledge.
In this sense, it is presupposed as a concrete possibility by Mendelssohn's
entire discourse, since he is attempting to have an effect on the world by
writing down his thoughts. It is more particularly presupposed whenever
he argues for the de jure imperative of a unification of knowledge and
power, i.e., whenever he says that we should affect others as much as possible only by means of rational discourse. For *should* certainly presupposes
can, at least in an Enlightenment text such as Mendelssohn's. The second
sense in which the de facto necessity of the unification of power and
knowledge appears in Mendelssohn's discourse is the converse, namely, as
the inscription of knowledge in brute reality, the triumph of pure power
over knowledge. In other words, whenever the impossible translation
between literal and figural occurs—and it occurs all the time as a displacement or replacement of one ontological status by the other, despite
its impossible or self-contradictory character, and therefore despite the
fact that it continues to fail to occur as a becoming-identical of these two
statuses themselves—there is no way to prevent the literalization of the
figural (or the becoming-power of knowledge, in the sense of the triumph
of knowledge over power) from being accompanied by (or understandable
as) a figuralization of the literal (or the becoming-a-knowledge-effect of
power, in the sense of the triumph of power over knowledge). For when
literal and figural are momentarily fused, who is to say which becomes the
other? If the *ethical* necessity of the impossible unification of the opposed
terms of literal power and figural knowledge is registered as the hope that

knowledge will progressively replace power, then the *real* necessity of this unification will have to be registered in the text as the appearance of violence within the ostensibly nonviolent play of the figures of knowledge. Indeed we can glimpse this appearance in various ways in Mendelssohn's text. For example, if the discourse of knowledgeable persuasion operates, as we have seen above, by means of the "artifice" (*Kunstgriff* [66; 134]) of metaphors, which fail to correspond to what we think we mean, and if we cannot know what metaphors the others attach to our own, then when we speak with the attempt to persuade, which Mendelssohn wants to see as the nonviolent activity of education (42–43; 112), we nonetheless participate in a play of power, or *performativity*, which doubly escapes the control of our knowledge. We participate in a poisonous discourse of figures the persuasive power of which is not grounded in any proper meaning, since proper meaning is only discontinuously related (that is, nonrelated) to the figures of its communication. This persuasive power, as blind power, is already and always the power of the "state" extending itself beyond its proper limits. From this point of view, "religious" groups, and this means all communities formed around discourses of knowledge, constantly exercise an illegitimate right to "excommunication," an illegitimate and blind power of inclusion and exclusion they do not control. Mendelssohn's reasons of truth are from the start figures that incessantly pass on the literally disfiguring power of their own motile, yet not necessarily living motivation.[34]

In sum, in Section I of *Jerusalem*, while arguing explicitly that church and state both are and should be *separate* and distinct kinds of institution (or ontological dimensions of the world), Mendelssohn intermittently completes this picture by allowing that, in addition, and as problematic as this may be, church and state at once are and always ought to be *unified*.[35] The question that he does not hereby solve is how this simultaneous affirmation and negation of the difference between church and state, an affirmation and negation taking place as both factual and normative propositions, are to be brought together under some harmonious heading. In Section II of *Jerusalem*, while maintaining a maximally discreet appearance, i.e., without making fully explicit that he is not only showing Judaism to be compatible with the separation of church and state (and the refusal of the right of excommunication to all religious groups) but demonstrating why Judaism is, in rational terms, *superior* to Christianity, Mendelssohn argues that Judaism, more than Catholicism or Protestantism, is able to accommodate these four positions on the state-church relation. Let us see how this argument takes shape.

Judaism as Synthesis of the Unity and Separation of Church and State

Mendelssohn persists in Section I—despite the undecidability of the church-state relation that repeatedly imposes itself upon his deliberations—in explicitly arguing for the separation of church and state. He thereby raises the expectation, particularly for the reader who does not consciously remark Mendelssohn's ambivalent appreciation of the ethical and real complexities of church-state power relations, that when he comes to discuss Judaism in the second half of *Jerusalem* he will have to demonstrate Judaism to be a pure religion devoid of political authority or power. If he argued this, however, then he would not only fail to address the double necessity of church-state unity but also grant Cranz's objections, Protestantize Judaism, and at the same time acquiesce to the demand for the unification of faiths which amounts, as he knows, to a reinstatement of a Christian theocracy under the name of a secularized discourse of Protestant conviction.[36] In order to avoid this aporetic trap, but also (half-unwillingly) to grant church-state unity a place (namely, a Jewish place) in his argument, Mendelssohn argues, rather surprisingly, that Judaism is neither a religion nor, although it comprises a divine legation, a politics.

On the one hand, it is neither a revealed religion nor a politics because it is *between* the two. Since Judaism leaves the individual totally free to explore the doctrinal dimension of the law by her or his own lights, it is, like a state that would not interfere with religion, completely compatible with natural religion. It thus could be said to overlap with natural religion or to include it nonexclusively within itself. But since it is a relatively powerless law, a law of mercy, like a religion that would exercise no power (possessing no power of excommunication, no power to exclude or include from its community), it is completely compatible with the secular state.

On the other hand, Judaism is neither a revealed religion nor a politics because it is *both*. As a revealed law, rather than a revealed religion in the narrower sense of a revealed doctrine, and yet a law whose prescriptive body (or power structure) carries veiled within itself an always implicit (and therefore never dogmatic) doctrinal dimension, Judaism embodies the unity of church and state in its most radical form, as Mendelssohn finds himself arguing, not quite comfortably, toward the end of Section II.

As a law situated *between* meaning and power, Judaism embodies, or allows fully the participation in, the (quasi-Protestant) separation of church and state, but as a *meaningful* law, Judaism embodies the (quasi-Catholic) unity of church and state. In this sense, Judaism appears as a kind of (non-Christian) synthesis of Catholicism and Protestantism that overcomes the limitations of each.[37] Let us look somewhat more closely at how Mendelssohn formulates these views.

Mendelssohn opens his argument on Judaism by showing why it is possible for him to adhere simultaneously to natural religion and Judaism. The reason is that Judaism, in distinction to Christianity, does not claim to offer its adherents revealed truth, only revealed law. It has no content concerning what is the case—it is the business of reason to discover such content—but only concerning what one should do.[38] Like the state, whenever separation of church and state is the order of the day, it withdraws from the space of the church, i.e., of knowledge, in order to allow free rein to reason there.

Ich halte dieses . . . für einen wesentlichen Punkt der jüdischen Religion, und glaube, daß diese Lehre einen charakteristischen Unterschied zwischen ihr und der christlichen Religion ausmache. Um es mit einem Worte zu sagen: ich glaube, das Judentum wisse von keiner geoffenbarten Religion, in dem Verstande, in welchem dieses von den Christen genommen wird. Die Israeliten haben göttliche *Gesetzgebung.* Gesetze, Gebote, Befehle, Lebensregeln, Unterricht vom Willen Gottes, wie sie sich zu verhalten haben, um zur zeitlichen und ewigen Glükseligkeit zu gelangen; dergleichen Sätze und Vorschriften sind ihnen durch Mosen auf eine wunderbare und übernatürliche Weise geoffenbaret worden; aber keine Lehrmeinungen, keine Heilswahrheiten, keine allgemeine Vernunftsätze. Diese offenbaret der Ewige uns, wie allen übrigen Menschen, allezeit durch *Natur* und *Sache,* nie durch *Wort* und *Schriftzeichen* . . . Man hat auf diesen Unterschied immer wenig acht gehabt; man hat *übernatürliche Gesetzgebung für übernatürliche Religionsoffenbarung* genommen, und vom Judentume so gesprochen, als sey es blos eine frühere Offenbarung religiöser Sätze und Lehren, die zum Heile des Menschen nothwendig sind.[39]

I consider this an essential point of the Jewish religion and believe that this doctrine constitutes a characteristic difference between it and the Christian one. To say it briefly: I believe that Judaism knows of no revealed religion in the sense in which Christians understand this term. The Israelites possess a *divine legislation*— laws, commandments, ordinances, rules of life, instruction in the will of God as to how they should conduct themselves in order to attain temporal and eternal happiness. Propositions and prescriptions of this kind were revealed to them through Moses in a miraculous and supernatural manner, but no doctrinal opinions, no saving truths, no universal propositions of reason. These the Eternal reveals to us and to all other men, at all times, through *nature* and *thing*, but never through *word* and *script*. . . . Invariably, little attention has been paid to this difference; one has taken *supernatural legislation* for a *supernatural revelation of religion*, and spoken of Judaism as if it were simply an earlier revelation of religious propositions and doctrines necessary for man's salvation. (89–90)

Thus, Mendelssohn rejects the prefiguration-fulfillment model for the specific reason that, in his eyes, there is a difference in kind, in intention, in orientation, between Judaism and Christianity, and not merely a difference in degree of realization. Judaism withdraws from the sphere of rational knowledge, even as it commands its adherents to explore that sphere on their own. Since it does not attempt to control knowledge, it is not guilty of the conflation of state and church; by withdrawing from the space of the church, it allows the church to become what it is—reason. In contrast, Christianity, insofar as it dictates doctrine to reason, is constitutively guilty of the conflation of church and state. In this sense, all Christianity is essentially Catholicism, according to Mendelssohn's characterization of the two Christian religions at the very beginning of *Jerusalem*, whereas the Protestant spirit, insofar as it tends toward the separation of church and state, is most adequately realized, in a sense, in Judaism. By conflating church and state, Christianity attempts to bind the spirit to specific forms of expression, and in this sense Christianity, and not Judaism, is the religion of the letter (or the religion that mistakes itself for a state). If the prefiguration-fulfillment model is not to be cast aside entirely, then it should evidently be reversed.

The withdrawal of Judaism from the space of reasoned belief does not entail that Jewish law has no cognitive content or meaning. Rather, Jewish law implies doctrinal truths, but it neither demands that these truths be accepted on "faith" nor definitively specifies their form. Judaism does not impose belief; it sets it free.

Although the divine book that we received through Moses is, strictly speaking, meant to be a book of laws containing ordinances, rules of life and prescription, it also includes, as is well known, an inexhaustible treasure of rational truths and religious doctrines which are so intimately connected with the laws that they form but one entity. All laws refer to, or are based upon, eternal truths of reason, or remind us of them, and rouse us to ponder them. Hence, our rabbis rightly say: the laws and doctrines are related to each other, like body and soul. I shall have more to say about this below. . . . But all these excellent propositions are presented to the understanding, submitted to us for consideration, without being forced upon our belief. Among all the prescriptions and ordinances of the Mosaic law, there is not a single one which says: *You shall believe or not believe.* They all say: *You shall do or not do.* Faith is not commanded, for it accepts no other commands than those that come to it by way of conviction [*Ueberzeugung*]. (99–100; 165–66)

As revealed law, Judaism withdraws its power from the space of knowledge, but it does not fail to indicate where knowledge may be sought. Judaism separates itself from the powerlessness of knowledge without setting itself up in opposition to that knowledge as blind power.

Indeed, as Mendelssohn argues, although Judaism is like a pure politics in that it withdraws from knowledge, it is, on the other hand, not like a politics at all, but rather much more like a pure discourse of knowledge, insofar as it withdraws tendentially also from the sphere of power, the proper sphere of the state.[40] Of course, it is important that Mendelssohn present Judaism in this way. For he has said that Judaism is compatible with church and state in being like a state that respects the separation of the church of knowledge from itself. He therefore runs the risk of having his interlocutors conclude that Judaism is merely a state, and so in this sense not compatible with the belonging of Jews to a secular German state. Mendelssohn suggests, therefore, in various ways that Judaism is not a state, not a politics, that its law is a powerless kind of law. For example, when recounting the fall of the ancient Hebrews into idol worship, he takes the occasion to emphasize the compassionate and loving aspect of their God (120–26; 185–91), in a manner reminiscent of his emphasis on compassion in *Letters on Sentiments.* If the law is a law of mercy, and God's justice the justice of his love (121ff.; 186ff. and 129ff.; 194ff.), then the law is not a matter of violence, as opposed to the nonviolence of faith, but rather of nonviolence. It is not imposed from without but from within. Punishment in Judaism, Mendelssohn argues, is not a matter of revenge, but of moral rehabilitation. The Jewish law, in short, is not a political law. Indeed, after the destruction of the Temple, punishments for transgressions against the law become *voluntary:*

Moreover, as the rabbis expressly state, *with the destruction of the Temple, all corporal and capital punishments and, indeed, even monetary fines, insofar as they are only national, have ceased to be legal.* Perfectly in accordance with my principles, and inexplicable without them! The civil bonds of the nation were dissolved; religious offenses were no longer crimes against the state; and the religion, as religion, knows of no punishment, no other penalty than the one the remorseful sinner *voluntarily* imposes on himself. It knows of no coercion, uses only the staff [called] *gentleness,* and affects only mind and heart [*Sie weis von keinem Zwange, wirkt nur mit dem Stabe gelinde, wirkt nur auf Geist und Herz*]. Let one try to explain rationally, without my principles, this assertion of the rabbis![41]

Thus, Mendelssohn emphasizes not only the nondoctrinal aspect of the law, its compatibility with the freedom of inquiry or religion in its rational purity, but also its noncoercive aspect, and so its compatibility with, its capacity to bend before, the coercive law of a secular state. Toward the conclusion of the text, indeed, drawing on the wisdom of the Jewish "founder of the Christian Religion" (132; 197), he says that the Jews must follow Christ's saying, "Render unto Caesar that which is Caesar's and unto God what is God's" (132; 197 and 139; 204), suggesting that what is God's is, at least for Jews, the Jewish law, even though he does recognize reluctantly that there is some potential tension involved in this attempt to divide one's duties between religion and state.[42]

Mendelssohn tries to position the Jewish law, then, in an intermediate position between state and church, literal letter and figural spirit, power and knowledge, and so on. Being distinct from, but not opposed to, both terms in each of these binary oppositions, the Jewish law would be perfectly compatible with both state and church, respecting the sovereign separateness of each sphere. And yet, as I have emphasized from the beginning, it is not enough for Mendelssohn to formulate the mere separation of state and church. He also wants to envision their harmonious unity. This unity is embodied for Mendelssohn also by the Jewish law, as we already glimpsed fleetingly in the passage above where Mendelssohn alluded to the Rabbinic view of law and doctrine as a unity of body and soul. On the one hand, of course, it is in ancient Hebrew culture prior to the period of the kings that Mendelssohn situates the historical moment when this unity is actually realized. On the other hand, despite the fact that this unity only existed for Mendelssohn in the "original" ancient form of that law, before the ancient Hebrews demanded any earthly king whatsoever, nonetheless the significance of the Jewish law in general as Mendelssohn portrays it in this text is that it not only divides but also unites, not only analyzes but also synthesizes, the spheres of state and church. For the "original" form of the law remains its ideal form, that as which it is supposed to be realized.

In order to explain how the unity of state and church (or power and knowledge, or life and doctrine, or behavior and reflection) is embodied in the ancient Jewish law, Mendelssohn describes it as a certain kind of writing, a "living writing." With this gesture, he decisively controverts the Pauline Christian tradition in accordance with which the letter kills, while the spirit gives life. The ceremonial law was originally a *living* writing because it constantly provided the occasion for the speech that was its necessary supplement: "The ceremonial law itself is a lively kind of writing [*eine lebendige, Geist und Herz erweckende Art von Schrift, die bedeutungsvoll ist*] that awakens mind and heart, that is full of meaning and awakens ceaselessly to meditations, and provides an occasion for oral instruction" (102–3; 169). Mendelssohn's determination of the precise character of this specific form of writing takes the form of a history of language as sensuous signs both audible and visual, because he explicitly recognizes the connection between the history of culture, especially religious culture, and the ideologies and practices of writing and representation with which culture and religions are bound up:

It seems to me that the change that has occurred in different periods of culture with regard to written characters [*Schriftzeichen*] has had, at all times, a very important part in the revolutions of human knowledge in general, and in the various modifications of men's opinions and ideas about religious matters, in particular; and if it did not produce them completely by itself, it at least cooperated in a remarkable way with other secondary causes. (104; 171)

In Mendelssohn's brief history of language and/as religion (104–17; 171–83), the language of visible signs, writing, is explicitly *not* conceived as secondary in any way with regard to speech (despite the traces of logocentric motifs which are elsewhere sufficiently evident in Mendelssohn's discourse [cf. 102–3; 169–70] and against which the traces of another discourse I am following here militate). Rather, speech and writing serve two different functions: the functions of communication with others and communication with oneself in the presence and the absence of the speaker, respectively. Thus, Mendelssohn from the start takes his distance here too from the tradition of Pauline semiotics that has done his people such an extended disservice. Indeed, the two extremes—materiality and abstraction—associated with (Jewish) writing in this tradition are, in his account, associated with two different kinds of writing, one of which turns out to be pagan, while the other turns out to be Christian. The passage from one to the other of these two different kinds of writing—the passage from hieroglyphics to alphabetic script—comprises the essential shift in Mendelssohn's version of the history of writing. Mendelssohn attempts to explain this shift as a rational innovation. Through the frequently repeated comparison of speech and writing, language users will have come to remark, he surmises, that both the audible signs and the written signs can be subdivided into elements which recur in different signs in different combinations, and that one can establish an arbitrary and limited system of correspondences between sounds and images which would provide a finite figuration of the infinite set of possible concepts. With alphabetic writing, one was able "to think the immeasurable as measurable [*das Unermeßliche als meßbar*], as it were to divide the starry sky up into figures [*in Figuren*], and so to situate each star, without knowing the total number of stars" (109; 175). In other words, alphabetization would allow for the apparent reduction of the unknown power of the skies of knowledge to the recognizable figures of the anthropomorphic will. The invention of alphabetic writing, then, achieves the abstract homogenization of speech and writing, the assimilation of each to the other, the identification of others with oneself and vice versa, or the effacement of the difference between presence and absence of the subject of thought. In this "history," however, the Hebrew language (and hence Hebrew law) comprises the moment of transition from hieroglyphic to alphabetic script and functions as a kind of *Mittelglied* (to use Kant's term for the faculty of reflexive judgment) between the two.

In order to understand what sort of *Mittelglied* the Hebrew language and its text comprise, we have first briefly to consider Mendelssohn's account of the disadvantages of the different kinds of writing (and religion) between which it discontinuously mediates. For Mendelssohn, the disadvantage of hieroglyphics, as of all forms of natural or mimetic visual signs, is that the concepts they are to represent are too easily confused with the things whose images are given in these signs. They are too close to the world of objects and so they tend to lead to superstition, which takes the literal letter—the material form—for the figural—spiritual—meaning, and thus turns the nourishment of writing into the poison of idolatry: "The images had lost their value as signs. The spirit of truth, which was supposed to be preserved in them, had evaporated, and the empty vehicle that remained behind was transformed into poison" (115; 181). The disadvantage of alphabetic writing, on the other hand, is that the figural, spiritual meaning usurps the place of the material letter entirely:

> Images and imagistic writing [*Bilder und Bilderschrift*] lead to superstition and idolatry, and our alphabetic scribbling [*unsere alphabetische Schreiberey*] makes man too speculative. It displays symbolic knowledge of things and their relations too openly on the surface, relieves us of the effort of penetration and research, and creates an excessively wide gap between doctrine and life. (118; 184)

In the case of hieroglyphics, doctrine disappears into life, and the two are too close together. In the case of alphabetic writing, life disappears from doctrine, and the two are excessively far apart. In the one case there is nothing but (what Mendelssohn has been understanding as) the literal letter, the blind power of a politics that does not know what it knows. State and religion are unified, as occurs also under the Catholic Church, according to the opening remarks of *Jerusalem*. In the other case there is nothing but the figural spirit, the all-seeing powerlessness of an apolitical discourse of pure reason incapable of having any effect upon the world. This is what would presumably happen with Protestantism, whose radical spirituality, or excessive evacuation of the world, would make it complicit with a state that expands to fill the power vacuum this spirit leaves. The spirit of such a Protestantism would constitute, even if by dialectical opposition, merely another version of the state-church unity of Catholicism it was originally meant to disrupt. (Like "autonomous art," such a spirit would confirm the politics of the status quo by removing itself from the scene.) Midway between the two, then, neither literal letter nor figural spirit, neither pure politics nor pure religious doctrine, the original Jewish law is situated. Mendelssohn continues in the passage just cited:

> In order to remedy these failings, the lawgiver gave this nation the ceremonial law. With the daily activities and passivities [*Thun und Lassen*] of the people, religious and ethical knowledge was to be bound up. The law did not force them into contemplation, it merely prescribed and proscribed what they could and could not do. The great maxim of this constitution seems to have been: *men must be forced into action, and only provided with occasions for contemplation.* (118–19; 184)

But this law, midway between action and thought, midway between forcing (*antreiben*) and informing (*veranlassen*), and precisely *as their unity*, would itself comprise the special kind of action it prescribes:

Human actions are fleeting, have nothing that remains or endures and that like imagistic writing could lead through misuse or misunderstanding to idolatry. But they also have the advantage over alphabetic signs [*Buchstabenzeichen*] that they do not isolate people, do not turn them into lonely brooders over writings and books. They force (or drive) people rather to communication, to imitation, and to oral, lively instruction. (119; 184)

To observe the ceremonial law, to confront its infinite (il)legibility, is neither to communicate with oneself nor to communicate with others, but rather something else. And this something else is conceived here as a combination that is perilously close to the combination of state and religion, or performance and figure, which Mendelssohn suggests ought (not) to occur in modern times: "Thus doctrine and life, wisdom and activity, speculation and communication were intimately fused, or at least they should have been according to the original arrangement and intention of the lawgiver. But, the ways of God are beyond research! here too, after a brief period, ruination set in" (119–20; 185). The unity of doctrine and life in Judaism qua ceremonial law obviously provides for Mendelssohn an image of the unity of church and state whose absence he at once wishes to affirm, in accordance with his main thesis, and to deny, in accordance with the insight he has into the problematic of the relations between church and state that exceeds the range of this thesis (just as it exceeds the terms in which the immediate social-political problems of the German Jews are posed in Mendelssohn's day). Despite his discomfort, he uses this demonstration of the life-doctrine unity of the Jewish law in order to suggest that, far from being mere "letter" opposed to Christian "spirit," Judaism provides the letter-spirit, figural-literal synthesis that the pure letter of Catholic hieroglyphics and the pure spirit of Protestant phonetic writing (which is the reversed mirror image of the Catholic letter) fail to realize, even if they "figure" it in their own, unrealized ways.

This demonstration having been obliquely accomplished, however, Mendelssohn must go on to deny the theocratic character of ancient Judaism:

But why, I hear many a reader ask, why this prolixity to tell us something that is very well known? Judaism was a hierocracy, an ecclesiastical government, a priestly state, a theocracy, if you will. We already know the presumptions which such a constitution permits itself.

By no means! All these technical terms cast the matter in a false light, which I had to avoid. . . . Why do you seek a generic term for a singular thing which has no genus, that levels with nothing, and is to be brought under a rubric with nothing else? This constitution existed only once; call it the Mosaic constitution, by its proper name. It has disappeared, and only the Omniscient knows among what people and in what century something similar will again be seen. (131; 196)

In the original constitution of Judaism, state and religion were "not united but unitary, not bound together, but the same" (*nicht vereinigt, sondern eins, nicht verbunden, sondern dasselbe* [128; 193]). As contemporary readers, we may find this denegational rhetoric patently unsatisfactory, although we need not therefore either condemn or denegate its unsatisfactory character in turn. For the historiography of the rhetoric of Jewish-German relations, it is above all necessary to have retraced with some degree of precision Mendelssohn's answer to the suspicion that, by presenting Judaism as a culture pervaded by a certain kind of spirit or spirituality, he had simply avowed Judaism to be destined to disappear into the truth of Christianity, generally, and into a Lutheran Protestant version of rationality, more specifically. Mendelssohn's gesture is to interpret Judaism as the synthesis of the Catholic letter qua unity of state and church, on the one hand, and the Protestant spirit qua separation of state and church, on the other hand.

The unity of the unity and disunity of knowledge and power that Mendelssohn tries to see as realized in Judaism repeats, in the final analysis, and on a higher level, the simpler structure of the unity of knowledge and power. For the *unity* of knowledge and power is ultimately, for Mendelssohn, their (Catholic) unity under the aegis of *power*, whereas their *disunity* is their (Protestant) disunity under the domination of *knowledge*. Since sobriety necessitates in this way the recognition that the Jewish unity of the unity and separation of knowledge and power in Mendelssohn's text is tantamount to the mere unity of knowledge and power, perhaps the most we can finally say about this Jewish unity is that it appears there— with the fleeting instability of a meteor. Cranz has written in the passage cited above that Mendelssohn should not be an "appearance which is allowed to disappear again immediately like a fleeting meteor" (76). And Mendelssohn, in turn, writes of the attempted legitimation of religious power, i.e., of any attempted legitimation of the politicization of education or of any exercise of power in the name of truth: "All believe that the meteor is visible, and attempt only, according to various systems, to determine its height. It wouldn't be unheard of, if an unprejudiced person, with much lesser talents, who was gazing upon the place where it was supposed to appear, persuaded himself of the truth: there is no such meteor anywhere to be seen" (84; 151).

The Ontorhetoric of "Refined Pantheism" in Moses Mendelssohn's 'Morning Hours, or Lectures on the Existence of God' (1785)

> It would not be the first famous struggle over which people have become divided, indeed have hated and persecuted each other, that turned out to be in the end a mere feud over words [*bloße Wortfehde*]. Language is the element in which our abstract concepts live and have their being [*leben und weben*]. They can exchange this element in order to alter themselves, but they can never leave it behind without being in danger of giving up the ghost [*den Geist aufzugeben*].[1]

The Pantheism Debate: Mendelssohn's Final "Dialogue" with Christianity

As I suggested at the outset of Chapter 1, merely by entering Enlightenment debates as a Jew, Mendelssohn performatively argues, or illustrates, that Judaism is compatible with rational spirituality or mind and, hence, that Jews can be humans. In response to this performance of himself as the rational, spiritual Jew—the Jew with a soul—Mendelssohn is greeted, not surprisingly, and fairly punctually (i.e., only two years after the publication of *Phädon*, in 1769), with Lavater's challenge either to prove the rational superiority of Judaism over Christianity or to convert. Of course, Lavater is himself much more an enthusiast than a rationalist, and the work by Charles Bonnet he recommends to Mendelssohn as proving the truth of Christianity is a work of empiricist rather than rationalist orientation in the methodological sense.[2] Nonetheless, apparently under the temporary influence of rational theology, and aware of its prevalence in certain circles of the Berlin Enlightenment, Lavater adopts, for the sake of attempting to convert Mendelssohn, the pose of a rationalist—in the sense of a believer in reason— who has found that rationality argues for Christian spirit, whereas Judaism reduces to irrationality and materiality.[3] And August Friedrich Cranz more or less repeats this challenge some thirteen years later in 1782, to be answered by *Jerusalem, or on Religious Power and Judaism*. In this text, as we have seen in Chapter 1, Mendelssohn argues that Judaism combines materiality and spirituality, prefigural letter and fulfilling spirit, and state and church (or the unity and disunity of state and church) more effectively than Christianity, either as Catholicism or as Protestantism. It is not the case, he points out, that the Jewish letter essentially disappears into the spirit of Christianity insofar as Judaism is (or becomes or avows itself to be, at least in part) rationally spiritual. Rather, the letter and spirit are undecidably one in Judaism, whereas in Christianity they are two, Catholicism embodying empirical letter and Protestantism embodying—if bodilessly—rational spirit.

Having published this argument late in his career, and somewhat reluctantly at that because he had always tried to avoid approaching debates on metaphysics in this particularist and violent way, Mendelssohn finds himself almost immediately approached by yet another importunate defender of the Christian faith, Friedrich Heinrich Jacobi. Jacobi *reverses* Lavater's earlier strategy (although he is to some extent a friend and ally of Lavater), attacking Mendelssohn's position, this time from what I would like to suggest is the *opposite* point of view. In accordance with shifting intellectual fashions in eighteenth-century Germany—more specifically the ascendancy in the 1780s of the *Sturm und Drang*—Jacobi attacks Mendelssohn from the standpoint of an irrationalist, pro-Christian and anti-Jewish empiricism, an empiricism that takes religious sentiment as its datum. By publicly advancing the scandalous claim that the recently deceased Lessing had once privately admitted to him to having been a closet Spinozist, Jacobi implies (and then goes on to argue) that the natural religion to which, in *Jerusalem*, Mendelssohn has committed himself on the level of doctrine, the sphere of rational inquiry Mendelssohn has shared with his friend Lessing as the explicitly affirmed site of their common humanity, is essentially a mere determinism, materialism, atheism, and immorality.[4] In short, reason is nothing other than the pure (or radical) impurity of the letter itself. While Lavater had suggested that the spirituality of reason must end up proving to be Christian, Jacobi argues that the spirituality of reason is a sham spirituality, that the spirit of so-called reason is actually pure letter. In place of the "false" spirituality of reason, which amounts for Jacobi to the masked instance of the letter, Jacobi argues for the "true" spirituality of inner feeling, irrational belief, which, as Thomas Wizenmann argues in the wake of the exchange between Jacobi and Mendelssohn, should ultimately be reduced to a belief in the letter of revelation itself.[5] Jacobi's logic, not quite beknownst to himself, is this: if spirit turns out to be letter, then letter—in the form of the empirical data of feeling—must be spirit.[6]

Jacobi represents, then, an emphatically pro-Christian version of sentimentalist empiricism: the letter of (inner) experience is truly spiritual, he assumes, while the spirit of theoretical reflection is mere mechanical letter. And yet, as a Christian empiricist (a "spiritual" materialist), Jacobi is very close to the position of a Jewish rationalist (a "material" spiritualist), his reversed mirror image. Perhaps Jacobi's aggressiveness toward Mendelssohn here is in part explained by the fact that the logic of Jacobi's rejection of rationalism—that the letter must be where the spirit resides—could as easily have seemed to command a preference for Judaism over Christianity as it commanded Jacobi's preference for faith in revealed religion over the reason (and the religion—natural and/or Jewish) that does without the letter of revealed truth.[7] Fortunately for Jacobi, the figure of Spinoza functions so well ideologically as the site of presumedly unambiguous materiality that it renders quasi-invisible the commitment to materiality—in this case, the materiality of sentiment—inherent in Jacobi's preference for faith in inner revelation over rational reflection.[8] At the beginning of the pantheism debates, when Jacobi accuses Lessing of having been a Spinozist, Spinoza is generally known in German intellectual circles not only as a Jew (if only in origin—yet when did origins stop determining essences?) but also as a materialist and atheist who reduces the idealities of God and human subjectivity to the materiality of the world substance.[9] In this context, to argue that reason leads to Spinozism is to argue with double persuasiveness that reason is the letter: reason is a materialist, Jewish plot against the spirit of belief.[10] How does Mendelssohn respond?

In his last major text, *Morning Hours, or Lectures on the Existence of God* (1785), in order to save Enlightenment reason from Jacobi's version of *Sturm und Drang* empiricist antirationalism, Mendelssohn tries to accomplish several things.[11] First of all, he develops an entire epistemology that turns, in a way that is crucial for our topic, around the relations between ontology and rhetoric. In the process of formulating this epistemology, which attempts to reconcile the claims of rationalism with those of empiricism, he unsettles or suspends the ontological stability of the proper and the improper. Second, while defending rationalist proofs of God's existence, and so demonstrating that rational theology in fact provides faith with a stable foundation,[12] he argues that the difference between Leibnizian theism (rationalism in a spiritual mode, or the "Christian" spirit of subjectivist monadology) and Spinozist pantheism (rationalism in a material mode, or the "Jewish" letter of objectivist cosmology) is an undecidable difference to which reason can well be indifferent.[13] (Beneath the surface of Mendelssohn's argument—setting aside for a moment the arguments in *Jerusalem* in favor of the enduring legitimacy of the revealed law—this undecidability evidently implies two things for the cultural crisis of the Berlin Jewish community, and more specifically for the conversion epidemic. First, conversion is conceivable or *possible*. But second, for the same reason, it is *unnecessary* or *senseless*, and so *counter to reason* insofar as it lacks any compelling philosophical justification.) Finally, Mendelssohn defends Lessing's legacy by arguing that, if Lessing was in fact a proponent of Spinozism, then it must have been Spinozism in this "purified" or "refined" sense, and not Spinozism in the sense of atheism and determinism.[14] In what follows, I will consider each of these points in turn. But before doing so, I will cast a glance at how Mendelssohn situates this text in its Preface with respect both to his own life's work and to the contemporary debates on rationalism and empiricism in philosophy. By situating his text in this way he also indicates how, at this point in his trajectory, he situates his life's work with respect to the philosophy of his day.

The Real World, or Metaphysics as a Woman Infected with the Plague

Mendelssohn opens his Preface by excusing himself for not being *au courant* with all of the recent developments in philosophy and by placing the blame for his lack of familiarity with these developments on an enigmatic nervous debility:

The following discourses *on the existence of God* contain the result of all that I have hitherto read or thought about this important object of our researches. For twelve or fifteen years I have found myself in the most extreme incapacity to extend my knowledge [*Unvermögen, meine Kenntnisse zu erweitren*]. A so-called nervous weakness [*Eine sogenannte Nervenschwäche*] to which I have been subject since then forbids me all spiritual efforts [*verbietet mir jede Anstrengung des Geistes*], and makes it almost more difficult for me to read the thoughts of others than to think for myself, which even seems strange to the doctors. I therefore know the writings of the great men who have come forward in metaphysics, the works of *Lambert*, *Tetens*, *Plattner*, and even the all-crushing *Kant* [*des alles zermalmenden* Kants], only from the insufficient reports of my friends or learned reviews, which are rarely more instructive.[15]

What is particularly remarkable about this opening passage is the way in which Mendelssohn characterizes his own vexed relationship with philosophy in terms of his physical-nervous affliction and vice versa.

First of all, he is apparently none too impressed by the medical-biological explanation of his difficulties, referring to them as a "so-called nervous weakness" ("sogenannte Nervenschwäche"). He does not seem to be completely unaware that these difficulties might well amount to a psychosomatic interpretation of his involvement with philosophy.[16]

Second, he gives us some positive sense of the connection between his "so-called nervous weakness" and the politics of religious culture in the current philosophical debates: (1) by dating the onset of the ailment around the time of the Lavater controversy; (2) by specifying that the ailment "forbids" him "all spiritual efforts"; and (3) by suggesting that he is forbidden not only to think but "almost more" strictly forbidden to "read the thoughts of others." Despite all the argumentative energy Altmann expends contesting the notion that Mendelssohn's illness is in large part psychosomatic (although Altmann may well take this approach, justifiably, in part to militate against anti-Semitic clichés about crazy Jews), it would seem that Mendelssohn furnishes us with some clues as to his own sense of the discursively-historically inscribed character of his affliction.[17] If Lavater invited Mendelssohn to convert because Mendelssohn was being too "spiritual" for a Jew, then after the encounter with Lavater, Mendelssohn certainly might have felt "forbidden"—be it by his Jewish conscience, by his desire to avoid conflict, by the Christian ideology around him, or by some combination of these factors—to do further "spiritual" work. And if reading the thoughts of others is not only dangerously self-assimilatory (insofar as these others are Christian philosophers) but also a matter of the constant transformation of letters into mentation or spirit, then reading the thoughts of others would doubly expose Mendelssohn to the danger of being called upon to convert.

Third, Mendelssohn characterizes his incapacity to extend his own knowledge in terms of the major philosophical dilemma of the age, a dilemma that is a displaced double of the impossible choice between (pre)figural letter and literal spirit: the alternative of rationalism or empiricism. More concretely, Mendelssohn makes use of the Kantian verb for the synthetic *extension* of our knowledge beyond the limits of the analytical, "erweitern," in saying that he is not able to "extend" his knowledge. Further, he characterizes his condition with respect to such extension by means of the very term he will apply at a certain point to "untruth" itself, "Unvermögen," as the incapacity to hold together the possible with the real. He thus apparently confesses to having been trapped ever since around 1770 in the untruth of the unreality of mere analytical formal reason, caught up in the impotent abstraction of rationalism. (Not only did the Lavater-affair begin in 1769 but also Kant's groundbreaking dissertation *De mundi sensibilis atque intelligibilis forma et principiis* was presented in 1770, with Markus Herz as respondent. The Lavater-business, which intensifies the letter-spirit crisis, and the movement of Kant toward his critical philosophy, which proposes a transcendental solution to this crisis [in the form of the crisis of the relations between the empirical and rational realms, sensibility and understanding], evidently combine to produce a kind of intellectual quasi paralysis in Mendelssohn from which he never completely recovers.)

Mendelssohn's entrapment in the rationalist world of analytical possibility can indicate that he is too much in philosophy to be out there in the real world, too utterly trapped in thought to be capable of gaining access to things ("Kenntnisse zu erweitern"). But it can also mean the opposite: he is too deeply ensconced in the real world to be out there in philosophy, too deeply caught up in the (material) history of rationalism to be able to move beyond it into the true spirit of current critical thinking. Mendelssohn acknowledges that he is either too much in possibility or too much in reality, too philosophical or not philosophical enough, thinking too much or too little, but he does not quite know which. In this sense, then, the text opens as the simultaneous problematization of the oppositions between images of sickly, nonphilosophical (or overly philosophical), breathless Jews and those of healthy, philosophically inspired (or metaphilosophically aerated) Christians and between philosophical-conceptual possibilities and the realities of the historical, natural, and social worlds. By raising the questions of these two sets of oppositions in one "breathless" breath, it raises the question of their interrelationship.

Moreover, Mendelssohn exacerbates the uncertainty about whether or not he is inside or outside the Jewish or Christian worlds, inside or outside the possible or the real, and inside or outside philosophy (of the possible or the real), by immediately adding to the confession of his inability to do philosophy in the current mode the opposite confession of his inability to *stop* doing philosophy, his inability to *stop* reading and thinking. We learn now that whatever it is that he can't get *into*, he can't quite get *out* of either.

Finally, to further complicate matters, Mendelssohn elaborates this confession through the development of a conceit comparing metaphysics to a dear, but diseased woman friend. In doing so, he overdetermines the several parallel polarities already at play by overlaying upon them those of masculine and feminine:

For me, then, this science still stands today at the point on which it stood approximately around the seventy-fifth year of this century; for it is since that time that I have been forced to stay away from her, although I have never been able to take leave of philosophy totally, as much as I have struggled against myself. Alas, she was in better years my truest companion, my sole consolation through all of the sufferings of this life, and now I had to avoid her on all my paths like a deadly enemy [*Todfeindin*] or, which is even more difficult, to shun her like a beloved infected with the plague [*wie eine verpestete Freundin*] who herself warns me to avoid all concourse with her. I was never sufficiently self-denying to obey her. From time to time secret transgressions occurred [*verstohlne Uebertretungen*], even if never without rueful penance [*reuevolle Büßung*].[18]

Mendelssohn introduces an ironic reversal of the traditional structure of Jewish-Christian relations that operates in terms of several parallel binary oppositions when he employs this extended metaphor of a diseased woman-friend to say that he cannot stop doing philosophy. The structure Mendelssohn displaces is evidently this: insofar as femininity is associated with materiality, and masculinity imaginarily endowed with the character of spirituality, then the relationship between Jews and Christians as one between material letter and intellectual spirit implies that Jews are feminine and Christians are masculine (for more on this topic, see especially Chapters 4 and 5 below).[19] Mendelssohn reverses this structure by making philosophy, which from the perspective of his cultural backgrounds belongs for the most part, medieval rationalism aside, to the Greco-Christian and non-Jewish world, into a woman. Consistent with this move, the woman—(Greco-Christian) philosophy—is connected with an implicitly venerealized plague: the medieval image of the Jew as cause of the plague is reversed into that of the Christian discourse of philosophy as carrier-cause of the plague. As a diseased seductress who warns one away but still lures one too, philosophy is like rhetoric or sophistry, as the Jews represented (and still represent) sophistry for a Christian discourse that was (and is) pervaded, not to say defined, by its mistrust of their wily, always (pre)figurative ways.[20] Of course, Mendelssohn manifestly uses an extended *metaphor* to characterize philosophy as a sophistically diseased woman. Further, he grants both that she appears as diseased only from *his* perspective and also that she warns him not to have contact with her. Hence, she is morally righteous. In this sense, Mendelssohn's reversal of the Jewish-Christian opposition here is ironic and self-ironic, which of course does *not* mean that it cancels itself out completely.

Thus, in contrast to his confident claim in *Jerusalem* that Judaism and philosophy as natural religion are completely compatible, Mendelssohn begins *Morning Hours*—in which he nonetheless proposes to defend natural religion—by acknowledging doubts as to whether philosophy will in the end prove entirely compatible with his continuing existence as a believing and observant (indeed, as a living) Jew. If philosophy leads to atheism, as from Mendelssohn's perspective both Jacobi and Kant argue, and if the activity of philosophizing inevitably exposes a Jew to the (explicit or implicit) demand to convert, either from the rationalist standpoints which Lavater and Cranz had occupied or from the irrationalist-empiricist standpoint which Jacobi now occupies, then perhaps philosophy will have to be abandoned after all. Despite this uncertainty, however, in *Morning Hours* Mendelssohn makes one final major effort to *reject* this conclusion by coming to the defense of rational theology.[21] Aware that his philosophy has been momentarily superceded by empiricism and irrationalism (which he calls "Materialismus" and "Schwärmerey"),[22] he proposes his own text as a testimonial "account" to be "left behind" (he speaks in terms of "Rechenschaft hinterlassen" [5]). He hopes that this testamentary account of a modified rationalism—one into which he tries once more, as he has repeatedly since *Letters on Sentiments*, to incorporate empiricist motifs—will foster a rebirth of rationalism. He sees such a rebirth as the necessary corrective to the excesses of the empiricism and irrationalism that, for the time being, seem to have superceded the old rationalism.[23]

Before moving on to discuss this defense of modified rationalism in natural theology, let us consider briefly its status, as Mendelssohn frames it in his Preface, in terms of the question of *figura*. Insofar as he means to occasion a rebirth of rationalism, Mendelssohn sets up his defense as a *prefiguration*. Indeed, the position of his text as prefiguration is one (witting or unwitting) implication of the title *Morning Hours*: morning is the self-anticipation of day. The treatise is to serve as the morning prefiguration of a later noonday fulfillment. To this extent, Mendelssohn plays his role as wise (dead) Jew to the end. And yet, here as often elsewhere, he subverts or slightly displaces and unsettles the categories of prefiguration and fulfillment that in turn prescribe and predetermine this role. The prefiguration here is both already *fulfilled*—a testamentary "Resultat" (3)—and *belated*—a work of mourning. It seems in fact a collection of mourning hours in which Mendelssohn mourns for the work and lives of his own generation, especially those of his friend Lessing and himself, the work and lives of a henceforth historical Enlightenment. Finally, it is the prefiguration of a return to the (rationalist) prefiguration prior to its fallen and false (empiricist) fulfillment. In order to retrace how the prefiguration proceeds, and so to "fulfill" it ironically in our turn by restoring its proper meaning, which we cannot avoid attempting to do, however "dialogically," let us begin by seeing how the epistemological preliminary section entitled "Preknowledge of Truth, Appearance, and Error" deals with the religio-culturally significant ontological and methodological uncertainties that the Preface announced.

The Ontorhetoric of Rationalist and Empiricist Truth: Three Models of the Unification of Possibility with Reality

In the preliminary, epistemological part of *Morning Hours* (the much larger second part deals with natural theology), Mendelssohn introduces three distinct models of truth, although he only characterizes two of them as such. Each of these models is charged with the task of articulating the unity of the rational and empirical dimensions. Mendelssohn introduces the first model explicitly as an "unfruitful" one, in order to replace it by the second, which he takes to be more "fruitful." As a result of the weaknesses of this second model, however, he is compelled to introduce further considerations, which it is necessary to understand as the proposal of a third model of the articulation that truth is supposed to accomplish. I will consider each of the models in turn. While none alone accomplishes the desired articulation, together they explicate *nolens volens* the ontological undecidability of the figural and literal.

According to the first model, truth (or true knowledge), is the correspondence between subject and object, thought and things, possibility and reality, essence and existence (10–28). Mendelssohn acknowledges explicitly from the start that this correspondence model of truth is questionable, even as he continues to try to provide it with a successful formulation. The source of his persistent doubts is simply the intractable rift between the possible and the real. At most, he suggests, we have immediate access to our concepts or representations of—the possibility or essences of—things, problematic though even the assumption of such access to concepts or representations may be, as he himself has acknowledged in *Jerusalem*. We certainly have no immediate access, however, to things themselves in their very presence. We therefore cannot compare our representations to these things in order to determine whether or not we have attained to adequate correspondence.[24] Still, to the extent that he attempts to render the correspondence model plausible, even as he doubts its capacity to assume a perfectly satisfactory form, Mendelssohn tries to graft an empiricist version of the harmonious agreements between the faculties of sense and between separate subjects (or repeated instances) of sensuous perception (15–17) onto a rationalist version of harmonious agreement between thought and thought.

The *rationalist* component of Mendelssohn's concept of truth operates, insofar as it attempts to reduce contingent reality to necessary possibility or ideality, in terms of the following ontological-rhetorical or ontorhetorical presuppositions. Figurality, or derivative impropriety, is predicated of or associated with the (contingently) real. Literalness, or originality or propriety, however, is predicated of the (necessarily) possible, that is, of thought, consciousness, the ideal, and so on. According to the *empiricist* half of the correspondence model, in contrast, the figural or derivative is associated not with the reality of things, but rather with the possibility of thought. The literal or original, in turn, is associated with reality or existence. The task of knowledge, insofar as it conceives itself as being faced with empirical reality, is to allow its own figures to be led back to an original literal reality from which they have strayed. The unification of these two sets of ontorhetorical presuppositions, however, is no easier to envision than the unification of the spheres of possibility and reality their combination is meant to achieve.

From an ontological point of view, then, the correspondence model of truth requires the (impossible) unification of possible and real, while from an ontorhetorical point of view, it requires the (equally impossible) unification of the reduction of figural reality to literal possibility with the reduction of figural possibility to literal reality.[25] Ontorhetorically, it requires the reconciliation of two equally (im)plausible and equally arbitrary ways of determining the modal status of figural and literal, as well as the reduction of figural to literal according to each of these determinations. Thus, Mendelssohn's attempt to make sense out of the correspondence model yields an exacerbated awareness of the ontological undecidability of figural and literal (as of rhetoric and philosophy, Jewish and Christian, and so on), as well as the awareness that our own knowledge always takes place in the undecidably figural-literal space of the possible-real.

Despite Mendelssohn's efforts to "save" the correspondence model (efforts which already suggest that he never quite manages to overcome that model), on the basis of his recognition of the fact that the absolute comparison of subject and object can never be made (or that the unification of rationalist and empiricist ontorhetorics can never be definitively achieved), he posits a *second* model or definition of the essence of truth, a model he wants to find more "fruitful," more reliable, more self-unified. This is the model of truth as the effect of the *positive force of the soul*:

> We can thus grant the validity of the general proposition: *Truth* [Wahrheit] is every act of knowledge, every thought which is the effect of the positive forces of our soul [*Seelenkräfte*]; insofar as it is, however, a consequence of incapacity [*eine Folge des Unvermögens*], insofar as it has suffered an alteration through the limitations of our positive forces, we call it *untruth* [Unwahrheit]. . . . Every human act of knowledge is thus in part true, in part untrue, for it is the effect of a force that has its borders and limits. (29)

The model of truth as force with which Mendelssohn replaces the correspondence model is supposed to unify truth with itself by reducing the incomparable, nonunifiable duality of possibility and reality to a unity, the unity of "force."[26] Even if knowledge remains divided between truth and untruth, force and nonforce, Mendelssohn has apparently unified the true part of knowledge with itself insofar as it is now that part of knowledge which is the effect of the combined force(s) of the (self-unified) soul. But despite the valiant effort represented by this shift from correspondence to psychic force as the formula for the essence and ground of truth, Mendelssohn is never able to disentangle it from the correspondence model it is supposed to supercede.[27]

Thus, it becomes necessary for Mendelssohn to propose a third model of truth:

What we have investigated until now was merely a matter of knowledge insofar as it is true or false. The true acts of knowledge themselves, however, differentiate themselves from each other in that they excite either pleasure or displeasure [*Wohlgefallen oder Misfallen*] in the soul. The beautiful, the good, the sublime are known by the soul with enjoyment and pleasure [*Lust und Wohlgefallen*]. The ugly, the evil, and the imperfect, on the contrary, excite nonenjoyment and repulsion [*Unlust und Widerwillen*]. . . . Both the faculty of knowledge and the faculty of approbation [*sowohl das Erkenntniß- als das Billigungsvermögen*] are, as you know from psychology, expressions of one and the same force of the soul, but different with respect to the goal of their striving. The former begins with things and ends in us, whereas the latter takes the opposite path, begins with ourselves and has as its goal external things. I will explain myself. /Every force is accompanied by the striving to bring thinkable accidents to reality [*denkbare Accidenzen zur Würklichkeit zu bringen*], either in the substance that possesses this force or in a substance outside of it, which is then considered the suffering one. The drive to knowledge [*Erkenntnistrieb*] is of the first sort. It presupposes the truth as unchangeable and tries to make the concepts of the soul harmonize with it. The goal of its activity is objective truth, and it attempts to bring to reality within the thinking being such predicates as are in accordance with that objective truth. By virtue of the drive to truth, we seek to bring our knowledge into correspondence with the unchangeable truth without regard for pleasure or displeasure. Not so with the expression of the drive to approbation [*des Billigungstriebes*]. When this drive is set into movement, its goal is not in us, but rather in the things outside of us; and it attempts to make those accidents real in outside things that are in harmony with our approbation, with our pleasure, with our wishes. The former wants to transform humanity in accordance with the nature of things, the latter wants to transform things in accordance with the nature of humanity. (61, 63–64)

True knowledge evidently requires both force and nonforce, to the extent that knowledge must both master the object (rationally) and allow itself to be mastered by the object (empirically). According to the model of truth as force, however, true knowledge divided between force and nonforce would be true knowledge divided into its truth and its untruth. In order to avoid this consequence, Mendelssohn divides the (quasi-rationalist) power and the (quasi-empiricist) powerlessness of knowledge into two forms of power: the power to desire and the power to know, respectively. He places one of these aspects of truth beside the other under the unifying heading of the soul.[28] Further, he at once acknowledges and effaces the internal disjunction between the power and the powerlessness of truth, a disjunction which in principle occurs in *all* instances of truth, by speaking of this disjunction as a difference between *different* "instances of truth" ("wahren Erkenntnisse"). The distinction between positive desire (or pleasure) and negative desire (or repulsion) is itself merely a displaced repetition of the distinction between knowing (or negating oneself in order to posit the object) and desiring (or negating the object in order to posit oneself in its place), which is merely a displaced repetition of the empiricist and rationalist aspect of the correspondence model.[29] The unity of true knowledge as force has apparently been saved, then, but only at the cost of a division of force within itself first into the forces (or capacities or faculties) of knowledge and desire, and then, within the force of desire, into positive and negative desire, attraction and repulsion.[30]

At their most advanced point, Mendelssohn's epistemological preliminaries, whose most simple outlines I have tried to sketch here, leave us exposed to their initial dilemma. In ontological terms, how does one establish a relationship between the possible and the real? And in more complex, ontorhetorical terms, how does one reconcile the (empiricist) notion of the figural-literal opposition as a possible-real opposition with the (rationalist) notion that figural is to literal as real is to possible? If Mendelssohn does not quite state the dilemma in the latter, ontorhetorical terms, he is nonetheless acutely aware, as he repeatedly states, in two different veins, that the epistemological and ontological problem with which he is wrestling is profoundly rooted in language.[31] On the one hand, he persistently attempts to clarify the philosophical vocabulary with which he is working, and even, like a good philosopher, to purify it of the metaphorical materiality that weighs it down and renders it opaque.[32] On the other hand, he acknowledges on a number of critical occasions, for example, just before concluding this epistemological first part, that the struggle between rationalists, empiricists, and those who, like himself, believe in both possibility and reality (he calls them "Idealisten," "Materialisten," and "Dualisten," respectively) may in the end be a struggle over words:

I fear that in the end the famous conflict of the materialists, idealists, and dualists would amount to a mere struggle over words [*einen bloßen Wortstreit*] that is more a matter for the linguist [*des Sprachforschers*] than for the speculative philosopher [*des speculativen Weltweisen*]. It would not be the first famous struggle over which people have become divided, indeed have hated and persecuted each other, that turned out to be in the end a mere feud over words. Language is the element in which our abstract concepts live and have their being [literally: weave]. They can exchange this element in order to alter themselves, but they can never leave it behind without being in danger of giving up the ghost. (61)

If the struggle between the materialists, idealists, and dualists is a struggle over how to define the relations between the figural and the literal, then this struggle is indeed a matter for the linguist, at least as long as the linguist is also a rhetorician. Moreover, this struggle over words is not, according to Mendelssohn, to be solved by getting beyond the figures of words to the literal content of thoughts themselves, but rather by coming to terms, if possible, with the impossibility of getting beyond words: by acknowledging the ineluctable yet undecidably and interminably duplicitous modality of the figural-literal. This is exactly what Mendelssohn expresses— if "figurally"—when he writes, playing with the conventional expression, that concepts would give up their *Geist*, their ghostly spirit, if they left language behind. Spirit depends on (being compromised by the) letter, in short, in order to be the spirit it is. The point, then, is not that the materialists, idealists, and dualists should not fight because they may be saying the same thing in different ways, but rather that they should not fight because none of them can actually, completely or finally, know what it is they are saying: they will all always be saying something different from what they mean to say.

When Mendelssohn turns to attempt, on the unsettling and unsettled ontorhetorical foundations of his epistemological preliminaries, some sort of "reconciliation" between pantheism and theism, it is a similar linguistic-rhetorical consideration to which he will have recourse. Whereas in epistemology the question has been whether or not there is an objective world out there that corresponds to the subject's knowledge, in theology the question will be whether or not the world of creation exists objectively outside of God's mind or merely in his thoughts. In other words, the theological question will be: Is God an idealist, a materialist, or a dualist? How will Mendelssohn handle this difficult and troubling conundrum?

Pantheism and Theism, or Fanaticism and Atheism:
The Word "In" as a Fundamental Catachresis

As opposed to the image of Spinoza that Jacobi is trying to exploit for counter-Enlightenment purposes, an image in accordance with which Spinoza is an atheist who collapses God into the world, Mendelssohn reads Spinoza as an acosmist who collapses the world into God.[33] Mendelssohn starts out, then, by reversing Jacobi's view of Spinoza. For Mendelssohn, Spinoza provides a description of the relation between God and world that is perfectly adequate, except that it is adequate only *prior* to creation, when the world still existed as a mere *possibility* or *essence* in the mind of God.[34] In other words, Spinoza is not too irreligious, but, if anything, too religious. Having opted for this acosmist interpretation of Spinoza, Mendelssohn goes on to evaluate Spinozism by comparing it with Leibnizian-Wolffian cosmology, which he takes to provide a description of the world in its relation to God *after* the passage of creation from possibility (or essence) into reality (or existence). Mendelssohn reduces the distinction between pantheism and theism, then, to that between the possibility and the reality of the world, between understandings of the world as existing *inside* and *outside* of God's mind. In other words, he reduces the distinction between pantheism and theism to that between the notions of God as idealist and as dualist. To put it perhaps more directly, he reduces it to the distinction between the idealist's view of the theocosmological relation, for whom not the world but only the mind in which it is represented is real, which in this case would be God's mind, and the dualist's view of that relation, for whom both representing mind and its represented objects are always real, in one sense or another.

Taking its departure from this construction of the pantheism-theism distinction, Mendelssohn's discussion of the distinction proceeds as an extended attempt to erode it, an attempt that comprises two main steps. First, he argues in various ways (in Chapter XIII), in defense of a Leibnizian-Wolffian perspective, that the objective and subjective things comprising the world cannot be meaningfully understood except as substances existing on their own. He tries to show, in other words, that Spinoza would have to acknowledge the existence of a world *outside* of the one substance of God.[35] Second, the shade of "Lessing" appears fictionally (in Chapter XIV) to provide a hypothetical defense of Spinozism that responds more or less point by point to the arguments Mendelssohn has advanced, showing that a pantheist can either controvert or absorb all of these arguments.[36] At the far end of this two-step discussion, a discussion with no decisive issue, Mendelssohn acknowledges, indeed attempts to enforce, a certain incapacity to decide between pantheism and theism. That is, he ultimately undermines the distinction between the two, not by claiming that there is no distinction to be made, but rather by suggesting that the distinction is *undecidable*. It rests, he argues at the conclusion of Chapter XIV, on the radical unreadability of a fundamental catachresis, what we might call the originary "preliteralization" or the "postfiguraliza-tion"—not yet quite literally either (pre)figural or literal—of an opposition between inside and outside that first establishes the very possibility of a relation between figural (possibility or reality) and literal (reality or possi-bility) as fundamental ontorhetorical terms.[37]

If my friend, the defender of purified Spinozism [*geläuterten Spinozismus*], admits all of this, as he, by force of his principles, certainly would have done, then moral-ity and religion are safe; and this school differentiates itself from our system merely in a subtlety that can never have practical consequences; in an unfruitful consid-eration: whether God has let these thoughts of the best coherence of contingent things shine forth, flow forth, stream forth, or with what image should I compare it [*ausstrahlen, ausfliessen, ausströmen, oder mit welchem Bilde soll ich es ver-gleichen*]? (for this subtlety can hardly be described in any other way than through images,) whether he let the light bolt away from himself like lightning or only light up within himself [*er das Licht hat von sich wegblitzen, oder nur innerlich leuchten lassen*]? Whether it remained a mere source [*Quelle*], or whether the source poured itself out into a stream? When one wants to make sensuously present for oneself, through the use of such imaginary turns of speech [*dergleichen bildlichen Redensarten*], production, creation, or making real, etc [*Hervorbringen, Erschaffen, Würklichmachen u.s.w.*]; it is hard to prevent misinterpretation or misunder-standing from extending the metaphor [*die Metapher*] beyond its borders and leading into digressions, into atheism or fanaticism, according to whether the mind inclines otherwise toward convulsive raptures or toward dry reflexion. In their consequences, the systems do seem far from each other, and yet at bottom it is the misinterpretation of the same metaphor that now puts God too imagistically [*zu bildlich*] into the world, now puts the world too imagistically into God. Upright love of truth leads soon back to the point from which one has departed and shows that one has merely entangled oneself in words. Renounce words and, friend of wisdom, embrace your brother! [*Thuet auf Worte Verzicht und, Weisheitsfreund, umarme deinen Bruder!*][38]

The relationship between pantheism and theism is finally undecidable or indeterminable, because there is no proper expression for the relationship between the world and its essential origin, between reality and possibility, figure and literal ground (or vice versa). And it is not merely that the appropriate imaginary representation of the (always already self-appropriated) concept of creation is not determinable, but that the *concept itself*—the most properly literal—is already improper or figural. For otherwise, Mendelssohn would not have spoken here of the sensuous representation of "production, creation, or making real, etc." ("das Hervorbringen, Erschaffen, Würklichmachen, u.s.w."), thereby indicating that it is also a question of the proper name for the concept, and not merely a question of the proper figure for its sensuous presentation. The hyperbolically figural, catachrestic, unrecoverably improper dimension thus pervades both the conceptual and the imaginal here, the possible and the real. We are between empiricism and rationalism, "in" neither the one nor the other. (The concept is imaginary, the image conceptual, and yet not quite, for each is "in" the other, the "figurality" of each consists precisely in its dependence upon its other, the entanglement of the sensuous with sense and of sense with sensuousness.) Hence, the ultimate "metaphor" here is simply "in"—in itself perhaps not so much a "metaphor" as a hyperbole, an excessive translation or an *over*passing. The misinterpretation of the metaphor of "in" constitutes the metaphor of the "in" itself. It is a misinterpretation because the one term is always being put "too" imagistically "into" the other term, the "into" is always too much. The hyperbolic metaphor or catachresis of the form-content distinction, the distinction between a containing outside and a contained inside, is responsible for the "false" alternative between pantheism and theism, or fanaticism (for which there is only a God who contains within himself a nonexistent world) and atheism (for which there is only a world within which God too exists as one being amongst others, even if the highest being: ontotheology), an alternative whose "falsity" consists in the fact that it is actually an undecidability.

"Refined Pantheism": The Rhetoric of Rational Theology Between Fanatical Figuralism and Atheistic Literalism

Having operated a rapprochement between pantheism and theism by way of their undecidable differentiation, Mendelssohn turns to the question of Lessing's relation to these two doctrines.[39] Anticipating Jacobi's public attack, Mendelssohn argues, as is well known, that Lessing has been a believer in that form of "purified pantheism," which, especially in terms of its ethical consequences, is compatible with theism, a pantheism which (excusably) errs in its concept of God only in the direction of enthusiastically giving God too much sway, denying any independent existence to the world outside of its creator.[40] As is less generally well known, Mendelssohn defends Lessing's theological views here in terms of rhetoric and again through arguments that unsettle the distinction between figural and literal, rhetoric and philosophy.[41]

First of all, due to its very "refinement,"[42] Mendelssohn's friend Lessing's "refined pantheism" ("der verfeinerte Pantheismus" [133]) hovers somewhere between what the text elsewhere calls the "overly refined sophistical grounds" ("die . . . überfeine[n] sophistische[n] Gründe" [125]) of nonrefined pantheism and what it again elsewhere calls the "overfine speculation"—(it asserts "daß der Unterschied blos in einer überfeinen Speculation bestehe" [133])—of those antipantheists who maintain an excessively rigid distinction between pantheism and theism. Between two symmetrically opposed forms of sophistical *raffinement*, Lessing's own "refinement" is situated on the edges of each.

But it is not only in this still relatively external way that the question of rhetoric enters into Mendelssohn's defense of Lessing. Much more intimately and particularly, in a discussion of his friend's conception of God as a God who condescends to participate in this world, a discussion which functions also as a characterization of Lessing's own Godliness, his own merciful or compassionate tendency to condescend and come to the defense of those in need (as for example Spinoza stood in need of a fair trial by the light of reason), Mendelssohn draws out the ethico-theological implications of the relation (without relation) between figural and literal, possible and real. "In all human actions that we can observe, we notice a sort of opposition between sublimity and condescension, dignity and confidence [*Hoheit und Herablassung, Würde und Vertraulichkeit*], which convinces us of the difficulty of combining both of these ethical traits in one character" (126). It is difficult, Mendelssohn argues, to combine height with lowliness, pride with humility, power with goodness. This difficulty is not only a practical difficulty but also a theoretical one. That is, it tends to block our attempts to achieve virtue as well as to conceive of the most perfect being. Moreover, Mendelssohn points out immediately that the difficulty is either due to, or at least confirmed by, language, in that language derives the conceptions of ethical height and depth from their physical equivalents and makes these ethical conceptions seem as rigidly opposed as their physical counterparts. He continues, "Language itself already induces us to make such an opposition, in that we compare the derived moral sense [*den abgeleiteten moralischen Sinn*] of words with their original physical sense [*ihrem ursprünglichen physischen Sinne*] and oppose height or sublimity to condescension" (126). Mendelssohn apparently wants merely to highlight that the figural, moral senses of height and depth are not completely analogous to the literal, physical senses of these terms. We must therefore not be misled, he suggests, by the physical metaphors. Rather we must separate thought from metaphorical language in order to begin to understand that, in ethical matters, to be high one must lower oneself, while in physical matters, this would be impossible:

When the physically sublime is lowered [*das physische Erhabene herabgelassen wird*], it ceases to be sublime, and thus one is inclined to assume the impossibility of the combination on the ethical level, although at bottom here precisely the opposite takes place; the highest ethical sublimity consists in lowering oneself, and dignity without confidence mistakes its true value [*Würde ohne Vertraulichkeit ihren wahren Werth verkennet*]. It takes no small refinement [*Verfeinerung*] of one's concepts to see this difference between the ethical and the physical and not to allow oneself to be blinded by the common prejudice. (126–27)

In ethical terms, the condition of ascent is descent.

However, when Mendelssohn goes on to develop this paradoxical structure of ethical verticality—that one must go down in order to go up—not only with reference to ethics in general (and to the virtue of Lessing in particular), but also with respect to theology, to the rational conception of God as grasped properly by Lessing, he points out that this reversal of sublimity into compassion has limitations symmetrically opposed to those of the separation of sublimity from all compassion:

The same difficulty of thinking these characteristics in connection with one another has led humanity from time immemorial, with respect to religion, onto opposite erring paths. One has either exaggerated the sublimity of the divine being, or exaggerated its condescension, now excluding God from all participation [*Mitwirkung*], now involving him to such an extent in all human actions that he also took part in human weaknesses. (127)

Thus, for Mendelssohn, if one removes God excessively from the world, making him too high, one ends up making him merely a part of the world, making him too lowly: a God lacking compassion is less than God. And this is the mistake that has been made by what Mendelssohn calls the "philosophers," although clearly this is also the mistake, from a Christian point of view, of the Jews. In order to avoid this mistake, God must be placed into the world and in this way enabled to be above it. Of course to place God in the world is to risk losing God altogether, making of him merely one being among others. Thus, the God who is constantly seen as intervening in the world, which Mendelssohn characterizes as the God of the "poets and priests" (and one might include here the Christian becoming-man of God as seen from a Jewish point of view) is not only robbed of some his dignity, becoming somewhat less than God, but also leaves the world bereft of God, for now wherever there is no miraculous intervention, God is not to be found (127–28). God in the world is less than God in a world bereft of God.

In short, to place God too exclusively above the world is to place God excessively down in the world (and this would be the mistake of the philosophers, the Jews from the Christian point of view, idealists, and Spinoza from Mendelssohn's ostensibly Leibnizian-Wolffian point of view). But to involve God too much in the world is to remove God excessively from the world (which would be the mistake of the poets and priests, the Christians from the Jewish point of view, materialists, and Spinoza from Jacobi's point of view). Up is down and down is up: out is in and in is out. Lessing's notion of God, however, avoids the two hyperbolic extremes of the God of the philosophers, whom Mendelssohn convicts of excessive sublimity, and the God of the poets and priests, whom he castigates in turn for hyperbolic condescension. Lessing's "God"—both Lessing and his God, Lessing or his God—intervenes in the world only noninterventionally and keeps out of the fray in a way that is nonetheless involved.

In what way, then, does this argument relate to rhetoric, except insofar as it begins with a traditional attempt to separate thought (in this case the thought of ethical and theological sublimity) from metaphor (here the metaphorics of high and low)? In order to answer this question, we have to reconsider in more detail, and marginally beyond Mendelssohn's most explicitly stated intentions, the implications of the passage adduced above on the difference between the thought of ethics and the metaphorics of high and low: Mendelssohn writes, "Language itself already induces us to make such an opposition, in that we compare the derived moral sense of words with their original physical sense and oppose height or sublimity to condescension" (126). The implications of this passage exceed Mendelssohn's apparent intentions here, issuing in a kind of performative paradox. Yet they do so in a way that is in uncanny accord with Mendelssohn's intermittent contestations of the border between figural and literal dimensions. For Mendelssohn's reminder that the height-depth contrast is "just" a metaphor when applied to ethical matters functions simultaneously as a reminder that the relationship between literal and figural is itself conventionally understood in terms of the metaphorical vertical spatialization of the ethical dimension. Literal meaning, in the sense of the spirit of an utterance, is understood at once as high and (therefore) as ethically good, while (pre)figural presentation, the material imagistic or referential form of thought, is considered to be both low and (therefore) relatively bad. (I adopt rationalist ontorhetorical presuppositions or terms here for the sake of simplicity, as also because this ontorhetoric figures most prominently in the passage under consideration.) If ethics is not understandable in terms of high and low (because high and low are "just" metaphors), then the relationship between literal spirit and figural letter, conventionally construed in terms of high and low, or heaven and earth, cannot be legitimately moralized on the basis of its vertical metaphorical representation (again, literal spirit as good because high or rising, figural matter as bad because low or falling). Thus, our conventional understanding of the relationship between ethics and metaphor (or our understanding of the ethics of metaphor), an understanding in terms of which the autonomous privilege of ethics or pure thought is here asserted, is itself an example or a result of the application of metaphor to ethics that this understanding here prompts us to condemn. Figurality is the vehicle of its own critique. Accordingly, while Mendelssohn suggests that the high-low metaphors do not enable us to account for the structures of the ethical and theological realms, he does not throw these metaphors away entirely, but instead attempts to work with them, to invert, displace, and complicate their application to the ethical and theological realms, as if thereby acknowledging the ineluctability of a figurality to whose disfiguring effects on the discourse of reason he wishes to alert his reader. In the wake of the explosion of this performative paradox, let us trace the rhetorical implications of Mendelssohn's assertion here that, in both ethics and theology, the condition of the possibility of ascent is descent.

On the level of the *figural*, i.e., on the level of *physical reality*, Mendelssohn argues, high is high and low is low, or literal is literal and figural is figural. Thus, on the level of the figural, the literal and the figural are to be kept rigorously separated.

On the *literal* level, on the level of *ethical spirit*, high is low (pride is sin) and low is high (humility is virtue): literal and figural are apparently to be confused or conflated. Indeed, literal and figural are to be confused or conflated here precisely in order to be kept the more separate and in order for their hierarchical relationship to be stabilized: high (power) must become low (compassionate) in order to remain or to become high (virtuous), while the low (humble) must become high (virtuous) in order not to remain low (sinful, materially bound).

This asymmetry cannot, however, be installed in a stable manner. If high is low and low is high, literal is figural and figural literal, then there is no way to prevent this from meaning that spirit is lost in matter, that matter usurps the place of spirit, as well as meaning that spirit is spirit insofar as it allows for matter, while matter is the proper vehicle and place of spirit. Moreover, Mendelssohn himself is no doubt aware of this consequence. For his ethico-rhetorical argument that condescension is necessary to ethical sublimity (126–27) issues in the slightly different theological argument (127–28) that both the refusal of condescension (i.e., of the being-in-the-world of God) and the acceptance of condescension constitute exaggerated extremes, equally false solutions to the problem of the definition of God's position with respect to the world.[43]

Thus, neither the (figural) separation of figural and literal, a separation which ignores the fact that the literal requires the presence and cooperation of the figural in order to be the literal it is, nor the (literal) conflation of figural and literal, which prevents us from isolating the literal in its radical spirituality, is adequate. We must instead adopt the perspectives of the figural and the literal at once: we must separate and conflate the figural and the literal, affirming their undecidable identity. And so, in terms of the undecidability of the figural and the literal, Mendelssohn argues for the undecidability of the distinction between the pantheistic conflation of God and world and their theistic separation.

The Twilight of Enlightenment: The Evening Hours of the Age of Mendelssohn

To conclude, let us consider the implications of *Morning Hours*, and so of Mendelssohn's legacy, for the theopolitical identities of Jew and Christian. Within Mendelssohn's discourse, the God of the philosophers and the God of the poets echo the conventional Jewish and Christian versions of God. Between the two, at the place of their undecidability, a position he delineates in terms of both Lessing and Rabbi Yohanan, for example, Mendelssohn tries to situate the divine world or the worldly divinity of rational theology.[44] Since Spinoza was a Jew, but of course also an excommunicated Jew who ended his life "blessed" by a Christian name, his position between Jew and Christian makes him a privileged figure for such an articulation, even if (and precisely because) Jacobi is in the process of exploiting Spinoza's Jewish background for the purpose of discrediting reason. Arguing that refined pantheism and refined theism, or refined fanaticism and refined atheism (unless it is the other way around), comprise an undecidable difference is tantamount to arguing that the place between literal and figural, between the immanence and transcendence of God, between incarnation and law, and thus between Christian and Jew, is "identical" with each of the terms it separates and unites. It is the constitutive border of their undoing. On the delineation of this twilight border, which implies that conversion is at once conceivable and senseless, Mendelssohn's career can be said to have exhausted and concluded itself.

Since Mendelssohn manifests an obsessive concern with suicide in some of his early texts, and since it has often been argued that Jacobi killed Mendelssohn with his provocation, it is necessary, in closing, to say a word on Mendelssohn's death. In the final analysis, on the one hand, Mendelssohn apparently ultimately does commit not only a kind of figural (or cultural) suicide but also a kind of literal suicide. Through his enthusiastic defense of natural theology he in effect weakens the Jewish revealed law even if without meaning to, by opening the door to a rejection of revealed law along with revealed religion. In this sense, he would inauguratively represent the cultural suicide of German Jewry. Further, he literally dies from a cold he catches going out in winter on foot and without an overcoat to take the short sequel of *Morning Hours*, entitled *To the Friends of Lessing*, to his publisher, Voss.[45] And so he literally kills himself, it seems, in defense of his friend, Lessing, as a representative of natural theology. On the other hand, Mendelssohn defends Judaism in *Jerusalem* as containing both spirit and letter. And when he defends "refined pantheism" in *Morning Hours*, he does so in a way that undermines Christianity at least as much as it undermines Judaism, insofar as it reduces the two, the religion of the "literal spirit" and that of the "(pre)figural letter," to the inconceivable border that constitutes their undecidable difference. In this sense, there is no figural suicide. As for the literal suicide, we do not finally know if Mendelssohn was killed by the aggression of Jacobi and his friends or if he simply died of "natural" causes. The notion of a literal suicide, although it is suggestive in light of Mendelssohn's discussion of suicide in *Letters on Sentiments*, can never become more than a hypothesis that may or may not accord with what "actually" occurred.

Neither merely affirming himself nor merely denying himself, then, from our perspective it appears that Mendelssohn attempted across the length of his career simply to present himself as one "Jewish" "human being" existing on the uncertain ground somewhere between "matter" and "spirit." Having presumed to embody implicitly the scandalous notion that a Jew could have spirit, he found himself compelled to argue repeatedly, against those who were outraged by this notion, that spirit was not the exclusive property of Christianity. Early on, against both a rationalist Christian discourse (as mouthed by Lavater and Cranz) and also a potential conflation, amongst Jews, of Enlightenment with the abandonment of Judaism, he had to argue that Judaism was highly compatible, perhaps even more compatible than Christianity, with rationality. In this way, he formulated Enlightenment as a Judaizing overcoming of the limitations of the Lutheran Reformation. Later, against the irrationalists (Jacobi and his *Sturm und Drang* friends), he had to argue that (what they wanted to frame as quasi-Jewish) rationality was not incompatible—indeed was less incompatible than irrationality, either as materialism or as *Schwärmerei*—with true religion and morals. In each case, whether while defending Judaism as rational or while defending rationality as religious (in terms of natural theology), Mendelssohn was compelled to show that what his opponents determined as the prefigural letter contained its spiritual other within itself, while showing that the ostensibly spiritual discourse which claimed to shun the letter was a pure form of the letter, and (provisionally) nothing more.

Thus, in connection with philosophical questions raised within rationalist discourse as it began to come undone, theopolitical exigencies pushed Mendelssohn, despite his relatively thoroughgoing inscription in Western metaphysics, to question in a persistent and far-reaching manner the metaphysical oppositions between rhetoric and philosophy, figural and literal, and the other oppositions with which these were bound up in late-eighteenth-century northern Germany. After his death in 1786, which, along with the death of Frederick the Great in the same year, signaled the end of both the intellectual core of the German Enlightenment and the end of political conditions favorable to its development, it was the late Kant and then the Romantic generation who would have to resume the interrogation of these oppositions where Mendelssohn and Lessing had left off.

PART II

ROMANTICISM

3

The Birth of German Romanticism out of the "Dialogue" Between (Protestant) Spirit and (Jewish) Letter

FRIEDRICH SCHLEGEL'S "ON LESSING" (1797)
AND ITS "CONCLUSION" (1801)

> When one hears the expressions, "his philosophy," "my philosophy," one always recalls the words of Nathan: "To whom does God belong? What kind of God is it who belongs to a human being?"[1]
>
> Unify the extremes and you will have the true middle.[2]

In the following readings, I will demonstrate that both the "life" and the "work" of Friedrich Schlegel, who here functions as a synecdoche for the discourse of German Romanticism, are powerfully determined by an extraordinarily insistent and self-conscious, if also defensively antimaterial, concern to transform the undecidability of (Jewish) letter and (Christian) spirit into their spiritual reconciliation. There is no better place to begin to carry out this demonstration than with Schlegel's essay "On Lessing."[3] The essay argues, as I will show, for the necessity of following Lessing in an attempt to go beyond the letter-spirit distinction in the interests of overcoming the Lutheran literalization of spirit. Schlegel's "life" while he is composing "On Lessing" also bears witness to an overwhelming desire to synthesize (Christian) spirit with (Jewish) letter: Schlegel sends this essay off to the printer in September 1797, one month after beginning to develop a relationship with Dorothea Mendelssohn-Veit, whom he has met at the salon of Henriette Herz in August 1797. The imaginative and conceptual preoccupations of the essay thus overlap in time—and, as I suggest, also in form/content—with the imaginative and conceptual preoccupations that will have constituted Schlegel's initial "romantic" interest in Dorothea Mendelssohn-Veit, alias Recha. In Chapter 4, we will look carefully at "On Philosophy: To Dorothea" and *Lucinde*, two texts Schlegel writes both for and on Dorothea during the early phase of their love affair. We will see there how his theory of religio-semiotic identity (i.e., of Judaic letter and Christian spirit), as this theory takes form in his early reading of Lessing, is expanded in these two texts into a theory of gender identity, which in turn mirrors Schlegel's relationship to Dorothea, as that of a Christian man to a Jewish woman. But before tracing this triple homology, we must clarify the early reading of Lessing. Who is Lessing for Friedrich Schlegel? And what role do the oppositions between Jewish and German, prefigural (or postfigural) letter and literal (or punctual) spirit play in Schlegel's relationship to Lessing, given that these are oppositions about which Lessing—the author of *Die Juden* and *Nathan der Weise*, of *Die Erziehung des Menschengeschlechtes* and *Ernst und Falk*, as well as the great public and private friend of Moses Mendelssohn—obviously had a fair bit to say?[4]

Lessing as "Prefiguration" of the "Spirit" of Romanticism

Two opposite versions of the Christian phonocentric hierarchy of voiced spirit over written letter impose themselves as possible paradigms upon Schlegel's written reading of Lessing even before it gets started: either Schlegel will restore Lessing's authentic voice and spirit to Lessing's writings, and thus apparently play New Testament to Lessing's Old Testament, or the living voice of Lessing's writings will be written down, re-presented (without presence), in a belated, derivative, and fallen form by Schlegel's text, in which case Schlegel will apparently play Old Testament to Lessing's New Testament, despite the fact that Lessing temporally precedes Schlegel.

Although these two versions of Christian phonocentrism are, in a sense, contradictory opposites, since in the one case we move from writing to speech, while in the other we move from speech to writing, still it is misleading to see them as implying mutually exclusive movements. The New

Testament may well accomplish for institutional Christianity the movement from the writing of the Old Testament to full speech, but it can do so only insofar as it presupposes that the Old Testament comprises a falling movement from an origin in full speech into the debasement of a writing. And conversely, the Christian notion of the Old Testament as a falling off in need of salvation through Christ's Word presupposes an origin in full speech that will have been restored. Each of these two versions thus includes the second, within and yet outside itself, as its marginal presupposition.

Similarly, Schlegel needs both of these paradigms to be operative simultaneously in the understanding of his reading of Lessing. It is not possible for him to have one without the other, even if there is some contradiction involved in their simultaneous invocation. If Lessing does not turn out to have been an authentic and inimitable voice, then the essay's topic (Lessing himself), although there is no problem in doing justice to it, is without interest. If Lessing *was* an authentic voice, then to hear that voice now is of the most pressing interest, yet the essay's portrayal of its topic must be radically flawed, must fail to render that voice adequately audible. Thus, Schlegel must at once play writing to Lessing's speech and speech to Lessing's writing. He must play Old Testament figure to Lessing's New Testament literal spirit, and New Testament spirit to Lessing's Old Testament, much as the New Testament has to begin by bowing to the authority of the Old in order to be able subsequently to appropriate that authority for itself. How does Schlegel go about this?

Schlegel begins by placing Lessing in a position of absolute priority, positing him as an authority without equal, a radical origin, while he places himself in the position of the secondary derivative, the writing that hopelessly lays claim to the status of an original speech it would emulate. As Schlegel tells us on the essay's first page, Lessing is nothing less than "the authentic author of the nation and the age [*der eigentliche Autor der Nation und des Zeitalters*]."[5] This implies, of course, that Schlegel is secondary and passive with respect to the original, active presence of Lessing. Moreover, Schlegel explains, also at the outset, that the novelty of his own essay will consist in the fact that it is an attempt "to characterize Lessing's spirit as a whole [*Lessings Geist im ganzen zu charakterisieren*]" (100). Indeed it will turn out to be a question of characterizing the whole of this spirit emphatically *as spirit*. But what does it mean, quite simply and (as it were) literally, "to characterize Lessing's spirit as a whole"? To "characterize" is, according to the etymology of the word, and prior to (or regardless of) whatever else Schlegel may say about it: to mark, to write, or to inscribe. To "characterize" a "spirit" is to write it down. Again, according to the best-worst traditions of Western metaphysics, writing holds always less than the whole of spirit. Schlegel thus sets himself up as playing a paradoxically belated arrival of the Old Testament to Lessing's unfashionably early New. His desire to "characterize" Lessing's "spirit as a whole" is impossible from the very start, to the degree that phonocentric conventions are in force. Finally, Schlegel no sooner states that he will attempt to characterize the whole of Lessing's spirit than he goes on to argue, ostensibly in favor of the legitimacy of such an attempt, that despite all the partial work on Lessing already published, there is still room for such a study as his own: such a nature as Lessing's "cannot be regarded too many-sidedly, and is thoroughly *inexhaustible* [unerschöpflich]" (100). Now, if Lessing's spirit is "thoroughly *inexhaustible*," then how can any attempt to represent that spirit *as a whole* possibly succeed? Clearly, Schlegel's attempt will remain an insufficient and fragmentary representation of a presence that will elude it. Schlegel's merely figural and derivative relation to a literal and originary Lessing, as well as his aspiration to an identification with that literal origin, are thus firmly established at the outset. His own text is squarely on the side of the letter, as a written-down reading bound to fail to grasp the totality of the spirit read.

How, then, does Schlegel proceed to operate a reversal and displacement of the polarities involved, putting Lessing in the position of writing (without allowing Lessing to lose thereby any of his originary authority), while he places himself in the originary position of speech (without ceasing to make reference to Lessing as the original representative of what he himself has to say)?[6] The main way in which Schlegel effects this reversal and displacement, this unsettling of the opposition between spirit and letter, is by locating Lessing's very spirituality *in traits normally associated with the letter*. If Lessing's radical spirituality inheres in the traits of what is generally determined as the letter, the more material dimension of language, then it must appear possible, conversely, for the lettered figurality of Schlegel's treatment of Lessing (as also for Schlegel's work of critical fragmentation more generally) to be granted the status of spirit. But there is a more radical consequence, one *too* radical even for Schlegel himself, who will insist despite everything on maintaining the priority of spirit. This consequence is the following: by situating (Lessing's) spirituality in the traits of writing, by thus arguing that writing is (or at least *can* be) more spiritual than spirit itself, Schlegel in effect unsettles the entire opposition between writing and spirit. He renders illegible and unsayable its very meaning, utterly unsituable its two constitutive terms. It is both to this most radical implication and to Schlegel's ultimate defense against it that we will have to attend most closely in what follows.

In what sense, then, does Schlegel situate Lessing's (Christian) spirituality in those aspects of Lessing's work which, at least in the Christian and secular worlds of Schlegel's day, tend quite consistently to be associated with the (Judaic) letter? As is well known and made quite explicit in the text, Schlegel's innovation in his reading of Lessing consists, first, in positing as essential the traits that had previously most often been considered inessential in Lessing's work, and, second, in valuing those traits positively whereas they had been valued more or less negatively in previous appreciations of Lessing's work.[7] But as is not generally remarked (because Schlegel sometimes makes it less than absolutely explicit), these traits are the traits of the (Judaic) letter.[8] Thus, Schlegel argues that Lessing is not essentially a poet, but rather a prose writer, not a creative genius, but a critical wit. Schlegel claims that this double trait—the "pedestrian" and therefore earthly, material "form" of prose as letter, and the (not very spiritual) spirit or intellectual "content" of wit—represents the strength of Lessing's mind or spirit.[9] But precisely because it is generally taken to represent unwholeness and its materiality, as well as parasitical belatedness with respect to the ostensibly "creative" nature of the absolutely spiritual origin, this trait is as unpopular and generally as unappreciated as the Judaic letter it resembles.

Wit [*Witz*] and prose are things for which only very few people have a sense, incomparably fewer perhaps than have a sense for artful completion and poetry. It is for this reason that there is indeed little talk of Lessing's wit and of Lessing's prose, in spite of the fact that his wit eminently deserves to be called classical, and that a pragmatic theory of German prose would, as it were, have to begin and end with the characterization of his style.[10]

The opposition here between wit and prose, on the one hand, and "artful completion and poetry," on the other, suggests that wit is a faculty of natural incompleteness, in the manner of the material letter. While wit is generally considered a form of spirit that is less spiritual than poetic genius (approaching as it does the mere manipulations of mechanical understanding), and while prose is considered less spiritual than poetry (for its associations with the purposiveness of communication, due to the assumption that it is used as a mere sensuous vehicle of the supersensuous rather than being fused and infused with the supersensuous), this nonspiritual content and form epitomize Lessing's spiritual strength.[11]

Further, Schlegel associates this wit and its prosaic form with *polemic*, in which Schlegel sees the center of Lessing's activities, his essential mode of relation with the world around him and, no doubt, also with himself. Wit (as spiritual content) and prose (as material form), then, are related to each other and to the surrounding world in a relation of negativity or struggle, whereas the spirit of "artful completion" and "poetry" are bound both to each other and to the world around by the bonds of a positive love. Yet, it is precisely in Lessing's *polemical* character, his hate, rather than his love, that Schlegel situates the very spirituality of Lessing's spirit.

Especially his polemic [*Polemik*] has itself been . . . so completely forgotten that it would be a paradox, perhaps, for many who think of themselves as admirers of Lessing, if one maintained that the ANTI-GÖTZE deserves amongst his writings the first place, not merely with respect to the *shattering* force of *rhetoric* [zermalmende *Kraft der* Beredsamkeit], surprising agility and glittering *expression*, but in its *geniality*, its *philosophy*, even in the *poetic spirit* and ethical sublimity of certain passages. Never did he write to such an extent out of his deepest Self [*aus dem tiefsten Selbst*] as in these *explosions* [Explosionen] that the *heat* of battle tore from him, and in which the nobility of his soul [*Gemüts*] streams forth so unambiguously in the purest glow. (106; emphasis added)

The polemic that Schlegel assumes here to be associated with (the letter of) rhetoric[12] becomes in Lessing, for reasons we will examine below, its opposite, the loving spirit of philosophy and its allied double, poetry. In Lessing, that is, spirit somehow appears in the guise of its opposite, the letter.[13]

The association of polemic—and of the witty prose with which it is intimately bound up—with the Judaic letter becomes explicit when Schlegel feels himself called upon to defend Lessing's polemical wit against the accusation of a lovelessness that would be tantamount to a lack of (Christian) spirituality.[14] Shortly after introducing the topic of Lessing's wit, Schlegel goes on to praise Lessing for having combined in his "Charakter" (105) a heterogeneous series of (perhaps mutually warring, yet) admirable personal traits.[15] What allows Lessing to possess all at once such a bundle of extraordinary qualities—to exist as the strewn letter or "character" he is—is the great "spirit" revealed in Lessing's polemical rage at falsehood:

Only *a great man* can possess these characteristics, a man *who has a soul* [*Gemüt*], that is, the lively activity and strength of the most inner, deepest spirit [*Geistes*] of God within the human being. One therefore should not have gone so far as to maintain that he lacks a soul [*Gemüt*], as they call it, because he had no love. Is not Lessing's hatred of unreason as divine as the most authentic, the most spiritual love [*die echteste, die geistigste Liebe*]? Can one hate in this way without a soul? . . . Some madmen of the narrow-minded and illiberal sort, who must of course have the same attitude toward Lessing as the Patriarch would have toward an Alhafi or a Nathan, seem to wish even to deny him all geniality because of this lack of love. (106)

Lessing's critical hatred or lovelessness must be seen as a proof of spirit itself, whereas in a certain conventional Protestant framework it would be taken precisely as proof of a "lack" of spirit.[16] Moreover, Schlegel likens this "lack" in turn to the "lack" that would be assumed by the narrow-minded Patriarch—i.e., by the orthodox Protestants of Lessing's day—to character-ize the dervish and, more importantly for our context, the Jew, Nathan/Mendelssohn, in Lessing's play). This reversal of a lack of spirit into its presence implies further the potential reversal of Schlegel's own position, notably, as a critic writing belatedly on Lessing's spirit, into the position of spirit.[17]

"A Main Trait in Lessing's Character": "Unlimited Contempt for the Letter"

Despite having already effectively unsettled the opposition between spirit and letter, Schlegel insists on presupposing the priority of spirit over letter. But in what sense of "spirit" can this term still retain a prior-ity over the term "letter"? We can approach this question by examining Schlegel's attempt to formulate the "common spirit" of all of Lessing's strewn characteristics:

How all of that which, in each of these areas, he is supposed to have been or actu-ally was, might hang together, what *common spirit* animates all [*welcher gemeinsame Geist alles beseelt*] that, *as a whole*, he really was, wanted to be, and had to become, on that question it seems no one has any judgment or opinion. . . . It is certainly praiseworthy that people have praised Lessing and continue to praise him. . . . But what would praise be without the strictest examination and the freest judgment? In any case, it would be unworthy of *Lessing*. . . . One ought now, finally, to risk the attempt to criticize Lessing in accordance with the laws he himself prescribed for the judgment of great poets and masters in art; wouldn't perhaps such a critique be the best kind of eulogy for him: to admire him and to follow him as he wished one would admire and follow Luther, with whom one could indeed compare him in more than one respect. (108–9)

Schlegel wishes to apprehend Lessing's spirit as a whole in such a way as to avoid imposing his own interpretation on that spirit as its fallen inscription or (belatedly) premature prefiguration. In order to achieve this goal, he will allow that spirit to judge itself and so to reestablish its own disrupted unity. In order to facilitate or to occasion the self-judgment of spirit, one need simply judge that spirit in accordance with its own law—with the law that spirit has established for the judgment of others—not in accordance with one's own. To grasp the spirit, one must simply apply to the spirit the law generated by that spirit itself, which in this instance means to fold its hermeneutics back onto its poetics.

Spirit and law (or letter) are to be (re)unified here in the judgment of a totalizing self-reading. Moreover, it is not by chance that such a model of reading is presented as having been applied, in Lessing's case, to Luther. For Luther is the exemplary spirit, the one for whom (or in whom) the law reduces essentially to spirit. A model of reading as the reabsorption of law back into spirit (in this case as the application of the law to the spirit) would be particularly appropriate when applied to Luther.

But what exactly are the "laws" Lessing prescribes "for the judgment of great poets and masters in art," and in what manner does Lessing "admire" and "follow after" Luther? How do the general rule and the particular (if exemplary) case cohere? Schlegel elaborates, "Those prescriptions are the following. 'One does not criticize [*tadelt . . . nicht*] a pitiful poet; one goes easy [*gelinde*] on a mediocre one; with respect to a great poet one is merciless [*unerbittlich*].' . . . On Luther he speaks thus: 'The true Lutheran seeks shelter not in Luther's writings but in Luther's spirit,' etc., ". . . In general *unlimited contempt for the letter* was a main trait of Lessing's character [*Überhaupt war unbegrenzte Verachtung des Buchstabens ein Hauptzug in Lessings Charakter*]" (109). According to Lessing's "laws," by varying one's approach in terms of the qualities of the textual object, one avoids inappropriate readings.[18] When reading a strong writer, one must hold that writer strictly to his or her principles. In the case of Luther, reading him the way he says one should read, one looks for the spirit, and not the letter. One reads figurally, not literally. Of course, the mere notion of reading an author only figurally—in terms of the spirit, not the letter—contradicts Lessing's notion of reading an author in terms of his or her own hermeneutics with a view to the rigorous concurrence of principle and performance. It is not possible to read with a view to the coherence of principle and performance, which is also the coherence of spirit and letter, as generality and particularity, without having a certain degree of respect—or *Achtung*—for the letter of the text.[19] One cannot read with a view to what is actually being said—to the supersensuous content of the text, beyond all limitations of sensuous form—without continuing to take into account precisely the semantic implications of all aspects of that form and thus, again, without having a certain kind of respect for the letter.[20] If Schlegel is not simply affirming one thing when he quotes Lessing on how to read Luther and another when he suggests that one must read great authors critically, then Lessing must mean (in Schlegel's discourse) something other than what he *seems* to mean when he says that one should seek shelter exclusively in Luther's *spirit*. What, indeed, is the "spirit" of this utterance?

What does it mean for Lessing to say that Luther's spirit, not his letter, should be respected? When Lessing says that Luther's spirit, rather than his letter, should be adhered to, that his language should be seen as figural rather than literal, the spirit that is to be followed and the language that is not to be taken literally are not just any spirit and language. They are the spirit as *the principle that the spirit, and not the letter, is the essential*, and the language that carries the imperative to follow the spirit, and not language in language itself.

Lessing thus occasions the self-reflexion of Luther, reads Luther in terms of his own law, which is the law of the inessentiality of the law. Precisely *because* he is a radically Lutheran reader of Luther, Lessing unsettles, suspends, and displaces Luther's message.[21] If we read "one must read figurally, not literally" *figurally*, if we try to take it seriously by not reading it literally, then we no longer know what it would—literally—mean to read figurally or literally. We are left in an aporetic uncertainty as to what the difference between the figural and the literal might be. And we are thus led back to a certain possibility of respect for the "letter" that Luther attempts to exclude. Such a respect for the letter would not be the kind that returns in Lutheran orthodoxy, like the return of the repressed, as Biblical literalism. This literalism accepts the Bible "literally" only in the sense that it assumes the spirit to present itself fully in the letter every time.[22] It thereby immediately effaces the instance of the letter as a moment of ineluctable opacity and a delay in the arrival of meaning.[23] Rather, such post-Lutheran respect for the letter, originating as it does in a suspension (although not an absolute effacement) of the hierarchical and teleological distinction between figural and literal, would respect the literal spirit as a mode of the figural letter, the proper as a variant of the improper, the original as a derivative of its derivative.

And to be sure, it is not by chance that the ethico-theological Ring-parable in *Nathan der Weise*—to which we will have occasion to return below—places emphasis on *works* as the realization of faith or grace.[24] Reading Luther figurally, Lessing apparently argues, and in this he is not far from Mendelssohn's account in *Jerusalem*, that the "essence" of spirit beyond all dogma resides in *action*.[25] The truth of a religion is here generated by the ethical *praxis* it generates. This means that the spirit of a religion is the work of its works, the law its letter actively spells out. For Luther, this would be tantamount to making the mistake (like the pre-Reformation church, or like the Jews) of placing one's emphasis on the letter of the law over its spirit. But Lessing takes us precisely—through Luther and in Lutheran terms—beyond Luther himself.

What, then, are the implications for the distinction between spirit and letter, which has already become thoroughly problematic in Lessing's own text, when Schlegel counsels us to take refuge in Lessing's spirit? Where exactly is one to situate the spirit of Lessing, when Lessing does so much to render the distinction between spirit and letter problematic? On the one hand, Schlegel ultimately comes down dogmatically on the side of spirit. The "unlimited contempt for the letter" that Schlegel counsels us to assume in Lessing's name is hardly a mild attitude. Indeed, in retrospect the implications of such a statement seem frightfully anti-Semitic. And this level of Schlegel's text remains effectively legible throughout. It is as if Schlegel were attempting to reverse Lessing's quasi reversal of Luther, to go back from "works" to "faith," from "letter" to "spirit."

On the other hand, "*unlimited*" contempt for the letter must be understood to include *above all* the contempt for any literalizing fixation of the distinction between spirit and letter. Accordingly, although Schlegel has been promising to deliver the "unity" of Lessing's "spirit," and although it therefore seems that he is about to situate the unity of Lessing's spirit in the contempt for the letter, in a moment of salutary modesty or sobriety he calls "the unlimited contempt for the letter" merely "*a* main *trait* in Lessing's *character*" (emphasis added). Although it is the site of the unity of Lessing's spirit, Lessing's radically spiritual contempt for the letter turns out to be—paradoxically—one mere *trait* of his *character*, that is, a fragmentary piece of the letter he is.[26] While Schlegel's text combats "literalism," and to this extent favors "spirituality," it is repeatedly compelled to situate "spirituality" in the very problematization of the relation between spirit and letter (and of their separate identities) while situating "literalism" in the false stabilization of that relation (as of those identities).

The Work that Is Not a Work: The Birth of the Fragment out of Lessing's Reading of Luther

To what sort of "works" will Lessing's "spirit" of polemical wit—this "unlimited contempt for the letter"—give rise, once this "spirit" has been defined as that which goes beyond the opposition between spirit (or faith) and letter (or works)? The "works" produced by this "spirit," or rather not so much *produced* by this "spirit" as *equivalent* to it, will have to be midway between works of faith and the faith of (or in) works.[27] They will have to combine a faith that is more or less than a faith with works that are more or less than works. Such works are the works of fragmentation. To anticipate a bit, the fragment is a work that is also not a work to the extent that it is neither whole, nor unitary, nor complete, nor the effect of a merely technical, intentional calculation. It is neither ethical nor religious, neither poetic nor philosophical, and yet all of these things—in part—at once. In order to see how Schlegel's concept of the work as fragment gains expression in the context of his reading of Lessing, and to see how this concept of the work as fragment answers to the demands that after Lessing must be made upon the work, let us consider the following characterization of Lessing at his best as a fragmentist:

An author, whether he be artist or thinker, who can put down on paper all that he is capable of or knows, is at the very least no genius. There are some who have talent, but such limited, isolated talent, that it leaves them quite cold, as if it were not their own, as if it were only externally attached or lent to them. Lessing was not of this type. *He was himself worth more than all of his talents.* . . . The most interesting and most fundamental of his writings are hints and suggestions, the most ripe and complete are fragments of fragments. The best of what Lessing says is what he casually throws into a few solid words full of force, spirit, and salt, as if he had just guessed at or invented it; words in which the darkest places in the realm of the human spirit are often lit up suddenly as if by a lightning bolt, the most holy things being expressed in a highly audacious, almost sacrilegious, manner, the most general being expressed in the strangest, drollest way. Isolated and compact, without any analysis or demonstration, his main principles stand there like mathematical axioms; and his tightest reasonings are usually like a chain of flashes of wit [*witzigen Einfällen*]. With such men, a brief discussion may often be more instructive and lead further than a long work![28]

Let us examine the structure of fragmentary writing here in its relation to the work-faith, letter-spirit polarity.[29]

On the one hand, Schlegel seems to be making the quite traditional claim that Lessing's spirit goes beyond what he has actually managed to hold fast in the letter of fixed language: the inner self or individuality of his "faith" is the essential thing, while the "works" produced out of this faith, which would in this case include the "talents" that express it, are the inessential, the mere "writing" of its "voice." Such a claim on Schlegel's part would amount to no more than the exploitation of the pathos of the Lutheran version of phonologocentrism to evoke a desire for the absent spirit of Lessing. Needless to say, there is nothing particularly unsettling about this sort of exploitation of the metaphysical presuppositions in terms of which we all still generally live.[30]

On the other hand, Schlegel claims there is a kind of writing—fragmentary writing—that can paradoxically accommodate *more spirit* than it can properly speaking accommodate. He thus implicitly differentiates fragmentary writing from both speech and also two other kinds of writing. To elucidate these distinctions, we must begin by briefly reconstructing the presuppositions these distinctions unsettle. Within everyday assumptions (which are also those of phonologocentric metaphysics), fragmentariness (discontinuity and incompleteness) is associated with writing in general, while wholeness (continuity and completeness) is associated with speech. The signifier in writing is taken to reveal a mere part of the signified, whereas the signifier in speech is taken to reveal the whole of the signified. Schlegel's notion of the fragmentary work unsettles these assumptions.

First, fragmentary writing in the emphatic sense, as Schlegel sees it exemplified by Lessing, is to be differentiated from *speech*, not because such writing says less than speech, but because it says more (and even if it were spoken out loud it would say more than speech as such, for the writing/speech distinction becomes purely "metaphorical" at this point). In Lessing, a brief remark, discontinuous and isolated, says more than a lengthy treatment in which each element of the signified would be represented by some element of the signifier. But second, Schlegel differentiates fragmentary writing in the emphatic sense also from *bad, unfinished writing*. Bad, unfinished writing is simply writing that fails to resist its character as writing, writing that fails to say all the spirit it means. Fragmentary writing, however, says more than it means, more than speech could say. Finally, Schlegel also differentiates fragmentary writing from what we normally think of as *finished writing*, whose banal pseudocompleteness consists in its pretense to accomplish a speechlike equivalence between signified and signifier, that is, spirit and letter, content and form. Writing that resists its own written character and manages to become speech is apparently "poetic" writing, but fragmentary writing says more than this sort of internally continuous or "poetic" discourse could say. Again, this is the case, despite the fact that Schlegel here uses phonocentric metaphors to say so, insofar as he says that a "kurze Unterredung" would be often more instructive than "ein langes Werk." "Long work" plays speech to the writing of a "short talk": the long work manages to express the *whole* of what it has to say, whereas the short talk says *more* than it says or has to say. The fragmentary work is even more finished than the finished work.[31] It says more than it can say by saying less in a specific yet enigmatic way, and by saying something other.[32]

In fragmentary writing, then, writing becomes more like speech than speech itself, the letter becomes more spiritual than spirit, the prefiguration more fulfilling than the literal fulfillment.[33] Fragmentary writing is a writing that is not a writing; and it is a spirit that is not a spirit, because the spirit is more tightly bound up with the letter there than spirit under normal circumstances or spirit as such.[34] The written fragment is both a work—the written letter of the law as law of realization—and less or more than a work. It is a faith—the "theoretical" essence of the work beyond the work—and the realization of the faith in makings (but makings which are only the makings of makings).[35] Lessing's lesson for Schlegel is that, in order to be adequate to the work-faith dialectic, the work must always be a *(w)hole*.[36]

'Nathan der Weise' (Nathan the Wise) as Exemplary Fragment: The Ellipsis of the Literal Spirit

Schlegel does not merely characterize Lessing's (exemplary) works in *general* as fragmentary (w)holes. He also characterizes some of Lessing's *particular* works in such terms. The last work by Lessing he discusses, devoting fully one-third of his essay to this work, is *Nathan der Weise*. Of course it is not only the position of *Nathan* in Schlegel's essay nor the amount of space it takes up that prompts us to look closely at Schlegel's reading of Lessing's play, nor is it even merely the play's content. Rather, beyond these factors, what makes it necessary for us to follow in detail Schlegel's reading of the play is the fact that he claims (toward the beginning of his discussion of *Nathan*) that this work is "the <u>work as such</u> [*das* Werk schlechtin] amongst Lessing's works in the sense determined above . . . the continuation of the *Anti-Götze*, Number Twelve." He also says, toward the end of the essay, that *Nathan* is made up of *two* works, comprising both the continuation of *Anti-Götze* and an additional work. Schlegel reads *Nathan* as comprising both less than a whole work (insofar as it is split in two), and more than a whole work (insofar as it comprises two works within one). Before leaving the early Lessing essay behind, it is important for us to see how Schlegel concretizes the necessary fragmentariness of the (non)work in his reading of this culmination of Lessing's spiritual endeavors. The question is not only what the play suggests *theoretically* about the status of works but also how it *performs* its theoretical suggestions by means of its own structure as work. In pursuing this question, we will have to continue to be attentive to the degree to which Schlegel follows through on his notion of fragmentariness and, thus, also to the point at which he defends himself against its more radical implications.

In his discussion of *Nathan der Weise*, Schlegel's opening gesture is to emphasize the play's radical spirituality, through which it distinguishes itself from a work like *Emilia Galotti*, which Schlegel considers a cold product of the mere understanding (and thus a work of the mere letter, a work in the pre-Lessing Protestant sense of the term).[37] "*Nathan* arose . . . , out of the soul [*Gemüt*] and penetrates again into it; it is, unmistakably, thoroughly glowing and inspired by the hovering spirit of God [*vom schwebenden Geist Gottes*]."[38] Both despite and due to the fact that he means to emphasize the spirituality of Lessing's play—that spirituality which, for Schlegel, precisely Lessing shows us paradoxically to exceed the opposition between letter and spirit—Schlegel makes the thesis of his discussion of *Nathan* the claim that the play is categorizable in terms of neither formal letter nor spiritual content, which here means also that it is neither a poetic nor a philosophical work per se.

Even if one could say with some justification, that it was the pinnacle of Lessing's poetic genius . . . philosophy has at least an equal justification to lay claim to the work for itself. (118)

A certain holy Something lives and hovers in *Nathan* with reference to which all syllogistic figures, as also all rules of dramatic poetry, are in truth mere bagatelles [*eine wahre Lumperei*]. A philosophical result or a philosophical tendency do not make a work into a philosopheme: nor do dramatic form and imaginative inventiveness make it into a poem.[39]

This gesture, insofar as it involves a rejection of both prescriptive genre-poetics and abstract philosophies in favor of something like an aesthetic hermeneutics, has often been understood, in organicist and individualist terms, as an instance of the Romantic advance over both neoclassicist rule-poetics and eighteenth-century didactical prejudices in the direction of the aesthetic appreciation of the wholeness and integrity of the individual work. The scholars of Romanticism tend to say in so many words of specifically Christian "inspiration" that in moving from neoclassicism to Romanticism, we move back from (bad, untrue, formalist, empty) culture—or should one say, "civilization"?—to good, true, substantial, full nature.[40] We move from the abstract materiality of "works" to the concrete spirituality of the individual's "faith," a faith we share by participating in the individual's affective experience. In Schlegel's characterization of Lessing's "individuality," however, the move from letter to spirit is the move from the letter of the letter-spirit opposition to its spirit, which is slightly more complicated and problematic, as we shall see.

In order to emphasize the misguidedness of attempting to determine *Nathan der Weise* as a poetic work in terms of its *generic* category, Schlegel quotes the play itself on the misguidedness of becoming fixated on the letter when one wishes to determine a human being's character in terms of religio-cultural identity. Lessing quotes Saladin as saying:

—Als Christ, als Muselmann: gleichviel!
Im weißen Mantel oder Jamerlonk;
Im Turban, oder deinem Filze: wie

Du willst! *Gleichviel! Ich habe nie verlangt,*
daß allen Bäumen Eine Rinde wachse.

—As Christian, as Moslem: Same difference!
In the white mantle, in the Moslem robe,
In a turban or a felt cowl: as
You like! *Same difference! I have never demanded*
That one bark should grow on all trees.[41]

Schlegel comments on this quotation, "But with respect to none [of Lessing's works] is the spirit of this sublime phrase—'same difference'—more thoroughly necessary for the audience than with respect to NATHAN" (118). With reference to Lessing's last play, Schlegel quite explicitly *models the generic indeterminacy of an individual work on the religio-cultural indeterminacy of an individual human being qua human being.* The individual spirit of the work as (non)work outweighs the question of its generic-formal letter, just as the individual spirit of a human being as a being-in-action outweighs the general letter of religio-cultural identity. But in each case, the spirit that outweighs the letter is the spirit that goes beyond the spirit-letter distinction. If the letter is the abstract, yet sensuous dimension, while spirit (in the narrow sense) is the concrete, yet supersensuous one, then the "spirit" (in the broad sense) of the individual (non)work that goes beyond letter and spirit (in the narrow sense) is that dimension of the individual which is neither abstract nor concrete, neither sensuous nor supersensuous, but simply other. Thus, Schlegel derives an aesthetic hermeneutics of the hybrid individuality of the (non)work from an ethico-theology of tolerance that is in turn based on the recognition of the undecidability of formal letter and spiritual content. Moreover, Schlegel cites Lessing's views on the generic indeterminacy of certain mixed works in order to provide this derivation with Lessing's authorization: "'In the textbooks [*Lehrbüchern*],' Lessing says . . . 'one may distinguish the genres as exactly as possible: but when a genius lets several of them flow together in one single work for the sake of higher intentions, then one should forget the textbook, and investigate merely whether or not the work has attained its intentions'" (119). Accordingly, the early Romantic ideal of the mixing of genres is at the outset not only bound up with but also in significant degree modeled upon the mixing of the different letters of diverse religions—including the letter of the religion of the letter, and the letter of the religion of the spirit—in what may be the one "spirit" of a humanity whose essence would reduce properly speaking to neither spirit nor letter.

In order to illustrate this mixing or dissolution of the genres, Schlegel argues, in the first half of his discussion of *Nathan*, not only against fixing *Nathan* within any poetic genre category but also against fixing it in the category or discursive genre of the poetic at all. He argues that the poetic dimension of the text is inessential, secondary, with respect to its philosophical dimension. He writes, "With liberal carelessness, like Alhafi's smock or the Templar Knight's half-burnt cloak, [the dramatic form of Nathan] is thrown over the spirit and essence of the work, and must bend and accommodate itself to the latter. . . . The dramatic form is mere *vehicle*; and *Recha, Sitta, Daja*, are indeed nothing but an *easel . . .*" (120–21). Moreover, rather than representing any poetic genre, *Nathan* is for Schlegel a text that has been "generated" and "animated" by "the enthusiasm of pure reason [*dieses vom Enthusiasmus der reinen Vernunft erzeugten und beseelten Gedichts*]" (119). It is the hyperspiritual expression of a man who has developed Christianity to the point where it becomes ironic ("er . . . im Christianismus sogar bis zur Ironie gekommen war" [119]). Where Christianity becomes irony, however, it is by no means undone, but merely raised to a higher power: the spirit takes its distance from the letter insofar as it recognizes its identity with the letter, but it takes its distance precisely through this recognition nonetheless. *Nathan* is thus a philosophical work that takes its distance from its poetic character or literariness insofar as it understands itself to be inseparable from that literariness. In this sense, *Nathan* is not a mere play at all. For this reason, Lessing can hope that it will be read as a philosophical letter written in the spirit of opposition to the letter itself:

Lessing himself contrasted with uncommon beauty the high philosophical dignity of the piece with its theatrical ineffectuality or counter-effectuality; and [he did so] with the piquant mixture of quiet, inward, deep inspiration and naive coldness that is proper to his tone: "It could indeed be . . . that my Nathan would have, on the whole, little effect if it came onto the stage, *which probably will never happen. Enough if it makes for an interesting read, and if amongst a thousand readers only one learns from it to doubt the evidence and generality of his religion.*" (121)

Having thus not only rendered indeterminate the specific poetic genre but also rendered doubtful even the general poetic character of *Nathan*, Schlegel turns, in the final pages of his essay, to the question of its status as a philosophical work in general and the question of its specific philosophical content. But the ideational, conceptual, or philosophical *content* of the play does not turn out, at least initially, and despite certain of the appearances generated by Schlegel's argument thus far, to be quite the essential *spirit* of its nonidentifiable formal letter. For Schlegel goes on to argue that the "meaning" of the play, its "message," can no more be finally determined as a unity than can its formal-generic category. Spirit here is not pure meaning or interiority. After discussing disparagingly a number of hypotheses that various members of "die logische Zunft" ("the logicians' guild" [121]) have offered concerning *Nathan*'s ultimate philosophical content, Schlegel proposes:

> One ought to give up the idea of reducing NATHAN to any sort of unity whatsoever or of being able to fence or stuff it into the guild of one of the faculties of the human mind that are hallowed by law or tradition: for through such a violent reduction and incorporation more will always be likely to get lost than the unity is worth in the first place. What do we get out of it, even if that which NATHAN wants not merely to *prove* but to communicate in a *living* manner—for the most important and the best part of it goes far beyond what dry proof is capable of—would allow of being summarized in a logical formula with mathematical precision? NATHAN would still maintain its place on the *common border between poetry and morals* . . . where Lessing liked to be early on in his career, and where he was playing already in the FABLES, which earn our respect as *preparatory exercises for the composition of Nathan's fairy tale of the three rings* . . . as great a thing as a human mind could ever produce. . . . (122)

Schlegel plays off the (ostensibly deadening) "law" of philosophical content against the "living" spirit of aesthetic-rhetorical form, just as, in his considerations on *Nathan*'s generic category, he had played off the categorical quibbling of prescriptive-formalist genre theory against the spirit of the individual work. In each case situating spirituality on the side of indeterminacy, Schlegel suggests first that the indeterminacy of *Nathan*'s individual content (as spirit) effectively undermines the pseudodeterminations of generic form (or letter), and then (conversely) that the indeterminacy[42] of individual style (here as spirit) effectively undermines the pseudodeterminations of conceptual content (here positioned on the side of the "law" of the human mind and hence also of its letter).[43]

    Nathan is thus situated on the "border" ("Rain") between poetry and philosophy, letter and spirit, where each internally unsettles the other. Schlegel's reading of Lessing's *Nathan*, and consequently of Lessing himself,⁴⁴ is an elliptical reading in an elliptical, double-centered sense. First, it is elliptical in the sense that Schlegel does not exactly give us the determination either of its formal or of its substantial essences, i.e., he passes over *Nathan*'s essential unity in a kind of silence. Secondly, it is elliptical in the sense that it posits *Nathan* as having *two* centers, as consisting in "two works" that have "grown together" and that can be seen as the "work" of the spirit and the "work" of the letter, respectively, although Schlegel characterizes both of these "works"—"works" that are indeed also not quite "works"—in terms of philosophical tendencies. He points out:

> It has not yet occurred to anyone to notice that, viewed by the light of day, NATHAN appears to contain *two main concerns*, and thus actually to have grown together out of *two works*. The first is of course the polemic against all illiberal theology, and in this respect not without certain side strokes that cut deep into the body of Christianity. . . . But not even the religious doctrines in NATHAN are purely sceptical, polemical, merely negative, as Jacobi . . . might seem to want to maintain. In NATHAN a quite definite, if not formal, type of religion . . . is set up as the Ideal quite decisively and positively; which always remains rhetorically one-sided as soon as it is bound up with claims to universality; and I do not know whether one can declare Lessing completely free of the prejudice of an objective and dominant religion, and whether or not he also applied and extended to individuals his great thesis . . . , that every formative stage of humanity as a whole has its own religion, whether or not he recognized the necessity of infinitely many religions. But isn't there also something completely different in NATHAN, again something philosophical, but something quite different from that religious doctrine to which Lessing's readers have clung, which even if it hangs together quite strongly with that doctrine is nonetheless quite distant from it and completely capable of standing on its own? Certain things point in this direction . . . such as the Dervish, who steps in with such firmness, and Nathan's story about the loss of seven sons and Recha's adoption. . . . What is it that stirs here if not ethical enthusiasm for the ethical force and ethical simplicity of good-hearted nature? . . . NATHAN THE WISE is not merely the continuation of ANTI-GÖTZE Number Twelve: it is also and every bit as much a dramatized *Elements of the Higher Cynicism* . . . [cynicism being that which appears as] every relationship, in which artificial nonnaturalness attains its pinnacle and in so doing jumps over itself and opens anew the way to a return into the unconditional freedom of nature. . . . (123–24)

The "two works" of which, for Schlegel, *Nathan* is composed are the polemic against illiberal theology and the affirmation of the ethical legitimacy of nature qua simplicity.[45] In terms of our linguistic-religio-cultural allegory, the former appears as the tendency of spirit or mind to deny all fixation of itself in the materiality of the letter.[46] The latter is precisely the opposed tendency of the material letter (which here appears as "nature") to take the place of or to assert itself as the spirit (which here appears in turn as "ethics")—"ethical simplicity of good-hearted nature"—or in a reversed formulation, the tendency of the letter now seen as artifice to become the free spirit of spontaneous nature—"artificial nonnaturalness attains its pinnacle and in so doing jumps over itself and opens anew the way to a return into the unconditioned freedom of nature." Both of the "works" *Nathan* contains are to some degree philosophical (Schlegel calls the second work "again something philosophical"). However, the former is religious ("religious doctrine"), while the latter is ethical ("ethical enthusiasm for the ethical force and ethical simplicity of good-hearted nature").[47] Insofar as they are both philosophical, they are predominantly spiritual, but the former provides us with the very *spirituality* of spirit. Being religious, the former concerns the divine, while the latter offers the *figural letter* of spirit because it concerns the human.[48] Here, the religious thought of a radical Protestantism is juxtaposed with an ethical thought that is explicitly traced to ancient cynicism. But this ancient cynicism, standing as it does here for the letter of nature or artifice, represents the same tendency as that represented so often elsewhere by the Judaic.[49] In short, Lessing's essence, the universalization of his particularity, or the entirety of his "spirit" as revealed in the essence of *Nathan der Weise*, is merely the struggle or interplay between— the antithetical identity of—content and form, spirit and letter, Protestant and Jewish.[50] In accordance with the concept of work it prescribes, his work is both more and less than a work. Its form and content are not organically articulated. The two main dimensions of its content represent in turn the dimensions of form and content and so are mutually at odds with each other to the precise extent that they are on terms of infinite intimacy.

Hyperbaton as Hypocrisy: The End of the Fragment as the Beginning of the Whole

Finally, how does Schlegel determine the status of his own work on Lessing vis-à-vis the fragmentary character of the (non)work Lessing exemplifies? First of all, Schlegel in a sense marks his text as fragmentary by breaking off, when the essay is initially published in the journal *Lyceum der schönen Künste* in 1797, with the comment that the conclusion will be provided in the next issue. Although he apparently means at first to supply this conclusion as announced, Schlegel ends up drawing out the completion of the essay for nearly four years, until he finally publishes it under the pressure of a deadline in *Charakteristiken und Kritiken* of 1801.[51] Despite the generalized character of both Schlegel's tendency to leave projects uncompleted and his difficulty getting along with editors and colleagues, it is quite plausible, given the importance of Schlegel's encounter with Lessing, to maintain that this delay of four years is a measure of how difficult the question of the proper termination of the Lessing essay actually is. Consider Schlegel's dilemma faced with this task. On the one hand, to write the conclusion will have been to make a whole out of what, according to the concept of the exemplary (non)work it argues for, ought to have remained a fragment. On the other hand, to leave the essay in fragmentary form will allow its readers to gain the impression that it still lacks completion, that it is not already complete in its very incompleteness. As a consequence of this dilemma, Schlegel is compelled to add a completion to the text that asserts both its own superfluity and its own necessity. I will complete this analysis of Schlegel's essay by discussing some of the main gestures through which he completes this essay, again in order to determine the limits of his notion of the fragmentary (non)work as spiritual mediation between letter and spirit.

Schlegel begins by reiterating what he finds most worthy of emphasis in Lessing's work. In this way, he briefly completes the essay "On Lessing" by summarizing it in order to say why he is not going to complete it in any straightforward way. Above all, it is in terms of Lessing's comment that "The New Gospel is coming" (from *Die Erziehung des Menschengeschlechtes*) that Schlegel attempts to sum up Lessing's value.

That is the thing that makes him so valuable to me; and if he had produced nothing of significance other than this one utterance, I would have to honor and love him already merely for this. And precisely *he* had to say it, he who lived totally in the clear understanding, he who was nearly without fantasy, except in wit, he had to say it, in the midst of the commonness that densely surrounded him, like a voice in the wilderness.[52]

The "New Gospel" Lessing announces is evidently the Gospel beyond the Gospel, the one that leads beyond the teleological opposition of letter and spirit. It is the Gospel whose spirituality consists in the fact that it takes the opposition between letter and spirit to be a figural letter signifying something other than what it seems literally to say.[53] And the reason why Lessing was the one who had to announce the coming of this New Gospel is that only someone opposed to *Schwärmerei*, a sober and in this sense marginally counterspiritual spirit, could have grasped the spirit beyond spirit that was a desideratum *now*, at this precise point in the history of the *Education of Humankind*. But what about the "form" of the work(s) in which Lessing's announcement of the coming Gospel appears?

In accordance with his emphasis on the announcement of the coming of the New Gospel as the essential "content" of Lessing's accomplishment, Schlegel goes on to emphasize to his readers precisely the mixed, heterogeneous, and, because for this discourse homogeneity and wholeness are quasi-synonymous, always fragmentary character of its "form":

> Just stop praising in Lessing only what he did not have and was not capable of . . . and if you finally want to fix upon that which actually came to ripeness and became quite visible in him, then leave him as he is, and take it as you find it, this *mixture of literature, polemic, wit, and philosophy*.
>
> It was precisely this mixture that drew me toward him early on and still binds me to him. (398)

What comes to "ripeness" or completion in Lessing is the sufficient homogeneity of radically hybrid discourse, the completion of the incomplete as such, the "ripeness" of ripening, the being-ness of becoming. How will Schlegel now articulate his own discourse with such a form of ripeness?

Consistent with his admiration and emulation of Lessing's accomplishments, Schlegel states toward the outset of the supplement to the Lessing essay: "But now I cannot finish in the manner in which I began at that time" (397). Having begun the originally published essay in terms of a notion of completeness that was eroded in the course of the essay's argument, Lessing cannot, indeed, complete it in the manner in which—that is, in terms of the formal presuppositions with which—he began. Instead, he will quite explicitly perform in various ways the heterogeneity and (in)completeness he affirms in Lessing. Before considering the *limitations* of Schlegel's commitment to this heterogeneous fragmentariness of the (non)work, let us look briefly at how Schlegel both performs and comments upon his performance of the (non)work in this supplementary "Conclusion" to the Lessing essay.

Concerning the performance, consider first certain relatively external, "formal" traits. The supplement to the Lessing essay contains: first a paragraph of prose; then a poem; then a page or so more of prose; then about ten pages of fragments (in the narrow sense of the term), mostly drawn from other sets of already published fragments; then about seven pages of prose; and then it ends with another poem. Three formal types—the letter (or is it the spirit?) of prose, the spirit (or should we say the letter?) of poetry, and the *Zwitterwesen* of what is "literally" a collection of fragments—are interspersed in such a way as to point incessantly to the place *between* partial letter and total spirit in which Schlegel is apparently interested. Further, in terms of the orientation of the "content," across all of these forms, there is a mixture of an "objective" attentiveness to Lessing and a "subjective" expressiveness whereby Schlegel presents directly his own views on various matters. This intermingling of self and other, subject and object, allegorically performs in another sense an intermingling of spirit and letter.

Concerning the way in which Schlegel repeatedly *announces* or *remarks upon* his performance—consider briefly just one example of such a remark. Immediately after saying that the "mixed" character of Lessing's texts was what kept him "bound" (as by irons or chains—"fesselt" is the word he uses) to Lessing, Schlegel goes on:

I would like to express, in my own way, the character of [this mixture], and my inclination toward it. How can this occur in any way better than through an anthology of my own thoughts that aim at it either internally or externally?

Let it be a pleasing sacrifice [*ein gefälliges Totenopfer*] for the immortal one whom I chose early as my guiding star [*Leitstern*].

Let me, too, follow the custom, which is becoming increasingly widespread, of loving allegorical names, and if others offer you blossoms or flowers in precious vessels, let me simply call this fragmentary universality *iron filings* [*Eisenfeile*] in order thus, through a symbol, to recall the dismembered quality [*das Zerstückelte*] of what seems to be formless form [*formlosen Form*], and yet at the same time to indicate with sufficient accuracy the inner nature of the material involved [*die innere Natur des Stoffs*]. (398)

Schlegel clearly announces that he not only admires and emulates but also feels some affinity with the mixed character of Lessing's writings ("inclination toward it"). The best way of writing (on Lessing) is thus to mix himself up (with Lessing) and to provide a heterogeneous mixture (an "anthology") of his own thoughts, which "internally" (in content) and "externally" (in form) point to the mixture of genres, that is, also to the undoing of the discrete identities of content and form. By calling his fragments "iron filings," Schlegel points to the "dismembered quality" of their "formless form," a form that must appear as formless insofar as it is already also content and so not mere form. But he also points to the "inner nature of the material," an inner nature which could not be more material—what is harder and more earthbound than "iron"?—and yet has a potentially spiritual dimension insofar as "iron" is susceptible of magnetization and thus capable of something like desire. Moreover, "iron filings" are what would result from trying to free oneself from "irons," in the sense of "fetters": they signify the tension between freedom (of spirit) and nonfreedom (as implied by submission to matter), a tension inherent more specifically in Schlegel's relation of being "bound" ("fesselt" [398]) to Lessing by his fascination with mixed discourse. "Iron filings" are form that is not form, matter that is not matter, and freedom that is not freedom.

However, despite the apparently strict rigor of Schlegel's commitment to the theoretical practice of the fragmentary (non)work, there is a limit. There is always in Schlegel, even in his most critically advanced phase which we are considering here, a moment of turning back from the thought of the fragment *as* totality—the interrupted work as work-faith, practico-theoretical balance—toward the thought of the fragment as what is *oriented toward* totality—the fragment understood as a work of the letter that can have value only insofar as it is oriented toward the telos of the whole understood as the assimilation of all works into an absolute work of pure faith. In the supplement to the Lessing essay, this moment is introduced through the figure of hyperbaton, a syntactical inversion, which here operates on the level of Schlegel's argument itself. The figural name is used by Schlegel himself in a letter on the "supplement" to his brother: "I couldn't revise [the Lessing essay], nor could I end it as it was, and so I will have to make use of the figure of hyperbaton" (XXXIV). This figure of hyperbaton will consist in placing the beginning at the end, so that the end is at the beginning. But it will also be bound up with an inversion of the argument on fragmentation Schlegel has thus far been pursuing in Lessing's wake. The beginning that now comes at the end will be the beginning of something rather different from the end that henceforth will have come at the beginning.[54] Let us retrace how this occurs.

After announcing (in the third prose section of the "Conclusion") that in the future he will renounce the criticism of modern literature in order to undertake two large and interrelated projects, the "History of Poetry" and the "Critique of Philosophy," he writes:

I have determined that the Conclusion of this fragment should be a Preface of the whole; for it was supposed, in accordance with the nature of the matter at hand, to be more a Postface than a Preface. But will you want to take even a series of studies to be a whole just because they have been animated by one spirit [*von einem Geist beseelt*] and have arisen within this spirit in a way not lacking in coherence? Let this be left to you and to your unconditional freedom of will. That unity of spirit, however, I can prove; in the unmistakable tendency of all those essays and in their unwavering maxim.[55]

The end of the fragment, then, is the beginning of the whole. But how are we to understand this here? If the fragment, especially when it is called *Bruchstück*, is necessarily the *end* of the whole, then this supplement to the Lessing essay was apparently to have been the end of the end. And if the whole is the *beginning*—because in this biblically inflected, phonologo-centric context we are assumed to begin in wholeness and only subsequently to fall into fragmentation—then what Schlegel is saying here is that the end of the end is the beginning of the beginning. Above all it is important to note here that *this is not at all consistent with the notion of the fragmentary (non)work*. The notion of the fragmentary (non)work between works and faith translates, in terms of ends and beginnings, into the notion that the end is the beginning and the beginning the end, the work the faith and the faith work. In contrast, what Schlegel is saying now is merely that the end of the end is the beginning of the beginning. And in saying this, he transforms the paradoxical structure of the fragment *as* whole into the truism that the fragment *belongs to* the whole. That is, to move outward from the fragment, to finish off the fragment from the outside and go beyond it, is to move toward, to begin to enter, into the whole—the beginning or the pure origin—to which it belongs. The whole is now both termination and telos of the fragment.

Indeed this is just what Schlegel spends the rest of this last prose section arguing for. The part (or letter), he asserts, is either an integral part of an infinite totality (or spirit) into which it teleologically disappears, or it is nothing and thus must be destroyed by the polemical power of that spirit itself.[56] The teleologically one-sided relationship between part and whole, letter and spirit, difference and identity, has been restored. Schlegel spells this out through his "proof" of the "unity of the spirit" by which the (serial) "whole" he is introducing will be animated: his determination of the "tendency" and the "maxim" of the planned series of studies.

The tendency is, Schlegel writes, "in spite of an often painstaking thoroughness [*Fleißes*] in details . . . nonetheless not so much judgmentally to evaluate as rather *to understand and to explain all as a whole.* . . ."[57] The whole to be grasped is associated with the spirit of the work, and it is not merely the whole of the work or author but the "immeasurable whole [*unermeßliche(. . .) Ganze(. . .)*]" (410), that Schlegel means to envision as the horizon of the appreciation of any given work. In order to arrive at the whole, however, one must find the "Mittelpunkt," which is "the organism [*Organismus*] of all arts and sciences, the law and history of this organism . . . its own science . . . *encyclopedia*" (411). Although—or rather precisely because—this science of the arts and sciences, of their abstract law and embodied history, does not yet exist, Schlegel claims that his "critical attempts" and "fragments" are interesting because they are formulated in the "spirit" of the same ("eben weil sie noch nicht vorhanden ist, diese Wissenschaft, darf ich für meine im Geist derselben entworfnen kritischen Versuche und Bruchstücke die ernstlichste Aufmerksamkeit und Teilnahme fodern" [411]). The part, which is also the letter, now assumes its significance from the whole to which it contributes and belongs. Parts that belong to the whole are evidence of "Genie" (410), whereas parts that do not are evidence of mere "Talent" (410), "which through being isolated betrays itself to be a false tendency of art and humanity" (410).

In order to function properly, this tendency to "understand" and "explain" with reference to the "whole" requires that some distinction be made between those things that refer, contribute, and belong to the whole, and those that do not:

True criticism [can] take no notice of works that contribute nothing to the development of art and science; indeed, a true criticism is not even possible with reference to that which does not stand in relation to the organism of formation and genius [*Organismus der Bildung und des Genies*], that which for the whole and in the whole actually does not exist.

In some cases it is not possible to dispense with a proof of non-existence and nullity . . . and thus the necessity of polemic is deduced . . . yet polemic is to me much more than that, much more than a necessary evil; when it is what it should be, it is to me the seal of the most lively effectivity of the divine in the human . . .

shouldn't that be the beginning of all knowledge, to separate the good from the evil? That at least is my faith. (410)

Schlegel's "tendency" to *understand* in the context of the whole requires as its constant accompaniment precisely the *judgment* that it excludes from itself. Understanding must rid itself, through polemical condemnation, of all that is not worth attempting to place in relation to the whole, all that is not even capable of any relation to rational truth. This activity of *judgment* is propelled by what Schlegel calls here his "maxim":

I have not so much striven to annihilate the great crowd of weak subjects that purposelessly carries on its nugatory activities within every sphere of art, but rather to extend the separation of the good and evil principles up to the highest levels of force and formation . . . for to this I found that I had a special calling. (412)

The polemical principle—the "most lively effectivity of the divine in the human"—here serves the principle of love as an extension of its spiritual force. The polemical principle *sacrifices* the negativity of the finite work, a negativity that it itself also represents (although it disavows any knowledge of this fact) to the degree that it is itself the "judgment" that the (loving) "understanding" and "explanation" of the "whole" has to exclude from itself in order to come into being in the full force of its pure positivity. The partial letter, as a trace of negativity, either enters into the spiritual, positive whole or is destroyed by the part of that whole which is its polemical negativity.[58] In one case, the (whole) spirit functions as the termination of the letter (*qua* part), while in the other case the spirit functions as its *telos*: in both cases, the spirit is (in one or another sense) its end. The end of the (fragmentary) end is the beginning of the (whole) beginning.[59]

Just as the double work to which Schlegel had reduced *Nathan*—the tension between the "religious" principle of the spirit and the "ethical" principle of the letter—was ultimately inscribed within an overarching philosophical spirit, so here the undecidable interplay between spiritual wholeness and alphabetic fragmentation is ultimately treated as an interplay whose absolute context is spiritual wholeness itself.[60] Schlegel's hyperbaton is finally hypo-critical, not in the sense of a moral fault, but in the "literal" sense of a lack of critical rigor. Against Schlegel's better "judgment," it operates the determination of the relationship between letter (as fragmentation, sensuality, and difference) and spirit (as wholeness, intellectuality, and sameness) *arbitrarily* as a *spiritual* relationship, whereas it is constitutively, structurally, undecidable: a relationship of neither spirit nor letter and both. To see how Schlegel's peculiarly tantalizing combination of rigorous critical vigilance and lack thereof extends itself, with respect to these same matters, into both his (theoretical and literary) presentations of gender and his—closely related—liaison with Dorothea Mendelssohn-Veit-Schlegel, we now turn to "On Philosophy: To Dorothea" and *Lucinde*, two texts written in sequence shortly after the initial publication of the ambivalently fragmentary essay "On Lessing."

4

Duplicitous Engenderments of the Literal Spirit

FRIEDRICH SCHLEGEL'S "ON PHILOSOPHY:
TO DOROTHEA" (1798) AND 'LUCINDE' (1799)

> But what should my spirit give to his son, who is, like him, as poor in
> poetry as he is rich in love?[1]

We have seen how Schlegel's attempt, in "On Lessing," to grasp spirit as spirit—to take spirit literally—leads him to suspend the distinction between spirit and letter—to take the letter (of the distinction between letter and spirit) spiritually or figurally—and yet to do so always with the intention of realizing spirit as such in its purest state.[2] Further, we have seen how, in the 1801 "Conclusion" of the Lessing essay, Schlegel's struggle to formulate the exemplary "spirituality" of what goes beyond the opposition between spirit and letter takes refuge in the notion that letter and spirit are one only in the sense that the letter always already alludes to the spirit it will have become in the end. Schlegel posits there, in other words, that difference is identical with identity only insofar as it is destined to become the identity it is not yet, or, in terms of the rhetoric of synecdochic metaphor: the part is a whole (and hence has a right to exist), only insofar as it has its telos in the whole that is no longer merely a part. In order to gain a more "comprehensive" view of the importance of Jewish-Christian "dialogue" both for Schlegel's early writings and for his life while he was producing these writings, it remains for us to consider in detail the two texts, "On Philosophy: To Dorothea" and *Lucinde*, in which Schlegel both publicly develops and theorizes about his relation to Dorothea Mendelssohn-

Veit. Here, we will see how Schlegel's attempt to formulate a theory of the necessary supplementation of literal spirit by figural letter comes to be expanded into, and overdetermined by, a theory of the necessary supplementation of the masculine by the feminine. In "On Philosophy," Schlegel articulates the religio-cultural and semiotic demand for the mutual supplementation of figural Jew and literal Christian with a gender-theory—as well as a "lived" desire—that argues for the mutual supplementation of feminine and masculine principles. Further, he accomplishes this articulation by means of a theory of the relations between philosophy and poetry. In *Lucinde*, Schlegel elaborates upon this constellation more fully, unfolding its implications across the entire semantic field of traditional rationalist metaphysics. While retracing the gender theory stated in "On Philosophy" and its elaboration in *Lucinde*, we will be particularly attentive to the ways in which the asymmetrical domination of spirit over letter, which emerged in the previous chapter, insistently and always problematically reappears as the domination of masculine over feminine in Schlegel's considerations on the category of gender, despite the rhetoric of androgyny that pervades those considerations.[3] Taking the texts in chronological order, we will begin with "On Philosophy" and then proceed to the discussion of *Lucinde*.

Androgyny and Philosophical Poetry as Judaeo-Protestant Syntheses in "On Philosophy"

Before entering into the argument of "On Philosophy," let us briefly consider the ways in which Dorothea Mendelssohn-Veit, Schlegel's addressee here, is entangled for him with the figure of Lessing, his transferential object in the texts we've examined thus far.

Dorothea is connected to the "life" and "work" of Lessing both by way of his "life" and by way of his "work." First, and most simply, Dorothea is the daughter of Lessing's double, Mendelssohn, the (almost secular Protestant) Jew. For Schlegel, who deeply regretted not having been able to meet Lessing,[4] she is thus an indirect connection to Lessing himself.

Yet, Dorothea serves for Schlegel as an indirect connection to Lessing not only because she is the daughter of his friend but also insofar as she is indirectly figured in Lessing's text.[5] Given that, as is well known, Lessing's last play, *Nathan der Weise*, was among other things a tribute to Mendelssohn, any of Mendelssohn's daughters could be readily associated with Recha, Nathan's adoptive daughter in Lessing's play, but especially the favored eldest.[6] As one will recall, Nathan illegitimately yet understandably raises Recha as a Jewess (even if Judaism here looks a lot like a universal rational ethico-theology), although he knows she is by birth a Christian. She ends up returning, as the sister of her would-be suitor and savior (the Templar Knight), to the Christian fold, in Arabian garb, a return to which Dorothea's conversion will ultimately correspond. Dorothea is a figure for Recha, then, with relation to whom Schlegel himself, her suitor and would-be savior, becomes a figure for the Templar Knight. Of course, as one might object, this would ultimately imply that Schlegel could not marry Dorothea because she would turn out to be his sister. But in a certain sense he ends up in something less than a marital relation with Dorothea—"figurally speaking"—both insofar as the Schlegels do not seem to have had a physically or even emotionally intimate relationship beyond the very early years, and insofar as they never had any children (whereas Schlegel himself posits in *Lucinde* that children are the touchstone of the reality of any marriage).[7] According to this scenario, finally, Lessing himself would be in the position of the Sultan Saladin insofar as the Sultan is the enlightened uncle of the Templar Knight, who spares the Knight's life when he still thinks the Knight is his Christian enemy, simply because the Knight reminds him of his brother. By means of these associations, Schlegel would become a kindred spirit with Lessing, playing nephew to Lessing's uncle, that is, displaced son to Lessing's displaced paternity. Further, in *Lucinde*, the narrator will characterize himself as the son of *Witz*, the same *Witz* in which Schlegel has situated Lessing's stylistic essence. And through the mediation of Lessing as *Witz*, Schlegel also gains a close bond of friendship, even familiality, with Moses Mendelssohn (as recent avatar of *the* Moses, even if he was often called "the German Socrates"), becoming at once his son qua nephew and (almost) his son-in-law. Finally, the fact that Schlegel will ultimately turn to serve the Patriarch (or to identify himself with the Patriarch) is inscribed in the structure of this play as well.

Given the complexity and intensity of Schlegel's investments in Lessing, in general, and in *Nathan der Weise*, in particular, and given that Schlegel met Dorothea in Henriette Herz's salon—in the house of Henriette's husband, Markus Herz, who was Moses Mendelssohn's last medical doctor and the one to bear authoritative public witness to his passing—given all of this, in short, it would have been indeed somewhat surprising if Schlegel had *not* fallen in love with Dorothea Veit. "Life" and "work," "reality" and "figure" interlacing inextricably here, Schlegel's reading lessons to Dorothea in "On Dorothea" as well as his reading of Dorothea in *Lucinde* will be guided by very much the same set of conceptual concerns as Schlegel's encounter with Lessing—with the notable addition, however, of an explicitly gender-theoretical anthropology that will ramify across the entire field of traditional metaphysics.

In order to approach the main argument of Schlegel's missive to Dorothea on the proper role of philosophy in her life, let us note two gestures—first merely a phrase, then a paragraph—toward the beginning of Schlegel's letter. Of interest is not simply *what* Schlegel has to say in this letter, but *how* he positions himself performatively with relation to his interlocutor. The referential-constative dimension of the letter will have to mirror its apostrophic-performative dimension, for the letter is precisely *about* how Schlegel as a man (and as a Christian) is positioned with respect to Dorothea Veit as a woman (and as a Jew). Through both of the gestures we will consider, Schlegel seems to switch places, to some extent, with his interlocutor, playing the Jewish parent to the Christian child, whereas one would expect that she should be playing the Jew to his Christian, and also parent to his child, for not only does the Jew come historically before the Christian but also Dorothea is older than Friedrich and already a mother at this time. That these structures have to be denegationally reversed testifies both to their presence and to the fragility and ambiguity of the typological teleology whereby the child term is supposed to become the "fulfillment" of its "prefigurative" parent. As realization of a mere anticipation, the fulfillment always becomes also, paradoxically, more anticipatory than the anticipation. From this perspective, the anticipation is more of a fulfillment than its fulfillment: the spirit is more letterlike than the letter. No wonder, then, if Friedrich will want to play parental Jew to Dorothea's childlike Christian. Let us see how this plays out in the text itself.

The first gesture I would like to consider is the opening phrase of the essay-epistle: "To what I told you about Spinoza, it was not without Religion that you listened."[8] Schlegel opens his letter by placing himself in the traces of Moses Mendelssohn. He makes himself into the ghostly after-life of the father of the addressee, picking up precisely where Mendelssohn broke off at the end of *Morgenstunden* after having defined for his quasi-fictional interlocutors the position of Spinozism in contemporary thought. (One of the "real" models—or prefigurations—of these "fictional" interlocutors was, as I have indicated, Dorothea herself, then called Brendel Mendelssohn). In that text, as we have seen in Chapter 2, Mendelssohn argued that the difference between pantheism—as the reduction of the spirit (or God) to letter (or creation), or, in slightly different terms, as the collapse of the two into an identity—and theism—as the tendential reduction of the letter to spirit, of creation to God as ultimate origin, or again, in a slightly different form, the maintenance of a sharp distinction between the two—is undecidable. We cannot know whether there is any difference between pantheism and theism; we cannot know whether spirit and letter (or identity and difference) are identical or different, because the letter blocks off all access to such knowledge. In picking up the thread of this discussion where Mendelssohn left off—a discussion one of the more important goals of which was to determine the legacy of Lessing—Schlegel will explain away the enigmatic undecidability with which Mendelssohn left us. And he will do so by means of a gender theory, a theory of how masculine spirit and feminine letter start out distinct and end up coming together. He thus poses in this text as the (at once filial and paternal) *realization* (or *fulfillment*) of the father's (Mosaic) *prefiguration*, that is, as the rendering meaningful, comprehensible, fully present, of the father's enigmatically self-withdrawing law of undecidability. Schlegel as Christian here realizes the spirit of the (Jew, Moses') law: the spirit makes it possible to know the identity that the law left in doubt, namely, the identity of letter and spirit, world and God, as the spiritually and indeed divinely androgynous identity of feminine and masculine principles.

But how is it possible and why is it necessary for Schlegel to pose in the paternal and therefore quasi-Jewish position as the realization of Moses's prefiguration? By identifying himself with the Mosaic text as its spiritual realization, Schlegel indeed lays claim at once to the "Jewish" and to the paternal/parental position. In turn, Dorothea, whom Schlegel will go on to render largely as a denizen of love and inward feeling, as is already announced in the passage above by the fact that she listens "not without Religion," occupies the "Christian" position and the position of the child. And yet, as Christian, playing opposite both Dorothea's Jewess and Moses Mendelssohn's Jew, and even as a Christ-figure playing opposite Dorothea's

"Madonna" (a figure that becomes explicit in *Lucinde*), Schlegel would by rights have to appear here as the son. How is it that the Christian child comes to occupy the position of the Jewish parent? This is made possible by the fact that the Jew stands, in Christian traditions, only for the *letter* of the paternal/parental law, its material, imaginary, infantile aspect, while the Christian stands, on the one hand, for the child as projective image of the law but, on the other hand, and essentially from the standpoint of Christian traditions, for the law of the law as its spirit. Thus, the material, imaginary, and infantile aspect of the Christian transforms itself into the spiritual, symbolic, parental aspect. The father is, indeed, to vary a Lacanian formula, the ghost or *Geist* of the father. Further, what makes this reversal of parent and child desirable or necessary for Schlegel is that the child as fulfillment is always also the realization of a *mere anticipation*, and so a fall away from the relatively fulfilled character of the originally unfulfilled anticipation.

But Schlegel does not content himself with occupying the position of the paternal law with respect to Dorothea Veit. He apparently continues, in the second gesture I wish to consider, to occupy the position of the *letter*, the *writing* of this law. A consideration of the passage two paragraphs further on in which this usurpation and reversal occurs—contrary to the most conventional expectations, given that Schlegel is the Protestant here, and Veit the Jew—will provide us with a glimpse into the full dialectical complexity of Schlegel's position at this time:

I still remember quite vividly my bold claim *that philosophy is necessary to women, because there is no virtue for them other than religion, to which they can accede only through philosophy*. I promised you then that I would prove this thought (as one calls it), or at least develop it somewhat more fully than can be done in a conversation. I am now coming to keep my promise; not really to show myself to be a man of my word, but rather solely and alone because I feel like it, even if only to tease someone so decidedly contemptuous of all writing and letteredness [*eine so entschiedene Verächterin alles Schreibens und Buchstabenwesens*] with my infatuated love of these things. You would perhaps prefer a spoken dialogue [*ein Gespräch*]. But I am, once and for all, an author. Writing [*Die Schrift*] has for me I know not what secret force [*geheimen Zauber*] perhaps through the twilight of eternity that hovers about it. Indeed, I admit that I wonder what secret force lies hidden in these dead traits [*welche geheime Kraft in diesen toten Zügen verborgen liegt*]; how the simplest expressions that seem nothing more than true and exact can be so meaningful that they seem to gaze out of bright eyes, or as telling as artless accents from the deepest soul. One believes oneself to be hearing what one is only reading, and yet someone who reads aloud can do nothing in the case of these actually beautiful passages other than strive not to ruin them. The silent traces seem to me a more appropriate covering for these deepest, most immediate expressions of spirit than the sound of lips. I would almost want to say in the somewhat mystical language of our H.: life is writing; the only human destiny is to dig the thoughts of God into the tables of nature with the engraving tool of the imaginatively forming spirit. But as far as you are concerned, I think that you will do complete justice to your part in this destiny of the human race if you sing as much as before, outwardly and inwardly, in the usual and in the symbolic sense being silent less, and reading now and then even in divine writings with a worshipper's awed thought [*mit Andacht*], not merely letting others read for you and tell you the tale. But especially, you must hold Words to be holier than you have heretofore. Otherwise, I would be in bad shape. For of course I can give you nothing and I must expressly require that you expect of me nothing more than Words, expressions for that which you long since felt and knew, only not in such a clear and well-ordered way. Perhaps you would do well to expect of philosophy itself also nothing more than a voice, language, and grammar for the instinct of divinity, an instinct that is divinity's germ and, if one has an eye to the essential, divinity itself. (42)

What is the meaning of the fact that, in this very complex passage, Schlegel stages himself, at the outset of his letter, as having a privileged connection to writing, while he stages Dorothea as being related to speech (or at most to reading, the movement from writing to speech)?[9] Two principal interpretations are possible. While both are plausible, neither has the power to cancel entirely the presence of the other.

On the one hand, Schlegel evidently identifies himself with writing and Dorothea with speech. In doing so, he reverses the Pauline schema according to which the letter kills while the spirit gives life, instead suggesting that the letter, because it has stability over time (Schlegel writes of "the twilight of eternity that hovers about it" [42]), offers the life of spirit. Speech, evidently because it flows away in time, is exposed (and exposes its speaker) to death. Pauline phonologocentrism is thus reversed into a kind of graphologocentrism, but it is reversed only in order for the Christian and male writer of the letter under consideration to be able to step into the "authoritative" position of the Jewish letter, from where he proceeds to condescend to the Jewish woman—however tenderly he may do so—about her relative incapacity to appreciate the eternalizing spirituality of the letter.[10] Schlegel usurps the position of the (Jewish) letter here precisely in the (unnamed) name of its hyperoriginary spirituality,[11] while he places Dorothea, who in her person is marked as and by that letter itself, into the position of a henceforth secondary speech.

What makes this reversal of positions *possible* is the fact that, as indicated above, the realization of the anticipation is more like the anticipation than the anticipation itself managed to be. What *necessitates* the reversal, however, is that, in being more like the anticipation than the anticipation itself, the fulfillment is also more anticipatory, a mere anticipation of the anticipation, a proleptic falling-off. It thus needs imitatively to usurp the anticipation.

On the other hand, it is possible, especially if one is rereading the text, to suppose that Schlegel does not identify himself with writing here but with the *lack* of writing, the *desire* for, or the *appreciation* of, the writing he neither has nor is. In turn, one could then suggest that Schlegel does not identify Dorothea with speech—or dialogue (and indeed it is a question here of what the dialogue could possibly be between dialogue and nondialogue, or speech and writing)—but with the *lack* of speech (the text explicitly remarks her silence), the *desire*, predilection, or preference for that dialogical speech from which she would, on this interpretation, be excluded. On the level of religio-cultural identity, this would mean that, because Schlegel is a Christian, he needs or wants, and is therefore fascinated by, the letter in which he takes no part (although it is paradoxically supposed to be an integral part of the spirit he embodies). Conversely, because Dorothea is a Jew—an embodiment of the figural letter—she needs to internalize precisely the spirit that supplements her. Each principle, in other words, would "naturally" tend toward its supplementary principle.

On one reading, Schlegel identifies himself with writing, while on the other, he differentiates himself from writing; on one reading, he identifies Dorothea with speech, on the other, he differentiates her from it. The tension between the two readings of this opening apostrophic gesture of Schlegel's text—after which he settles into the development of the content of his message, shifting largely from the apostrophic (or second person) to the representational (or third person) mode—is the tension between identity and difference. Through the ambivalence of this opening gesture, the text performs the undecidability of identity and difference, as the undecidability of fulfillment and prefiguration. The difficulty one has imagining that such a performance could have been calculated by Schlegel himself as a conscious, intentional subject testifies to the difficulty, for any subject, of sustaining without lapse the tension of such an awareness of the undecidability between identity and difference. Moreover, the fact that, while Schlegel's early works incessantly point to the necessity of this undecidability, even as they seek to overcome it, his later works (from about 1804 on, as we will see in Chapter 6 below) attack with increasing vehemence and explicitness any possible affirmation of this undecidability, provides further evidence of the difficulty of sustaining such awareness (an awareness however that we urgently need, today, to learn how to bear). Having remarked, in its tortuous duplicity, this important opening gesture on Schlegel's part, let us proceed to consider the gender theory that "On Philosophy" spells out, in particular with a view to its implications for the letter-spirit, Jewish-Christian opposition in its (impossible) dialogue with itself.

Schlegel's explicit main object in "On Philosophy" is to develop for Dorothea his thesis that women need philosophy in order to arrive at religion, which is ostensibly their only virtue.[12] In order to develop this thesis, which here means to contextualize it within a broader conceptual framework, Schlegel sketches out and coordinates with each other a gender theory and a theory of the relationship between philosophy and literature (here called poetry), or science and art. In other words, he presents a theory that defines in terms of gender the relations between philosophy and poetry, while conversely it defines gender in terms of the relations between philosophy and poetry. Fortunately, Schlegel is not so simplistic here as to establish a mere one-to-one correspondence between the masculine-feminine and the philosophy-poetry opposition. Unfortunately, however, his schematization is perhaps not quite so complex as one might have hoped.

The framework he sets up is as follows: the starting point for femininity is earthly materiality, while its destiny is religious spirituality, to which philosophy is to lead. The starting point for masculinity, in contrast, is spirit, while its destiny is action in the material world, to which poetry is to lead (42–44, 53 passim). Poetry, then, is what women have and men need, while philosophy is what men have and women need. Or, to put things the other way around: what it means to be a woman is to possess poetry innately while standing in need of philosophy; to be a man is to possess philosophy, and yet have dire need of poetry. Poetry, as the (allegorical) passage from spiritual to material, is the means to the realization of masculinity on its path from an anticipatory spirituality to a fulfillment in the material. In turn, philosophy, as the (symbolic) passage from material to spiritual, is the means to the realization of femininity on its path from a material anticipation to a spiritual fulfillment. Schlegel's rhetorical-philosophical theory of gender, then, posits the feminine both as prefigural letter and as the passage from prefigural letter to literal spirit, while it posits the masculine both as spiritual fulfillment and as the passage from prefigural *spirit* to literal, fulfilling *letter* (see Figure 4).

According to this structure, philosophy and poetry are in a mutually complementary and circular relationship, as are masculinity and femininity: each ends where its binary other begins. In terms of a humanistic gender theory that combines descriptive and normative dimensions, the ideal humanity is androgynous: "Only soft masculinity [*sanfte Männlichkeit*] . . . only independent femininity [*selbständige Weiblichkeit*], are the right, the true, and the beautiful" (45). In order to move toward this perhaps infinitely unattainable (and perhaps therefore all-too-safe) goal, men must cultivate their poetic sensibilities and capacities, which at the outset are inferior to those of women, while women must study philosophy in order to raise themselves up above the "Weltmeer" (43) of material, domestic concerns in which they are otherwise in danger of drowning.

But what does Schlegel's position in this essay imply for the relations between letter and spirit, Jews and Germans/Christians? How does it overdetermine, and how is it overdetermined by, these relations? Earthliness is aligned as materiality with the letter, which is aligned with Judaism; spirit is opposed to letter and aligned with Christianity.[13] The implications of these alignments can be summarized as follows. As far as gender theory is concerned: in their origin (or their existence), women are letters, pure figural materiality; in terms of their end (or their essence), women are spirit, radical spirituality. As for men, in their original existence they are already spirit, while in their ultimate essence they will have become the materiality of the letter. Women thus begin as Jews (i.e., women) and end up as Christians (i.e., men), while men begin as Christians (men) and end up as Jews (women). It is the business of philosophy to make Christian men out of Jewish women, and conversely it is the business of poetry to make Jewish women out of Christian men.

These positions seem at the outset quite simply symmetrical. But the apparent symmetry of these positions is deceptive (see Figure 5). Assuming that anticipatory existence (or origin) and fulfilled essence (or end) may be

	anticipation ——————→ fulfillment	
feminine	material ——————→ spiritual	
	philosophy	
masculine	spiritual ——————→ material	
	poetry	

FIGURE 4. Schlegel's Gender Theory

aligned here with letter and spirit (and this alignment is imposed by the force of the tradition Schlegel inherits, for which the telos is always spirit), when men are said to *exist* spiritually, this means that even in their material figurality they are already spirit. If men become letter in becoming their essence, then even as letter, men are still essential (i.e., spiritual). In other words, it is precisely as essences (or spirits) that they become letter: men begin as spiritual letters and end up as material (or lettered) spirit. For women, this combination of spirit and letter at each pole of their development does not obtain. Women begin their existence (or simply they exist) as letter; in their very material figurality, they are material figures. And women end as their spiritual essence, i.e., their end is being-spiritual in their very spirituality (or essence). In other words, men are chiasmically totalized, and their trajectory is characterized by the continuous maintenance of this totality, but at the same time they are always inwardly divided, always comprised of some sort of combination of letter and spirit. Women, in contrast, are never total, and their trajectory involves a radical break, the leap from pure material letter to pure spiritual essence. Yet on both sides of this leap, women are internally homogeneous, purely self-same.

How should we understand this asymmetry? It compensates men for their internal dividedness by giving them a certain stability and totality that endures across the masculine trajectory from beginning to end, while it makes women buy their wholeness or homogeneity at any given point with a partiality and a developmental trajectory that render them always incomplete in a way that is not characteristic of men. Men, in other words, are androgynous all along, unchangingly, while women are androgynous only across the trajectory they cover, that is, never all at once.

What are the ramifications of this asymmetrical establishment of the relations between the genders for the relations between the *religious groups*

Since anticipation (existence) = letter
while fulfillment (essence) = spirit:

	anticipatory ⟶ letter	fulfilling spirit
feminine	material ⟶ letter	spiritual spirit
masculine	spiritual ⟶ letter	material spirit

FIGURE 5. Letter and Spirit in Schlegel's Gender Theory

with which the genders are implicitly associated? Insofar as the positions of anticipation and fulfillment that are traditionally marked as letter and spirit are in addition (and consequently) marked as Jewish/feminine and Christian/masculine, respectively, what follows for the religio-cultural overdetermination of the distinct trajectories of men and women? (See Figure 6.) Let us start by considering the man. As a man, that is, as a spiritual being, the man is in origin the Christian man. Because a Christian man is such in his *existence*, or in origin, one can say that a Christian man is a Christian man insofar as he is a Jewish woman, or in his Jewish womanliness (because existence as letter is always Jewish and feminine). When the Christian man—any man, or any Christian—becomes material (becomes a Jewish woman) in his *essence*, he becomes a Jewish woman insofar as he is a Christian man, or in his very Christian manliness (because essence is associated with Christianity and masculinity).

The situation for the woman, however, is rather different. The woman, as woman (as a material being, a figural form), is in her origin a Jewish woman. The Jewish woman—any woman, or any Jew—is a Jewish woman only insofar as she is a Jewish woman, in her materially figural existence or in her Jewish womanliness itself. When (after reading philosophy) the Jewish woman—any woman, or any Jew—becomes a Christian man in essence, however, she becomes a Christian man only on the level of her Christian manliness, that is, her essentiality, which is now all that she has or is.

The asymmetrical violence of both gender relations and their homologous and overdetermining religio-cultural relations sheds light, further, on

Since letter = Jewish and feminine
while spirit = Christian and masculine

	anticipatory ⟶	fulfilling
	Jewish femininity	Christian masculinity
feminine	Jewish woman ⟶	Christian man
	as Jewish woman	as Christian man
masculine	Christian man ⟶	Jewish woman
	as Jewish woman	as Christian man

FIGURE 6. Jewish Femininity and Christian Masculinity in Schlegel's Gender Theory

the relationship between the author and addressee of this letter, Friedrich Schlegel and Dorothea Veit. The Jew and the woman as Jewish woman must entirely annihilate themselves in order to become the Christian and the man, the Christian man. The Christian and the man, however, as Christian man, can indeed become the Jew and the woman, i.e., the Jewish woman, without giving up their identities as Christian man.[14] Indeed, the Christian man includes within himself, so to speak, at all moments, the Jewish woman. Hence, Schlegel in one sense has no need for Dorothea, because he already *is* her (in part).

In another sense, the religio-cultural implications of Schlegel's gender theory prescribe, or at least describe, as follows the "necessity" (and ambivalence) of Schlegel's choice of a Jewish woman as his object of desire. While according to his schema the notion of a Christian woman or a Jewish man would be excluded as a contradiction in terms (because the feminine and Jewish are originally material, the masculine and Christian originally spiritual), by virtue of this contradiction and on another level the Christian woman and the Jewish man represent ideal forms of achieved androgyny. The Christian woman and the Jewish man are thus at once excluded from the system and idealized. Since Schlegel posited androgyny as the ideal, and since as a Christian man, Schlegel was, so to speak, a pure spirit, he apparently needed the doubly material supplementation of a Jewish woman in order to attain together with her the androgynous balance his text proposes as ideal on the level of its theoretical desire. But since this androgynous ideal, this double oxymoron of the Christian woman who is a Jewish man, is also excluded from Schlegel's system of gender, one can understand something of the (massively denegated) ambivalence with which Schlegel always seems to have approached (the prospect of) his union with Dorothea.

Finally, let us return now to reconsider the duplicity of Schlegel's opening gesture, whereby he seemed at once to identify himself with writing and to differentiate himself from writing, at once to push Dorothea into the space of a debased speech and to differentiate her from a speech marked as the proper object of her desire. In light of Schlegel's theory of gender, the duplicity of this gesture becomes comprehensible in a new way. We can now see that Schlegel speaks as the Christian man or spiritual being whose destiny it is to enter, through poetry, into the space of the Jewish woman qua earthly letter. He can speak (as Figure 6 indicates) at all points along this trajectory from both positions at once. This explains the apparent usurpation and spiritualization of the position of the Jewish letter on Schlegel's part. Correspondingly, as a Jewish woman, the quintessence of both Jew and woman, Dorothea exists in the form of the material letter that anticipates its spiritualizing annihilation. In the self-abnegation that she apparently performs in her life and that Schlegel almost taunts her with in this text,[15] one can perceive concretely her inhabitation of this position. The gender theory that Schlegel develops in "On Philosophy," then, renders apparently comprehensible and manageable the undecidability of identity and difference (another name for the undecidability of spirit and letter) by turning this undecidability into the narrative of an apparently circular trajectory whereby each term is destined to turn into the other. The turn from spirit into letter becomes the developmental trajectory of masculinity, while the turn from letter into spirit becomes the developmental trajectory of femininity. The circular totality of these two trajectories taken together—the name of this totality is "complete humanity"—renders apparently comprehensible as a narrative sequence (even if an infinite and circular one) the endlessly static structure of a repetitive break that the undecidability as such presents and withdraws from our grasp.

The points of articulation between these two trajectories remain, however, unsoldered by Schlegel's gender theory as it is articulated in "On Philosophy." The masculinized woman is not quite the same as the not-yet-feminized man, nor is the feminized man the same thing as a woman not yet trained in masculinity, as Figures 5 and 6 make clear. The absence of any (religio-)sexual, letter-spirit relation is not overcome by Schlegel's androgynous gender theory. And the privilege of (Christian male) spirit is left intact to the degree that in the final analysis the only properly androgynous position is that of male, Christian spirit. Since Schlegel develops this gender theory much more extensively and intensively in *Lucinde*, the text that comprised his next major project after the composition of "On Philosophy," one might imagine that he overcomes the limitations of "On Philosophy" in his novel. It is necessary, therefore, for us to demonstrate that Schlegel does not manage there to solder these two joints of gender, nor to overcome the destructive contradiction of the privilege granted to spirit ostensibly beyond spirit. Instead, he develops this disjointedness and contradiction into a full-blown, but always unstable, metaphysics in quasi-fictional form. If, in his later years, he turns to the Catholic Church as a support and guide, it is no doubt due to the very instability of the metaphysics *Lucinde* develops and displays.

Metaphysics in 'Lucinde': Spiritualizing Syntheses of (Christian) Masculine Spirit with (Jewish) Feminine Letter

Allow me to summarize briefly in this section the reading of *Lucinde* that follows. As was the case in "On Lessing" and "On Philosophy," Schlegel's starting point in *Lucinde*, insofar as the novel can be read as an allegory of the relations between (masculine, Christian) spirit and (feminine, Jewish) letter, is the recognition of a certain dialectic or undecidability: to wit, the spirit becomes letter—dead matter—when it refuses any contact with the letter, just as the letter takes on a ghostly spirituality—a dead abstractness—when it externalizes all spirit. Since the novel, like those essays, is written from the point of view of masculine and Christian (which here means late Protestant) spirit, its main concern is the danger of the becoming-letter of a would-be exclusively spiritual position. Accordingly, the spirit of its protagonist, Julius, is constantly undone by a splintering of consciousness into material fragmentation precisely due to excessive inwardness. Lucinde appears in turn as a woman whose materiality tends toward a certain spirituality, which the novel treats as nonproblematic: the proper destiny of matter in this text is its spiritualization. The self-lettering, or self-littering, of Julius's spirit, however, is supposed to be overcome by means of his relationship with Lucinde, contact with whose very materiality is supposed to allow Julius's spirituality to stabilize itself by a kind of contrastive combination. But the relationship between Julius and Lucinde does not quite turn out to stabilize this spirituality in such a way as to protect it from self-(de)materialization. In order to secure itself against dissolution into the materiality on which it borders, Julius's spirit continues to have to negate that materiality (and by thus inflating itself to negate itself).

This negation or denegation of the material, feminine letter in the self-affirmation of spirit, even if ostensibly beyond the limits of the opposition between spirit and letter, is repeatedly carried out as the novel unfolds. Indeed, in a manner that tends toward an abstract saturation or totalization of the semantic field, Schlegel carries out this post-Enlightenment version of the repudiation of the feminine (and Judaic) principle of the material letter not only in terms of a definition of the human, or an anthropo(gyneco)logy, but also in terms of each of the thematic domains of traditional rationalist metaphysics. As I will show with reference to four illustrative chapters, Schlegel's narrative of the dialectical ravishment of letter by spirit is recounted not only in *anthropo(gyneco)logical* terms but also in *ontological, psychological,* and *cosmotheological* ones. Each account confirms the others, for each mirrors the structure and fundamental concerns of them all. But further, the ontological account "anchors" the gender categories in the modal categories of contingent and necessary; the psychological account "concretizes" these modal categories "subjectively" in terms of the poles of desire and satisfaction; and the cosmotheological account "concretizes" them "objectively" in terms of the poles of nature and divinity. The mutual determinations and overdeterminations of each of these accounts of the spirit-letter dialectic lend a degree of systematic totality to the novel's otherwise willfully chaotic and fragmented form. But what creates this totality is unfortunately the incessant denegation of its necessary undoing by the infinitely fragmenting force of the letter in its various avatars. Before considering each of these scenes, it is necessary to confirm, by looking at the narrative of Julius's life leading up through the development of their relationship in "Lehrjahre der Männlichkeit," that the novel indeed establishes Julius and Lucinde in the positions of spirit and letter, respectively.

Inwardness in Pieces Meets Materiality that Breathes

Throughout the novel, but in particular detail in the chapter titled "Lehrjahre der Männlichkeit," Julius is presented as having been in his youth so inward, so wholly spiritual, that this very inwardness and spirituality tended to flip over into their opposite extremes, becoming the externality of material fragmentation.[16] For example, at the outset of the "Lehrjahre" we are told that "a love without object [*eine Liebe ohne Gegenstand*] burned within him and undermined his inwardness [*zerrüttete sein Innres*]" (35). The inward demand of this love without object is so absolute that it cannot make any sort of connection with an external, objective, or relative existence. Because it wants *all* of the world, it remains utterly *without* world: "He had the sense that he wanted to embrace a world but could catch hold of nothing" (36). But this worldless inwardness nonetheless reverses itself into an excessively worldly externality, as Julius's spirit strews itself into fragments of sensuous materiality: "And hence he became more and more savage [*verwilderte*] out of unsatisfied longing [*Sehnsucht*], became sensuous out of despair over the spiritual [*am Geistigen*], behaved imprudently to spite fate and was actually unethical with a kind of loyalty of spirit [*Treuherzigkeit*]" (36). In the company of others, Julius is lonely, because he is lost within himself. Yet, when he is alone he loses himself in fantasy, which takes him paradoxically out of himself, albeit in a manner that remains devoid of both reality and coherence: "all that he loved and thought of with love was torn off and separated. His entire existence was in his fantasy a mass of fragments without connection."[17] And this excessive intensity of an indeterminate desire is constantly tearing Julius apart throughout his development until he meets Lucinde. At one moment, we read, "The rage of dissatisfaction tore his memory to pieces [*zerstückte seine Erinnerung*]; he had never had less an overview of the whole of his self [*vom Ganzen seines Ich*] than he had now" (46). And shortly thereafter: "A confusion of all pains tore his inwardness savagely and the sickness of the spirit [*die Krankheit des Geistes*] gnawed ever more deeply and secretly at his heart. It was more a madness of feeling than of the understanding" (47). Finally, just before meeting Lucinde, Julius is still characterized as losing hold of affective bonds because of the overwhelming power of "the inner sea of general inspiration [*allgemeiner Begeisterung*]" (50).

While Julius is thus construed as an example of the excessive wholeness of spirit that keeps tearing itself apart into strewn materializations of the letter, Lucinde appears as the instance of the letter that nonetheless inclines toward its own spiritualization. While his identity continually deteriorates into difference, her differentiality is continually realizing itself as identity.[18] For example, Julius learns from Lucinde what it is to have a unified, self-identical subjectivity:

Through what his womanfriend had revealed to him it became clear to the young man that only a woman can be properly unhappy or properly happy [*recht unglück-lich ... und recht glücklich*], and that women alone, who have remained natural human beings [*Naturmenschen*] in the very lap of human society [*mitten im Schoß der menschlichen Gesellschaft*], have the childish sense with which one must accept the grace and gift of the gods. . . . He recognized now that love, which for the feminine soul is an indivisible, thoroughly simple feeling [*ein unteilbares, durchaus einfaches Gefühl*], is for the man a mere alternation and mixture [*nur ein Wechsel und eine Mischung*] of passion, friendship, and sensuality; and he saw with happy astonishment that he was quite as infinitely loved as he himself loved. (54–56)

Women are opposed to men here as natural unity to social differentiation. Natural unity is the oneness of a spirituality that continues to arise out of roots firmly planted in the material world, whereas social differentiation is an abstract materiality, a strewn litter of arbitrary laws that arises out of the spirit precisely when it lacks a material ground.[19]

The initial effect of the contact between Julius and Lucinde is that— in accordance with their respective religious and gender identities—Lucinde becomes even more spiritual than she already was, while Julius becomes in various ways more material.[20] Thus "her spirit [*ihr Geist*] blossomed through contact with his own" (56). Julius in turn begins to finish *works*, albeit works with a "Christian," lawless coloring, suggesting that he is now learning to give himself up provisionally to the materiality of the letter so as to be able to realize his spirit ultimately all the more purely as spirit:

Julius finished a number of things. His paintings came alive [*belebten sich*], a stream of animating light [*ein Strom von beseelendem Licht*] seemed to pour itself over them and in fresh colors the true flesh blossomed. . . . The forms themselves did not perhaps always correspond to the accepted laws of an artistic beauty [*Gesetzen einer künstlichen Schönheit*]. What recommended them to the eye was a certain stillness and grace [*Anmut*], a deep expression of contented, happy being [*Dasein*] and an enjoyment of this being. They seemed animated plants in the godlike form of humanity . . . and so his life too became for him a work of art . . . it became light inside of him, he saw and could oversee all of the masses of his life and the outline of the whole clearly and correctly, for he stood in the middle. (56–57)

Julius becomes more spiritual now by virtue of his increased rootedness in the material and affective worlds.[21]

It is precisely this intensification of Julius's spirituality, however, that should make us suspicious. For the insistence on the spirituality that Julius gains through his contact with Lucinde must lead to a renewed denegation of the material, and so to a renewed implosion of pure spirituality, a renewed fragmentation of the self-identical spirit. And a certain tendency toward excessive spirituality reveals itself early on. While Julius is supposed to have gained a new sense of "tenderness" (57) from his life with Lucinde, still this "tenderness" expresses itself in an abstract, Platonizing manner that completely ignores the specificity of those toward whom it is directed. It is characterized as "a contemplative joy [*anschauende Freude*] in the beauty of the human, which remains for all of eternity, while the individuals disappear; and a lively and open sense [*ein reger und offner Sinn*] for the innermost in himself and others" (57–58).

The excessively violent character of Julius's desire to reduce the world of the others to the inwardness of his own spirituality,[22] a repetition of Julius's original condition, is revealed by the terms in which Julius states his preference for Lucinde over all of the others: "But he found total harmony also in this respect only in Lucinde's soul, where the seeds of all that is glorious and all that is holy merely waited for the stream of his spirit [*den Strahl seines Geistes*] in order to unfold themselves into the most beautiful religion" (58). Whereas other people, including men, do not without further ado consent to be the prefigurative, semiotic seeds brought to full realization as religion by Julius's spirit, Lucinde does consent. She is not more inward or spiritual than the others, but in a certain sense precisely *less* so, because she doesn't contribute any spiritual sunlight of her own, but rather grows up toward the light of Julius's spirit and thus allows his light to realize itself in her.[23] Julius affirms the writing of finite nature for which Lucinde stands only in order to posit an infinite content within this finite nature, a purely spiritual content that defies expression, an inexpressible essence of things, a *Ding an sich* that is pure *Geist*:

We are grateful and contented with the will of the gods, which they have so clearly indicated in the Holy Scriptures of beautiful Nature [*in der heiligen Schrift der schönen Natur*]. The modest soul [*Gemüt*] acknowledges that it is its natural determination, just like all things, to blossom, to ripen, and to wither. But it knows that one thing in it is immortal. This is the eternal longing [*die ewige Sehnsucht*] for eternal youth, which is always there and always escapes. . . . something always gets left behind that cannot be externally presented because it is entirely inward. The spirit of the human [*Der Geist des Menschen*] is its own Proteus, it transforms itself and does not want to be called to account to itself as it attempts to grasp itself. (59)

The privilege of spirit is stated in this passage through the very attempt to do justice to the letter. Even here, the dimensions of anthropo(gyneco)logy, ontology, psychology, cosmology, and theology all appear in the statement of this privilege, but intermingled. In the remainder of this chapter, we will consider a series of passages in which these dimensions are highlighted more or less separately, in order that the systematic coherence and full semantic range of Schlegel's asystematic text should come into clear view.

Wit as the (Phallic) Essence of Humanity: The Spiritualization of the Letter in Anthropo(gyneco)logical Terms

In the chapter on the "Dithyrambic Fantasy about the Most Beautiful Situation," Schlegel's treatment of the relation between letter and spirit is stated as a gender theory in explicitly *anthropo(gyneco)logical* terms. The question—"What is it to be human?"—is answered here in terms of a theory of androgynous humanity that anchors this humanity in wit. Julius describes the enactment of wit in the mutual imitation of the sexes as an allegory of "complete, whole humanity" (10, 13). Wit becomes thereby the human faculty par excellence insofar as its realization in the form of the "wittiest" situation is at once a presentation, if in allegorical form, of humanity itself. The destiny of *humanity* is presented in this situation, and wit is the name for the play of this destiny in its most human form.[24]

Whereas Schlegel's androgynous or anthropo(gyneco)logical gender theory in "On Philosophy" theorized the mutually imitative interdependence of the genders in terms of the pedagogical effects associated with the discourses of poetry and philosophy, here he dramatizes that imitative interdependence as the realization of wit. The treatment in *Lucinde* is consistent with the earlier treatment, since wit is indeed to be situated somewhere between poetry and philosophy, being more conceptual than poetry and more literary or figurative than the latter. But it goes beyond that earlier treatment in the unfolding of Schlegel's thought on the letter-spirit distinction insofar as its much larger scope allows it to treat explicitly and in detail the metaphysical themes that in "On Philosophy" could be at best fleetingly addressed. To begin, however, with the dramatization of witty humanity as the *mise-en-abime* of the sexual difference: How does the "wittiest" situation unfold, and how does the interplay of feminine, Jewish letter and masculine, Christian spirit yield there to a predominance of the latter?[25]

The chapter is framed by remarks that highlight the tension between representation and presence both in terms of writing and in terms of erotic desire. At the end of the preceding chapter, "Julius to Lucinde," the "Dithyrambic Fantasy" is introduced as a text Julius wrote in her room with Lucinde's (phallic) feather pen to console himself for her absence. Writing is here presented as a replacement for erotic activity, and the instrument of (de)sexualized writing, the pen as phallus, is a replacement-phallus borrowed from the woman, but it is the phallus with which the woman borrows the (phallic) thoughts of the man, writing them down, and so it is essentially a phallus borrowed back from a borrower. When the text of the "Dithyrambic Fantasy" begins, Julius writes as if he had just read Lucinde's inscription of the "wittiest" situation, which was in turn originally Julius's idea.

A large tear falls upon the holy page that I found here in your stead. How faithfully and how simply you inscribed it, the bold, old thought of my most dear and most secret plan. In you it grew large and in this mirror I do not hesitate to admire and love myself. Only here do I see myself whole and harmonious, or rather completed, whole humanity in me and in you. For your spirit too [*auch dein Geist*] stands definite and perfected before me. . . . The most fleeting and holy of those tender traits [*Zügen*] and expressions of the soul . . . are the common atmosphere of our spiritual breathing and life [*unsers geistigen Atmens und Lebens*]. (10)

While the idea of the unification of the sexes comes from Julius, its inscription stems from Lucinde, as convention compels us to expect. Its inscription by Julius is a repetition (and therefore a kind of imitation) of Lucinde's inscription (or imitation) of his idea. And while he writes, following her example, she appears to him, in what is his properly original mode of being, as spirit. Seeing himself, writing, in the mirror of her writing, he sees also her as spirit mirroring his spirit. In the mirror of her writing, Julius sees both himself and her fused in the one, "completed, whole humanity" (10). And as the paragraph closes, Julius emphasizes—again, not surprisingly by now—the spirituality of their relationship. Although a slight trace of the letter appears in the word "Züge," even here the trace is to some extent dissipated by the connotation of a "breeze" (in "Zug") that carries it off tendentially in its train.[26]

The spiritually inflected unity of Julius and Lucinde as figures of spirit and letter claims to be so total here that it cannot fail to continue to reveal, despite itself, hints of an imaginary aggressivity that will take the form of an aggression against Lucinde as figure of the letter. At the pinnacle of one of the repeated crescendos of unification, Julius writes, "I can no longer say, my love or your love; both are the same and completely One, as much love one way as love in return. It is marriage, eternal unity and connection of our spirits [*unsrer Geister*] . . . for our whole eternal being and life" (11). This affirmation of absolute unity is immediately followed, however, by Julius's imagining of both his own death and Lucinde's, in terms of the carpe diem theme, but in an asymmetrical manner. He asserts that they should drink the rest of their lives quickly, as one would drink wine "before the most noble spirit [*der edelste Geist*] of the wine" (11) escapes. According to this image, one drinks the material wine, to be sure, but one does so nonetheless only for the sake of its "spirit." And while Julius claims that he would be prepared to drink with Lucinde a glass of poison in the same way—life being the poison one drinks in order to gain the spirituality of death—he also imagines that, if he happened to die first, Lucinde would throw herself upon his funeral pyre. This gesture on Julius's part must be appreciated in all the force of its proto-Wagnerian, imaginary aggressivity:

I know, you too would not want to outlive me, you would follow your precipitous mate even in his coffin, and out of pure desire and love you would climb down into the flaming abyss into which a raging law [*ein rasendes Gesetz*] compels Indian women, destroying and desecrating the most tender sacraments of the free will through crude intention and command. (11)

Not only does Julius's prediction about Lucinde double as a gentle command in its turn but also he himself has not gone so far as to suggest that he would follow her to the grave if she happened to die first, only that they should die together. Further, by having Julius attack the notion of a rigid "law," Schlegel takes an indirect swipe at Dorothea's Judaism by means of his protagonist. Schlegel's later text on ancient Indian culture places that culture in the position hitherto reserved by Christianity for the Jews. From here to Wagner's Brünnhilde and beyond, the figure of the Jewish woman as Indian woman will intermittently haunt the German Romantic imaginary. The unity of the purely spiritual fire burns slightly out of control here, turning into aggression against Lucinde insofar as she resists, in her very material existence and qua Jewess, absorption into the purely spiritual essence that Julius, despite his (always provisional and instrumental) affirmations of sensuality, ultimately represents.

The fantasy of the wittiest situation is thus prepared—or as one might say, "prefigured"—by a series of remarks that explicitly idealize (while they implicitly problematize) the seamless unity of Julius and Lucinde in terms of spirit and letter. The situation itself is inserted within this context as the attempt to cool the intolerable heat of the lovers' mutual presence, to place some distance between the two. On the one hand, Julius asserts that nothing can separate the two, because the further apart they get the more powerfully they are drawn toward each other. Slightly formalized, this means that distance is impossible because distance always dialectically implies proximity. Difference implies and includes identity. The presence of the letter immediately entails its spiritualizing effacement. Conversely, Julius suggests that the reason why distance cannot distance the two lovers from each other is that for them presence is too present: "How could distance distance us, since presence is for us, as it were, too present [*Wie könnte uns die Entfernung entfernen, da uns die Gegenwart selbst gleichsam zu gegenwärtig ist*]?" (12). If presence is too present, then it forces the lovers apart. Proximity implies distance, or identity presupposes or entails difference: spirit must inscribe itself as letter in order to be spirit. The lovers play the game that constitutes their "wittiest" situation in order to "cool" the "heat" of this excessive presence, to distance themselves from the proximity that implies distance, to supplement proximity with the distance that prevents distance, to supplement identity with the difference that prevents difference, to supply for the burning fires of pure spirit the coolness of the letter in order to prevent the fires from completely burning themselves out:

We must temper and cool its consuming fire by joking around and so the most witty amongst the forms and situations of our joy is also the most beautiful. One amongst them all is the most witty and most beautiful: when we exchange our roles and compete with childish pleasure to see who can most deceptively ape the other, whether you succeed better in imitating the protective robustness of the man or I in imitating the attractive self-abandonment of the woman. But do you know that this game has charms for me which are quite different from its own? Moreover, it is not merely a matter of the pleasures of exhaustion or the presentiments of revenge. I see here a wondrous allegory—rich in sense and full of meaning—of the perfection of the masculine and feminine to complete, whole humanity [*die Vollendung des Männlichen und Weiblichen zur vollen ganzen Menschheit*]. There lies much therein, and what lies therein will certainly not stand up as quickly as I when I lie beneath you (in defeat). (12–13)

The play of substitutive representation, wherein each of the lovers plays letter to the other's spirit, becomes itself a substitutive letter—an allegorical form—standing for a spirit or meaning, the meaning of the unity of masculine and feminine in full humanity, which itself does not immediately appear. The rhetorical, figural instance of imitative wit, which proceeds by metaphor or analogy, is to "cool" the fires of the literal spirit of their love, so that its (imaginary) violence should be tamed. And so the spiritual content of their unity is bound up in the formal letter of their mutual metaphorization.

However, the spirit continues to assert itself against its defeat through the *mot d'esprit* of the end of the passage: "Es liegt viel darin, und was darin liegt, steht gewiß nicht so schnell auf wie ich, wenn ich dir unterliege." The phallus of Julius stands up and protests—it is a matter of an *Aufstand*—out of his relatively failed impersonation of the feminine, in response to Lucinde's more successful impersonation of the masculine. Where the letter (Lucinde) becomes more like the spirit (Julius) than the spirit is like the letter, when the letter shows itself to have more imitative flexibility and hence more spirituality than spirit, the response of spirit is not mere capitulation (figured as the connotations of flight and desire of the "standing up" of Julius at the end of the passage). It is also a (self-ironic, yet not self-canceling) defiant display of phallic power, a "masculine protest" of the sort that would have made Alfred Adler proud. The apparent spirituality of *Witz*, its persuasive performativity, protests against and resists its figural materiality. It appears as Julius's virtue that he is not capable of imitating a woman as well as Lucinde imitates a man. And even aside from the sense in which his *Aufstand* is phallic, through the boldness of the acknowledgment of his flight from Lucinde's manly womanliness, his masculinity reasserts itself as self-mastery and ambiguous display.

The "witty" synthesis of masculine spirit and feminine letter in the scene of their mutual imitation effects the spiritualization of the letter, then, in anthropological terms as the sign of full humanity. In the coda that Schlegel attaches to this chapter, Julius crowns this spiritualization in his proleptic response to Lucinde's objection to his publication of their intimacies. "How can one want to write what one is hardly even allowed to say, what one really only ought to feel?" (13). By being put in the position of raising this objection, Lucinde is, on the one hand, aligned with the inwardness of pure spirituality, while Julius is aligned with the externality of material writing, objectification, and so forth. (We see again the ambivalent usurpation of the Judaic letter we saw above in the opening paragraphs of "On Philosophy.") But Julius defends himself, in part by pointing to the "loutish enthusiasm" (13) of the man "who happily blurts out all that is tender and holy . . . and in a word is easily divine to the point of crudeness."[27] The careless spontaneity of the man in his externalization of the internal is precisely the culmination, within this chapter, of the spiritualization of writing: writing, as the externalization of the interior, comes thus to be situated beyond the artificiality of works in the Judaeo-Enlightenment sense, whereas the discreet silence of bourgeois values is equated with such works. As externalization, writing is realization or fulfillment. It thus occupies the position of Christian spirituality, whereas pure inwardness occupies the position of mere potential, prefiguration, Judaic anticipation.[28] Still, to do justice to the dialectical sophistication of Schlegel at this point, the spirituality to which Julius lays claim is, or at least attempts to be, *beyond* the opposition between potential and real. Julius signals this by answering Lucinde in such a way as to parody and to chaoticize by exaggeration her concern with appropriate modalities: "I answer: if one feels it [*Fühlt man es*], one must want to say it [*so muß man es sagen wollen*], and what one wants to say, one is allowed also to be able to write [*darf man auch schreiben können*]" (13). The play of feeling, wanting, being allowed to, and being able to—*fühlen, wollen, dürfen, können*—points to the difficulty of determining the borders between the modalities of possibility, reality, and necessity, such that the distinctions between writing and speech, or writing and silence, cease to appear to be masterable by a dialectics that would operate in terms of the oppositions between real and possible, contingent and necessary, prefiguration and fulfillment, existence or essence, and so on. Such chaoticizing parody thus renders apparently "necessary" and so more "spiritual" Schlegel's position "beyond" the opposition between spirit and letter, the position from which he letters the spirit in order the better to have "spiritualized" it in the end. But what exactly would it mean, at this point in Schlegel's novelistic discourse, to be necessary or contingent? What is a necessity that lies beyond the opposition between necessity and contingency? How exactly, in short, is the question of ontological modality to be articulated with the anthropo(gyneco)logical theory into which Schlegel extrapolates his views on the semiological and religio-cultural distinction between letter and spirit? Schlegel addresses this question rather explicitly in the brief chapter called "Eine Reflexion."

The Masculine as Determined to Determine the Feminine as Indeterminate, or the Spiritualization of the Letter in Ontological Terms

The reflexion announces itself as an attempt to understand why people endlessly make love or copulate, and simultaneously why the spiritual and the physical endlessly appear to come at once together and asunder as they do. The ambition of this reflexion is hence to circumscribe the sexual relation as a relation between thought and existence and vice versa. Since the relation between thought and existence is what Schlegel calls destiny or determination (*Bestimmung*), the sexual relation appears here as nothing less than this destiny or determination. That is, the constitutive components (and the deconstitutive opponents) of ontological necessity are both explicitly gendered and in turn determine the genders themselves. The relation between being and sex is reflexive, like that between each of these terms and itself.

In order to render somewhat accessible Schlegel's formulation of what turn out to be the three main components of determination and their relations with the two components of gender, masculine and feminine, it is important to point out that Schlegel refers to the masculine and feminine essences and genitalia as the "nameless." He thereby manages to be suggestive without appearing too crudely inappropriate and to refer at once to the most spiritual (or divine) and material (or earthly) aspects of both masculine and feminine. Schlegel thus provisionally implies that, in a perfect symmetry, both the masculine and the feminine contain spiritual as well as material dimensions. Yet, as I read the following passage, the feminine becomes spiritual only insofar as it has been mastered by and assimilated into the masculine as the supplementary border between masculine activity and masculine passivity, the passage from one to the other. Insofar as this feminine border remains only a border, outside the proper space of the masculine spirit, its sole characteristic is that of the material letter.

Das Denken hat die Eigenheit, daß es nächst sich selbst am liebsten über das denkt, worüber es ohne Ende denken kann. Darum ist das Leben des gebildeten und sinnigen Menschen ein stetes Bilden und Sinnen über das schöne Rätsel seiner Bestimmung. Er bestimmt sie immer neu, denn eben das ist seine ganze Bestimmung, bestimmt zu werden und zu bestimmen. Nur in seinem Suchen selbst findet der Geist des Menschen das Geheimnis, welches er sucht.

Was ist denn aber das Bestimmende oder das Bestimmte selbst? In der Männlichkeit ist es das Namenlose. Und was ist das Namenlose in der Weiblichkeit?—das Unbestimmte.

Das Unbestimmte ist geheimnisreicher, aber das Bestimmte hat mehr Zauberkraft. Die reizende Verwirrung des Unbestimmten ist romantischer, aber die erhabene Bildung des Bestimmten ist genialischer. Die Schönheit des Unbestimmten ist vergänglich wie das Leben der Blumen und wie die ewige Jugend sterblicher Gefühle; die Energie des Bestimmten ist vorübergehend wie das echte Ungewitter und die echte Begeisterung. (72)

Thought has the peculiarity that, aside from itself, it prefers to think about what it can think about without end. For this reason, the life of the educated and reflective person is a continuous formation of and reflexion upon the beautiful riddle of his determination. He determines it ever anew, for precisely this is his entire determination, to be determined and to determine. Only in its very seeking does the human spirit find the secret it seeks.

But what, then, is the determining or the determined itself? In masculinity it is the nameless. And what is the nameless in femininity?—the undetermined.

The undetermined is more richly secretive, but the determined has more magical force. The charming confusion of the undetermined is more romantic, but the sublime formation of the determined is more genial. The beauty of the undetermined is transitory like the life of flowers and like the eternal youth of mortal feelings; the energy of the determined passes by like an authentic storm and authentic inspiration.

The masculine appears here not only as the (actively) determining but also as the (passively) determined instance, while the feminine appears only as the undetermined. That which is determining (or determinant), comprising a kind of subjective self-necessitation, evidently determines the undetermined or indefinite—the contingent—in order to transform it into the determined, that which has objective necessity. The masculine freely and so out of self-necessitation leaves itself to act on the feminine, which lies outside of necessity, in order to return to itself as the henceforth objective necessity of the determined. The feminine gives itself over to the masculine in order to be used by the masculine as the mediation of the return of the masculine to itself.[29] The feminine becomes the masculine in being acted upon by the masculine and returns to itself—and here the crucial asymmetry asserts itself that Julius explicitly denegates—only by losing itself into masculinity as the *determined* aspect of the masculine. Whereas the masculine passes through the feminine in order to return to itself, incorporating the feminine into itself in the process, the feminine returns to itself in its encounter with the masculine only by taking leave of itself and disappearing into the masculine. That is, it either never leaves itself and so leaves itself, or it returns to itself because it never returns.

Accordingly, insofar as, in terms of gender, for Schlegel the masculine is always (despite certain appearances) the privileged form of spirit, while the feminine is the privileged form of the letter, we are to understand his ontological allegory of masculine and feminine as implying also an allegory of spirit and letter. The spirit as determining force determines the indeterminate letter in order to return to itself as determinate spirit. Yet the letter never enters as such into the space of destiny or determination that is comprised by the determining and the determined, subject and object. For the letter remains "the undetermined," that which has in itself no determination, no destiny, no necessity: the feminine letter is the contingent as such that is excluded from the ontological necessity into whose self-relation it disappears by enabling it.

The necessity consequently imposes itself on us to examine somewhat suspiciously the passages such as the following where Julius claims that the relations between the two genders are strictly symmetrical: "With eternally unchanging symmetry both strive in opposed ways to approach and to flee the infinite. With quiet, but certain progress the undetermined extends its innate wish [*erweitert das Unbestimmte seinen angebornen Wunsch*] from the beautiful middle of finitude into the borderless" (73). In other words, the dimension of the letter extends into the dimension of the spirit. The signifier is always already a signified. "The completely determined [*Das vollendete Bestimmte*], on the contrary, throws itself through a bold leap from the blissful dream of infinite willing into the limitations of the finite deed and continually grows, refining itself as it does so, in generous self-limitation and beautiful sufficiency" (73). The determined, then, circles incessantly from its infinitude (its spirituality or meaningfulness) back through the finitude of the undetermined (and meaningless) letter and toward itself, reencountered qua determined. The apparent symmetry between these two strivings, then, is actually an asymmetry. While the undetermined extends its finitude into the space of infinity, infinitely gaining contour, it also loses its contour as precisely that which is without contour, loses again and again all possibility of grasping itself as such, namely, as the ungrasped. In contrast, the determined "nimmt . . . immer zu," augments itself,[30] gives rise to itself anew with every recirculation. Again, the masculine (Christian) spirit goes out of itself toward the feminine (Jewish) letter in order to prevent itself from losing itself (for a determining instance without an indeterminate instance outside of itself to determine would itself become indeterminate). In contrast, the feminine (Jewish) letter goes out of itself to be absorbed into the self-mirroring process precisely of that spirit.

But where or how do this indeterminate contingency and determinant-determined necessity appear in the realm of beings? Schlegel's novel provides a double answer to this question: once in terms of "subjectivity," or psychology, and once in terms of "objectivity," which here involves both world and God, or cosmology and theology.

Contentment as Fulfillment, Longing as Prefiguration, or the Spiritualization of the Letter in Psychological Terms

In the brief chapter entitled "Longing and Contentment" ("Sehnsucht und Ruhe"), Schlegel provides more succinctly and directly than anywhere else the psychological version of the answer to this question. In this dawn-song scene, the two lovers are standing at the window,[31] watching the sunrise through its panes. As they watch the day arrive, they "dialogue" about the sexual relation by discussing the enigmatic intimacy between longing and contentment, between desire, which translates indeterminate contingency here, and satisfaction, which translates the determining-determined synthesis of necessity.[32] In this little chapter, it is the interplay of the titular opposition, longing and contentment, with the correlative opposition between day and night that we have to retrace in order to see how longing, which functions as the feminine, dependent state of mind, is to be transformed into the contentment of masculine autonomy.

Lucinde initiates the conversation by asking Julius—whom the author places in the position of the subject supposed to know—why she feels deep longing amidst such cheerful contentment ("Julius . . . warum fühle ich in so heitrer Ruhe die tiefe Sehnsucht?" [78]). Clearly, "longing" is to "contentment" as "prefigurative anticipation" is to "literal, spiritual fulfillment," albeit on a psychological register the significance of which we will specify in a moment. Given this set of correspondences, Lucinde must be understood as asking here why, although she has been taken up into the space of what should be her fulfillment, that is, although she has disappeared (or although she expected that she would have disappeared) into the male, spiritual, Christian space of her beloved Julius, she still feels unfulfilled. On the one hand, she feels unfulfilled because she has remained merely "herself," the embodiment of the feminine, material, and Jewish principles, in short, the embodiment of the prefigurative or anticipatory letter whose meaning in this subjectifying context can be nothing other than "longing." Therefore, she has not entered into the peace of the (male, Christian) spirit at all. On the other hand, having been absorbed into the peace of that spirit, she feels unfulfilled because she has been effaced. From this point of view, her "longing" registers a dissatisfaction over, and a refusal of, the effacement itself.

Julius's response to Lucinde's complaint—uncomprehendingly acute— is: "Only in longing [*Sehnsucht*] do we find contentment [*Ruhe*]. . . . Indeed, contentment is only this: when our spirit [*unser Geist*] can long and search undisturbed, where it can find nothing higher than its own longing" (78). While Lucinde says that, despite the contentment, she still feels an enigmatic longing, Julius responds that contentment is found only in such longing. That is, he reinterprets her longing as contentment, her lack as fullness, her absence as presence, her desire as the object of her desire. This move is meant to confirm the chiasmic structure of the heterosexual couple as Schlegel conceives it: the woman is anticipatory longing, the man fulfillment; but the woman finds herself in the man (and hence longing in contentment), while the man finds himself in the woman (contentment in longing). But within this apparently symmetrical solution, an asymmetrical tension emerges: the self of woman is longing or lack of self, while the self of man is contentment, self-possession. Julius finds fulfillment—and himself as fulfillment—in longing insofar as longing is for him a matter of pure spirit, the pure expansion of spirit within and as the space of an infinite and infinitely self-same interiority. As the form of pure spirituality, then, longing becomes Julius's contentment. This transformation is only possible, however, insofar as longing is from the very start conceived of as a mode of spirit, as a mode of fulfillment. It is only possible insofar as "longing"—although it functions as an equivalent of the letter—is never encountered as letter, as materiality, as whatever it might actually be, independently of all belonging to longing (or desire or "love"). And yet, the transformation of longing into fulfillment, the absorption of longing into fulfillment, can have no meaning here *except* as the absorption of letter into spirit. For the telos, or the point of the novel, is precisely to achieve this absorption.[33] As I have suggested above, excessive spirituality and subjectivity, in which Julius is represented as having spent his youth drowning or floundering, can only be corrected, according to the novel itself, by such an absorption. Despite the appearance of this absorption having been accomplished through their love, Lucinde indicates in this scene that she still remains outside of it. She is still "longing" because she has not been encountered in or as what she is, namely, something other than (at least the *spirit* of Julius's) "longing."

To Schlegel's credit, Julius's response to Lucinde's complaint fails, at least at first, to prove persuasive. Lucinde grants only qualified assent to Julius's suggestion that contentment is to be found in longing. And her qualification amounts to the reminder that contentment is to be found in longing precisely and only from his point of view within the structure they (unevenly) share. "Only in the peaceful quiet of night [*Ruhe der Nacht*], Lucinde said, do longing and love [*die Sehnsucht und die Liebe*] glow and glimmer, bright and full, like this lordly sun.—And during the day, Julius answered, the happiness of love shimmers palely, just as the moon casts only a sparing light" (78). The opposition between day and night enters here as a double of the opposition between longing and contentment, or a new avatar of the opposition between anticipatory, material difference and fulfilling, spiritual identity. Julius has maintained that contentment is to be found in longing because longing and contentment are one, that the experience of the differential letter and the identical spirit are the same in spirit. Lucinde has suggested however that only more longing is to be found in contentment, which amounts to saying that longing and contentment are two, or that the relationship between difference (or the letter of longing) and identity (the contentment of the spirit) is dominated by the differential letter. Since day is the realm of differences, and night the realm in which differences are effaced, when Lucinde grants that longing and love can light up like the sun only at night, she is saying that longing and contentment can coincide, or that difference can identify itself—difference and identity thereby becoming one—only in the realm of indifference or identity that is represented here by the night.

While Julius again uncomprehendingly expresses his emphatic agreement, going on to describe in lyrical transports the way in which their amorous unity takes place "only in the night," Lucinde responds with an indication that he does not seem to have gotten her point. Indeed, she does so rather bluntly, by suggesting that he is only projecting his narcissistic phantasies onto her:

Not I, my Julius, am the one whom you paint as being so holy; although I would like to complain like the nightingale and, as I deeply feel, am only consecrated to the night. It is you, . . . the wondrous flower of your phantasy [*die Wunderblume Deiner Phantasie*], that you see in me, who is eternally yours, when all the hustle-bustle has been veiled [*wenn das Gewühl verhüllt ist*] and nothing common distracts your high Spirit [*Deinen hohen Geist*]. (78–79)

Still not quite getting the point, Julius chooses to attribute Lucinde's observation not to her psychological or cultural-critical perspicacity but to her false modesty, which he tells her to drop and to stop flattering *him*. Having thereby to some degree neutralized Lucinde's objection, Julius goes on to argue that there is indeed a connection between night and day—himself and her world—and that this connection furthermore is she herself: she represents him, the self-identical night, within the world of the differential day, as his priestess, and thus mediates between himself and her, the inward night in which spirit dwells and the outward day in which matter rules: "Consider that you are the Priestess of the Night. In the ray of the sun itself the dark glow of your full locks, the bright blackness of your earnest eyes, your stature [*der hohe Wuchs*], . . . the majesty of your forehead and all your noble members proclaim it" (79). Lucinde represents the night in the day, then, by virtue of her dark hair and eyes, as well as the nobility of her bearing. In her very body, she represents the beyond of the body, the night of the spirit (of identity), as the blackness of letters represents the spirit of the life beyond life (or beyond death) on the whiteness of the page (i.e., in the realm of the visible). Julius makes Lucinde his representative in the realm of the day, the countermaterial material or letter that represents his spirit out there in the world of the day amidst its deathly differentiations.

She, however, refuses this position by claiming to be embarrassed by his praise, which is tantamount to telling Julius that the day—that is, her own perspective—makes it impossible for her to accept what he is saying.

In fact, the chapter does not overcome this impasse. For Julius repeats at this juncture that his love for her is not "idle fantasy" ("eitle Phantasie" [79]), but rather "longing" endlessly unarrived at, that he is with her to the degree that he is not, or that their difference is an identity. And in turn she simply resigns or relapses into a naïve acceptance of her role, repeating the obligatory formula for her position in the structure: "Whatever it is, you are the point in which my essence comes to rest [*Sei's was es sei, Du bist der Punkt, in dem mein Wesen Ruhe findet*]" (79).

From this point on, through developments we need not follow in detail, the text repeats the trajectory we have traced thus far: the feminine is defined as self-differential longing, the masculine as self-identical contentment; the nonidentity of the two positions is announced from the feminine position; and this announcement is resisted from the masculine position. In this repetition, there does seem to be a moment when Julius acknowledges a moment of identification with longing (or the feminine, Jewish letter) in such a way that this longing is not translatable into contentment (or the masculine, Christian spirit). "O eternal longing [*Sehnsucht*]!—But finally the day's fruitless longing [*Sehnen*] and idle blindness [*eitles Blenden*] will set and be extinguished, and a great night of love will eternally feel content [*sich ewig ruhig fühlen*]" (80). But here, too, longing retains or recovers its identity as contentment in the form of the telos of the afterlife. After the final setting of the sun of differentiation, the final dissolution of its law, longing will disappear into the quiet it is its destiny to become: letter will have become spirit at last.

Fatally, as when she resigned herself to or relapsed into (the denial of) the impasse in the sexual relation the first time around, so here Lucinde herself agrees with, or capitulates to, Julius's conclusion. She inscribes herself, at the end of the dialogue, in the position of the woman as self-effacing signifier of the man, the position of the letter that has been spiritualized without remainder, the position of the German Jew devoted without reserve to the project of assimilation: "That is how the feminine soul [*Gemüt*] in my love-warmed breast feels, when I am allowed to be as I am. It longs only for your longing, is content where you find contentment [*Es sehnt sich nur nach Deinem Sehnen, ist ruhig, wo Du Ruhe findest*]" (80). The difference between longing and contentment within Lucinde is effaced here to the degree that her identification with Julius is emphasized. Her internal doubleness is neutralized or overcome insofar as this doubleness finds itself mirrored as *one* doubleness in the *one* who is a double of herself, and who includes the doubleness of the couple within himself. Anticipatory or prefigurative difference of the feminine, Jewish letter finds its "fulfillment"—and is effaced—in the speculative identification with the masculine, Christian, spiritual identity of its difference, an identification here situated in the second-person singular pronoun of an unfortunate apostrophe.

Pantheism Proven by the Making of Babies, or the Spiritualization of the Letter in Cosmotheological Terms

How, finally, do the contingency of the letter and the necessity of the spirit appear in the realm of "objective" beings? Schlegel answers this question, with particular clarity of outline, in cosmotheological terms in the chapter entitled "Two Letters." Schlegel figures the *establishment* of the letter-spirit, Jewish-Christian, feminine-masculine, contingent-necessary relation in the first of these two epistles as the becoming-pregnant of the woman. In this letter, Schlegel explicitly overdetermines the figure of pregnancy in philosophical terms as a cosmotheological synthesis—an empirical proof of the pantheistic hypothesis—by aligning mother with the (contingency of) *cosmos* as earth or nature, father with the (necessity of) *theos* or divine spirit. In the second epistle, Schlegel figures the *interruption* of the letter-spirit relation as Julius's imaginary loss of the mother, that is, as his fantasy of the death of his pregnant beloved, which signifies the loss of the world as loss of the feminine, Judaic letter. We will return to this second epistle below. Before doing so, it is necessary to retrace the (fictional) argument of the first epistle, where the identification of mother with the objectified longing of the earth, father with the objectified contentment of the divine spirit, occurs within the second of two quasi-dialectical steps.

On the Pleasures of Insemination:
"Now I love the earth"

Julius's initial response to the news of Lucinde's pregnancy, in the first of the quasi-dialectical steps I have in "mind," is to turn affirmatively toward the natural earth out of a kind of grateful identification, an identification due to his persuasion that nature has confirmed his bond with Lucinde, her representative.

You're going to be a mother!

Farewell to you, longing and also to you, soft complaint, the world is beautiful again, now I love the earth, and the sunrise of a new springtime raises its rosy-streaming head over my immortal existence. If I had laurels I would weave them around your forehead, to consecrate you to a new seriousness and activity; since for you too a new life is beginning. In turn, give me the myrtle crown. It is appropriate for me to decorate myself youthfully with the image of innocence, since I dwell in the paradise of nature. What was between us before, was only love and passion. Now, nature has bound us more intimately together, totally and indissolubly. Nature alone is the true Priestess of Joy; only she knows how to create a marriage bond. Not through idle words without blessing, but through fresh blossoms and living fruits out of the fullness of her force. In the endless changes of new figures formative time weaves the wreathe of eternity, and he is holy who is touched by the happiness of bearing fruit and being healthy. . . . I want to plant the earth, I want to sow and reap for the future and the present, I want to use all of my forces as long as day lasts and then refresh myself in the evening in the arms of the mother who will eternally be my bride. Our son, the little serious devil, will play about us, and think out various schemes against you with me. . . . Frivolously I lived without touching the surface of the earth and was not at home upon it. Now the holy sacrament of marriage has given me the rights of citizenship in the state of nature. I am no longer floating in the empty space of a general enthusiasm [*Begeisterung*], I take pleasure in friendly limitation, I see the useful in a new light and find everything truly useful that marries any sort of eternal love with its object, in short everything which serves an authentic marriage. The external things themselves inspire respect in me, whenever they are thorough in their way. (61–62)

If the bond between Julius, as supersensuous and therefore supernatural spirit, and Lucinde, as natural letter, had already been established before on the level of spirit—which here appears as the mere subjectivity of passionate love—now this bond has been established on the level of natural letter—which appears as the organic objectivity and actuality of new life. Moreover, in a gesture rich with (self-impoverishing) consequences, Schlegel *privileges* this objective unity over the subjective one. While this gesture is not surprising to the degree that it acknowledges the insufficiency of an exclusive emphasis on the spiritual dimension (an insufficiency on which Schlegel has been insisting for some time), it *is* odd insofar as Schlegel asserts that the unification of spirit and letter must take place *above all* in the name (or on the level) of *the letter itself*. In terms of the marital *exemplum*: marriage is not marriage except insofar as there are children.

One very striking implication of this position, no doubt subsequently very painful to Schlegel—although it is nowhere mentioned in the secondary literature, as far as I can determine—is that Schlegel's marriage with Dorothea, which will in fact remain childless, must therefore be invalidated in Schlegel's own eyes—undone as a marriage of (Christian, masculine) spirit and (Jewish, feminine) letter—in terms of his own theory of marriage as publicly propounded in *Lucinde*. We will return to this below.

The second implication of Schlegel's surprising decision to elevate (through Julius) the materiality of the natural letter to the status of the *proper*[34] is that he makes himself thereby appear as the *Jew* with respect to whom Dorothea—the "earthly" woman—would be the *German/Christian*. (Since Judaism is traditionally considered within Christianity to be not only material but also abstract, as opposed to the ostensibly spiritual and concrete character of Christianity, it is always possible for Christian spirituality to become confused with Jewish abstraction, one cause of the paranoid form Christian anti-Semitism takes.) This implication is made fairly explicit when Julius writes that he is becoming "at home" ("einheimisch") on the earth and that the holy bond of natural marriage has given him "the rights to citizenship" ("das Bürgerrecht") in the state of nature. Insofar as the synthesis of spirit and letter must occur under the dominance of both terms—otherwise, how could it be a synthesis?—this scene performs one aspect of the synthesis that, by reading Lessing, Schlegel discovered it would be necessary to seek: namely, the material aspect, which Schlegel's attempt to formulate the synthesis as an ultimately *spiritual* one has obliged him to deny at every turn. While the letter must indeed become spirit in order for the two to be one, it is equally the case that spirit must become letter. Schlegel's position requires him both to acknowledge this intimate mutual dependency of spirit and letter and at the same time to deny it. Yet, in this particular context it seems that, because "nature" is not only the *material* opposite of *spirit* but also the *real* opposite of the *unreal*, the concrete realization of mere abstract possibility, Schlegel can affirm through Julius the becoming-natural of spirit without seeming to notice that there is any dire threat involved. Or can he?

As Julius's letter to Lucinde continues—and here we begin to consider the second of the two quasi-dialectical steps mentioned above—he does appear to harbor reservations about entering into the realm of the letter, hesitations in his love of the earth, which he expresses in various ways. First, he expresses them *nolens volens* in a comically indirect manner, in terms of his concern about the grapevines that he and his beloved wish to cultivate upon the rural property they plan to occupy with their child: "One more thing" ("Noch eins"), he adds, when writing to her of this property: "Don't trim [or circumcise: the word, *beschneiden*, cuts both ways] the grape-vines too much. I write this only because you found them a bit too wild and exuberant and because it might occur to you to see the little house from all sides thoroughly clean" (63). Thinking ahead, Julius (as representative of Friedrich) draws the line just before circumcision—and even where it is only a question of grapevines![35] Moreover, he continues to argue (in psychological and hermeneutical terms) for his unity with Lucinde, claiming to be the fulfillment Lucinde merely anticipates. "There is no ecstasy and no love whatsoever in me that does not lie hidden already in some depth of your being, you infinite and happy one! . . . O, Love! believe me, there is no question in you that does not have its Answer in me" (63–64).

It cannot be the case, therefore, that the spirit will find fulfillment in its condescension to the level of the letter. Rather, it will become letter only in order to unfold itself all the more vigorously as spirit. And so—to cite a third example of Julius's recoil from his becoming-earthly, one even more obviously denegational than those adduced thus far: Julius characterizes the change that has come over him first of all as "a general softness and sweet warmth in all capacities of the soul and spirit [*Vermögen der Seele und des Geistes*], like the lovely exhaustion of the senses that follows upon the highest life" (63). But he hastens to add that this softness only confirms the hard telos of his fraternal masculinity[36]: "And yet it is anything but softness. Rather, I know that I will pursue all that is my calling [*meines Berufs*] from now on with greater love and fresh force. I never felt more confidence and courage to be effective as a man amongst men, to begin and follow through on a heroic life and to act in brotherhood with friends for eternity" (63–64). It is in the context of this deliberation that cosmotheological considerations enter. The tension between masculine and feminine comes to be overdetermined as one between the *divine* and *natural* dimensions of a hypothetical *pantheistic totality* about whose possibility Julius is enthusiastically ambivalent. He now expresses his unwitting resistance to the Judaizing, feminizing materiality of his pantheistic paradise by splitting that paradise into the two separate realms of *cosmos* and *theos*, realms henceforth to be comfortably ordered within a neatly hierarchical binary opposition. Commenting upon the "heroic life" he now feels the courage to lead (as if in a "prophetic prefiguration" of Schlegel's later political engagement under the Restoration), Julius clarifies the distinction between his proper "virtue" and that of his beloved in terms of "divinity" and "nature": "That is my virtue; thus is it fitting for me to become similar to the gods. Your virtue is quietly to reveal, like nature, as the priestess of joy, the secret of love, and in the midst of dignified sons and daughters to consecrate beautiful life as a holy festival" (66). Julius becomes like the gods—radically spiritual—by passing into contact with the letter. As a result of her contact with the (masculine) spirit, Lucinde too becomes more spiritual (for this is her "end"), and yet in an earthly mode (earthliness being her "original nature"): she reveals the "secret of love" but does so "like nature." Again, the polarization in force is not symmetrical. Not only Julius but Lucinde too, as the *natural* component, has her "end" in spirituality or divinity, yet Julius ends up there as if returning to his own home, while Lucinde serves that end from the distance of her earthly place of fallen manifestation.

Finally, lest one imagine that the figurality and literality of language are not directly involved in this discussion, *language* calls attention to itself as a homologous overdetermination of the cosmotheological, typological, and gender-theoretical tensions already at stake here when Julius writes to Lucinde that their love actually corresponds to an expression he had read in a French book, "They were the universe to each other" ("Sie waren einer dem andern das Universum"):

How it struck me, moving me and making me smile, that what stood there so thoughtlessly, merely as a figure of hyperbole, had become literally true in us [*was da so gedankenlos stand, bloß als eine Figur der Übertreibung, in uns buchstäblich wahr geworden sei*]!

Actually, even in such a French passion it is literally true [*buchstäblich wahr*]. They find the universe in each other because they lose all sense of everything else.

Not so with us. Everything that we otherwise loved we now love even more warmly. The sense of the world has finally dawned on us. You have come to know through me the infinity of the human spirit [*die Unendlichkeit des menschlichen Geistes*], and I have understood through you marriage, life, and the lordly splendor of all things [*die Ehe und das Leben begriffen, und die Herrlichkeit aller Dinge*].

All is animated for me, speaks to me, and all is holy. When people are in love as we are, nature in the human being returns to its original divinity. Pleasure becomes again in the lonely embrace of the lovers what it is in the great whole—the holiest wonder of nature; and what for others is only something of which they rightly feel they ought to be ashamed becomes for us again what it is in and for itself, the pure fire of the most noble life-force. (67)

Julius distinguishes—good German patriot that he is—between the figural, hyperbolic sense of the expression in the context of the French book, on the one hand, and its literal truth as realized in his German relationship with Lucinde, on the other. He thus invokes the separation of figure and letter. (This notion of their separation is conventionally sanctioned by logocentric discourse along with the notion of their inseparability, even if this discourse silently stipulates further that the two conventions may not be invoked simultaneously.) But he invokes this separation in order to lay claim to the *reality* associated with the letter (as opposed to the *unreality* of the figural) while distancing himself from the *materiality* which its figurality always also implies. Julius's claim that the figure has here become literally true is itself, of course, an instance of the "thoughtless" use of a "figure of hyperbole." Julius even registers his recognition of this fact by modifying his formulation and acknowledging that the figural, hyperbolic French use of the expression has a kind of literal truth about it, but he goes on to deny this recognition again by drawing what is supposed to be a fundamental distinction between the French meaning of the expression and its German one. Namely, in the French case, the lovers forget the rest of the world for each other, and so the part replaces the whole, whereas in the German case, they discover the world through each other, so the part enhances, "warms" the whole. The part actually presents the whole, rather than merely representing it. In French, a synecdoche is not a metaphor, but a metonymy, whereas in German, a synecdoche is actually a metaphor, hence no longer a figure at all.

But again, to claim that synecdochic representation can actually be the presentation of the whole, to affirm the fragment as an adequate presentation of the whole, is to practice hyperbole, to fall prey to the rhetorical materiality of language precisely in the linguistic act by means of which one denies that materiality.[37] And the hyperbolic character of Julius's claim becomes unmistakably apparent in that his explanation of *how* the two are "the universe to each other" divides the universe into *two pieces*, the spiritual and natural, spirit hovering hierarchically over nature. That is, Julius presents the German realization of this French prefiguration in his own relationship with Lucinde not as a unitary structure in which two pantheistic universes metaphorically mirror and fulfill each other, as the expression would seem to demand, but rather as a split structure in which a divine spirituality *finds itself* in an earthly nature, while this nature *loses itself* in the spirituality it contemplates. The triumph of pantheism is stated in terms of the uneven and denegated battle or polemic between *theos* and *cosmos*. If Julius discovers through Lucinde "marriage and life . . . the lordly splendour of all things," the lordly splendor he discovers is a spiritualizing splendor of "animation" ("everything is animated for me") that consists in a return of nature to its "original"—final—"*divinity*."[38] In contrast, when Lucinde discovers the "infinity of the human spirit" through Julius, she does not discover the *thingliness* of spirit as one would expect (insofar as only this would be the symmetrical opposite of the spiritual "lordliness of things" which Julius discovers through her). Instead of the thingliness of spirit, the materiality and finitude of mind, she discovers spirit as such in its very infinitude. In short, divinity finds itself in earthly nature here just as spiritual meaning finds itself in the letter of its material signifier: by effacing the disturbingly foreign presence (and the internal splitting) of that in which it literally appears, and without which its appearance would be literally impossible.[39]

The Fantasy of the Loss of the Mother: "I hated everything earthly"

Julius's joy over the announcement of the coming birth of his child is followed in the second of the "Two Letters" by his despair over the imaginary threat of the death of the mother.[40] This second letter serves, intentionally or not, as an illuminating reflexion upon the first: it explains why, despite being overjoyed about the pregnancy of his beloved, Julius recoiled from the affirmation of nature and turned away from the notion of his inscription in its materiality, a notion he took this pregnancy to imply.[41] Before unfolding the main associative implications of the fantasy of the death of the beloved as it is deployed in this second letter, let us very quickly restate its trajectory. The (inner) process Julius recounts there, addressing himself to Lucinde, apparently in order to illustrate "die Allmacht der Fantasie," is as follows: Julius read in a letter from Lucinde's sister the news of Lucinde's (never explicitly specified) illness; he thereupon imagined that she was going to die, then went so far as to imagine her dead and buried, himself desperate, considering suicide, then rejecting the idea and deciding to live out the rest of his now-meaningless life, purely out of a sense of duty; he lived on (in his imagination) for awhile, practiced his profession as if in a dream, but slowly came to be tempted again by suicide, and then suddenly, just as, in his imagined future, he was looking forward, with a sweetly luxurious sense of longing, to a self-imposed death, he received news that Lucinde had recovered, and was awakened out of his imaginary despair with a jolt.

What are the implications of the story of this waking nightmare? How does it serve to explain Julius's surreptitious recoil from the letter of nature in the previous epistle? And to move toward answering these questions—what does the death of Lucinde signify? The death of Lucinde signifies, obviously, the loss of the woman, the mother, the material, natural world, and the Judaic letter. Because Julius, as man, father, spiritual, supernatural, and Christian being depends for this identity on some kind of intimate yet external contact with his binary opposite, the loss of the woman (and of all that she stands for) means nothing less than the loss of Julius himself. When Julius imagines himself losing Lucinde, in order to protect himself against this loss he turns—playing a kind of *fort-da* game *avant la lettre freudienne*—against all that she has represented. This turn begins, indeed, with his decision to imagine her already dead once he hears that she is sick, rather than wait for her death to impose itself on him from without, against his will.[42] The turn reasserts itself after her imagined death as Julius's hatred of life, his (nihilistic) affirmation of the suffering and sickness of nature: "I was sick and suffered a lot, but I loved my sickness and welcomed the pain itself. I hated everything earthly and was happy that it was punished and destroyed" (70). Since the woman—the material letter of a Jewish mother nature—can be taken away, Julius decides to turn against her in advance, rejecting nature and affirming its destruction. Since the letter might get lost or be misunderstood, why not destroy it in advance?

Moreover, as the terms of our analysis thus far would make us suspect, Julius's turn against the letter of earthliness entails his refusal of *works* in favor of a more purely spiritual affirmation of radical faith. As Julius puts it, if in a somewhat self-aggrandizing fashion (especially in light of the difficulty with which Schlegel himself finished works):

Slowly the years flowed away, and effortfully one deed after another, one work and then another met its goal, which was as little my own as I took those deeds and works for what they are called. They were for me mere Holy Figures [*heilige Sinnbilder*], all relations to the one beloved, who was the mediatrix [*die Mittlerin*] between my dismembered ego and indivisible eternal humanity; all of existence [*das ganze Dasein*] a continuous religious service of lonely love. (71)

In the context of Julius's rejection of nature, works become meaningless in themselves, mere "figures" ("Sinnbilder") for the "beloved" who links, like a mediating spirit, the fragmentary subject to the totality of his social, human world.[43] Yet even such symbolic works, totally subordinate to Julius's faith in his beloved, are not in any way sufficient. "Finally I perceived that this one was the last. . . . My course was ended, although not completed. The best force of life was gone and art and virtue still stood eternally unattainable before me. I would have despaired had I not seen both present and deified in you, blessed Madonna! and you and your mild divinity in me" (71).

In Lutheran fashion, Schlegel condemns works as cause for despair over the impossibility of perfect accomplishment, while giving a proto-neo-Catholicizing twist to the condemnation, by means of his sentimental transformation of his beloved into a figure for the mother of God. In order to escape the loss of the imaginary other, one negates that other, even at the cost of negating oneself: "Then you appeared before me, significant, and waving me toward death [*winktest tödlich*]. A heartfelt longing for you and for Freedom had already gained possession of me; I longed for my beloved old Fatherland . . . as I was called back into life through the promise and certainty of your recovery" (71). If the first of the "Two Letters" tells of Julius's surreptitious recoil from the identification with nature he there expressly affirms, then the second of the letters tells us the (at once infantile and unwittingly self-destructive reason) why: it is better to destroy or to reject on one's own that on which one depends than to allow it to be taken away by someone or something else.

The "furchtbare Allmacht der Fantasie" (68) that Julius says he wishes to illustrate by means of this little story, then, is much like Freud's infantile "Allmacht der Gedanken." It is the fearful power of fantasy to rid itself of the imaginary other in order not to have to be exposed to the danger of depending on that other for its own—one's own—always imaginary or phantasmatic existence.

After Jena: Childlessness and the Logic of Conversion

As I have suggested above, the episode on Lucinde's pregnancy (along with her imagined loss) in "Two Letters" is important not only because it demonstrates the cosmotheological (and in this case pantheistic) dimension of the (im)possible relation in which Schlegel places the genders of the letter and spirit. Nor is it merely the fact that the life-and-death stakes of this relation become perfectly manifest in "Two Letters" that gives them their significance. Rather, beyond these two matters, the episode of the pregnancy is "crucial" because it sheds ominous yet clarifying light on the future convergences, divergences, and conversions of Friedrich and Dorothea. In *Lucinde*, Schlegel makes the generation of a baby the crucial touchstone—soon to become for him the tombstone—of a mixing of the genders (as mixing of letter and spirit, signifier and signified, work and faith, Judaism and Protestant Christianity, and so forth). This concern in *Lucinde* should no doubt be read not only "immanently" but also against the background of the relatively high numbers of illegitimate children being born to mixed Jewish-Christian couples at this time.[44] Whereas marriage (conditional upon religio-cultural homogeny) was usually taken to legitimate children, Schlegel reverses the pattern in characteristically antinomial fashion: for him, the child legitimates the marriage. The fulfillment legitimates the prefiguration. The spirituality of natural union thus legitimates as a supplementary origin the materiality of merely cultural, artificial, institutional union. Once Schlegel has posited this structure, the lack of literal reproductive fruitfulness in the form of a baby necessarily places in question the possibility of the relationship between a man and a woman, which means also the possibility of any presentation of meaning itself, any form-content synthesis whatsoever.[45]

In light of Schlegel's metaphysically burdened ideology of gender mixing, the fact that Dorothea and Friedrich never had any children, except purely spiritual-textual ones, must be seen as one of the more important overdetermining factors in Dorothea's and Friedrich's decision to convert to Catholicism and marry for their second time less than a decade subsequent to the publication of *Lucinde*. Even before that, it must have enhanced their need to marry—hoping against hope—in the first place, as initially occurred under Protestant auspices in 1804. Once this marriage had occurred, however, it must have contributed to rendering necessary a second marriage surpassing the imperfect character of this first one. For the Schlegels had to perfect their act of marriage: nothing less than the life of meaning and the meaning of life of both partners depended symbolically upon it. The first marriage was flawed in two senses at once. First, despite its materiality qua institutional ritual, since the first marriage (subsequent to Dorothea's conversion to Protestantism), insofar as it was a *Protestant* ceremony, was carried out in the name of spirit alone and so took into account only Friedrich's original identity, not Dorothea's, this marriage still required a supplement of materiality. Marriage in the spirit alone could not take Dorothea into account. Insofar as it was a *ceremony* at all, however, a material act on the level of the letter of the work, the first marriage already implicitly departed from the space of Protestant spirituality in its most radical sense, and yet it did not own up to its necessary material dimension. It comprised only the Schlegels' first step, then, toward the fulfillment, as it were, of their (henceforth merely prefigurative) Protestant marriage in a Catholic marriage. In a Catholic marriage, the ceremonial character of the act would not have to be denegated—at least not so obviously as in the case of Lutheran Protestantism—but would instead appear (i.e., claim) to be fully fused with the spiritual inwardness or meaning of the event, thus giving Dorothea's Jewish origins as well as Friedrich's Lutheran origins, works as well as faith, their due. As a middle ground between the Protestant spirit and the Judaic letter, the Catholic Church would ultimately provide a consoling (if illusory) confirmation of the possibility of the connection—of each sex with the other as of meaning with linguistic form—of which Dorothea and Friedrich lacked proof in the form of biological fusion. And it was only on the basis of such a connection that it was possible for Friedrich to imagine his own spirituality, since he had already come to the firm conclusion that there is no spirit without letter, that spirit without letter becomes pure letter. If there turned out to be no relation between him and Dorothea, this would mean, paradoxically, that he was she, or at least that he was what she, in her negative aspect, represented: the dead letter, the Judaic materiality of death itself. Schlegel attempts to avoid this eventuality through the neo-Catholic turn, as I have argued elsewhere with reference to a work from the moment of the Schlegels' Catholic conversion in 1808, *Über die Sprache und Weisheit der Indier*, where ancient Indian culture supplants Jewish letter, so that Jewish letter may fuse with Protestant spirit in order to give rise (in a "logical" rather than a "historical" consequence) to the Catholic Church.[46] Below, however, I will demonstrate the neo-Catholic turn more precisely and explicitly than was possible in the reading of the text on ancient Sanskrit culture, turning to consider in Chapter 6 Schlegel's rereading of Lessing from 1804, where—strikingly—he explicitly returns to his elective paternal mirror-image, but now in order to read in Lessing's radicalization of Luther the inauguration of a return to Catholicism beyond the Enlightenment culmination of the Reformation.

Before proceeding to consider the moment of the neo-Catholic turn, however, in Chapter 5 I will examine Dorothea's indirect response to *Lucinde* in her own novel of 1801, *Florentin*, where she provides ample evidence of the absolutely central importance of the rhetoric-philosophy opposition for her relationship with Friedrich, as the relationship between a Jewish woman and a Protestant man.

Resisting "Fulfillment"

THE UNDECIDABLE LIMIT BETWEEN
FIGURAL AND LITERAL IN DOROTHEA VEIT'S
'FLORENTIN: A NOVEL' (1801)

"Florentin was nowhere to be found."

Florentin. Ein Roman. Erster Band,[1] the only novel among Dorothea Veit's many published works, appeared in 1801 with no indication of its author. Friedrich Schlegel, however, was named on the title page as its editor, or *Herausgeber*. Veit's context while she was composing this text, along with a number of the thematic and formal traits of the text itself (the limit between text and context being understood here as constantly shifting) makes a contextual reading of this text potentially "fruitful" (I use this organicist term here, where it is most appropriate) for my attempt to trace German-Jewish "dialogue" in the literary-philosophical space around 1800. As anyone who is reading this book in a semilinear manner will be well aware by now, Veit was the eldest daughter of Moses Mendelssohn, who had died in 1786. While writing *Florentin*, she was living in "wilder Ehe" (i.e., "sin") with Friedrich Schlegel. The mother of two children, in 1798 she had divorced their father, Simon Veit—an apparently kind but unintellectual Jewish banker who had been chosen for her by her father when she was nineteen and to whom she had been married for sixteen years—in order to be able to live out her relationship with Schlegel. She would convert to Protestantism in order to marry Schlegel in 1804 and then go on to convert to Catholicism with him (and remarry him) in 1808. In this chapter, we will examine how, within this situation, in the most "promising" moment of the epoch of emancipation, Veit takes up in *Florentin* a critical position on the rhetoric of Jewish-German cultural dialogue. Before entering into the interpretive discussion of this first volume of *Florentin*, which as it turned out—like Friedrich's *Lucinde*—was never to be followed by a second volume, let me begin by providing, with as little commentary as possible, a brief overview of its somewhat indeterminately developed characters and fragmentary plot. Such an overview is all the more necessary here as one can hardly assume this novel to be universally familiar either to a broader readership or even much more narrowly to German or Jewish Studies scholars today.

Prolonged Engagements and Problematic Couples

The title character of the novel, its "hero," as Dorothea calls him ironically in a draft she wrote for the Preface of the never-completed continuation of the novel, is a man without identity who wanders through Germany, in search of his origins, with the (apparently somewhat vague) intention of going to America to fight on the side of the Republic. At the outset of the novel, while crossing alone through a forest on his travels, he becomes involved quite by chance with a family of the nobility by saving the father of the family, Count Schwarzenberg, from an angry wild sow[2] that has attacked him while he was out hunting. Implored by Schwarzenberg to accept his hospitality as an expression of gratitude for having saved his life, Florentin consents to a brief stay with the family. Having met the Count's charming wife Eleonore and eldest daughter Juliane, as well as the daughter's fiancé Eduard von Usingen, Florentin consents to stay on with the family until the upcoming wedding of Juliane and Eduard. In the days and weeks spent awaiting the wedding, which gets postponed somewhat mysteriously at the epistolary bidding of Juliane's beloved Aunt Clementina (Schwarzenberg's sister and Eleonore's friend), Florentin wins over the entire family, as in a mild, good-natured version of Pasolini's *Teorema avant la lettre*. In particular, he forms strong, passionate, and somewhat ambiguous friendships both with the creative and coquettish Juliane and (less passionately) with her nice but somewhat dull fiancé, Eduard. Not surprisingly, given this setup, much of the dramatic tension of the novel turns around the many implicit questions concerning the eventual fate of this amicable threesome. Can Juliane be fulfilled by Eduard? Will she ultimately marry him, or will she end up running off with Florentin? And would she be more fulfilled by a life with Florentin? What exactly is meant by fulfillment in love? Can she and Florentin be just friends? How will Florentin (and also Eduard) handle the situation, and how *should* they handle the situation?

One day during Florentin's stay, he, Juliane, and Eduard take a long walk in the country, a romantic excursion during the course of which Florentin tells the story of his life's adventures in search of his origins. This narrative, to aspects of which we will return below, fills about one-third of the originally published text. Once Florentin has finished recounting his story, a storm forces the friends to spend the night at the house of a miller. In a critical conversation with Florentin at the miller's house, Eduard expresses both his own attachment to Florentin and his jealous anxiety about Juliane's desire for the latter (about which he has hitherto kept silent).

The next day, the young people return to Juliane's parents' castle. The day of the wedding soon arrives. At the last minute before the ceremony, Florentin runs off, apparently disgusted over the alienating formality of the institutionalization of desire. He takes refuge provisionally at the home of Juliane's mysterious, old, sick Aunt Clementina (again, her father's sister and her mother's friend), who has largely raised Juliane, and who is herself quasi boycotting the wedding, because she feels that Juliane is too young to know what she is doing.

At the estate of Aunt Clementina, while he is waiting to meet the fragile, aged woman, Florentin encounters another not-so-happy nascent couple, Betty and the Cavalry Captain Walter. This couple is much more unambiguously exploitative than the ones it mirrors in exaggerated form— the "real" couple, Juliane and Eduard, as well as the potential or virtual couple, Juliane and Florentin. The Captain is a brute and a tyrant, and Betty only stays with him as a way of attempting to recuperate the loss of her purity that occurred when she capitulated to his sexual advances. Betty is thus not only the victim of an oppressive marriage but also the victim of seduction or rape that Juliane might have become at Florentin's hands, had he even attempted to overcome her, which did not occur. On one occasion, indignant over the Captain's jealously brutal mistreatment of Betty, Florentin verbally defends Betty's honor. Angered, the Captain smolders, until one evening, shortly after Florentin has made the acquaintance of Clementina in an enigmatic scene of suggestively high emotion, the

Captain provokes Florentin to a fight. Florentin deftly disarms the Captain and throws the Captain's sword, now broken into several pieces, at his feet. At this moment, the young newlyweds arrive at their Aunt's house amidst the tumult and confusion of the scuffle. Florentin seems to have run off, for he is nowhere to be found. The first part of the novel (the second part of which was never completed) thus breaks off.

'Florentin' as Dialogical Response to 'Lucinde'

How does Veit's novel, from the distance of its own singularity, respond to and correspond with Schlegel's novel, *Lucinde*? In posing such a question, I assume, along with most other readers of *Florentin*, that Veit's novel in part answers to, and defines itself with relation to, both *Lucinde* and Friedrich Schlegel.[3] Indeed there seems ample ground for such an assumption. The "author" of *Florentin* is—even if in an ultimately indefinable way—the "referent" and the "addressee" of *Lucinde*. And the (never fully constituted) discourse of love in which both Friedrich and Dorothea are involved posits at least the possibility, if not the assured reality, of the reciprocity of love or the mutual substitutability of those who love. It is consequently unavoidable to read *Florentin* as both addressing itself to and referring to Friedrich Schlegel and his *Lucinde* in turn. In addition, due to the notion of necessary reflexivity that, by the time of *Florentin*'s composition, had already been developed by Friedrich and the other Romantics around *Athenäum*, one must read the novel as addressing itself and referring to the *question* of whether or not and under what conditions it might be possible to dialogue with the object it reads.

To begin to read *Florentin* as a (highly self-reflexive) reading of *Lucinde* that is a writing of (and to) Friedrich Schlegel, we must ask ourselves how Dorothea Veit approaches the task of positioning her own text *as the writing of a reading*. As what sort of *reading* does Veit conceive her reading of Schlegel and his text? In light of the historical record and the literature on the relationship between Dorothea and Friedrich Schlegel, it seems unambiguously clear that, in general in her relationship with Schlegel, of the two main dimensions of the rhetoric of cultural dialogue as I initially sketched them in the Introduction, Dorothea emphasizes the dimension of self-effacement. She reads *herself*—at least, she tries to read herself—in terms of the *other*, and *not the other* in terms of *herself*. She thus endows her own language with the status of *figurality*, of derivativeness and anticipatoriness, while endowing the language of the privileged other, in this case Schlegel, with the status of *literalness*. A line from a letter from 1806—the year in which the French occupation of Berlin inaugurated the decline of Berlin Jewish salon culture as part of a general upsurge of nationalist feeling—expresses this position with particular clarity (and there are a plethora of such passages from the letters and memoirs of others, from the time Veit and Schlegel met in 1797 on, through which to demonstrate the same point): "I seek to make all of my thought conform to your own and to understand you completely."[4] Veit endows her life, insofar as it comes to comprise a reading of Schlegel's own, with the status of a figural reading, in the specific sense of a reading that takes itself to be a mere figure of its literal object (an empiricist, realist reading), a signifier willing and able to efface itself before the signified that sustains it.

The secondary literature provides two main views of this general stance toward Schlegel, a stance that took on the proportions of abjectly idealizing happy servitude. Veit has frequently been praised as saintly and just as frequently bemoaned or berated as pitiful or misguided, sometimes by the same scholars, no doubt with some justification on all sides.[5] Again and again she insists that she finds her fulfillment in Friedrich, in his work and his love, and yet throughout their lives together Friedrich seems to have behaved in a manner that was anything but fulfilling. He had difficulty completing work he'd projected, he made little money while accumulating substantial debts, and he was not particularly sensitive, caring, or loving toward Dorothea as his beloved and then wife, or at least he does not seem to have been consistently so. Meanwhile, she slaved over publications to make money, kept house, supported and defended Schlegel in all of his endeavors, and never wavered from her position of absolute affirmation and devotion. So why exactly did she allow herself to become fixed into—if not fixated upon—such a position?

My suggestion is that in order to understand how Veit can become stuck in such a position, especially insofar as one attempts to gaze upon it through the lens of *Florentin*, one has to take into account the rhetorical-hermeneutical-typological sense in which Schlegel is the literal "fulfillment" or "realization" of the "prefiguration" she represents (even if these are not always the precise words she uses), in addition to the religio-political, the gender-political, and the aesthetic-generic implications of this sense.

Both as a woman and as a Jew, within the dominant discourse, which she to a great degree internalizes, Veit has virtually no chance of conceiving herself as anything other than the *figural* anticipation (or falling off) of which Schlegel is the *literal* fulfillment (or origin). Hence, her very pronounced tendency to a kind of self-abnegation, despite the fact that she is one of the brightest and most highly educated women of her day and is doubtless also aware of this.[6] On the other hand, however, I will try to show here that she resists this prefiguration-fulfillment model by conceiving prefiguration as fulfillment, fulfillment as prefiguration. In other words, she suspends the teleological linearity of the progression from prefiguration to fulfillment by situating the essential existence of both terms on the undecidable limit where they meet and come asunder. This limit—in its limitless instability—would be the site of (cultural) dialogue as Veit formulates it in *Florentin*.

My reading of *Florentin* here will try to show how Veit attempts to circumscribe such a limit in this novel.[7] I do not, of course, mean to suggest that the mere fact of Veit's having made such an attempt in the aesthetico-theoretical sphere of novelistic production would somehow make Veit's actual self-subordinating relationship to Friedrich Schlegel "okay." Nonetheless, it is important to understand how, even as she consents to inscribing herself in this self-subordination, Veit resists this inscription by attempting *to rethink and to disrupt the traditional Western rhetoric of figural and literal expression*—as well as the most crucial metaphysical variations on the theme of this opposition. In terms of Veit's private life, *Florentin* can thus be seen as Veit's attempt to reconceive Friedrich Schlegel not as fulfillment pure and simple but as a *figure* of fulfillment, or as "figural fulfillment," while reconceiving herself not merely as prefiguration but as the *fulfillment* of prefiguration, or as "fulfilling prefiguration." In terms of Veit's thought, more generally, the novel can be seen as an attempt to articulate a critique of the teleological passage from figural (back) to literal as a *flawed* model of "fulfillment." Whatever the "aesthetic" flaws of the novel might be—as if "aesthetic" were a predetermined category on which we could all depend—in any case it bears witness to Veit's energetic attempt to think through the question of figural fulfillment. As such, it commands our interest and respect as a serious thought-experiment in "novelistic" form (we will return to the question of genre below).[8]

In the following, the way in which I demonstrate both *that* Veit is attempting to determine the limit-concept of figural fulfillment and *how* she is doing so is by retracing how she positions her "hero" Florentin. More precisely, I argue that, evidently in the attempt to construct a model of this undecidable limit, she positions Florentin consistently *between* figure and literal fulfillment. Moreover, she does so not only in the "literally" rhetorical guise of this opposition but also in its transfigurations or translations into some of the principal conceptual oppositions of her day, within the discourses of theology (Protestant and Catholic, Christian and Jew), psychology (will and inclination, masculine and feminine), and cosmology (finitude and infinitude of the world).

By going "beyond fulfillment," Veit will have proposed a solution to the problem of the rhetoric of cultural dialogue that is also a dissolution— or a precipitation out of solution—of the solution itself. For what is neither figure nor fulfillment cannot, of course, be a fulfillment. It can only appear to be *beyond* fulfillment at the price of appearing also to be *this side* of fulfillment, that is, at the price of appearing to be precisely *unfulfilling*. The place of the undecidability in question is the place where fulfillment is not only more but also less than itself. While such a place is not simply untenable, it is also always only tentatively tenable. Like truth, it is always pending, expending, and upending itself: it can only be insistently pursued, never secured in the mode of a possession. One will not be surprised, then, that beyond the novel's end, Florentin relapses from his interliminal position back into the figure-fulfillment model. He thereby prefigures the real relapse through which Schlegel will have fulfilled Veit's text with his own texts, and with particular clarity those from 1804 on.

Florentin Between Figures of Sense and the Sense of Figures

Throughout the novel, Florentin repeatedly and explicitly embodies what we are considering here to be the principle of rhetoric. Rhetoric takes in *Florentin* not only the form of persuasive power in words (of which Florentin is a kind of master, for example, as improvisor of songs to guitar accompaniment that read as tight lyrical compositions) but also the forms of the persuasive power of images in painting (Florentin makes his living for part of his life as a portrait painter and as a painting instructor) and of sounds in music (he improvises songs of great magic on the guitar).[9]

Florentin is not only a skillful *manipulator* of forms of appearance but he is also perforce *immersed* in them thoroughly because he possesses no knowledge of his origins or essence, of his essential origins or original essence. Lacking all knowledge of who he might be, he is the essentially anonymous one, essentially without essence or name,[10] who not only *will not*, but *cannot*, appear as who he is. He can only appear in the masks of others, as a mere figure of himself. As if to highlight this characteristic, Florentin appears on a number of occasions in the novel explicitly "incognito." For example, when he attempts to save his sister from the cloister,[11] he does so "incognito" (61). When he gets into trouble in Venice by saving his English friend, who has just stabbed someone at the gambling table, here too he is masked, attending a Carnival Ball (67–69). Finally, on the excursion he makes with Juliane and Eduard, all three are "incognito" (90), the woman disguised as a man while the aristocratic class position of both members of the couple is covered up. In the dangers that arise during this excursion—the dangers of the confusion of identities and of the jealous fears to which the specter of such confusion gives rise—the novel must be seen as registering the contagious tendency of the "improper." Actively and passively, then, as both user and sufferer of the transfigurative powers of appearance, Florentin is closely associated with rhetoric, figuration, the material letter, and all that they entail in the discourse we are tracing in this study.

On the other hand, insofar as Florentin is living his life in search of his true identity, and insofar as those around him also seek his essence beneath the forms into which he seems to withdraw, the novel posits Florentin as *disidentified* with rhetoric. It posits his spiritual core as free from, and other than, the letter of his external life that embellishes and obscures that core. But the best way to demonstrate briefly, within the context of the present study, the sense in which this spiritual inwardness of Florentin doubles the material exteriority of his aesthetic charm is to consider his troubled relationship with the Catholic Church, as he represents it to his friends in his autobiographical narrative during their excursion into the country.

As he recounts, his surrogate mother has raised him and his sister in accordance with the directives of a Catholic (more specifically a Benedictine) Prior,[12] with the intention of having the children become priest and nun respectively. This connection with the Catholic Church functions above all, within the heavily Lutheran atmosphere from out of, and into, which Dorothea Veit's fiction emerges, as a connection with the

letter of the law, the material reality of works that Luther sought to supple-
ment with the inwardness and spirituality of faith, as in a renewal of the
Christian ("inner" and "universalist") fulfillment and overcoming of the
Jewish ("outer" and "particularist") prefiguration. Not surprisingly, given the
Lutheran and/or rational-theological character of the milieu—late-
Enlightenment/early-Romantic Berlin, Dorothea Veit being the eldest
daughter of Moses Mendelssohn[13] (and thus also to some extent of Lessing's
Nathan and, therefore, figuratively of Lessing himself), while Schlegel was
the son of a prominent preacher—the influence of the Catholic Church on
Florentin's childhood turns out to have been extremely negative, indeed
traumatic. While still a child, Florentin takes his distance from the outer
strictness, the oppressive violence of the prescriptions of the church. To
escape this violence, Florentin has developed—consciously and program-
matically and yet also of necessity—a split between his inner and outer
selves, the spiritual self of his true thoughts and the material self of the rit-
uals he has been obliged to perform, the life he has been obliged to lead.

The decisive break occurs after Florentin is severely punished for
interrupting his reading aloud—while having his "capacity to read" (48)
tested by his mother and the Prior—of a poem in praise of the happiness
of childhood. Being in disagreement with the contents of the poem,
Florentin suddenly becomes unwilling to perform it for the adults. He
refuses to provide them with the self-congratulatory pleasure the poem's
happy recitation promises to afford them by functioning as a performative
proof of the poem's truth.[14] At first, he is unwilling to have inside and outside, understanding and behavior, spirit and letter fail to coincide while
performing their apparent coincidence (as the happiness of the child reading and the happiness of childhood the text celebrates, and also as the voic-
ing of the written text). He is unwilling to become a hypocrite, to say what
he does not mean and not to say what he does mean, to assent to the claim
that writing is speech when what he experiences is a disjunction between
writing and speech as a disjunction between imposed behavior and feeling.
Yet, upon reflexion he realizes that the adults are hypocritical in a still more
extreme sense. They flatter themselves with illusions about the ideality of a
childhood, while at the same time they perversely attempt to destroy its
naïve insouciance. The child Florentin decides then to become a hypocrite
only in the more "honorable" sense of capitulating in act wherever
absolutely necessary while remaining free in thought, that is, in the sense
of being only externally hypocritical while internally refusing to lie to him-

self. "I attempted in every way to maintain my independence in my interior the more I was compelled to order my actions and my exterior life in accordance with their will" (49). Whereas the outer self continues to conform to the demands of the adults who represent the church, the inner self develops and maintains its independence. The notion that such a break between inside and outside would result from a Catholic (or Jewish) upbringing belongs, again, to the idiom of Lutheranism to which Veit is at this time still (and with acute intensity) trying to accommodate herself, and for which the excessive emphasis on the figural letter of "works" (as opposed to the literal spirit of "faith") wrongly privileges the outside in place of the inside. The result of an exposure to this imbalance in Florentin's case is its coming to be doubled by its opposite. Privateness, mistrust, and unhealthy aloneness continue to mark him throughout his life. The other characters in the novel even regard these traits at once as fascinating signs of his superiority and as frightful signs of his morally questionable suffering, of a kind of illness, a melancholic separation. Raised within a rhetorical-ritual exteriority[15] from which he recoils into an excessive philosophical interiority, Florentin stands on—and stands for—the torn limit between letter and spirit, figural and literal expression.

The Secular Exacerbation of Jewish Exile: From Literal Christian to Figural Jew and Beyond

Florentin's rebellious relation to his Catholic upbringing splits him not only between (prefigural, rhetorical) letter and (fulfilling, philosophical) spirit and between externally imposed, explicit Catholicism, and internal, implicit Protestantism, but also along the fault line of one more religio-cultural opposition, that between (figural) Judaism and (literal) Christianity. Florentin is figurally a Jew both because his Catholicism is already (from a Protestant point of view) a figural Judaism, and because his very dividedness between inside and outside is (from a Christian point of view) an essentially Jewish trait. And he is literally Christian insofar as he has been raised Catholic.

Given that his partial identification with the Christian has been thus far sufficiently established, then, in what ways—beyond the literal Catholicism and the dividedness of spirit—can Florentin be said to be associated figurally with Judaism?[16] First of all, Florentin is marked by the Judaic simply insofar as his aesthetic talents assume a rhetorical (dis)coloration by comparison with the ostensible purity and candor of discourses of knowledge, scientificity, philosophy, and so forth. That is, he is figurally Jewish— potentially Jewish or quasi-open to the suspicion of being Jewish—because he is (literally) *figural* and because, just as "all men are mortal," so "all Jews are figural," which means that some of those who are figural are Jews. Secondly, however, the most obvious sense in which Florentin is a figural Jew is that he is a wanderer, without home or identity, and in this exilic *destinerrance*, he is like the Jews.[17] Of course, if he has no identity, then he cannot be strictly speaking Jewish, and if he does not know where he comes from, then he cannot know himself to come from Palestine as his most proper place, as would at least any orthodox Jew. Still, this lack of knowledge about his origins means that Florentin's Christian identity too is placed in question (it is just a matter of upbringing, not "nature"), and the possibility of his being literally, that is, originarily or by birth, a Jew is opened up. More to the point and beyond this, insofar as he is the wanderer bereft of origins, Florentin can be read as a secularized *radicalization* or exacerbation of the Jew, who has lost not merely the Temple and the Land of Israel, *but Judaism itself, the textual-ritual body of Judaism* (seen as a cultural identity or as one particular formalization of the imaginary), where this body would have (long since) come to function as the supplement of the Land of Israel (and of the Temple within it) under conditions of sustained exilic dispersion.[18] Florentin is thus a figure for the Jew who has become so Jewish that he or she is no longer Jewish, the figure that has become so radically figural it is no longer properly speaking figural at all (because it is no longer oriented toward an original literality of sense), the improper and derivative use of language that has become so radically improper and derivative it can no longer be measured against the proper. He is a figure for the figural letter that has become so independent of its literal spiritual meaning that it is almost but not quite self-sufficiently literal again. It is pure dissemination.[19]

But his "literal" (and vexed) relation with Catholicism and his "identity" as the one who is without assured identity, origin, or end, are not the only aspects of his determination that confer upon Florentin this status of "figural Judaism" that we are reading here as a hyperfigurality—and thus also an exacerbation of exile—located somewhere in the abyssal space between figurality and literality, Judaism and Christianity, "properly socalled." What further confers, but also complicates, this status is a certain set of traces of Florentin's *literary precursors* inscribed in his situation.[20]

These traces complicate Florentin's religio-cultural status because they make him not only figurally Jewish but also figurally Christian and thus unsettle further the oppositions Florentin is supposed to mediate between or evade. What traces do I have in "mind"?

Insofar as the text begins with his sudden, unexpected, and unintentional arrival on the scene to save the day, Florentin is a strikingly close relative of two characters in Lessing's plays. As has not been sufficiently emphasized in the literature on *Florentin* (because source studies have tended to focus on Goethe and the Romantics), these characters (and these plays in general) form important biographico-textual backgrounds to Veit's novel. The characters are themselves particular tropes on the figure of the Romantic hero of longing, whose longing here becomes an ethico-theological longing for the overcoming of reified religio-cultural distinctions. The first of these characters is the Jewish hero—the (anonymous) "Traveller"—in Lessing's play, *The Jews* (1749), who saves the Baron[21] at the outset from two robbers (the equivalent of the wild sow at the outset of *Florentin*) and then goes on to become—almost—the prospective husband of the Baron's daughter, an eventuality which becomes unthinkable when it is revealed that he is a Jew. The second of these characters is the Knight of the Templar Order in *Nathan the Wise* (1779), who—as I mentioned in Chapter 4 in terms of Friedrich Schlegel's evident identification with this character—saves Nathan the Jew's stepdaughter, Recha, at the outset from a fire that has engulfed their house in flames and then goes on to become— almost—her prospective husband, until it is revealed at the last minute that he is her (Christian) brother.[22] In the function of ironic savior, who tends to replace what he is there to return to its place, that is, savior as supplement, Florentin replaces both Lessing's traveling Jew and Lessing's errant Knight.[23] Replacing them, he saves them in turn. Because the one who saves and thereby displaces the Father is, for Christianity, Judaism, and for Judaism, Christianity, in each case the symbolic order of the one lending support to and undermining the symbolic order of the other, the passage of Lessing's dramatic development from the Jewish "Traveller" to the Templar Knight is a logical one. By resembling at once Christian Templar and Jewish Traveller, Florentin is drawn into the orbits of both of their religious identities at once, an elliptical orbit, which leaves him figuratively-analogically related to both.[24] Finally, because the ambiguity of Florentin's position as "savior" of father or daughter is enhanced by these implicit allusions to both "salvations" in Lessing's plays—so that Recha and the Baron become conflated and thus reinforce the conflation of Schwarzenberg and Juliane, Mendelssohn and Dorothea—these allusions lead us on from the (theopolitical) question of the religio-cultural (non)identity of Florentin to the (psychopolitical) question of his gender (non)identity.[25]

The Sexual Exacerbation of Secular Exile: Florentin Between Masculine (Will) and Feminine (Inclination)

What in fact are the psychosexual implications of Florentin's intermediate or liminal position between the two rhetorical terms—figural and literal—around which the rhetoric of cultural dialogue turns? In other words, how does this rhetorical position translate at once into the facultative determinations of the soul that are at stake in Veit's novel and into the gender determinations of the (sexed) psyche that correspond to these facultative determinations? And what is the historically situated sexual politics implied by the psychology of facultative and gender determinations in Veit's novel? Let us begin with the latter, more "worldly" question, in order to approach the former, more "theoretical" one.

Dorothea's novel comprises, in part, and like many other literary texts of the period, a critical study of the use of women as means to familial alliances in Veit's day.[26] Especially among the wealthy Jewish families (which were needless to say by far the minority of Jewish families) and the aristocratic Christian ones they aspired to imitate, young women were often exploited by being married off apparently before they were ready to know or to declare their "own" desires. Companionate marriages were not yet, for these privileged social groups in particular, the order of the day. In Lacanian terms, Veit's novel is a study—obviously strongly colored by Veit's own biography—of the subordination of the young girl to the Name of the Father, first the Name of her own Father, then the Name of the Father of her husband, the Father her husband also is (or is "supposed" to represent, as happens for example when the title page of *Florentin* indicates that it is "herausgegeben von Friedrich Schlegel").[27] To translate these psychoanalytic terms into rhetorical ones, the novel is a study of the ideological mechanisms of the control of the imaginary (or *figural*) order by means of the symbolic (or *literal*) order seen as its mastering frame. Within this relationship between imaginary or figural (here of course also the feminine, the daughter) and the symbolic or literal (the Father and Fiancé), I will try to show that Florentin is inscribed as the one whose presence recalls the inter-rupted or broken character of the closure of patriarchal-familial power. More precisely, Florentin plays the role of a kind of nonimaginary anti-symbolic order, a meteoric fragment of what Lacan called the "Real." (In modal terms, as suggested in the Introduction above, one would say he rep-resents the "necessary" and "impossible.") He signifies what exceeds both the (literal) order of the signifier as *nom-du-père* and the (figural) order of imaginary disfiguration that can be said to underlie and constitutively undermine the grammatological order of the signifier (or again, *langue* as social law). How does the literal-figural, symbolico-imaginary field project itself as gender identity in this novel, then, and where does Florentin fit in?

It is above all the parental couple, Count Schwarzenberg and his wife, Eleonore, who provide the positive models of masculine and feminine in the novel. This becomes quite explicit without delay on Florentin's first day in their household. Veit's narrator takes as its starting point the Schillerian version of gender identity as developed for example in "Über Anmut und Würde" ("On Grace and Dignity"). Focalizing through Florentin, the third-person narrator describes the house of the Schwarzen-bergs, as Florentin first perceives it, in precisely such terms: "As it were the serious will [*der ernste Wille*] of the man, softened by the more pleasant inclinations [*die gefälligere Neigung*] of the woman of the house" (17). Or as Schwarzenberg puts it: "The man is concerned with war, in peacetimes with hunting, while the house and the *internal* economy belong to the woman" (19–20; emphasis added). Masculine duty or will and feminine inclination combine in this household to produce an impression that is "anmutig," graceful. Veit thus tilts the Schillerian ideal of a combination of feminine grace and masculine dignity lightly (gracefully) in the direction of feminine grace.[28] The feminine, as (the) nontotality (of essentially dis-tracted inclination, or *Neigung*), "totalizes" totalization (of will) and non-totalization. In the case of the Schwarzenbergs the man helps his wife at home and learns from her about the domestic space, just as the woman has joined her husband, who is a General, in war, and shared with him the per-ils of struggle on the political outside. In a socially acceptable version of Friedrich Schlegel's "Dithyrambic Fantasy about the Most Beautiful Situation," the genders combine to produce a higher, androgynous (albeit nominally feminine) unity. This androgynous (yet feminine) unity is not, however, the conjunctive unity of a metaphorical identification but the dis-junctive unity of a metonymical juxtaposition.

The disjunctive character of the synthesis becomes explicit when the novel concretizes the principles for which the Schwarzenbergs stand as man and woman, in the form of their different tastes in questions of interior design. Their positions on interior design turn out to diverge in accordance with the historical categories of ancient and modern, categories which in this case mean as much as "medieval" and "postmedieval." Florentin says to Eduard on the first morning of his stay at their castle: "This castle is an excellent monument of its century; it makes me happy to see it so well preserved and so utterly without any modern additions. This surprises me all the more as the rest of the furnishings in general are, in accordance with today's taste, elegant and delicate, rather than rich and costly as in the old days" (26). In response, Eduard informs him that the Count prefers "to retain in its original form that which testifies to the age of his family" (26), whereas his wife prefers the modern. The one prefers a heavy richness, the other a light elegance. Each respects the other's taste, and so the two are combined.

But this combination does not amount to an identity nor to a seamless and easy harmony: "Those who have not had an opportunity to get to know the inner realm [*das Innere*] here find it strange, and take the liberty to mock the mixture [*das Gemisch*] of archaic and modern taste. . . . But he who knows humanity will soon discover the harmony in these apparent dissimilitudes [*das Übereinstimmende in diesen anscheinenden Ungleichheiten*]" (27). The Romantic notion of *mixture* thus takes the form here of the relationship—"peacefully juxtaposed [*friedlich nebeneinander*]" (27)— of old and new. But this relationship is also a nonrelationship, a relationship reminiscent of Lacan's strikingly categorical and (yet) enigmatically suggestive formula for the nonrelationship between the sexes: *il n'y a pas de rapport sexuel.* Masculine metaphoric literalism (as *unity* with past traditions) and feminine metonymic figuralism (as modernizing *detachment* from the past) meet here only insofar as they diverge.[29] The tensions of nonrelation between Eduard and Juliane—tensions which comprise precisely "das Innere" of this family whose feminizing harmonization as the metaphor *of* metonymy can only occur by means of the denial of its bigendered and therefore always both metaphorical *and* metonymical character—will gradually reveal this disjunctive character of the symbolico-imaginary synthesis, but not without the help of Florentin, at least as an instrument of explication and recall.

Indeed, how does Florentin function here? Where does he fit into this model of gender identity? Does he represent will or inclination, continuity and pastness or discontinuity and futurity, metaphor and metonymy? Clearly, in *his* case more than elsewhere, these decisions are not easy to make. He is always loyal to his friends and heroically conscious of his duty, but at the same time he is frivolous and fanciful, irresponsible, impulsive, and hedonistic. Likewise, he is drifting around the world in search of his roots. In this sense, he is attached to the past, but since he has no idea where his roots are, he is radically detached from the past, even if he also carries it within himself: he is all futurity, even going so far as to say to Count Schwarzenberg that his Fatherland will be the land in which, one day, he becomes a father.[30] Florentin is thus *neither masculine nor feminine and both*, in terms of the way the novel characterizes these gender positions. He embodies—or he suffers his identification with—the impossible relation of those terms between which there is no relation. This enables him to function as a disruption or provocation of the system, which is a system of the regulated interplay of these positions, although to function in this way is also for him an exclusion and a disablement.[31] He cannot supplement the woman's *Neigung* with his *Wille*, because he has too much *Neigung* of his own, as it were. Nor can he turn his *Neigung* in the direction of the men, although Eduard seems at times to want this very much (and Juliane even becomes jealous, or at least claims she is, shortly before her marriage), because he has too much *Wille* and *Pflichtbewußtsein* for things to be able to go in that direction. Thus, when Florentin arrives on the scene at the Schwarzenbergs' he arrives like the return of what the symbolico-imaginary system has had to exclude in order to constitute itself in the first place as a system of identities in interplay. He returns as the (Lacanian) Real in the sense of the combination *in one place* of the two gender principles whose interplay only enters into the system on condition that, at the outset and in the final analysis (within the system), each principle can be assigned to only one of the individuals in any given (dual) interaction.

But let us not forget that the psychological instances of masculine will and feminine inclination correspond to ontorhetorical poles and thus to ontorhetorical attitudes. In terms of such attitudes, the "masculine" desire of a unity with past traditions corresponds to *literalism*. Count Schwarzenberg wanted "nothing [to] be moved from its place, and nothing still left over from the old days [to] be given a new shape" (26–27). In contrast, the "feminine" break with traditional furnishings concretizes as a psychosexual identity what one can call an attitude of *figuralism* in the sense that it affirms discontinuity (loss of the old, gain of the new, without exchange) as a form of translatability literalism denies. Florentin's "impossible" and "necessary" position split between the masculine, the external *reality* of war and the hunt, and feminine, the internal *potentiality* of home as source, develops, finally, in a psychosexual register his "impossible" and "necessary" position split between literalness and figurality.

What is the appropriate *world* for such a subject? In what world does such a subject live? Will this world be seen as a literal ground against which the figure of the subject stands out? Or will it be construed as the mere prefiguration or figural falling off from an ultimate and originary literality of the subject? If, as is to be expected given how we have been reading *Florentin* so far, it is neither, then how will Veit manage to delimit the world in this way?

The End of the Novel, the End of the World: Between the (Literal) Totality of the "Story" and the (Figural) Infinity of the "True"

The world in which Florentin lives, of course, is the world of the novel, *Florentin*. One can anticipate, then, that the delimitations of this world will depend on the delimitations of the novel, that the novel's discourse on its own limits—wherever such a discourse might be situated—will speak of the limits of the world (the world in which the novel finds itself, the world from which it cuts itself off, or the world it imaginarily constitutes). One can hypothesize that the genre theory that governs the production of the novel will implicitly presuppose and therefore explicitly, if perhaps partially, state a kind of cosmology, a theory of the world. How, then, does this novel determine its own closure or lack thereof? And what are the implications of this determination for the delimitation of "world" the novel implies?

To take as our point of departure the question of the novel's sense of its own (in this case, *lack* of an) ending: in the posthumously published notes for a dedication of the novel to the editor (Friedrich Schlegel), Veit attempts to justify her failure to round off (the world of) her novel in some sort of "satisfying" way.[32] In order to accomplish this self-justification, she is compelled to indicate, if only fragmentarily, the way in which the compositional passage from the idea for a work to the finished work is conventionally understood, and to differentiate herself from this conventional understanding (which to some extent she also attributes to Friedrich Schlegel, her ostensible or perhaps real interlocutor). Since her understanding of the passage from idea to work turns out itself to be another conventional understanding, she is, in effect, playing off two conventional understandings against one another.

The one who now left me no peace [*keine Ruhe*] until I had expressly completed [the story], according to the ways of the world, was you, and I humbly obeyed; for it certainly was not my will. For me, in my way, while I still carried it around with me in secret, and silently developed it, now in this way, now in that, and while my phantasy, hindered by nothing real, bothered by none of those things that get in one's way in the world, mixed in with it all manner of lovely little bright things . . . it was more complete than now, when I see that I have achieved so little of what I actually intended, and my little images appear even to me as utterly foreign. . . . I always thought I was writing exactly what I was in the process of thinking, but it was an illusion; up in front of my pen the correct word hovered; back behind it stood then quite different words I could no longer recognize, like when someone wants to grasp a ball of mercury between his fingers . . . until they have become mere parts and he cannot rediscover the whole. . . . It seemed to me as if I had to ask myself what a *satisfying conclusion* might be. What appears so to most people does not appear so to me. Alas, out there in reality, in certainty, that's where all melancholy and all dissatisfaction begin. My reality and my satisfaction lie in longing and expectation [*Meine Wirklichkeit und meine Befriedigung liegt in der Sehnsucht und in der Ahndung*].[33]

On the basis of this passage, let us attempt to schematize, in ontorhetorical terms, the conventional understanding of the compositional process against which Veit is objecting here and then to determine to what position her objection to this conventional understanding must lead. According to what she considers to be the conventional, commonsense understanding, insofar as we can reconstruct it on the basis of Veit's indications, the compositional process consists in two phases—the phase of composition (or becoming or writing) per se, and the phase of the existence (or being or being-read) of the work—phases between which the momentary passage is the composition of the *end* of the work itself. For each of these phases, a different ontorhetoric reigns.

For the phase of composition, common sense invokes a variant of what we have determined above (see the Introduction, as well as Chapter 2) as the ontorhetoric of empiricism: the *idea* of the work is determined as *figural* possibility or anticipation, whereas the written *realization* of the work in the world is determined as *literal*, and thus as the proper, the origin to be returned to. Once the final touches have been applied to the work, however, it is as if common sense suddenly shifted to the ontorhetoric of rationalism. The *realized*, written work is now (in being read) the mere *figural* anticipation and possibility, while the *ideal* existence of the world figured by the work is now its *literal* heightened reality, precisely its world. Prior to composition, literal worldliness is on the side of the material or the real, while subsequent to composition literal worldliness is on the side of the spiritual or the ideal. The place of the turning from one ontorhetorical model to another is the critical site of the ending, the finishing touch. How can we now situate Veit's position with relation to this conventional, commonsense understanding?

By insisting that the idea is more "real" than the realized work, and that the process of composition is more "worklike" than the work itself, Veit does not simply reverse the positions of the terms reality and ideality. Beyond this, she reverses and displaces by implication the entire conventional understanding of the compositional process, which, as we have just sketched it, is simply mobilized or brought into motion but not quite exhausted by the punctual assumption that the ideal is in fact less real than the real. Thus, when Veit reverses the values of ideal and real, the domino effect of implications that follows upon this gesture produces the following: in the compositional process, the idea (or phantasy or imagining) with which one begins is the literal truth, whereas the realization or writing down of the idea in the world is a figuralization of this truth that is at once a falling away. In turn, once the composition has been finished, the written work (in being read) is not the mere (self-effacing) prefiguration of an ideal world in the reader's imagination through which this prefiguration would be fulfilled, but rather the written work (in its very unreadability) is the literal reality, the dead materiality of language to which the apparent effects of meaning are ultimately reducible and by which these apparent effects of meaning are generated and led astray. Veit thus reverses what we have been calling the conventional, commonsense understanding of the passage from composition to work, invoking the ontorhetoric of rationalism for the process of composition, the becoming of the work, while she invokes the ontorhetoric of empiricism for the work itself (in its being read). But clearly, what she claims to be her "own" understanding here is itself also conventional, and so she should be seen as reversing one conventional understanding by means of another one.[34]

To what does this reversal lead? Is the understanding that privileges the finished work simply being scrapped for the one Veit claims as her own? The mere fact that Veit still writes the novel at all—that she strives for some degree of externalization and realization—argues against such a hypothesis. Is Veit, then, simply criticizing the conventional understanding in *theory* while leaving it intact in *practice*? The fact that Veit does not finish her novel, but rather leaves it in fragmentary disarray, ending the work in the middle of the process of its composition and yet continuing to work on its extension after it is over without ever finishing the sequel, argues against this alternative exaggeration. Apparently, Veit's reversal of the conventional understanding *adds itself* to that understanding, leaving Veit's novel poised— impossibly—on the edge of the writing and the reading of the work, and thus also on the edge between two opposed models of the writing and the reading of the work, on the edge of the failure of the work to be finished, on the one hand, and the finishing of that failure, on the other. Because the novel is a microcosm, this teetering poise of the novel on the abyssal edge of itself counts also for the world henceforth on edge.

Veit supports her fragmentary aesthetico-cosmology of the novel by illustrating it with a figure drawn from the (properly improper) worlds of childhood and femininity. Brief consideration of this figure will help clarify the sense of Veit's preference for the unfinished as a preference for the endless finishing of the unfinished. That is, it will help clarify the sense of Veit's position on the edge between infinity (or the unfinished) and totality (its finishing off).[35] The figure she develops here is an analogy between a doll and its clothing and the work and its ending.

I'm like one of those little girls who would rather play with a naked doll's body that they can dress up differently every hour, in order to give it a completely changed form [*eine ganz verschiedene Gestalt*], than play with the most gloriously and perfectly clothed doll onto which the pieces of clothing, and thereby forever its completed destiny [*ihre vollendete Bestimmung*], have been sewn.[36]

A doll without clothing is better—not, of course, insofar as it remains without clothing, but because it can be dressed up in an infinite number of outfits without any one of them being the last, without any one of them becoming the doll's own and only outfit. Just so, a work without ending is better not because it remains completely without end, but because it is and is not without end. It never has an end that sticks, but every reading gives it an end. This endlessness of ending (assuming a potential infinity of readings) is indeed the only thing that could prevent the work from having an end, for as soon as it had no end at all it would end precisely at the limit where its absent end began.[37] Further, as the only endlessness there is, the endlessness of ending ensures that *both* models of the passage from idea to finished work will be endlessly interrupted, even as they are endlessly put into effect.[38] The fragmentary text thus remains endlessly suspended between its reading and its writing.

Such a suspension has an important advantage over supposedly closed texts: it makes explicit the (impossible) structure of the rhetoric of hermeneutics on which the rhetoric of cultural dialogue is based, quite simply the structure of the "either me or you and not both." The text that lacks an end functions like a parody of the text that lacks an interpretation. If I must give your text an ending, then I can hardly forget that I have had some part in producing the resultant whole, and I can therefore only with difficulty claim that the text I've produced is yours, which is precisely the moment when violence (incessantly) enters into the rhetoric of hermeneutic dialogue. Veit's aesthetico-cosmology of the fragmentary turns this violence into play by placing it in the position of having to become a parody of itself—now adding not merely meaning but part of the story as well. Veit's suspension of the epistemological pseudovalidity of understanding thus provides the sketch not only of an aesthetico-cosmology but also of a theory of communication, insofar as the unfinished novel is an example of the unfinished message in general.

Veit does not content herself with an apology for her failure to finish her novel. She goes on to consider the specific kinds of endings that count as satisfying to those who are in favor of (satisfying) endings and to argue that such endings are not only unenjoyable but impossible.

Usually . . . the only kind of novelistic closure that one finds satisfying is the kind where the most interesting character gets either married or buried, and people will complain that they are not completely satisfied here [*zur völligen Ruhe kommt*] in either of these two ways. How you will judge of this, I am curious to hear; as far as I am concerned, however, I must admit that I am never completely satisfied [*nie ganz beruhigt*] when the poet leaves nothing for me to think out or to dream out for myself. . . . I ask again: What ought to have become of this man you call the hero? Married? Can we be satisfied by that? Do we not see in the cases of Eduard and Juliane that often that is where all suffering and all confusion just begin? Death! Yes, that would really be an ending of a novel by which we would have to be satisfied. But here I must repeat my complaint and my regret that this book has been called a novel, and not, as it really is, a true story. (158)

The two main endings of novels, Veit argues, at once amusingly and plausibly, are the marriages and the deaths of their heroes. In marriage, identity is achieved between the hero and his beloved as a figure of his world, whereas in death, absolute difference supervenes. The ending of a novel occurs, then, as the achievement of absolute identity or absolute (and absolutely self-identical) difference, metaphor or metonymy, as the purely literal (the metaphorically self-same), or as the purely figural (the metonymicity of a substitution that combines separate terms across an unbridged distance). At the end of the novel, Florentin neither marries nor dies, he is simply nowhere to be found, which is neither here nor there. And Veit argues that his marriage would not, in any case, have meant the end of his struggles, for—as we see in the examples of Eduard and Juliane (and as Veit both recalls from her marriage with Simon Veit and doubtless foresees for her marriage with Schlegel)—to get married is by no means to find one's proper meaning, to be metaphorically united with one's world without remainder and thus finally to have a world one can call one's own.[39] Nor could Florentin's death have meant the consummation or crowning of his struggles, but merely their interruption, because death is the *end* of the search for meaning, not the *attainment* of meaning itself; it is the end of world, not world as end or end as world. It is not the achievement of the self-identity of absolute difference, but the event of something assimilable as neither identity nor difference. The only conventionally sanctioned endings of novels could not have been plausibly employed in Veit's novel for the simple reason that they are always implausible.

Thus it is that Veit calls her novel a "true story." It does not lie about its failure to attain its closure, the final totalization of its "hero" as the coming into being of its henceforth total "world." As its readers have unanimously remarked and generally complained, any number of potential analogies and familial relationships between characters remain suspended somewhere between identity and difference, metaphor and metonymy.[40] The fact that *Florentin* is not called a "true story," but rather a "novel" is for this reason ironically *appropriate* to its truth. This truth is the truth of the impossibility of properly naming oneself (or another) with one's proper (or another's proper) name, the impossibility of being one with and through the world of names one finds and is called upon to read.

The world of Florentin is neither infinite nor total, neither open nor closed, neither given in fact nor suspended in pure possibility; it is fragmentary.[41] It is given, yet remains suspended in its eventual sense; and it breaks off, yet insists on continuing; it is totalized, yet as a mere piece of itself toward which it continues to strive. Thus, if Florentin neither dies nor marries at the end of the "true story," if he finds his proper meaning neither in the unity with another nor in the disengagement from himself, if he finds his proper meaning neither in pure unity nor in pure disunity,[42] he is in another sense, a sense perhaps a bit more obviously "figurative," *marrying and dying continuously* throughout the "novel."[43] This "novel" would be a "true story"—a true fiction or fictional truth—that is constantly ending and beginning again, constantly undoing both fiction and truth through the living-dying of its "hero"[44] and constantly resuming again only to undo itself in turn, like Penelope's tapestry in an eternal expectation of an absent Ulysses with whom *this* Penelope would also be identical.

□□

For me, therefore, the book is here at its end, for Florentin's influence did not reach any further than this. For the rest, of course, we know that he in fact no longer played with the serious, but truly realized his decision, that which, as far as he was concerned, was his fate: rejecting the refinements and advantages of culture, he returned to his beloved primitives. He was the principal leader of an entire nation that honored him as a divinity. Once more the family saw him on their estates as the emissary of his people, and he returned again when they tried to move him to stay. Since then we know nothing more of him. He may still be alive, telling his grandchildren about the miracles that bring unhappiness and the brilliant abjection [*die unglück-bringenden Wunder und das glänzende Elend*] of the Europeans. (158–59)

After she has indicated that her novel has no end and that it must (continue to) end in order not to have an end, Veit respects the rigor of her own thought, consents momentarily to function as her own first reader, and gives her novel—in spite and because of everything—a hypothetical ending beyond its ending. "The reason why one cannot tell what happened next," she tells us, "is because this is what happened next. . . ." But what happened next? What turns out to be the external limit of Florentin's existence, the place where his story must stop because he is no longer himself?

This limit—the limit of the limit—is the *relapse* into the naïve figure-fulfillment model whose immanent interruption Florentin has "figured" all along. By no longer playing with what is serious, but actually realizing his decision as his fate (his subjectivity as his objectivity, or the two synthesized into one overarching necessity), Florentin *renounces* his position *between* seriousness and nonseriousness (as, for example, philosophy and rhetoric), *between* realization and its prefiguration as possibility. From the textual fact that Florentin "returned" to the "primitives" and became their "principal leader"—functioning as fulfilling ground of their prefigurative anticipation—we can infer that the "refinements" of culture Florentin rejects (à la Rousseau) are here the duplicities of the undecidable that he has been hitherto living out. Accordingly, the rejection of the "miracles that bring unhappiness and the brilliant abjection of the Europeans" sounds the note of a cultural pessimism that posits its own unity with the figures of nature as their totalizing meaning. For not only is Florentin now the leader but further *he* is the one who tells *them*, "his beloved primitives," that they have it better than the Europeans who languish in a dangerously contagious undecidability. Florentin is a colonist from the world of undecidability, occupying what is ostensibly the world of the figural and claiming to be an emissary from the immanent-transcendent Land of *Aufhebung*. That is, he is a colonist who, in the position of the literal possibility of spirit, has come to fulfill the merely figural reality of the "primitive," their natural gift, their being as matter with the potential for potential (yet as matter nonetheless).

But who are the "primitives" more specifically? Indians, of course, American Indians to be more precise (Florentin has said at the novel's outset that he meant to go help the colonies against the English oppressor). That is, they are European colonists in America qua Native Americans qua Indians. Further, because these American Indians occupy, for post-*Florentin* Florentin, the place of prefiguration which, for Christian Europe, had belonged to the Jews, they are so to speak *Jewish* American Indians. Thus, beyond the end, vacating the position of the undecidable limit between prefiguration and fulfillment, letter and spirit, Florentin goes off to become the fulfilling spirit of the "Indians" (themselves New World avatars of their pre-Old World origins), who are here, from the standpoint of Florentin, being conflated with the Jews and determined as the legitimate subject-objects of their own self-colonization. This development strikingly anticipates or "prefigures" Friedrich Schlegel's own. In the next few years, he will turn increasingly to the study of the "Indians"—this time, the ancient Eastern ones—who will come by 1808 to prefigure the "stable" Judaeo-Christian, figural-literal synthesis Schlegel already firmly situates in the Catholic Middle Ages, henceforth to be restored. Elsewhere, I have examined in detail this "fulfillment" of Veit's "prefiguration" of the relapse from critical undecidability. Here, I will look not at a text from the moment of "literal" conversion but at one from the phase of Schlegel's reorientation, a crucially transitional text, the commentaries on Lessing that Schlegel wrote to introduce the various sections of the Lessing anthology he edited in 1804, entitled *Lessings Gedanken und Meinungen*. This will allow us to see how, as he turns toward Catholicism, Schlegel attempts to justify this turn, as he had attempted to justify the fragmentary and hybrid socioaesthetics of the *Athenäum* period, by showing it to be a necessary consequence or realization of Lessing's authoritative prefiguration.

Protestant Negativity as "Prefiguration" of Neo-Catholic Positivity in Friedrich Schlegel's 'Lessing's Thoughts and Opinions' (1804)

The distance between Schlegel's essay "On Lessing" of 1797 (along with its "Conclusion" of 1801) and the longer, though fragmentary group of texts accompanying the anthology of Lessing texts that Schlegel edited in 1804 is bridged by two very important common traits. The bridge is drawn asunder or exploded, however, by two crucial differences.[1] As for the *continuities*: first, Schlegel still attempts in 1804 to read Lessing's project as a prefigurative justification of his *own*; second, he still situates Lessing's exemplary character in the opposition to the apparently paradoxical return of the repressed letter within the theopolitical symptomatology, as it were, of Protestant orthodoxy.

The rather drastic *differences* between the earlier Lessing texts and the later ones are as follows. First, Schlegel now goes so far as *to reverse* Lessing's radicalization of the Protestant dissolution of positive religion, turning this radicalization into a proto-Neo-Catholic turn back toward the pre-Reformation church. In these later texts, the Catholic Church is already beginning to appear as the solution to the problem of the relation between letter and spirit,[2] and Lessing is being presented as the one who initiated the discovery of this solution. In stark contrast, as one will recall from Chapter 3, Schlegel argued in "On Lessing" with reference to *Nathan* that, if anything, Lessing's strewing of the centrality of the one authoritative church did not go quite far enough. Second, Schlegel now no longer reads Lessing's fragmentary forms as a quasi-secular middle ground between works and faith (as in "On Lessing"), nor even as an anticipation of the total work of art (as in the "Conclusion" of 1801). Rather, he reads them as forms that due to their radical dialogicity serve as the appropriate vehicle for the movement of human reason on the properly regressive and self-negating path of its return to the one transcendent revelation, the revelation on which, he now thinks, the medieval European order was rightly founded long ago.

Lessing's Thoughts and Opinions marks the turning point, in Schlegel's religio-cultural development, from the pantheistically and aesthetically inflected secularized (post-)Protestantism of his work leading up to the "Athenäum" (and also up to his early erotic alliance with Dorothea Mendelssohn-Veit) to the Neo-Catholicism of his later phase. He will speak out increasingly boldly in favor of this Neo-Catholicism as he approaches his and Dorothea's conversion of 1808. In order to begin to see how, during the process of his gradual conversion, Schlegel formulates his Neo-Catholic ideology in terms of a rereading of Lessing, let us consider the essay Schlegel situates toward the end of the anthology of *Lessing's Thoughts and Opinions*, entitled "On the Character of the Protestants" ("Vom Charakter der Protestanten").

From Protestantism to Catholicism: Spirit as 'Polemos'

In this essay, which functions in the anthology as an introduction to the section that includes *The Education of the Human Race, Ernst and Falk*, and *Nathan the Wise*, Schlegel begins by positing that Lessing is an exemplary Protestant. In his attempt to explain what this means, he situates the essence of Protestantism in polemic. "Polemic [*Polemik*] is essential to all Protestants, to all those who fight error, indeed their whole character is enclosed in this concept. Polemic is the principle of all their striving and the form of all their effectivity [*alles ihres Wirkens*]. . . . polemic and the spirit of Protestantism are utterly one and the same."[3] The spirit of Protestantism, then, the very spirituality of spirit, resides in polemic.[4] And polemic, Schlegel goes on to say, resides in negativity. In order to clarify what Protestantism as polemical negativity is all about, Schlegel invokes the opposition between Catholicism and Protestantism, which he develops as an opposition between "positive" and "negative" religion.

Schlegel associates "positive" religion (Catholicism) with poetry and "negative" religion (Protestantism) with philosophy, pointing out that even in the ancient Greeks this double tradition can be found. The poetic tradition affirms "the form of allegory and the pious belief in the old fables." The philosophical tradition, in contrast, opposes "the old belief and the slag that is indeed bound up with it," and is characterized by an "unconditional rejection [*unbedingtes Verwerfen*] of this belief, which is often even extended to all imagery and allegory [*auf alle Sinnbildlichkeit und Allegorie*]." "Catholicism is poetical religion, Protestantism the religion of philosophy."[5]

As will already be evident, in addition to the Greek correspondences Schlegel makes explicit, this opposition implicitly replays, within the Christian tradition, the opposition traditionally posited by Christianity between Judaic letter and Christian spirit. But as may not be so immediately evident, it replays that opposition in a reversible or undecidable way. Insofar as it is opposed to rhetorical figures, such as allegory, Protestantism or negative religion is anti-Jewish; by comparison, Catholicism or positive religion, siding with "allegory" and "old fables," is positively Jewish. But insofar as it is opposed to images per se ("Sinnbildlichkeit"), Protestantism is aligned with Jewish, monotheistic radicalism; in contrast, Catholicism, with its affirmation of images, appears as either pagan or quintessentially Christian, but in any case not as Jewish.

The undecidability of these alignments, however, is simply a manifestation of the more important undecidability of each of the binary oppositions involved. Why is the opposition between negative and positive religion undecidable? How, for example, does the structure of Protestantism, since Protestantism is Schlegel's theme here, ensure that it encloses its other within itself? As we saw already in "On Lessing"—even though there Schlegel did not quite explicitly determine Protestantism as polemicism—Protestantism only remains itself insofar as it never halts the movement of its essential contempt for the letter (where the letter is conceived as the bad aspect of self-identity, the nonidentity of identity). If it stops undoing and exceeding itself, then it fails to remain itself and becomes "literally" its own enemy. Protestantism must always go beyond itself to become itself (anew), spirit must always go beyond itself (i.e., its literal self or lettered self) and become (or at least allow for) letter in order to maintain itself as spirit.[6] Its tendency to become (the) letter (of antiliterality) must be countered by a more radical spirituality, that is, by its paradoxical willingness to become letter.[7] Thus, "True polemic is infinite, steadily progressive in all directions."[8] Like Romantic poetry (according to the famous *Athenäum* fragment 116), true polemicism only attains to itself in going beyond itself.

How does Lessing exemplify or illustrate the polemical essence of Protestant spirit? Being a true Protestant, Lessing goes beyond the point where most (bad) Protestants stop. He goes beyond the letter of a dogmatic faith that belies the spirit of Protestantism. That is, he goes beyond Protestantism itself.

[Lessing] was precisely a good Protestant because he did not insist rigidly on the doctrinal propositions [*Glaubenssätzen*] of the Protestants, but maintained instead the old maxims of freedom and in this way wanted to enliven the spirit of Protestantism anew [*den Geist des Protestantismus von neuem beleben wollte*].

This is why he struggled so energetically against that which is only letter [*Buchstabe*] in the doctrine [*Lehre*] of the Protestants, and against the all too crude and bodily way [*die allzugrobe und körperliche Art*] in which they understand and apply to the Holy Scriptures the concept of the eternal, ubiquitous word of God; and even defends, on the contrary, the Catholic rule of belief according to ancestral tradition and the agreement of the best in the community. (87)

Lessing is such a good Protestant that he goes beyond its letter, namely, the excessive dissolution of the letter with which it dogmatically contents itself.[9] But whereas in "On Lessing" this only meant that Lessing read Luther in terms of Luther's principles, according to the "spirit" (as problematic as that was), now it means *Lessing is such a good Protestant that he verges upon becoming a Catholic.* He is so firmly devoted to "spirit" that he rebels against the "letter" (or "law") against "letter" (and "law") to affirm the "letter" (or "law") of a "rule" ("Regel") of belief that is not simply belief itself.[10]

Moreover, to the degree that Catholicism appears, from a German Protestant perspective, like a kind of Christian Judaism, one should not be surprised to see Schlegel proceed to indicate that *Lessing also verges upon becoming a Jew—and (associatively) hence also a Moslem or a Spinozist*:

The true Protestant must also protest against Protestantism itself, whenever it wants to reverse itself into a new Pope-dom and letteredness [*neues Papsttum und Buchstabenwesen*]. . . . For this reason the Protestant, along with Lessing, out of hatred for the non-genuine and the intolerant aspects of Christianity, can even take into its protection Judaism, praise Mohammedanism and, praying alone before pure reason and pure love along with Spinoza, cast off all sensuous images [*alles Sinnbild verwerfen*].[11]

Taking Protestant spirit literally, Lessing turns against the letter of its dogmatic refusal of all letter, at least provisionally or partially embracing the letter in the forms, for example, of Judaism and Catholicism (as well as Islam) in order to undo the unwitting embrace of the letter that the orthodox Protestant rejection of these religious cultures accidentally constitutes.

This movement of self-excess, however, does not lead to a state of rest, but rather calls forth further movements of self-excess.

All of this is very close to his principles; as long as he has not become indifferent, one may not believe that the religious principle has died within him, nor may one take the transitory crisis of the inner struggle [*die vorübergehende Krisis des innern Kampfes*], before it has been decided, to be the final result and an enduring denial. As long as there is *still something merely negative and finite* [irgend etwas bloß Negatives und Endliches], as long as *not every enveloping veil has been transfigured and thoroughly penetrated by spirit* [noch nicht jede Hülle verklärt und von Geist durchdrungen] and the word of God become all-present, as long as even *the possibility of a dead and dried-out letter* [nur noch die Möglichkeit eines toten und dürren Buchstabens] is present, *the evil principle* [das böse Prinzip] is still in existence, against which to struggle, without rest and without pity, is the high calling of *polemic*; once this has been overcome, then it may be the last duty of polemic *to annihilate itself* [sich selbst zu vernichten]. (88; emphasis added)

Lessing's polemic continues to oppose the letter with which, in order to escape identification with that letter, it has identified itself. Moreover, as Schlegel (perhaps unintentionally) makes clear, in opposing this letter, Lessing's polemic opposes *itself*, for Schlegel now calls the letter "irgend etwas bloß Negatives"—"anything negative at all"—but evidently nothing could be more negative than the principle of negativity itself.[12] Lessing's polemic, indeed polemic in general as the principle of negativity, will be in a position to negate itself only when it has already negated itself ("has been overcome"). Its finitude will have to be, in principle, infinite, even if Schlegel contradicts himself here by envisioning a moment when this finitude will have come to an end.

Yet this contradiction is not an aberrant passage, but rather an indication of where Schlegel is heading. There are already ample signs that in Schlegel's case the endlessness of this polemical dialectic of letter and spirit will shut down a bit early, signs that there is a suicide of mind in store,[13] signs in short that Schlegel is giving up on Protestant spirit and turning to Catholicism (in its pre-Reformation form) as the (phantasmatic) sublation of Protestant and Jewish, spirit and letter in their "purest" or most radical forms. We have already seen a hint of this in Schlegel's reading of Lessing as having embraced Catholic notions of "ancestral tradition." Let us look at one further passage in which such signs appear.

The passage occurs when Schlegel is arguing that, precisely because it must always be going beyond itself in order to maintain itself, Protestantism—spirit as such—is constantly in danger of dissolving into pure nothingness, either by turning into a political, worldly engagement, or by refining itself out of existence. Protestantism has at once too much and too little letter. Its spirit therefore cannot avoid repeatedly deteriorating into two forms of the letter: radical politics, which is tantamount to a certain kind of materialism or literalism; and pure self-dissolving inwardness, which always leads to the mere residue of a dead letter, a body without mind lying inert on the page of history.

According to Schlegel, the only way to fight these two self-negations of spiritual negativity is by pursuing

a third path . . . the only true one, the return to the primitive and positive [*zum Primitiven und Positiven*]. The original [*Das Ursprüngliche*] in all things is certainly the best, and to all innovators, when they—often not wrongly—find that which is old reprehensible, one can say: Just go still further back, and put in place of what is old that which is even older, the oldest and primary [*das Alleralteste und Erste*], and you will certainly find the right and true. . . . Incontrovertibly there was, in Christianity too, an epoch in which it was not yet Catholic or Protestant in the current sense of these words; but both at once, even if Church history were too incomplete to show evidence of this epoch.[14]

Here, Schlegel proposes that we go back to a Catholicism—to a "positivity"—that precedes the Reformation split between Catholic and Protestant, positive and negative, back to a spiritual letter that precedes the splitting apart of spirit and letter. In this way, he believes, one can avoid the twin excesses of Protestantism, the dissipations of spirit either in excessive interiority (the self-dissolution of mind) or in excessive exteriority (radical politics ultimately seen as a kind of "bad" anarchy). But Schlegel's infinitely regressive imperative—"Just go still further back"—cannot stop with medieval Christianity except by an act of arbitrary, dogmatic decision. Why not go back to the ancient Hebrews, and from there to pagan Mesopotamia, and so on? The fact that it stops at this moment makes it fairly clear: what Schlegel seeks here is a synthesis of, a middle ground between, "Judaism" and "Protestantism," the extremes of works and faith, letter and spirit. By stopping at this arbitrarily chosen symbol or figure of such a middle ground, Schlegel's *infinite* regressiveness becomes *finite*, authoritarian reaction. The German Romantic spirit has now become the spirit of German Romantic Neo-Catholicism.

Schlegel thus attempts to make his nascent Neo-Catholicism appear as the realization of Lessing's prefigurative turn away from Protestant literalism to a more rigorous supplementation of the Protestant spirit with the letter of the law. It is a testimony both to Schlegel's fortitude and to his rhetorical force that he manages—against all textual odds—to render somewhat plausible here the notion of Lessing as his precursor: "To have at least begun to move in the direction of this regressive path [*Rückweg*] in religion, which is the only path that can save us from double downfall, indeed to have been perhaps the first amongst the Protestants to move in this direction, this is Lessing's achievement" (89).

Dialogical Negativity in the Service of Monological Positivity: On the Appropriate Form of Polemical Spirit

Having considered the spiritual "content" Schlegel now finds in Lessing, that is, polemical negativity, it is imperative that we examine what Schlegel at this point considers to be the "form" appropriate to this polemical negativity. This will also incidentally provide us with an opportunity to illustrate in a very direct way the titular thesis of the present study. It turns out, conveniently, that this "form," the letter of the spirit's polemic against the letter (of) itself, is "dialogue." Schlegel explicitly invokes "dialogue" as the appropriate form for a philosophical (spiritual) synthesis of spirit and letter, a philosophical synthesis now furthermore subservient to an incipiently Neo-Catholic notion of revelation. He opens his argument for the exemplary character of Lessing's (and by implication also his own) nonsystematic and dialogical form by stressing its superiority to the systematic, monological form of philosophical presentation typified by the works of Fichte. Since he embeds this argument in a textual performance of dialogicity wherein he addresses, in an attitude of partially feigned fawning, Fichte himself, it behooves us to begin by looking at the structure of Schlegel's performance of his dialogue with Fichte here, in order to see what notion of dialogue it generates.[15]

At the outset, *Lessing's Thoughts and Opinions* determines itself as a *dialogical* text to the extent that it opens with a dedicatory section "To Fichte."[16] In the process of justifying this dedication and the dialogicity it brings into play, Schlegel explains why dialogue is the privileged form of philosophy. In doing so, he makes polemical use of the teleological rhetoric of prefiguration and fulfillment that structures the (impossible) dialogue between Jews and Germans we have been tracing.

Schlegel opens "To Fichte" with a contrast between the "philosophical spirit" (46) and "a strictly scientific philosophy" (46). While the former is "in itself incontrovertibly of incalculable value" (46), it needs the latter in order to become real and useful in the world and in order to have the stability it needs in order to endure: "But for the world . . . [the philosophical spirit] can only become properly and enduringly effective and useful when its effects have been secured and grounded by the presence of a strictly scientific philosophy. Otherwise its most beautiful results must soon lose themselves in the general mass and be forgotten" (46). Schlegel positions scientific philosophy here as the realization and completion, the supplementary fulfillment, of the mere philosophical spirit. He goes on to say, "This is the reason why I am dedicating the present attempt to you, honorable friend, rather than to anyone else" (46). On the one hand, Schlegel will speak to Fichte of Lessing in order to honor Fichte with the recognition that Fichte himself is the realization of Lessing's beginning. On the other hand, Fichte's "strictly scientific philosophy" functions here as the formal letter that only secondarily fixes the "philosophical spirit" and, hence, always represents the same danger as writing—the danger of a supplemental materiality (and radical destabilization or debasement) of mind. Schlegel addresses Fichte as the "realization" of the philosophical spirit both in the positive and negative senses. Fichte is the one who literally realizes the potential of that spirit; but he is also the one who debases that which is properly speaking purely ideal by inscribing it in reality (thereby merely re-presenting, as writing, in its absence the presence of speech or belatedly prefiguring the ideality of creative faith in the materiality of a mere system of conceptual law).[17] Since Schlegel's gesture toward Fichte is thus so treacherously ambivalent—so underhandedly polemical—as to induce us to doubt whether we have read him right, it will be worthwhile to see it "realized" once more as the first two pages of "To Fichte" unfold.

Two paragraphs later, Schlegel is still tortuously telling Fichte why he is addressing this text on Lessing "first of all" ("zunächst" [46]) to him because in this way . . . I have an opportunity to reveal my conviction that such miscellanies and fragments of philosophy as Lessing, in an unfavorable and insipid epoch of literature . . . , was able to leave behind only gain their full value when in the same literature that which they lack, or that which they silently presuppose, has finally become present. Only where the first principles of the true, whose discovery or reconstruction the age owes above all to you, have been taught in a strictly scientific method of philosophy, only then are the freer productions and results of the merely natural philosophical spirit in their place.[18]

Again, Schlegel implicitly invokes the ontorhetoric of partial, potential prefiguration and total, real fulfillment, figure and ground, positing Lessing as the (Jewish or Old Testamentary) prefiguration of Fichte, who thus occupies the position of (Christian or New Testamentary) fulfillment. But Schlegel again immediately proceeds to subvert this teleology, going so far as to grant the fragmentariness of the merely "natural" philosophical spirit à la Lessing priority over the fullness of Fichtean systematic rigor.[19]

But these [freer productions of the merely natural philosophical spirit] can never be taken to be superfluous, no matter how clearly the principles of knowledge have been presented, no matter how perfect method has become. For knowledge is, as is well known, not a mere *mechanism*, but it proceeds only from one's own *free thinking*. . . . what good would the fullness of that which has been perhaps already thought by others do if the force of the thinker itself did not become excited and active ever and again? For this is the only way in which this force is capable of appropriating the thoughts of others for itself and drawing some advantage from them. At least on the current level of spiritual development, it can seem neither strange nor superfluous if the friend of philosophy thinks of all imaginable ways . . . of gaining access to the human *spirit* and of *awakening* it finally from its slumbers. *Freer forms* are generally *more effective* in this than the completely *strict method*, because the latter presupposes to be already present that to which almost everyone still needs to be educated.

But hardly any German writings are more appropriate to the task of exciting and educating this *spirit of thinking-for-oneself* [Geist des Selbstdenkens] than Lessing's.[20]

Schlegel here grants to the fragment a greater pedagogical efficacy and a greater freedom than to the systematic whole, an efficiency and freedom which unite the fragment more intimately with spirit than the systematic whole, making the fragment the very spirit of spirit, the awakening force par excellence. He even goes so far as to oppose the awakening power of spirit to philosophical systematicity, as an implicitly organic force to one explicitly called mechanical.[21] In the process, again, Schlegel is also under-handedly and defensively aggressing or insulting—polemicizing against—Fichte, putting Fichte "in his place" as the secondary anticipation not only of Lessing but also, because Schlegel is so strongly identified with Lessing's mode of writing, of Schlegel himself.

In both of these examples, the dialogue between Schlegel and Fichte sets up a dialogue between Lessing—as surrogate for Schlegel—and Fichte, but this latter dialogue represents in turn a dialogue between dialogue and monologue. (As we will see, Schlegel characterizes Lessing explicitly as an eminently dialogical thinker.) Further, this dialogue between (Lessing's) dialogue and (Fichte's) monologue is a *polemic*, in which each term claims the status of spiritual speech in the face of which the other would appear as material writing. As Schlegel presents things, from Fichte's point of view, dialogical fragmentation is the (unachieved) writing of which monological system would be the (achieved) speech. From Lessing's point of view, dialogue is the living speech that systematic monologue only fixes in an inadequate, no longer spiritual form. By arranging this structural polemic in narrative form—first monologue is provisionally privileged in Schlegel's praise of Fichte, and then dialogue wins out in his praise of Lessing—Schlegel presents the appearance of having overcome its—in principle, endless—oscillation. Dialogue appears to be more monological, the splitting of the word more whole, than the monologue of the whole word. But because monologue is exorcised from dialogue in the movement by which dialogue claims to go beyond monologue (claiming to go beyond monologue by virtue of including monologue, its own other, dialogically within itself, whereas the reverse is not the case), dialogue becomes monological in the moment of its triumph over monologue. Dialogue exceeds monologue only in order to become immediately monological in its turn. Fichte's mechanical systematicity is wiped off the map and thus unwittingly reinstated. The surreptitious teleological subservience of dialogue to monologue is at work not only performatively, in Schlegel's polemical address of his Lessing text to Fichte, but also in Schlegel's more explicit theoretical formulations on the superiority of dialogue as appropriate polemical form.

In contrast to the form of systematic philosophy, which represents *mere* letter,[22] according to Schlegel the form of Lessing's text *fulfills* the letter—or so at least it will appear at first—by spiritually combining letter with spirit. This form of Lessing's text, which thus merits being called "the inner form of his thought [*die innere Form seines Denkens*]," is "dialogue" (*Gespräch*).²³ In turn, dialogue is defined as the combination of the characteristics of poetry and prose, art and science, into a higher unity:

> Der Unterschied der Prosa und der Poesie besteht darin, daß die Poesie darstellen, die Prosa nur mitteilen will. Zwar wie überall, so gibt es auch hier für das Entgegengesetzte einen Punkt, wo die Grenzen sich ineinander verlieren. Im Gespräch, im dialogischen Kunstwerke zum Beispiel, ist es eigentlich die gegenseitige Gedankenmitteilung der Redenden, welche selbst der Gegenstand der Darstellung ist.—Dargestellt wird das Unbestimmte, weshalb auch jede Darstellung ein Unendliches ist; mitteilen aber läßt sich nur das Bestimmte. Und nicht das Unbestimmte, sondern das Bestimmte ist es, was alle Wissenschaften suchen. In der höchsten aller Wissenschaften aber, die nicht irgend etwas einzelnes Bestimmtes lehren soll, sondern das Bestimmen selbst überhaupt zu bestimmen hat, ist es eben deswegen nicht hinreichend, das Gedachte schon fertig zu geben. Es will diese Wissenschaft nicht dieses oder jenes Gedachte, sondern das Denken selbst lehren; darum sind ihre Mitteilungen notwendigerweise auch Darstellungen, denn man kann das Denken nicht lehren, außer durch die Tat und das Beispiel, indem man vor jemanden denkt, nicht etwas Gedachtes mitteilt, sondern das Denken in seinem Werden und Entstehen ihm darstellt. Eben darum aber kann der Geist dieser Wissenschaft nur in einem Werke der Kunst vollständig deutlich gemacht werden. (48)

The difference between prose and poetry consists in this, that poetry wants to render present, while prose only wants to impart. As elsewhere, so here there is a point where the borders between opposed terms lose themselves in each other. In dialogue, in the dialogical artwork, for example, the speakers' mutual imparting of thoughts is actually the object of presentation.—The indeterminate is presented, which is why every presentation is an infinite one; only the determinate, however, can be imparted. And not the indeterminate, but the determinate, is what all sciences seek. In the highest of all sciences, however, which should not teach anything determinate in particular, but which should determine determination itself in general, it is thus not adequate to provide the thought already in a finished form. Such science wants to teach not this or that thing that has been thought, but thinking itself; for this reason its imparting is necessarily also presentation, since one cannot teach thinking except through act and example, by thinking in front of someone else, not by imparting a finished thought, but by presenting thinking in its becoming and origination. But for precisely this reason the spirit of science can be made completely clear only in a work of art.

In this rich passage,²⁴ dialogue is determined as the presentation of communication or imparting, as the exemplary performance of constative thought.[25] Presentation (*Darstellung*) is the concretization of an indeterminate abstraction (or feeling), while imparting (*Mitteilung*) is here the universalization of a particular experience so as to enable its shared comprehension by others. In terms of the problematic of spirit and letter, then, poetry (or art) is the passage from spirit to letter, writing as the material presentation of the spirit, while prose (or science) is the spiritualization of materiality, speech or reading aloud as the passage from letter to spirit.[26] Because each of these passages is undecidable, the "realization" of each is their combination into one: the dialogue between two different figures as the mutually positive-negative interplay between principle and performance, spirit and letter. As Schlegel argued in "On Lessing" that *Nathan the Wise* comprised two different—but in each case, philosophically and hence spiritually determined—works, so he argues here that the dialogical moment comprises two discourses, science and art. But these two discourses are tilted in the direction of spirit insofar as what they present in their unity is "determination itself . . . [or] thinking itself." On the other hand, just as, on the level of the performance of the dialogue with Fichte, Lessing's dialogicity paradoxically reinstates monologue insofar as it realizes spirituality, so too, on the level of the theoretical definition of dialogue we have been citing, dialogue reinstates monologue. Here, dialogue reinstates monologue insofar as, in dialogical communication, presentation finally dominates the imparting of communication: "The . . . imparting of thoughts is actually the object of presentation. . . . its imparting is necessarily presentation. . . . not by imparting a finished thought, but by presenting thinking." Where the spirituality of the communication of thought is *presented*, it is as if speech were written down: dialogue—the dialogue of thinking—realizes itself as monologue—the monologue of the letter.

Thus, for Schlegel in the anthology of 1804, Lessing's significance consists in his mastery of both the "content" of polemical "spirituality" and the "formal" "letter" of dialogue, as that formal letter which, by refusing or failing to gain total focus as the expression of merely one discrete thought, ostensibly presents "thinking" itself, the interplay between thought and expression. For Schlegel, Lessing's self-canceling or quasi-formless forms exemplify the letter that effaces itself in order to give way to the pure—polemical—"spirituality" it contains, a "spirituality" that represents in turn the synthesis, on a higher level, of letter and spirit. But as we saw with respect to the figure of *polemic* (in the discussion of "On the Character of the Protestants"), so too we will see with respect to the figure of *dialogue* (in the final section of *Lessing's Thoughts*, "On the Form of Philosophy") that Schlegel not only puts a stop at an arbitrarily determined point to the endless play of negativity but also invokes, as the denegational guarantee of the ostensible nonarbitrariness of this point, the Church as figure of the utterly spiritualized letter of revelation. The endless writing against writing of polemical dialogue turns out to be organized around an end, to have a teleological orientation. The task of thought will be that of merely clearing a path, through the refuse of centuries of misunderstanding and decay, to the revelation of a scripture—a writing that is immediately speech—at which point it must (suicidally) stop thinking. Philosophy will have to sustain itself only provisionally, until revelation has been finally unearthed anew. Let us look at how Schlegel presents this position.

The last section of the anthology, "On the Form of Philosophy," in which Schlegel states even more explicitly than before that dialogue is the proper form of philosophy (99), consists in a philosophical paean to "dialogue," which takes place within an invented extension of Lessing's dialogical text, *Ernst and Falk: Dialogues for Freemasons*, into a post–French Revolutionary moment. Whereas Schlegel's post- and counterrevolutionary Ernst bemoans the deterioration of the ethical-political sphere, his equally backward-turned Falk is mainly worried—although he acknowledges Ernst's concerns—about the deterioration of the religious culture.[27] Falk, however, proposes that philosophy is in a position to cure both of these ills, to minister both to the ailing external letter of society and to the internal spiritlessness of the age.[28] In order to effect this cure, philosophy must subserve revelation and take us back to a medieval, pre-Reformation, European order. The new idealism must

lead back from all sides to that old, divine Idealism, whose dark origin is as old as the first revelations, the Idealism which one needs . . . only to discover and to rediscover, which . . . stepped forward to interpret and to confirm the old revelations with new divinities, and whose richest fullness of heavenly illumination . . . unfolded itself in a particularly lordly form in the One German Spirit of by-gone days.

Once complete, science will necessarily lead us back to these oldest secrets of divine truth. (98)

Thus, in this final text of the anthology, Schlegel is reversing, in Lessing's name, the thrust of both *The Education of the Human Race* and *Ernst and Falk*. Whereas in *The Education of the Human Race* Lessing characterized revelation as a pedagogical path to the autonomous reason of humanity, Schlegel is making philosophical reason a path to revelation.[29] And whereas in *Ernst and Falk*, Lessing had polemicized against the reactionary turn to the image of the Templar Knights within some of the Freemasons' lodges, Schlegel gives his Falk the last word in his text, allowing him to argue there in favor of just such a turn back to a medieval model of European spiritual and political order.[30]

But why is dialogical form, which ought to conduce to an *infinite* process of thought, essential to the accomplishment of this finite task with which philosophy is now charged? The answer is: because it is a form that is almost no form at all. The bright flames of philosophy[31] are exposed to a double danger; only a form that is almost formless allows them to escape. On the one hand, the fire of spirit must be stabilized, provisionally protected from burning itself out too quickly. On the other hand, the fire must be preserved in a material form that is delicate and flexible enough not to extinguish that fire.

Die Philosophie ist ein himmlisches Licht, ein göttliches Feuer; aber so wie auch dies heilige Element, wo es ganz frei und ungebunden wirkt, nur vorübergehend entflammt oder zerstört, und nur da wo es in den höheren Bildungen auf ein gewisses Maß beschränkt und an eine bestimmte Gestalt gebunden ist, als sanfte Lebenswärme heilbringend erscheint; so verschwindet auch der philosophische Geist, so selten er erscheint, ebenso schnell wieder, ohne bedeutende Wirkung zu hinterlassen, außer wo eine kunstgerechte Form und Gestalt das flüchtige Wesen fest hält und bleibend macht. Nicht die Philosophie selbst, aber ihre Dauer und ihr Wert hängt ab von ihrer Form. Die Wohlfahrt der Menschen und die Begründung aller höheren Wissenschaft und Kunst ruht auf der Philosophie, der Bestand dieser aber auf ihrer Form. Wie wichtig also, und wie bedeutend ist die Form der Philosophie und wie groß ihr Wert![32]

Philosophy is a heavenly light, a divine fire, but just as, when this holy element acts completely freely and unbound, it flames up only fleetingly or destroys, and only appears as the soft salvific warmth of life when it is limited, in higher formations, to a certain measure and bound to a determinate form, so too philosophical spirit disappears [*so verschwindet auch der philosophische Geist*], as seldom as it appears, just as quickly again, without leaving behind any significant effect, except where a skilful form and image [*kunstgerechte Form und Gestalt*] holds onto the fleeting essence and makes it enduring. Not philosophy itself but its continuation and value depend upon its form [*Form*]. The well-being of humanity and the foundation of all higher sciences and arts depends upon philosophy, and the stability of philosophy depends in turn upon its form. Therefore, how important, how significant is the form of philosophy and how great its value!

Philosophical form is the letter in which the spirit of philosophical content is to be preserved, but the only appropriate letter will be one that is virtually (but only virtually) self-suspending. Dialogue is appropriate and necessary to philosophy precisely because it is a quasi-self-suspending material form.[33]

Nonetheless, "dialogue" is not so perfectly serviceable to the spirit as Schlegel would like, and its imperfection extends in two directions at once. On the one hand, there would be no point to Schlegel's initial, in part genuinely positive characterization (in "To Fichte") of Fichte's system as fulfilling "letter," if the more dialogical mode of a Lessing were totally and unambiguously sufficient, in Schlegel's view, as a material form for the (philosophical) spirit. Indeed, the very fact that dialogical textuality is *adequate* to spirit by being self-suspensive is the reason why it is *inadequately* preservative or protective of spirit. Dialogical writing burns itself out. On the other hand, at the end of "On the Form of Philosophy" Schlegel finds it necessary to insist that even when the form is adequate, even when the most consummate dialogical art is brought to bear upon the composition of a philosophical text, still philosophy does not have its "essence" in its *Darstellung* (that is, its containment in the letter) but in its *Mitteilung* and its life (100–101). The essence of philosophy is spirit, which of necessity withdraws from even dialogical form, insofar as this form is a (material) form at all, a letter, a reality without absoluteness or absolution. Even the dialogical text, insofar as it is letter at all, is not adequate to the spirit itself, and spirit escapes all adequacy of presentation. Dialogue can never be dialogical enough. For this reason, and in this sense, spirit—the end of philosophy—remains for Schlegel a secret—a *Geheimnis*—inimical to all expression, all form:

Thus, philosophy is a beautiful secret [*schönes Geheimnis*]; it is itself mysticism, or the science and art of divine secrets. . . . Far be it from us to want to expose to the crowd, in public speeches and writings, the mere purposes of true philosophy, never mind its entire content. First the Reformation, and then even more the Revolution, have taught us all too clearly what comes of an unconditional commitment to the public sphere [*unbedingten Öffentlichkeit*]. . . . Of course, the first level of all mysteries can be imparted to anyone without danger. . . . It can and may be said that it is [the] definite purpose [of the new philosophy] to restore the

Christian religion, and to confess, once and for all, its faith in the truth that has been stepped on for so long. It can and may be said that it is the express purpose of the new philosophy to call forth once again the old German constitution, i.e., the realm of honor, freedom, and loyal custom, by forming the sensibility on which true, free monarchy rests, which must lead back the improved human being to this original and alone ethical and sanctified form of national life.— . . . but how much else, which is equally necessary . . . is still held back, which would be desecrated in being said, and which I must prevent myself here from even indicating any further? (100–101)

In the final analysis, even the dialogical letter of the philosophical text is both *not letter enough*, that is, insufficiently literal (or literate) to contain the spirit, and *too much of the order of the letter*, that is, too literal (or literate) not to displace that spirit with its own materiality:

It is not in writings, therefore, and letters and systems [*Nicht in den Schriften also und Buchstaben und Systemen*] that philosophy is contained: the infinite spirit [*der unendliche Geist*] does not let itself be bound and tied up so tightly. It wants to expand and impart itself [*mitteilen*], to be lively and effective and to receive effects in turn, and to bond with everything that is like itself. What we could call something like the form of philosophy in truly scientific works is only an imitation of that original form of philosophy or the philosophy of life itself; the mysteries are this original form of philosophy, a sacred and secret union of those who have been initiated into the highest knowledge. . . . For this reason all true philosophers have always formed . . . an invisible, but firmly closed union [*Bund*] of friends. . . . (101–2)

This "invisible, but firmly closed union," this monological community of the secretly revealed spirit, at the end of the polemical dialogue of letter and spirit, is Schlegel's odd trope on Lessing's notion of an eternal freemasonry. In four years, Schlegel's conversion will link him to a *visible* form of such community. He will have found, if not inner peace, at least the external figure of a spiritual home.

PLATE I. *Martin Luther,* dressed in the confession of faith of the Holy Bishop Athanasius and framed by the Apostolic and Nicenian confession of faith. BPK, 1999.

PLATE 2. *Moses Mendelssohn.* Anonymous oil painting. BPK, 1999. Märkisches Museum.

PLATE 3. *Moses Mendelssohn at the Berliner Gate in Potsdam.* Engraving by Lowe after a drawing by Daniel Chodowiecki (1792). BPK, 1999. Photo: Ruth Schacht (1978). Staatsbibliothek preussischer Kulturbesitz zu Berlin, Mendelssohn-Archiv (hereafter M-A).

PLATE 4. *Gotthold Ephraim Lessing*. Steel engraving by A. H. Payne after a drawing by Storck from early nineteenth century. BPK, 1999.

PLATE 5. *Meeting of Lessing (standing), Lavater (right), and Mendelssohn (left) in his house.* Woodcut (1856) after a painting by Moritz Oppenheim. BPK, 1999. M-A.

PLATE 6. Scene from production of *Nathan the Wise* in Deutsches Theater Berlin, Sept. 7, 1945, with Paul Wegener as Nathan (*left*) and Eduard von Winterstein as the Lay Brother (*right*). Direction: Fritz Wisten; Set: Willi Schmidt. BPK, 1999. Photo: Willy Saeger.

PLATE 7. *Johann Kaspar Lavater.* Etching. BPK, 1999.

PLATE 8. *Friedrich Schlegel.* Woodcut after Bürkner. BPK, 1999.

PLATE 9. *Dorothea Schlegel.* Painting by Anton Graff. BPK, 1999.

PLATE 10. *Heinrich Heine visiting Karl and Jenny Marx in Paris* (1844). Drawing by Shukow. BPK, 1999.

PLATE 11. *Richard Wagner.* Photo-postcard (circa 1870). BPK, 1999.

Da lieg auch du — dunkler Wurm!
Den gleißenden Hort heb' ich hurtig.

128. C. v. Grimm. Schalk. Leipzig. 1879

PLATE 12. *Siegfried-Wagner unearths the Nibelungen-treasure.* Caricature by Grimm, published in 1879 in Leipzig, the *Schalk.* BPK, 1999.

PLATE 13. *Richard Wagner as Shoe-fetishist.* Caricature (1881). "Hm, hm, let me at least admit it to myself 'sub rosa': This Chancellor of the Reich is, as far as state matters are concerned, aside from me the foremost man in Germany! Truly, truly, if I didn't already have to bear the weight of both the musical world and the finest satin coats and shoes, I would indeed want to be Bismarck!"

PLATE 14. *Sigmund Freud stepping onto a Lufthansa airplane.* Photo (1929). BPK, 1999.

PLATE 15. *Sigmund Freud in his consulting room in Vienna, Berggass 19.* Photo (circa 1935). BPK, 1999.

PART III

POST-ROMANTICISM

The Reversal of Emancipation on the Left

KARL MARX'S "ON THE JEWISH QUESTION" (1843)

> In the final analysis, the *emancipation of the Jews* is the emancipation of mankind from *Judaism*
> —Marx, "On the Jewish Question"[1]

From the Neo-Catholic but also post-Enlightenment standpoint that Schlegel adopts definitively with his conversion in 1808, Catholicism appears as the synthesis of a Protestant (male) spirit with Jewish (female) letter. Schlegel reasserts in a new way the medieval version of the assimilation of the Jewish prefiguration into its Christian fulfillment. Perhaps surprisingly, however, Schlegel's Neo-Catholic position is double-edged to the degree that its claim to have absorbed Judaism into itself is accompanied by a relatively liberal attitude toward the emancipation of the Jews: Schlegel supports Jewish emancipation. However "reactionary" the post-1808 Schlegel's position is in certain regards, his position is "progressive" insofar as he affirms the granting of civil rights to the Jews, understanding the Jews as a religiously defined community, rather than a political entity. As one could argue also with respect to the eighteenth-century French "Catholic Vindications of Israel," the reassertion of Catholicism from the Enlightenment forward, which must insist, against the Lutheran Reformation's reduction of the Catholic Church to the status of a mere *prefiguration*, that the Catholic Church is already a *fulfillment*, requires the reassertion of the notion that Judaism is the prefiguration of (Catholic) Christianity.[2] As such a prefiguration, Judaism can command a certain degree of respect and toleration, and in any case inclusion within the domain of the human. In accordance with this logic, Schlegel's Neo-Catholicism needs Judaism, as well as the quasi-pagan, self-dissolving spirit of Protestantism, in order to define itself against the two as their sublation. This is one important reason why, during the Vienna Congress and afterward in his time in Frankfurt, Schlegel defends not only the freedom of religion, in general, but also the freedom to practice Judaism, in particular. In his work for Metternich on drafts of a constitution, for example, under the rubric of "religious constitution," Schlegel argues for three main points: (1) that all Christian religious parties should have equal civil and political rights; (2) that the Catholic Church should be restored in Germany; and (3) that the Jews should be granted civil rights.[3] Moreover, Schlegel defends these principles not only in his drafts of a constitution for Metternich but also in his journalistic articles on the politics of religion under the emerging, post-French-Revolutionary European order.[4] Of course, when he defends the freedom of religion as well as the emancipation of the Jews, this defense should be understood as treacherous—"sophistical," "Jesuitical," or "Jewish"—for he takes these positions in order that the truth of Catholicism should have an opportunity to emerge out of the free interchange between the partners involved and ultimately assert itself against them. Further, to emancipate the church from the state is ultimately to subordinate state to church, as Schlegel is well aware. Ultimately, Schlegel believes one should found the state upon the church. Nonetheless, it is important to note that Schlegel's Neo-Catholic phase remains explicitly within the discourse that affirms the emancipation of the German Jews.[5]

From Neo-Catholicism to Neopaganism:
Options for the Post-Romantic Position

The same cannot quite be said for the two anti-Jewish discourses we examine in the chapters that comprise Part III, discourses which I treat as synecdoches of the German post-Romantic situation and which signal or emblematize the end and indeed the reversal of the discourse of emancipation. Both cases—those of Karl Marx and Richard Wagner—have to do no longer with Neo-Catholicism but with a theologically invested worldliness that can be characterized as neopaganism. From the standpoint of such a neopaganism, which in these cases is also explicitly a humanism, as we shall see, the emancipation of the Jews from the Germans appears as its reverse: the emancipation of the Germans (or, in the case of Marx, society and humanity generally) from the Jews. But Jewish-German emancipation—either as the emancipation of the Jews or as that of the Germans—is in all cases conceived as the opportunity to become one's oppressor, the opportunity to be included in that from which one has hitherto been excluded and to become that to which one has been opposed and by which one has been enslaved. The emancipation of the Jews always accordingly meant the becoming-German of the Jews, which never appeared particularly scandalous to the Germans or even, for that matter, to most of the Jews involved in the discussion. The emancipation of the Germans from the Jews will consequently and implicitly mean the becoming-Jewish of the Germans, if only because this is the structure of the notion of emancipation being invoked. Needless to say, this sense of the emancipation of the Germans from the Jews as the becoming-Jewish of the Germans will have to be disavowed or denegated wherever such emancipation is proposed. We will return below to the marginal or fleeting return of this repressed figure in both Marx's and Wagner's discourses against the Jews. But before examining these discourses, which represent the two political extremes of neopagan humanism, we should ask: Why is it that the turn from Neo-Catholic Romanticism to the neopagan humanisms of the immediately post-Romantic age (which I would also call, following Nietzsche in *The Case of Wagner*, the age of decadence and its contestation) ultimately entails not so much a rejection as a radical *reversal* of the notion of Jewish emancipation? What does it mean, at this point in Judaeo-Christian history, for a German to say—without quite saying so—that in order to become free, in order to become themselves, the Germans must not only free themselves from but also *become* the Jews?

The sketch of an answer to these questions has to begin with a renewed consideration of the rhetorical wheel of Judaeo-Christian (mis)fortune I presented in the Introduction.[6] Due to its position as the fulfillment of the (Neo-Judaic) Enlightenment fulfillment of the (Lutheran) Reformation spirit, (Neo-Catholic) Romanticism is fulfilled in turn by a repetition of the Reformation discourse. In other words, when Romantic Neo-Catholicism reflects upon its own displaced repetition of the medieval triangular scenario, it is compelled to consider the possibility that it has its destined end in—that it is realized, fulfilled, or superceded in turn by—a repetition of the Reformation scenario. However, because the Neo-Catholic position has claimed Christianity for itself in a post-Reformation situation, superceding Protestantism along with the Neo-Judaic Enlightenment, the post-Romantic renewal of the Reformation—taking Romanticism at its word, granting it the Christianity it wishes to possess—repeats the Protestant discourse as an overcoming of Christianity (and thus of Judaeo-Christianity) altogether.[7] In the post-Romantic German nineteenth century, Protestantism is reborn in a more radically secular humanist form and, thus, in a specifically neopagan form (see Figure 7).[8] This rebirth can take on both left- and right-wing characteristics, both ascetic and aestheticist traits, and a relatively optimistic or a relatively pessimistic tone, depending on the case.[9] It begins in two versions: on the one hand, there is Hegel's critique of the Romantics, the influence of which extends through the works of Young Germany and the Young Hegelians, in a tradition whose pagan references tend to go in the direction of classical antiquity; and on the other hand, in a counter-Hegelian direction, there are Schopenhauer and his descendants and kindred spirits, where the pagan authority is situated in the preclassical Orient. The two politically and metaphysically extreme mid-nineteenth-century articulations of this discourse, optimistic internationalism and pessimistic nationalism, each of which mixes in complex ways asceticism with aestheticism, are represented here by the anti-Jewish texts of Marx and Wagner.[10]

Once neopagan secular humanism establishes itself as the fulfillment of Romanticism, however, it cannot help but look forward, in structural and therefore in temporal terms, to its fulfillment by the (Neo-)Judaism that is now in the position of *littera*, or the pre-prefiguration with which the whole process begins. Caught between a prefigurative Catholicism that, ever since the Reformation, has counted as quasi-Judaic, and a pre-prefigurative Judaism that precedes this Catholicism and proceeds upon pagan polytheism, German post-Romantic radical humanism seems to be surrounded by Judaism.[11] For neopaganism to liberate itself from its bondage to the tendential Judaism of Neo-Catholicism (and after all, Friedrich Schlegel was the husband of a Jewess and a defender of emancipation, i.e., a "Jew-loving" Catholic, as seen from the perspective of anti-Semitism) is for it to liberate itself into the possibility of its self-fulfillment *as* Judaism, the possibility of its return to its literal, material, and even positionally pagan origins in Judaism (for the position of *littera* is "originally," in the medieval discourse, that of the pagan). While the description of this

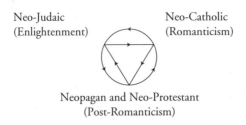

Neo-Judaic (Enlightenment)   Neo-Catholic (Romanticism)

Neopagan and Neo-Protestant
(Post-Romanticism)

FIGURE 7. The Judaeo-Christian Triangle in the Post-Romantic Context

structure is hardly meant to excuse the particularly rabid form that anti-Semitism assumes in mid- to late-nineteenth-century Germany, it may help to explain its broadly popular apparent persuasiveness there.

One further general trait of the reversal of the emancipatory discourse by post-Romantic neopaganism remains before we look more closely at Marx's and Wagner's arguments. The mid-nineteenth-century critique of the Jews differentiates itself to some degree from earlier critiques through its strong emphasis on the identification of the Jews with money and capital.[12] There are above all two reasons for this, one discursive, the other sociohistorical. As for the former, because the neopagan discourse of the post-Romantics can no longer draw directly on Christian religious anti-Judaism, the question arises as to how such a discourse will defend itself in apparently secular-humanist terms against the Judaism from which it feels it is destined to liberate itself (as well as destined, despite itself, to become). The answer, as we shall see in what follows, is relatively simple: it will defend itself in terms of anticapitalism, on the basis of a pseudosecularizing transformation of the notion of the dead letter of the law and its works into the notion of the dead matter of abstract money and its egoistic pursuit. The Christian notions of the loveless and faithless Jew will be adapted to—overdetermined by—the secular humanist and pseudomaterialist vocabularies of a bourgeois age: the Jew will be (primarily) the one who puts money in the place of feelings, as the Jew used to be (primarily) the one who put law in the place of faith.[13] Concerning the sociohistorical reason for this shift, whereas during the age of absolutism the problem for progressive social consciousness was a strictly *political* problem (how to overcome the opaque power of the aristocracy and the monarchies), during the age of the bourgeoisie the problem for social progressives becomes increasingly an *economic* problem (how to overcome the opaque power of the bourgeoisie, which is more an economically than a politically defined class). For these reasons, in the ideologically "forward-looking" thinkers of the nineteenth century the figure of the evil Jew is no longer above all associated with the political instance of the law, but rather mainly with the economic instance of capital. The abstract materiality of the Jew—a very old story—is now with a vengeance the abstract material-ity of the Jewish capitalist.

Thus, as modernization and industrialization advance across the nineteenth century, the twin eternal specters of bad (mechanical) material-ity and bad (abstract) intellectuality turn around capital as their concept, and the Jew functions as the ideological exemplum of this concept. Good materiality is then isolated as that materiality grasped in its truth by socio-historical realism (for the left) or as the earth and blood of the nation (for the right), while good intellectuality appears as either scientific critique (for the left) or the spirituality of natural feeling (for the right). Both political extremes of anti-Semitic neopaganism share the (secularized Christian) identification of the Jew with capital as a figure for bad material abstraction (and thus as a figure for the figural). They replace the attempt to found a politics on the strictly theological basis of revealed religion, which was still Schlegel's *desideratum*, with the attempt to found a politics on a strictly post-Judaeo-Christian, scientific-historical basis, variants of which extend from the historiography of class struggle to the historiography of race struggle.[14] Both remain, however, within a strictly ontotheological horizon. Having said this much in general terms, we can now turn to a more detailed presentation of the arguments of Marx and, in Chapter 8, of Wagner on the status of the Jews with respect to the politics of class and the politics of nation, respectively.

Marx: From the Secularization of the State to the De-Judaization of Humanity

While he is in the process of developing his early critique of Hegel's *Philosophy of Right*, Marx writes his essay "On the Jewish Question" as a review of Bruno Bauer's texts on "The Jewish Question" and "The Capac-ity of Present-Day Jews and Christians to Become Free."[15] In his review-essay, Marx situates the question of Jewish emancipation within the hori-zon of the broader question of the possibilities offered by political emancipation in general, where *political emancipation* means the emancipation of the political from religious commitments, the establishment of a secular state along Hegelian lines. As is well known, Marx attacks the notion of a merely *political* emancipation as conceived in Young Hegelian terms by Bauer, and he attempts to replace it with the nascently Marxist notion of a more thoroughgoing or total *human* emancipation.[16] Marx's critique of political emancipation argues that this notion of emancipation remains *theological*, while the human emancipation he proposes would be not only metapolitical but also *nontheological* or *posttheological*. In order to examine critically Marx's reversal of emancipation, then, we will have to evaluate his attempt to formulate this reversal in terms that exceed all he knows as theology, especially the Catholicism or Judaized Christianity that characterizes the Romantic prefiguration of the post-Romantic period. Before turning to this examination, however, it is necessary to say a brief word about Hegel's position on Jewish emancipation, specifically as it appears in his *Philosophy of Right* within the context of his discussion of the relations between church and state.[17] It is "crucial" to recapitulate Hegel's position here, not only because Marx's critique of the Jews makes up part of his early critique of Hegel's *Philosophy of Right* but also because Hegel's remarks there on the relations between church and state are directed precisely against the Romantic Neo-Catholicism of Schlegel and his theopolitical allies: this text by Hegel provides us with our best possible place of crossing from Schlegel to Marx.

In the *Philosophy of Right*, Hegel occupies the same position as Schlegel to this limited degree: he also supports the civil emancipation of the Jews.[18] He occupies a radically different position insofar as he supports the separation of church and state, that is, a secular politics, in the sense of the emancipation of state from church, against Schlegel's attempt to reproduce the medieval subordination of state to religion, an attempt that proceeded in a surreptitious or sly manner to the degree that it took the form of the disingenuous affirmation of the mere emancipation of the church from the state.[19] Hegel articulates this critique of the political theology of Romantic Neo-Catholicism in such a way as to *replace* the politicized church of the Middle Ages with the secular state.[20] Of course, to *replace* the medieval church with the modern state, to formulate the status of the modern state in a way similar to the way in which the status of the church was defined in the Christian Middle Ages, is to risk *repeating* the essential

structure of Catholicism in only superficially secular terms. Marx's early critique of Hegel in turn must be understood as including, perhaps even cen-
tered around, the claim that Hegel is "guilty" of such a repetition. In the
first half of his critique of Bruno Bauer's essay on the question of Jewish
emancipation, Marx suggests that Bauer's Hegelian conception of the secular state remains a theological conception. Somewhat more specifically, he
suggests that this conception repeats in a modern or pseudomodern form
the structure of the medieval church-state relations it means finally to overcome. Before focusing on the ramifications of this critique for Marx's views
on Jewish emancipation, let us see how this critique is stated and structured, while evaluating its capacity to escape the repetition of theology it
condemns in Hegel.

We do not convert secular questions into theological ones. We convert theological
questions into secular questions. . . . Bauer . . . transforms the question of Jewish
emancipation into a purely religious one. The theological scruple as to whether the
Jew or the Christian has the better prospect of salvation is here reproduced in the
enlightened form: Which of the two is *more capable of emancipation*? It is thus no
longer the question: Does Judaism or Christianity emancipate? but rather, on the
contrary: Which emancipates more, the negation of Judaism or the negation of
Christianity? . . . For the Jew it is still a matter of *professing faith*, just not in
Christianity, but rather in dissolved Christianity. . . . Bauer views the ideal and
abstract essence of the Jew, his religion, as his whole essence. . . . We are trying to
break the theological frame of the question. The question concerning the Jew's
capacity for emancipation becomes for us the question: What specific *social* element is to be overcome in order to abolish Judaism?[21]

In terms such as these, Marx repeatedly claims throughout his essay
that he will be going beyond theology to a radically worldly human position, or to what I am calling here one version of neopaganism.[22] Marx's
claim remains, however, highly problematic everywhere in his discourse in
ways that have "crucial" implications for his views on Jewish emancipation.
One of the senses in which Marx remains beholden to, or inscribed within,
theological discourses, is this: the structures of (Judaeo-)Christian figural
interpretation significantly determine the manner in which he situates his
own, ostensibly posttheological, discourse of human emancipation with
respect to the theological discourses (including the discourse of political
emancipation) it would overcome. We will see how this is the case in just
a moment.

First, it is necessary to see that the prefiguration-fulfillment model already enters into the construction of "On the Jewish Question" as the constitutive model of *political* emancipation, defining the relation between religion (or the religious state) and state (in the sense of the secular state). According to Bauer, the state must become secular, and individuals must renounce their commitments to religion in order to enter this state: they must consent to confining their religious commitments to the private sphere of civil society.[23] For Marx, the relation between religion (or civil society) and state in Bauer's Hegelian political theory is structured as the relation between material prefiguration and spiritual fulfillment, a relation in which, from Marx's standpoint, the fulfillment remains a misleading or false one.[24] Accompanied at a distance by civil society, the secular state accomplishes what politicized religion (or the religious state) was always meant to accomplish.[25] It becomes the site of identity and community, while civil society occupies the site of difference and atomistic individuality.[26] On a diachronic level, then, the secular state becomes the fulfillment of the religious state that prefigures and precedes it in temporal-historical terms.[27] Homologously, and on a different, synchronic level, the secular state is the fulfillment of the civil society into which the religious state will have been banished through the very constitution of that secular state. "The political state relates to civil society as spiritualistically as heaven relates to earth. It stands in the same opposition to civil society, and it overcomes this society as religion overcomes the limits of the profane world, i.e., in that it must once again recognize, establish, and allow itself to be dominated by, this society" (225; 355). For Marx, in Hegelianism the state is supposed to overcome [*überwindet*] and spiritually realize civil society just as, in traditional religion, heaven was supposed to overcome earth, but this overcoming and realization remain just as questionable and problematic for Marx in the case of the relation between state and civil society as they did in that of the relation between heaven and earth.

Before moving on, let us briefly reconsider this structure in terms of ontotheology, in order to clarify the theological stakes here in philosophical terms, in addition to the religio-historical and rhetorical terms we have thus far invoked. The separation of civil society, as the space of (beliefs in) God, absolute Value, or the highest being, from the state, or the sphere of actual Being itself, establishes for Bauer a harmonious division of ontotheological labor.[28] The ontotheological totality is achieved through an analytical separation of the (true) *ontos* of state from the (false or illusory) *theos* of society.[29] Because Bauer's epistemology or ontorhetoric is of the materialist-empiricist variety, the theologico-ideal realm of society is seen as the mere *figure* of the political-material realm of the state, which functions as the *literal* term: to separate the figural from the literal allows the literal to come into its own, to become literally what it is. Society and state thus comprise one internally differentiated theological-ontological whole.

Figural interpretation plays an important role, however, even beyond this construction of political emancipation as the separation of state from civil society—a construction which, after all, Marx felt he could still blame on the residually theological thinking of Bauer and his master, Hegel. In Marx's own critique of political emancipation as theological, all-too-theological, Marx construes also the relation *between* political and human emancipation as a teleological, rhetorico-philosophical one between an anticipatory prefiguration and its fulfillment.[30] For Marx, political emancipation, because it is still theological, achieves only in a partial and flawed manner what human emancipation, which overcomes theology, will achieve completely and perfectly.

The *political* emancipation of the Jew, the Christian, or the *religious* man generally is the *emancipation of the state* from Judaism, from Christianity, from *religion* in general. In a form and manner corresponding to its nature, as a *state* the state emancipates itself from religion by emancipating itself from the *state religion*, that is, by confessing no religion, but rather confessing itself simply to be a state [*indem der Staat als Staat keine Religion bekennt, indem der Staat sich vielmehr als Staat bekennt*]. *Political* emancipation from religion is not complete and consistent emancipation from religion because political emancipation is not the complete and consistent form of *human* emancipation.

The limits of political emancipation are seen at once in the fact that the *state* can free itself from a limitation without man *actually* being free from it, in the fact that a state can be a *free state* without the human being becoming a *free human being*. . . . The state can thus emancipate itself from religion even though the *overwhelming majority* is still religious. And the overwhelming majority does not cease being religious by being religious in *private*. (223–24; 353)

This means that political emancipation only achieves in a *mediated* manner, through an abstract and limited representational form or figure—as when the letter binds the spirit, or when the church stands between man and God—what human emancipation will achieve *immediately*.

Man frees himself from a limitation *politically, through the medium of the state* [*durch das* Medium des Staats], by overcoming the limitation in an *abstract, limited,* and partial manner, in contradiction with himself. Further, when man frees himself *politically,* he does so *indirectly* [*auf einem* Umweg], through an *intermediary* [Medium], even if through a *necessary intermediary* [notwendiges Medium]. (224; 353)

In accordance with its mediated character, the discourse that reigns when the secular, politically emancipated state has been installed in its separation from civil society is for Marx, like the Jewish or the Catholic one, a discourse not of philosophical truth but of "sophistry." "Certainly, the *bourgeois*, like the Jew, participates in the life of the state only in a sophistical way just as the *citoyen* is only sophistically a Jew or bourgeois; but this sophistry is not personal. It is *the sophistry of the political state* itself" (226; 355). Moreover, this prefiguration-fulfillment relation is analogous in an additional sense to the relation between Judaism and Christianity (which is in turn the model for the relation between Catholicism and Protestantism), especially as it generally appears in the later works of Hegel. As Judaism operates a separation of God and world/man which Christianity attempts to reverse and overcome by means of the worldly becoming-man of God, so political emancipation establishes a rift between state and civil society which human emancipation overcomes by means of the dialectical synthesis of state and civil society. This synthesis fulfills the separation it reverses, by achieving the chiasmic absorption of the individual into the collective and of the collective into the individual (241; 370).

Further, like the synthesis of God (or church) and human world (or subjectivity) on which it is patterned, the synthesis of state and civil society is ontotheologically invested in a way that reverses, and then envisions the fusion of, the terms Bauer established. Given that for Marx the state relates to society as does heaven to earth, the state stands in, first of all, for God as highest being, while civil society stands in for the Being of the human world understood as the whole of the extant. This means that for Marx the false religiosity of civil society is the truth of the illusory secularism of the state under the conditions of the division of state from civil society. The *figurality* and religiosity of civil society according to Bauer's discourse is for Marx the *literal* "truth" of the *figurality* of the secular state, which Bauer took to have been *literally* achieved by the separation of church and state. Beyond this, however, while preserving the materialist-empiricist ontorhetoric that Bauer already adopted, Marx posits the literality of the material only in the achieved synthesis of secular state and religious civil society, while he posits the figurality of the ideal in both state and civil society under the conditions of their division. Human emancipation, or the Revolution, will have named in Marx's discourse the establishment of the ontotheological fusion of the highest being with Being itself in the name of the mere Being of human society.

In sum, the allegory of figural interpretation with which Marx confronts us in the first part of his essay is as follows. Religion as such (or politicized religion, the theologically invested state) *prefigures* the political state. The political state provisionally *accomplishes* this prefiguration by separating itself from it, that is, by separating secular-collective politics from religious-individual civil society. This political state *prefigures* in turn the *achievement* of humanity through the revolutionary reunification of civil society with the state.

To restate this summary in terms of the Judaeo-Christian discursive history that is structured by these relations of prefiguration and fulfillment: the state that is either explicitly controlled by or explicitly controls, and thereby remains implicitly controlled by, religion (the medieval or the [post] Reformation state) is structurally *Jewish*. The secular, political state of Hegelian provenance that replaces this theopolitical state is structurally (if not ideologically) *Catholic*; it repeats the Judaism of the theological or religious on a higher level, for the religiosity it casts out persists and continues to affect it on the supplementary level of civil society. Finally, the human emancipation that will succeed upon this structurally Catholic, secular political state is structurally *Protestant*. Yet, in its programmatic, (anti)theological intentional sense, it is radically atheist or pagan, because it achieves what the still-prefigurative political emancipation meant to achieve: total freedom from the material violence of religious delusion, a freedom that in this case takes the form of a total fusion of private and public.

Before going on to examine the residually theological dimensions of the negative characterization of the Jews in the second half of Marx's article, let us briefly take a look backward to see how Marx's neopagan, Neo-Protestant construal of the relationship between church and state relates to the Enlightenment Neo-Judaism of Mendelssohn and the Romantic Neo-Catholicism of Schlegel. Such a brief look back will provide another perspective on the still-theological character of Marx's analysis. In *Jerusalem*, as will be recalled from Chapter 1, Mendelssohn set up the church-state opposition as a spirit-letter or reason-power opposition, and placed Judaism in the center of that opposition—on the site of the hyphen, as it were—where the unity and disunity of the polarity were combined. From Mendelssohn to Marx, passing by way of Schlegelian Romanticism and Hegelian post-Romanticism, two notable displacements of the same set of elements have taken place.[31] First, these relationships have been reversed: the church-state opposition appears in "On the Jewish Question" as a letter-spirit or power-reason opposition, and not the other way around. Religion has become the religion of unreason, and the state has become the state of reason. The realms of freedom (or spirit) and necessity (or letter) have switched places in the passage from the age of absolutism to that of ascendant capital. For in the wake of Hegel's critique of formalist and subjectivist "moralities," Marx identifies the church with the private sphere qua realm of individual violence and mediation, while he identifies the state with the public sphere of common meaningfulness, although he goes beyond Hegel by requiring a further *Aufhebung* of the resultant opposition between public and private. Second, Marx places Judaism, as we will see in more detail in a moment, in the position of the letter of the church and thus sees it as embodying—more than any Christian faith—the violent materiality of the ostensibly nonpolitical.

Like Mendelssohn, Schlegel defined the relation between church and state as one between spirit and letter. In contrast to Mendelssohn, however, in his nostalgia for a balance he ultimately felt had been fleetingly attained and then lost in the Middle Ages, Schlegel wished in his Neo-Catholic phase to found the letter of the state on the spirit of the church while lending the church the power it needed to determine the shape of the state by giving it some materiality of its own. Hence, he affirmed Catholic hierarchical authority as opposed to an Enlightenment-style religion of reason.[32] Marx displaces Schlegel's Romantic Neo-Catholicism not only by initially positing church as letter and state as spirit but also by placing Schlegel's Neo-Catholic synthesis in the position of the state, just as he places Mendelssohn's Neo-Judaic synthesis in the position of the church, while he situates his version of Neo-Protestant neopaganism in the position of mediating synthesis, of a truly spiritual materialism.[33]

We have thus far seen three senses in which Marx remains beholden to the theology he abhors. First, he construes the passage from political to human emancipation in terms of the Christian tradition of figural interpretation. Second, Marx's attempt to radicalize Bauer's secular materialism or empiricism remains faithful, against its will, to the residually theological idealism or rationalism of Bauer's theory by envisioning human emancipation in terms that are, like Bauer's, not merely ontological but specifically ontotheological. Third, Marx's characterization of church-state relations shares the main elements of the Neo-Judaic Enlightenment and the Neo-Catholic Romantic models we've examined in Parts I and II while rearranging them such that they make up a Protestant model disguised in pagan garb. Having established to this extent that Marx's critique of the division of state and civil society is still theological and idealist, we are now in a position to see how Marx's critique of *Judaism* fits into this still-theological critique of the theological character of the split between civil society and state.[34] More specifically, we will examine the way in which Marx sacrificially externalizes the theological or precritical character of his would-be materialist-empiricist analysis, that is, its excessive ideality or abstractness, which (oddly) doubles as its excessive materiality, by attributing it to—or blaming it on—the Jews. Jewish materialism will turn out to be bad because it is too materialist by virtue of not being materialist enough, while Marx's materialism will turn out to be good because it is more than materialist by virtue of being not quite materialist. Let us see how the Pauline (a)theism of this structure—the sacrificial externalization of the self-differentiality of "materialism" by means of its projection onto the Jews—develops out of Marx's "materialist" analysis of the Jews.

In the attempt to "break the theological frame of the question" of Jewish emancipation, a frame Bauer had ostensibly left intact by remaining within the purview of political emancipation, Marx claims he will try to understand the sociohistorical reality of the Jew, instead of his religious identity.

We are trying to break the theological frame of the question. The question concerning the Jew's capacity for emancipation becomes for us the question: What specific *social* element is to be overcome in order to abolish Judaism? . . .

Let us consider the actual, worldly Jew—not the *sabbath Jew*, as Bauer does, but the *everyday Jew.*

Let us look for the secret [*Geheimnis*] of the Jew not in his religion but rather for the secret of the religion in the actual Jew.

What is the worldly ground of Judaism? *Practical* need, *self-interest* [Eigennutz].

What is the worldly cult of the Jew? *Bargaining* [Der Schacher]. What is his worldly god? *Money* [Das Geld].

Very well! Emancipation from *bargaining* and *money*, and thus from practical and real Judaism would be the self-emancipation of our time . . .

Thus we perceive in Judaism a universal, *present antisocial* [gegenwärtiges antisoziales] element, which has been driven to its ultimate height through the historical development to which, in this negative respect, the Jews have busily contributed, a height at which it necessarily must dissolve itself.

In the final analysis, the *emancipation of the Jews* is the emancipation of mankind from *Judaism*. (243–44; 372–73)

To what extent does the transition from a theological (or idealist-rationalist) to a secular (or materialist-empiricist) point of view actually occur here? First, the renunciation or destruction of one frame of reference does not, of course, dispense with the necessity of framing, and so of mediation, representation, figuration, and so forth. Insofar, then, as Marx continues to participate in mediation, representation, and figuration, he continues to participate in what he characterizes as the still-theological character of the secular state, the sense in which it requires of us belief in things that are unreal. On the other hand, Marx claims to give us the secular reality of the Jew—"the actual, worldly Jew . . . the worldly ground of Judaism . . . the worldly cult . . . his worldly God"—and so the immediate presence of the Jew without any mediation or re-presentation whatsoever. This claim, in turn, must be understood as not only grotesquely naïve or self-disingenuous but also precisely *theological*, and more narrowly *ontotheological*, as we suggested above. To be able to stake the materialist-empiricist claim to immediate knowledge of the Jew's reality qua social function, Marx must be able to gain *immediate* access to the *totality* of relations between the (figural) theological realm of social reality and the (literal) ontological realm of the state (according to Bauer's construction), or between the (literal) ontological realm of social reality and the (figural) theological realm of the state (according to Marx's provisional reversal of Bauer's construction). On the level of "human emancipation," of course, Marx envisions the *synthesis* of both of these versions of the state-society relation into one ontotheological, politico-social totality.[35] He does so in the name of an ontological concept of reality (or being qua totality of present beings) into which the (illusion of) God has been pantheistically reabsorbed.[36] Thus, according to both his notion of theology (as mediation) and our (post-)

Heideggerian notion of theology (including even secular transformations of ontotheology), Marx's secular materialism (or realism or empiricism) is still theological (or idealist or rationalist).

The dogmatism or idealism of Marx's decision in favor of materialism not only commits Marx to a theological epistemology, the religion of a certain version of "scientificity," but also skews his approach to the Jewish question in various ways. First, due to his dogmatically or metaphysically materialist-empiricist ideology, he fails to consider the role of religion—as belief, interiority, thought, or discourse—both on the part of the Jews and the part of the Christians, in the determination of the history of their interactions. He is not interested in "the sabbath Jew [*den Sabbatsjuden*]" except as a pure effect of "the everyday Jew [*den Alltagsjuden*]." Even in the absence of the insights of structuralism, however, such disinterest should have been rendered impossible by the formative influence of Hegelian dialectics alone. What Marx is consequently unable to consider is the importance of what one sometimes calls, even if insufficiently, the history of ideas (later characterized by Marxist thought as part of the superstructure) in the history of the socioeconomic (or the base). In this context, he is unable to consider the possibility that the gravitation of the Jews toward the commercial professions during the rise of capitalism is as likely to be an effect of purely "religious"—discursive-conceptual—relations as it is to be an effect of so-called social realities. Christianity "historically" leaves open to Jews certain positions, which the Jews then adapt themselves to occupy. Christianity does so, and the Jews of Europe adapt themselves to these positions, as a result of the ideological determinants of these religio-cultural groups that are not purely social or economic but also conceptual-affective, and so on. Whether the "history" of Judaeo-Christian relations is to be regarded as "material" or "ideal" is an undecidable question, as can only be shown by such critical, ontorhetorical preliminaries as Marx fails to discover (or to rediscover, for example, in Kant) due to his haste to move (with and against Hegel) beyond "theology."

Second, Marx's dogmatic, theological pseudomaterialism provides us with a "worldly ground of Judaism" that is manifestly not "worldly" or historical at all, but rather psychological. Marx's theory of Judaism is an idealist-psychologistic theory. It is not a matter of cosmological, but of psychological essences, to speak in the language of traditional, pre-Kantian *metaphysica specialis*. The "Judaism" Marx envisages is hence not a "specific *social* element [*besondre* gesellschaftliche *Element*]" at all, except in the sense of an element of the social that is not social, indeed, an element that is, as Marx goes on to say, "antisocial." For the "worldly ground of Judaism" is "practical need," or "self-interest." The Jew is thus characterized not only in psychological terms but also *as* the psychological dimension within the social, the individual within the collective, the nonmateriality of the material. If there is some subjectivity or ideality—which also means, for Marx's discourse here, religiosity—in Marx's objectivist secularism, then it is due to the Jews, who represent precisely the principle of (bad) subjectivity, ideality, and religiosity.

Third, Marx's unwittingly idealist materialism casts out not only (its own) "bad" ideality qua self-interest or the insistence on self-sameness but also its opposite, "bad" materiality or self-differentiation, i.e., non-self-interest, in the name of the Jews. The problem with the Jews is that they are material (or empirical) and materialistic (or empiricist qua "practical"), and Marx execrates the material in this "bad" sense. In other words, the Jews are not only to be empirically, materially grasped in Marx's text but also they are to be grasped and criticized *as* the empirical and material. This implies that they are to be grasped precisely from the standpoint of what is *not* empirical or material, but rather ideal, not "self-interested," but rather altruistically interested in the welfare of others as in the welfare of a collectively self-same sociopolitical subject. This association of the Jews with materiality gains expression in passages such as the following:

When society succeeds in suspending [or sublating] the *empirical* essence of Judaism [*das empirische Wesen des Judentums*]—bargaining and all its conditions—the Jew becomes *impossible* [unmöglich] because his consciousness no longer has an object, the subjective basis of Judaism—practical need—is humanized, and the conflict between the individual sensuous existence of man and his species-existence is suspended [*aufgehoben*].

The *social* emancipation of the Jew is the *emancipation of society from Judaism*. (248; 377)

To emancipate the Jews—to emancipate them from themselves and to emancipate society qua humanity from them—requires the suspension of the "empirical" essence of the Jew. But this phrase, "the *empirical* essence," refers here not only—explicitly—to the actual existence of the Jewish essence, but also—implicitly, or by a kind of "rhetorical" play on words—to the existence of the Jew as the existence of the one whose essence it is to be empirical or material, and hence to the existence of existence qua given-ness of appearance, inessentiality, and difference. "Bargaining"—the "empirical essence" of the Jew—implies first of all the relativity and sus-pension of value and, hence, the differentiality of value, its material non-self-identity, and instability. The suspension of the "empirical" essence/exis-tence of the Jew means the suspension of the "empirical" (the relative, the material, the self-different or transient), an empirical suspension of the empirical, no doubt, or a pagan suspension of the pagan in the total spiri-tuality of a state that has absorbed into itself the differentiations of civil society or individuality (and vice versa). In other words, the Jews and/or Judaism—in an undecidability of thing and concept—are responsible for the very difference that makes it impossible to decide, for example, whether it is Jews or Judaism that we are to designate as the responsible party. By undoing the Jews and/or the "economic" sphere or the "civil society" they embody, "we" can regain our proper state of pure identity, pure human-worldly self-immediacy, in which public and private are fused in a seamless totality. Such is the logic of the nascent "materialist" discourse of Karl Marx, a partial childhood convert from the world of difference, the world of written "marks," to that of identity, the world of revolutionary speech.[37]

Marx's idealist materialism still plays out the ideology of Pauline Christianity, which—as we have seen repeatedly—posits itself as the good synthesis of spirituality and concretion and opposes itself to Judaism as the bad splitting of spirituality qua abstraction from concretion qua material-ity. Marx makes Judaism responsible for bad ideality and bad materiality, each in connection with splitting and difference. In turn, he makes his ver-sion of Neo-Protestant neopaganism, or more specifically his nascent dialectical materialism, responsible for the good ideality (or collective commitment) and good materiality (or sense of sociohistorical totality) which anticipate the ultimate historical synthesis of state and society.

If I have thus far shown how Marx's views of the Jews are not only theological, in general, but also adhere to the pattern of Pauline Christianity, specifically, then it remains to show more clearly the sense in which Marx's would-be secularism or paganism tries to renew not only paganism but also—if unwittingly—Protestantism. The discussion above of the role of figural interpretation in Marx's construal of the passage from political to human emancipation already suggests that Marx is in a Protestant position.[38] But the Protestant character or dimension of Marx's paganism, its position between the Catholicism of the Romantics (and, for Marx, in a metaphorical or derivative sense, of Hegel as well), on the one hand, and the possibility of a telos that would consist in a return of Judaizing Enlightenment, on the other hand, becomes much more clear if we take a close look at Marx's characterization of the Jews. In the turn from the critique of the separation of civil society and state to the critique of the Jews, Marx not only characterizes Judaism as one "social element" but also as the totality of modern society itself: *Judaism has taken over Christianity*. In this claim, we can see a return of the Protestant argument or fear that (in the first instance Catholic) Christianity has become Judaized.

The Jew has emancipated himself in a Jewish way not only by appropriating financial power [*indem er sich die Geldmacht angeeignet*] but also because, with and without him, money has become a world power, and the practical Jewish spirit has become the practical spirit of Christian peoples [*der praktische Judengeist zum praktischen Geist der christlichen Völker geworden ist*]. The Jews have emancipated themselves insofar as the Christians have become Jews. . . . Indeed the practical domination of Judaism over the Christian world [*die praktische Herrschaft des Judentums über die christliche Welt*] has achieved the unambiguous, normal expression in North America that the very *preaching of the Gospel*, Christian ministry, has become an article of commerce and the bankrupt merchant takes to the Gospel while the minister who has become rich goes into business. (244; 373)

As far as Marx is concerned, the entire "Christian" world has disappeared into the material, theological discourse of Judaism: money talking, chattering on, saying nothing; money talking tautologically about money. The Jew has already radically emancipated himself, making the Christians into Jews, turning their theoretical standpoint into his practical one, turning their altruism into his egoism, and turning their political world into his theological-economic civil society, in which religion is economics and economics religion.[39] This situation is from Marx's standpoint (if often only implicitly) structurally medieval, or Neo-Catholic. But Marx even explicitly indicates here that this is so, by saying that while politics stands "ideally" above the power of money, it has actually become the feudal "serf [*Leibeignen*]" (245; 374) of that power.[40] The apparent Christianity of the secular political sphere, or the public arena, is actually the Catholicism, that is, the Judaized Christianity of the religion of individualism as the economism of civil society.

But further, in accordance with the post-Reformation triangulation of Judaeo-Christian relations, if the Christians have become Jews, then the Jews have become pagans. "Hence, the Jew's monotheism is actually the polytheism of many needs, a polytheism that makes even the toilet an object of divine law."[41] The unworldly world of the realized secular state, then, would be a Catholic, Jewish paganism. In contrast, the radically worldly and atheistic or pagan humanism Marx is proposing in the name of "human emancipation" would comprise the realization of the human spirit as a renewed Protestantism, because it is structured as the overcoming of the implicit Catholic, Jewish paganism of that secular state. As the Reformation placed Protestantism in the position of the (implicitly) pagan synthesis and overcoming of both (in a different sense, pagan) Jews and (Catholic) Christians (see Introduction, Figure 3), so Marx's secularism positions itself between and beyond Neo-Catholicism and Neo-Judaism.

The fact that the Jews, as *littera*, are associated here with paganism does not, however, mean that Marx's renewal of Protestantism is not in other respects sympathetic to, indeed identified with, the image of paganism. This identification appears, moreover, not only in realist and secularist motifs but also in the motif of a polytheistic nature.[42] Here is where the (in part, Feuerbachian) *naturalism* that Marx shares with his (anti)decadent contemporary, Wagner, becomes explicit:

Money is the jealous god of Israel before whom no other god may exist. Money degrades *all the gods of humankind*—and converts them into commodities. Money is the general, self-sufficient v a l u e [*W e r t*] of all things. Hence it has robbed the whole world, *the human world as well as nature*, of its proper value. Money is the alienated *essence* of man's labor and existence [*Daseins*], and this alien essence dominates him as he worships it. (246; 374–35; emphasis added)

In place of the abstraction and relative value of money qua artificiality, Marx's neopaganism would restore to itself the concretion and absolute value of inner and outer nature (or essence), "all the gods of man," which will later be called "use-value."

Finally, as is to be expected, in accordance with the position of this simultaneous renewal of paganism and Protestantism between figures of Catholicism and Judaism, Marx claims that Christianity has become Judaized. "Paradoxically" he also envisions human emancipation implicitly as a realization of Judaism. That is, Marx aspires to the *escape* from Judaism as a mode of *access* to it. He attempts to *differentiate* himself from Judaism in order to become *identical* with it, to replace it, "supplementarily":

The unfounded and groundless law of the Jew is only the religious caricature of unfounded, groundless morality and of law in general, the caricature of merely *formal* ceremonies encompassing the world of self-interest.

Here also the highest relation of man is the *legal* relation [*das* gesetzliche *Verhältnis*], the relation to laws which apply to him not because they are laws of his own will and essential nature [*seines eigenen Willens und Wesens*], but because they *dominate* him and because the fall away from them will be *avenged*.

Jewish Jesuitism, the same practical Jesuitism [*Der jüdische Jesuitismus, derselbe praktische Jesuitismus*] Bauer finds in the Talmud, is the relationship of the world of self-interest to the laws governing it, and the cunning circumvention of these laws constitutes that world's main art.

Indeed, the movement of the world within its laws is necessarily a continuous suspension [*Aufhebung*] of the law.[43]

While the Judaism of a world split between state and civil society constitutes the continuous and simultaneous positing and suspension of an *improper* law, that is, a continuous paganism, the protesting, revolutionary movement toward human emancipation will apparently amount to the positing and maintenance of a *proper* law (a law beyond all law). It will establish a law, Marx implies, that is the law of the "will and nature" of its subject, and it will no longer need to subvert this law, because this law will be truly its own. Replacing heteronomy with autonomy, replacing the law of the subject with the subject of the law, Marxism will realize the original intentions of the heteronomy that prefigures it: it will realize Judaism and so realize itself *as* a Judaism. Its revolutionary emancipation will truly leave Egyptian bondage behind, this time the Egyptian bondage of the Jewish law itself. If the Hegelian theorization of the secular state fell back unbeknownst to itself into the Judaism of Catholicism, then the Marxian overturning of Hegelianism will provide the properly pagan-Protestant solution that looks forward into the realization of itself as the spirit of the law. Marx's Neo-Protestant neopaganism will realize itself as the true Judaism.

What is more, the denegated aspiration of Marxism toward the Judaism it casts out appears not only as an aspiration to establish the true law beyond all law but also as a desire for materiality and practicality, including those of rhetorical language. The bad practicality and materialism of Judaism will one day find its fulfillment in the good practicality and materialism of Marxism. Thus, for example, even play with words, rhetorical hieroglyphics, is apparently no longer such when Marx indulges in it, as is suggested by the phrase "empirical essence of Judaism" above and also by the quasi-untranslatable line toward the end of his essay, "Die Veräußerung ist die Praxis der Entäußerung" (248; 376), "Selling is the practice of externalization/alienation." The Judaism of such sophistry is evidently the "philosophical" or "true" Judaism of Marx's Protestant, pagan, spiritual nature. Thus, Marx envisages and broaches emancipation from Judaism implicitly as the same becoming-Jewish that he also explicitly fears.[44] To speak in psychological terms, fear of the Jews, envy of the Jews, Jewish self-hatred, and Jewish self-aggrandizement converge here in a curious way. But this psychological convergence is prescribed—largely, if not totally—by the discursive-historical position of Marx's text in this proto-Modernist moment at the (seemingly endless) end of Judaeo-Christian history. The internationalist solution to the problem of history as class struggle proposes its own version of the final solution of the Jewish question, and a version that, despite its radically secular and materialist pretensions, remains theological through and through.

8

The Reversal of Emancipation on the Right

RICHARD WAGNER'S "JUDAISM IN MUSIC" (1850)

> Quite imperceptibly the "Creditor of Kings" [*der "Gläubiger der Könige"*] has become the King of Creeds [*Könige der Gläubigen*], and we really cannot take this monarch's pleading for emancipation as otherwise than uncommonly naïve, seeing that it is much rather we who are shifted into the necessity of fighting for emancipation from the Jews [*um Emanzipirung von den Juden zu kämpfen*]. According to the present constitution of this world, the Jew in truth is already more than emancipate: he rules, and will rule, so long as Money remains the power before which all our doings and our dealings lose their force.
> —Wagner, "Judaism in Music"[1]

At the opposite end of the political and metaphysical spectrum from Marx, Wagner represents, in our account of the end of emancipation in the post-Romantic period, a right-wing, idealist version of the same movement of reversal. Wagner's infamous essay "Judaism in Music" has been the object of the serious attention of some fine scholars, especially in recent years, who have justified its infamy and to some extent explained the context of its origins, its connections with Wagner's operatic works, and its effects on reactionary ideology in the Germany of our own waning century.[2] Despite such work, much of the largely (and often willfully) naïve international opera-going public continues to denegate the significance of Wagner's anti-Semitism. In addition, the members of this public—as well as many "art lovers" beyond the more narrow world of opera buffs—tend to view great art uncritically as a gift of pure Feeling or Sense descending from a Nature on high. Moreover, in the scholarship, the connections between naturalist/nationalist aestheticism and anti-Semitism in Wagner are only rarely drawn in terms of rhetoric and its ontology.[3] Given this situation, the production and dissemination of one more critical reading of the role of anti-Semitism in Wagner's aesthetics, this time in the specific terms of the history, rhetoric, and ontology of figural interpretation, is perhaps justified as a way of closing.

In retracing the outlines of Wagner's essay, my general view, in terms of the historiography of aesthetic and religio-cultural movements, will be that, while still in part clinging to the (medievalizing) naturalism of Romanticism, Wagner moves beyond Romanticism and transforms it into a post-Romantic neopagan secular nationalism. This development ultimately culminates in the would-be Aryan transfiguration of Neo-Catholicism that is *Parsifal*. In order to make this transformation seem necessary, Wagner attempts to make the Jews responsible for the *artificiality* of art in the Romantic period, that is, what we are characterizing as the Neo-Catholic period, while making the Germans responsible for the (neopagan-Protestant) *naturalness* of art. This naturalness, moreover, he everywhere presupposes to be the essence of art, its most essential possibility, as exemplified by his own artwork of the future.

With regard to the topic of rhetoric, I will emphasize specifically, on the one hand, that through this attempt Wagner reveals himself to be inscribed in, and to extend, the rhetoric of *figura* as it has dominated the Jewish-Christian relation since the beginning. Accordingly, in his discourse artificiality is associated with the *figural*, material dimension, while nature is linked to the *literal* dimension, which is here also spiritual, in accordance with the ontorhetoric of rationalism/idealism. On the other hand, I will show how his own variant of this rhetoric of *figura* belongs to the post-Romantic—that is, specifically Protestantizing and paganizing—version of Pauline idealism. Within the Lutheran-pagan context of this attempted ideological naturalization of art, Wagner's desire to free the Germans from Judaism appears "paradoxically" also as his (fearful) desire to transform the Germans into Jews, to make of the Germans a supplement of the Jewish origin.[4]

Wagner develops these views of Jews and Germans with respect to art by characterizing Jews as the exterior of art that is currently found improperly on its interior. More specifically, he argues, on the one hand, that Jews do not belong within the space of art, yet, on the other hand, that they have come not only to reside in, but to control, this space. But before following the development of this argument, we have to see how Wagner introduces it by stating what he means to accomplish in this essay and then by situating art in a preliminary way with respect to politics and religion.

Wagner begins his attack on the artificial with the opening gesture of his essay, through which he states his intentions: he places his remarks at once under the sign of the natural, as opposed to the artificial, and under the sign of true, unconscious feeling, as opposed to false, consciously rhetorical manipulation. Although Wagner aims to "clear up the matter lying at bottom of" a recent debate in the "Neue Zeitschrift für Musik" over the question of "an 'Hebraic art-taste'":

> It will not be a question . . . of saying something new, but of explaining that unconscious feeling [*die unbewußte Empfindung*] which proclaims itself among the people as a rooted dislike of the Jewish nature [*als innerlichste Abneigung gegen jüdisches Wesen*]; thus, of speaking out a something really existent, and by no means of attempting to artfully breathe life [*künstlich beleben*] into an unreality through the force of any sort of fancy. Criticism goes against its very essence [*ihre Natur*], if, in attack or defence, it tries for anything else.[5]

Like a good naturalist irrationalist, but an irrationalist who preserves the logocentric privileges of natural breath as spirit, Wagner will base his remarks on an "unconscious feeling" "rooted" in the "people," and not create the fake and nonpopular (or elitist) illusion of spirit—not "artfully breathe life into an unreality"—where no basis for that spirit is actually or literally present. The Jewish "nature" will be clarified in a natural way, and this Jewish "nature" will turn out to be the nonnature, the self-excessive nature, indeed the antinature, of artificiality.

Before clarifying the nonnatural "nature" of the Jew, Wagner moves to limit his topic to art. This shift is itself manifestly sophistical or disingenuous, because art here does not represent one limited field alongside others, but rather replaces and sublates into itself the two fields of state and church, or secular and sacred, that together traditionally totalize the universe of the human by dividing it into the realms of world and God.

> Since it here is merely in respect of Art, and specially of music, that we want to explain to ourselves the popular dislike of the Jewish nature [*den Grund der volksthümlichen Abneigung . . . gegen jüdisches Wesen . . . erklären*], even at the present

day, we may completely pass over any dealing with this same phenomenon in the field of Religion and Politics. In Religion the Jews have long ceased to be our hated foes—*thanks to all those who within the Christian religion itself have drawn upon themselves the people's hatred.* In pure Politics we have never come to actual conflict with the Jews. (79–80; 85–86; emphasis added)

Like Marx, then, Wagner attempts to move beyond the realms of religion (or church) and secular world (or state). Both Marx and Wagner attempt to go beyond not only religion but also politics (Marx wanted human, not political emancipation) to a totalization of the theopolitical domain. In Marx, this domain ultimately becomes the natural telos of proletarian internationalism (as fusion of state and civil society, overcoming of their unnatural division), while in Wagner, it appears as the natural state of German art. This is why Marx and Wagner are neopagan, rather than simply secular: their worldliness is religious, just as their religiosity is worldly. The conflict between state and church—played out, in the authorial figures we have considered thus far in this study, in terms of the oppositions between letter and spirit, form and content, figural and literal—will be transformed or sublated in Wagner into a conflict between the two aspects of art, its naturalness (as positive spiritual content) and its artificiality (as negative material form).

Having said that he would "completely pass over any dealing with this same phenomenon in the field of Religion and Politics," Wagner nonetheless says a few things about religion and politics on his way to the topic of art of which we should take note because these things suggest that Wagner's art doesn't only cancel, but also maintains, the religion and politics from which it separates itself by negation. Concerning religion, in the first edition of 1850 Wagner writes, in the place of the above italicized passage (from the edition of 1869, which I am otherwise citing here), that the Jews are no longer foes in religion: "Thanks to our pietists and Jesuits [*unsern Frömmlern und Jesuiten*], who have led the Folk's entire religious hatred toward themselves, so that with their eventual downfall Religion, in its present meaning (which has been rather that of Hate, than Love), will presumably have also come to naught [*ebenfalls untergegangen sein wird*]!"[6] Both radical Protestantism and radical Catholicism, the two extremes of the splitting of Christianity into figures of the literal and figural, respectively, are objects of Wagner's (and the Folk's) execration. Together, these extremes represent for Wagner the principle of lovelessness, hatred, or discord: the self-differentiation and self-materialization of spirit tantamount to the Judaization of Christianity. Wagner attempts instead—as he spells out in 1849 in the "Wibelungen" essay, developing a position to which Schopenhauer's philosophy will lend support from 1852 on—to realize the intentions of Christianity by returning it to its "true" Aryan pagan essence, that is, by removing the false admixture of Judaism that has divided this Aryan essence from itself in the bastard forms of traditional Christianity.[7] If the later Wagner excises this passage on the pietists and Jesuits, he no doubt does so for strategic reasons, in the desire to avoid insulting his Christian supporters by leaving undetermined just who the (Judaized) Christians are who have "drawn upon themselves the people's hatred."[8] What the passage helps us to see, however, is this: for Wagner, despite his denegations, religion is not external to art, but rather to be realized in art and as art. Art, as we will see, is for Wagner the appropriate mode of the presentation of nature as the absolute principle of unification—love. Religion is to art, therefore, as Judaism was to Christianity. Jewish love-lessness, a traditional theological characteristic that Wagner essentialistically situates in the Jewish (non)nature, is for him at once what has ruined Christian theology and what for the time being is still ruining contemporary art, preventing the latter thus far from *realizing* the loving intentions of Christian theology in the form of the Wagnerian total work of German art. Wagner's aestheticism is not a secular evasion or overcoming of religion, but rather its Neo-Protestant, neopagan *Aufhebung*.

As for the *politics* about which Wagner will not speak in "Judaism in Music," he is even more loquacious on this subject than he is about religion. We must listen carefully to what he says here, because it is in his remarks on this subject that Wagner formulates his desire to reverse the emancipation of the Jews, even though this emancipation has not yet occurred on a political level.[9] Wagner begins here by mentioning the main alternative to emancipation, namely, exile, in the form of the proposal that the Jews might leave Europe, under the leadership of Rothschild, to resettle in Palestine. Not surprisingly, Wagner expresses regret that this proposal has not been realized. What is above all significant about Wagner's regret, however, is that he expresses it by alluding directly to the money-lending capacity of the Jews and, thus, by alluding more indirectly to the anxiety of indebtedness (or influence, and hence of finitude) that is the principle psychic effect of the prefigural function of the Jews within Christianity: "We have rather had to regret that Herr v. Rothschild was too keen-witted [*zu geistreich*] to make himself King of the Jews, preferring, as is well known, to remain "the Jew of the Kings."[10] If the indebting Jew has thus remained in Europe, then the project of emancipation has done nothing, Wagner argues, to solve the problems posed by that presence. If emancipation has failed, he continues, then this is because "we" (80; 86) Germans never really wanted to emancipate the Jews in particular, but were only interested in "an abstract principle" (80; 86) or "a general idea [*Gedankens*]" (80; 86), whereas "we" (80; 86) continued to feel an "involuntary repellence [*das unwillkürlich Abstoßende*]" (80; 86) at the Jews, an "instinctive dislike [*instinkmäßige Abneigung*]" (80; 86) which must henceforth be given due respect. The abstraction of the idea of Jewish emancipation is insufficient, however, not simply because it is not concrete but also because, as abstraction, it is precisely a Jewish idea. A Jewish idea has thus usurped a German reality.

Wagner makes use here of the stereotypical, irrationalist equation of the Jews with the abstract and material rationality of liberalism, or more broadly of the Enlightenment tradition. This equation is utterly ideological, insofar (for example) as abstract rationality and Judaism are neither necessarily conjoined nor necessarily disjoined. At the same time, it is partly accurate in terms of the history of Judaeo-Christian ideologies, but only insofar as the Enlightenment discourse in Germany tends momentarily, if largely unwillingly, to privilege Neo-Judaism as the (phantasmatic) realization of Protestant reason, as I argued in the Introduction and illustrated in detail in Chapter 1. In terms of the cliché of the calculating Jew, then, Wagner argues that the "Jewish" idea of emancipation has usurped the German idea (of nonemancipation, it would seem, either of the Jews or in general, but this remains indeterminate in Wagner's text), just as the abstract law always tends to become the literal truth of the Christian faith that attempts to supercede the law by announcing *itself* as the literal truth of that law's figures:

To our astonishment, we perceive that in our Liberal battles we have been floating in the air and fighting clouds, whereas the whole fair soil of material reality has found an appropriator [*der schöne Boden der ganz realen Wirklichkeit einen Aneigner fand*] whom our aerial flights have very much amused, no doubt, yet who holds us far too foolish to reward us by relaxing one iota of his usurpation of that material soil [*durch einiges Ablassen von diesem usurpierten realen Boden*].

Quite imperceptibly the "Creditor of Kings" has become the King of Creeds, and we really cannot take this monarch's pleading for emancipation as otherwise than uncommonly naïve, seeing that it is much rather we who are shifted into the necessity of fighting for emancipation from the Jews. According to the present constitution of this world, the Jew in truth is already more than emancipate: he rules, and will rule, so long as Money remains the power before which all our doings and our dealings lose their force. . . . That the impossibility of carrying farther any natural, any "necessary" and truly beauteous thing [*Natürliches, Nothwendiges, und wahrhaft Schönes weiter zu bilden*], upon the basis of that stage whereat the evolution of our arts has now arrived, and without a total alteration of that basis—that this has also brought the public Art-taste of our time between the busy fingers [*die geschäftigen Finger*] of the Jew, however, is the matter whose grounds we here have to consider somewhat closer. (81; 87)

The reversal of literal into figural and of figural into literal is here characterized, on the one hand, as the "usurpation" of the (German) material ground by the (Jewish) immaterial. Jewish immateriality and abstraction has thus replaced German materiality. On the other hand, Jewish materiality—the materiality of the Jewish letter, which here appears in its nineteenth-century form as money—has also replaced German immateriality, for money has come to control art. That is, matter has replaced spirit. Just as spirit is always indebted to the material letter, so the German, that is, the pagan-Christian, or natural art, always "owes" money to the Jew, a priori. And this is so, as the chronically indebted Wagner knows but does not wish to know, regardless of whether or not one owes anyone any money at all. If the Jews are held responsible for all abstract materiality or material abstraction, the initial form of which is taken to be the dead letter of the law, and if money functions, within capitalism, as an exemplary form of abstract materiality or material abstraction, then one "owes" the Jews money in general and therefore all money, all one's money, because they are transcendentally responsible for money as such. Furthermore, from the perspective of this crazy anti-Semitic transcendental logic, the abstract character of the materiality of the native soil, of nature itself, i.e., the lack of any immediate meaningfulness of culture as nature, is precisely due to the Jews. That is, even the embarrassing silliness and implausibility of nationalism can be attributed to the Jews, according to this "logic," and so the nonnationalist concept of "emancipation" becomes a "Jewish" idea.[11]

Because Jews control the Germans, and because the notion of the emancipation of the Jews is itself a Jewish idea, this notion must for

Wagner be reversed into that of the emancipation of the Germans from the Jews: "It is much rather we who are shifted into the necessity of fighting for emancipation from the Jews" (81; 87). While this seems to suggest that the Germans must simply be free of the Jews, the structure of the thought is a bit more complicated.[12] As I've suggested above, the mid-nineteenth-century reversal of emancipation involves both a desire to free oneself from the Jews and a desire to become one of the Jews, or one with the Jews, a desire to replace the Jews. Just as Jewish emancipation meant that Jews should become citizens in the German lands, so the emancipation of the Germans from the Jews must mean that the Germans should become citizens in the Jewish land, that they should become Jews—or more precisely, Zionists! In the case of Wagner, this ambiguity is exacerbated by a further one. Namely, as has been much discussed, Wagner is not sure that he is *not* the illegitimate son of a certain actor named Geyer (meaning "vulture"), who may, as far as Wagner knows, have been a Jew.[13] Insofar as he is both a German Christian and the (at least figural) son of Geyer, to the rotting carcass of whose name we will return below, Wagner is a Jew divided from himself. In order to become (imaginarily) one with himself, he must both get completely free of Judaism and become completely Jewish. This double bind reinforces the double bind implied by the German "necessity of fighting for emancipation from the Jews." Envy of the prefigural origin as well as fear and hatred of it patently overdetermine each other within this structure.[14]

All of Wagner's remarks on religion and politics here should not mislead us, according to Wagner, about the topic of his essay: "We may completely pass over any dealing with this same phenomenon [viz. the popular dislike of the Jewish nature] in the field of Religion and Politics" (79; 85). The legitimation of this feeling with respect to art is merely the legitimation of an aesthetic phenomenon with respect to the aesthetic (for art is about feeling: "Music is the language of passion [*die Musik ist die Sprache der Leidenschaft*]" [86; 92]), and a legitimation which simply takes the form of a capitulation to the feeling ("if we avow it quite without ado" [82; 88]). The feeling legitimates itself by being deeply felt: the aesthetic generates its own necessity, absolutely. And the self-affirmation of this feeling will allow the Germans to "win" the "forces" they need for "this war of liberation" (82; 88) from the Jews. Clarifying by feeling their hatred of the other, the Germans will evidently render more pure and more homogeneous their love of themselves. But according to Wagner, the self-enactment of this feeling will have nothing to do with either politics or religion, state or church, power or the spirit of love. There will be no theopolitics here, only aesthetics, which thereby comes to occupy the place of theopolitics as a supplement in the Derridian sense.

The self-denegating, supplementary sublation of theopolitics into aesthetics will proceed not only by showing how the Jew has ruined, or threatens to ruin, German aesthetics, but by developing (that is, performatively describing) German aesthetics—German feeling—tautologically *as* the feeling of fear and hatred of the Jew. The Jew is opposed to German feelings because German feelings are the feelings of the hatred of the Jew. And this is so because the Jew is opposed to German feelings. But what is the Jew? Wagner's dogmatic phenomenology, or his phenomenology-without-*epokhé*, of German feeling(s) begins by describing its object, the Jew, as that which is not capable of being present either objectively or subjectively, either as represented or as representer, within the field of art, or again within the (theopolitical) field of feeling, nature, or Germanness. The Jew is properly the outside of art.

For Wagner, the Jew is incapable of being represented in the field of the arts in either visual or aural terms, either as image or as speech. The Jew is thus first of all excluded from art by being excluded from the two *spiritual* senses of sight and hearing. In each case, by an apparent paradox, the naturalness of the Jew asserts itself, but only in the sense of the brute materiality of the Jew, a materiality that, because it is always somehow either too much or too little, is characterized as something radically *unnatural*. For example, the "outward appearance" of the Jew is taken to be "instinctively" disagreeable. And this appearance is described as an "unpleasant freak of Nature [*unangenehmen Naturspieles*]" (83; 89), in the sense of a game nature plays at a distance from its proper or serious functioning, as rhetoric occurs at a distance from the serious business of philosophy or art. This appearance, then, "can never be thinkable as a subject for the art of re-presentment [*als ein Gegenstand der darstellenden Kunst denkbar*]" (83; 89), either in plastic art or on the stage (whether as character or actor).

Because the Jew is outwardly unnaturally natural or material, he is also inwardly so: "Neither can we hold him capable of any sort of artistic utterance of his [inner] essence" (84; 89). Because outer and inner, or objective and subjective, aspects coincide, because form and content are one, where the outer form is unnaturally natural, so is the inner content.

Wagner's organicist, literalist-symbolist aesthetic ideology in this way both provides him with the passage from the Jew's appearance to his speech and provides us with a further clue to the logic of his conceptualization of the Jew: the Jew is nonorganic, the one whose interior and exterior do not coincide. Yet, even in the Jew both outside and inside coincide in this, that they do not coincide either with each other or (therefore) with themselves. Thus, both the outside and the inside of the Jew are to be excluded from the organic, natural realm of (symbolic) art.[15]

The level on which this non-self-coincidence that the Jew abstractly embodies (or allegorically personifies) appears most significantly for Wagner's analysis, however, is the level of speech, as the level of the ostensibly immediate, external self-presentation of pure interiority. Music, however, as the highest of the arts, is "the language of passion" (86; 92; I have changed Ellis's "speech" to "language" here, although the point would be that Wagner makes no distinction between "speech" and "language" in the case of what he considers to be natural or organic subjectivity). For this reason, the inadequacy and self-inadequation of the Jew's speech will immediately provide a fortiori sufficient proof of the Jew's incapacity to be in the essence of art, to be at the musical center of the arts. The problem with the Jew's speech is that it is never his own: the Jew always speaks the language of the other, the language that is not his property or properly his. In short, the Jew speaks improperly, or figuratively, derivatively, rhetorically:[16]

Der Jude spricht die Sprache der Nation, unter welcher er von Geschlecht zu Geschlecht lebt, aber er spricht sie immer als Ausländer. . . . Zunächst muß im Allgemeinen der Umstand, daß der Jude die modernen europäischen Sprachen nur wie erlernte, nicht als angeborene Sprachen redet, ihn von aller Fähigkeit, in ihnen sich seinem Wesen entsprechend, eigenthümlich und selbständig kundzugeben, ausschließen. Eine Sprache . . . ist nicht das Werk Einzelner, sondern einer geschichtlichen Gemeinsamkeit: nur wer unbewußt in dieser Gemeinsamkeit aufgewachsen ist, nimmt auch an ihren Schöpfungen Theil. Der Jude stand aber außerhalb einer solchen Gemeinsamkeit, einsam mit seinem Jehova in einem zersplitterten, bodenlosen Volksstamme, welchem alle Entwickelung aus sich versagt bleiben mußte, wie selbst die eigenthümliche (hebräische) Sprache dieses Stammes ihm nur als eine todte erhalten ist.[17]

The Jew speaks the language of the nation in whose midst he dwells from generation to generation, but he speaks it always as an alien . . . that the Jew talks the modern European languages merely as learnt, and not as mother tongues, must necessarily debar him from all capability of therein expressing himself idiomatically, independently, and conformably to his nature. A language . . . is not the work of scattered units, but of an historical community: only he who has unconsciously grown up within the bond of this community, takes also any share in its creations. But the Jew has stood outside the pale of any such community, stood solitarily with his Jehova in a splintered, soilless stock, to which all self-sprung evolution must stay denied, just as even the peculiar (Hebraic) language of that stock has been preserved for him merely as a thing defunct.

The figurality or impropriety of the Jew's speech has, not surprisingly, two dimensions. Not only is the Jew not rooted in the soil of history and community, and so *abstract*, but also he is too deeply rooted, and so *material*, in a different sense. Wagner characterizes the "purely physical aspect of the Jewish mode of speech [*die rein sinnliche Kundgebung der jüdischen Sprache*]" (85; 91) as repellent to the Euro-Germanic soul. He points out that two thousand years of culture have not succeeded "in breaking the remarkable stubbornness [*die sonderliche Hartnäckigkeit*] of the Jewish *naturel* [*Naturells*] as regards the peculiarities of Semitic pronunciation."[18] Here again, the Jew appears as both too abstract and too material to be concretely spiritual in the good sense of the Indo-Germanic, European Christian traditions.

Finally, Wagner's naturalist-nationalist aesthetic sublation of theopolitics is also a *humanism*. The exclusion of the Jews from art as from nature is synonymous with their exclusion from the realm of the human as human nature. The Jew is both unnaturally natural and materially immaterial, and as such—and as in Marx also—he is *not human*:

If we hear a Jew speak, we are unconsciously offended by the entire want of purely human expression in his discourse [*so verletzt uns unbewußt aller Mangel rein menschlichen Ausdruckes in seiner Rede*]: the cold indifference of its peculiar "blubber" ["Gelabbers"] never by any chance rises to the ardour of a higher, heartfelt passion. (85; 91)

The Jew is not human, because he is cold, passionless, has no feelings (feelings requiring the fusion of abstract and material qua concrete spirit that is denied the Jew).[19] He is therefore incapable of dialogue with a non-Jew: "He is incapable of replying in kind. Never does the Jew excite himself in mutual interchange of feelings [*Empfindungen*] with us, but . . . only in the altogether egoistic interest of his vanity or profit."[20] The exacerbation of nondialogue by the one-sided rhetoric of *figura* is here blamed by Wagner, without further ado, on the Jews, on their inhumanity. Being outside of the musical self-presence of the voiced spirit, the Jew is inhuman. Conversely, being outside of the human realm of the (dialogical) speech of sympathetic feeling, the Jew is incapable of song and, hence, of music. "Song is just Talk aroused to highest passion: Music is the language of passion" (86; 92); music is spiritual, literal language.

If the Jew is, on the one hand, by nature (by virtue of the unnatural nature of his nature) excluded from art, where art is conceived as the sphere of materiality dissolved in its own immanent spirituality, then, on the other hand, the Jew has "nevertheless been able in the widest spread of modern art-varieties, to wit in Music, to reach the rulership of public taste" (87; 93). Properly speaking, because he speaks only improperly, situated on the exterior of art, the Jew has nonetheless managed not only to enter into the interior of art but also to appropriate that interior—that interiority—for himself. So it is necessary for Wagner, in the next step of his "argument," to explain how the essentially nonartistic Jew has been able to both "become a musician" (87; 93) and take over music and the arts more generally.

Wagner begins his explanation by describing not so much how the Jew has been able to "become a musician," but rather how he has been able to present the *appearances* of becoming a musician while actually failing to do so. In order to describe this process, Wagner describes both what sort of Jews have become (apparent) musicians, and what sort of (apparent) musicians these Jews are. Once he has accomplished this, he can address the question why this sort of (apparent) musician has become powerful on the contemporary German scene.

To begin with the first of these subordinate concerns: the cultured Jews, those who have cast off their Judaism and yet failed to take on any intimate or real connection with the European-Germanic culture around them, have occupied the field of the arts and more particularly of music (87–88; 93–94). In some cases, they have become thinkers who have a merely reflective and abstract relation to things.[21] In others, they have become artists. But what sort of artists do these rootless figures caught between an abandoned Judaism and an unattainable Christian European identity become?

The art of the cultured Jews is one of imitation, the reuse of the carcasslike forms of others without any reference to content (88–89; 94–95). Even when they seek for some sort of sustenance, ground, spirit, or content in their own cultural roots, being incapable of relating to the contents of European-Germanic culture, they find only the radical formalism, the radical rootlessness, of their own culture—the dead letter of a decayed synagogal musical tradition (90; 96–97). The nonspiritual nonnature of this tradition, which is "reflective" rather than "instinctual" (91; 97), dominates the noninstinctual instincts of the Jewish musician, such that the synagogal musical features, dead material-formal patterns that they are, permeate his compositions despite his best intentions and most acute awareness.[22] The Jew "merely listens to the barest surface of our art [*Kunstwesen*], but not to its life-bestowing inner organism [*lebengebenden inneren Organismus*]" (92; 98), because he can only understand what answers to his own musical tradition, a tradition of surface, appearance, mere material form. The Jew mistakes the "most external accidents" of the non-Jewish musical traditions for their "essence" (92; 99) and thus produces a distorted version of them in his own music, "as though a poem of Goethe's, for instance, were being rendered in the Jewish jargon" (92; 99). As an apparent musician, in short, the cultured Jew is a formalist.

The reason why the Jew can appear to be a musician "today," according to Wagner, is that the music of "today" is bogged down in the dead, imitative formalism that proceeds upon the exhaustion of substantial content, and so of living forms, which was brought to completion by Beethoven.[23] Indeed, the music of "today," like the music of today's "today," is what some might today call "postmodern": "So does the Jew musician hurl together the diverse forms and styles of every age and every master. Packed side by side, we find the formal idiosyncrasies of all the schools, in motleyest chaos" (92; 99). In such a soulless mixture, there is neither "passion" ("Leidenschaft") nor "calm" ("Ruhe"), only "prickling unrest" ("prickelnde Unruhe") or "sluggishness" or "inertia" ("Trägheit").[24]

But why exactly has German music fallen prey to the formalism that makes it a prey to Jewish exploitation? Here, in its culminating moment, Wagner's argument encounters a decisive aporia. If he blames the downfall of German music on the Jews, then he acknowledges that the Jews are stronger or more active than the Germans, the letter more spiritual or positive than the spirit itself. However, if he makes the Germans take responsibility for the downfall of their own music, then he shows German music to be internally flawed and thereby exonerates Judaism. How does Wagner deal with this dilemma? By having it both ways—naturally! After discussing the cases of Mendelssohn-Bartholdy and Meyerbeer, Wagner attempts to address this problem in bringing his essay to a conclusion (98–100; 105–8). Insisting upon the "ineptitude of the present musical epoch" (98; 105), Wagner chooses to emphasize, on the one hand, that the downfall of music in this time is due to its own "inner death" (99; 106). On the other hand, he argues that the Jewish musicians of the day not only have *not* helped it to become strong but also have attached themselves to it like worms parasitically living off a dying body and completing its destruction. The death of German music is its own "inner death," but death itself is Jewish, not German. The death of German music is thus its immanent Jewishness, and the life of Judaism in German music is the life of the death of that music, the life of the death as such of life as such.[25] The life of the Jews, like that of worms on a corpse, is the life of death as the "incapacity for life [*Lebensunfähigheit*]" (99, 106):

Hätten die näher erwähnten beiden jüdischen Komponisten in Wahrheit unsere Musik zu höherer Blüthe gefördert, so müßten wir uns nur eingestehen, daß unser Zurückbleiben hinter ihnen auf einer bei uns eingetretenen organischen Unfähigkeit beruhe: dem ist aber nicht so; im Gegentheile stellt sich das individuelle rein musikalische Vermögen gegen vergangene Kunstepochen als eher vermehrt denn vermindert heraus. Die Unfähigkeit liegt in dem Geiste unserer Kunst selbst, welche nach einem anderen Leben verlangt, als das künstliche ist, das ihr mühsam jetzt erhalten wird. . . . Dieser Kunst konnten sich die Juden nicht eher bemächtigen, als bis in ihr Das darzuthun war, was sie in ihr erweislich eben offengelegt haben: ihre innere Lebensunfähigkeit. So lange die musikalische Sonderkunst ein wirkliches organisches Lebensbedürfnis in sich hatte, bis auf die Zeiten Mozart's und Beethoven's, fand sich nirgends ein jüdischer Komponist: unmöglich konnte ein diesem Lebensorganismus gänzlich fremdes Element an den Bildungen dieses Lebens theilnehmen. Erst wenn der innere Tod eines Körpers offenbar ist, gewinnen die außerhalb liegenden Elemente die Kraft, sich seiner zu bemächtigen, aber nur um ihn zu zersetzen; dann löst sich wohl das Fleisch dieses Körpers in wimmelnde Viellebigkeit von Würmern auf: wer möchte aber bei ihrem Anblicke den Körper selbst noch für lebendig halten? Der Geist, das ist: das Leben, floh von diesem Körper hinweg zu wiederum Verwandtem, und dieses ist nur das Leben selbst: nur im wirklichen Leben können auch wir den Geist der Kunst wiederfinden, nicht bei ihrer Würmer-zerfressenen Leiche.

Had the two aforesaid Jew composers in truth helped Music into riper bloom, then we should merely have had to admit that our tarrying behind them rested on some organic debility [*organischen Unfähigkeit*] that had taken sudden hold of us:

but not so is the case; on the contrary, as compared with bygone epochs, the specific musical powers [*das individuelle rein musikalische Vermögen*] of nowadays have rather increased than diminished. The incapacity lies in the spirit of our Art itself [*Die Unfähigkeit liegt im Geiste unserer Kunst selbst*], which is longing for another life than the artificial one [*das künstliche*] now toilsomely upheld for it. . . . The Jews could never take possession of this art, until that was to be exposed in it which they now demonstrably have brought to light—its inner incapacity for life [*ihre innere Lebensunfähigkeit*]. So long as the separate art of Music had a real organic life-need [*ein wirkliches organisches Lebensbedürfnis*] in it, down to the epochs of Mozart and Beethoven, there was nowhere to be found a Jew composer: it was impossible for an element entirely foreign to that living organism to take part in the formative stages of that life [*ein diesem Lebensorganismus gänzlich fremdes Element an den Bildungen dieses Lebens theilnehmen*]. Only when a body's inner death is manifest [*der innere Tod eines Körpers offenbar ist*], do outside elements win the power of lodgment in it—yet merely to destroy it [*nur um ihn zu zersetzen*]. Then indeed that body's flesh dissolves into a swarming colony of insect-life [*wimmelnde Viellebigkeit von Würmern*]: but who, in looking on that body's self, would hold it still for living? The spirit, that is: the life [*Der Geist, das ist: das Leben*], has fled from out that body, has sped to kindred other bodies [such as that of Wagner?]; and this is all that makes out Life [*und dieses ist nur das Leben selbst*]. In genuine Life alone can we, too, find again the ghost of Art, and not within its worm-befretted carcase [*nur im wirklichen Leben können auch wir den Geist der Kunst wiederfinden, nicht bei ihrer Würmer-zerfressenen Leiche*].[26]

At the culmination of his argument against the Jews, Wagner suggests, trying to save (German musical) face, that the outside can only come inside when the inside has gone outside. On the frontier where this outside and inside go past each other in the process of switching places, he makes the Jews assume responsibility for the death of the German (as German music), its going outside, even as he denies their capacity to control or undo the life of the German (as the life of its music). That Wagner is externalizing his own Judaism here is clear through the close functional analogy between the "worms" in this passage and the Jewish "vulture"—*Geyer*—he thinks or fears he is. Vultures prey on the dead as the insects here feed on the essentially already dead body of German music. That Wagner is, in the same gesture, externalizing his own Christianity is no less patent. Christianity preys, like a vulture, on the dead body of Judaism. If the spirit lives off a dead letter, then it lives as a vulture. While recalling Daumer's Jewish cannibals, Feuerbach's Jewish gourmands, and the blood-drinking Jews of medieval superstition, Wagner the fanatical vegetarian cannot help but recall also his own bloodthirsty self not only as (possible) half-Jew but also as (possible) half-Christian.[27]

What, then, will be the fate of (German) art now that it has died a (Jewish) death? Wagner tells us here that, when art dies, when organic, natural life dies, its spirit passes into other life, other bodies. Clearly, Wagner means to suggest that his body, the body of his musical corpus, will henceforth carry the reincarnated, living spirit of German art. As his English translator helps him to say, however, no doubt unwittingly, there is a curious ambiguity in this (re)discovery of the spirit of art in life. "In genuine Life alone can we, too, find again the ghost of Art, and not within its worm-befretted carcase." On the one hand, this means that life is the spirit of art and, thus, that art is ultimately nature, that form has its origin in content, that art imitates or expresses the nature or life that is its origin. On the other hand, the *Geist* of art here, as Ellis points out through his translation, is also a ghost. It is not only an original spirit but also an afterlife, the living on of one dead. If what we find in life is the ghost of art, then life or nature imitates art, is the afterlife of art. Moreover, if the conventionally posited artificiality of art is its distance from life (or nature), then life (or nature) is here, in this passage in Wagner, doubly artificial: it imitates or expresses—it is the place of the "ghostly" or artificial derivative of—an art which itself exists prior to, or independently of, nature, an originary artificiality. Life is the artifice of artifice, the imitation of an originary imitation. In life we find the ghost of art. With this unintentional conclusion, Wagner—the body of this life where art's ghost will be found—overcomes and replaces the Jews as the place where death becomes more alive than life. Because he not only overcomes but also replaces the Jews here, Wagner is compelled to repeat and intensify his (sacrificial) polemic against the Jews from this point on, to the end of his (wandering) career.[28]

Without once looking back, take ye your part in this regenerative work of deliverance through self-annulment [*an diesem, durch Selbstvernichtung wiedergebärenden Erlösungswerke*]; then are we one and un-dissevered [*einig und ununterschieden*]! But bethink ye, that one only thing can redeem you from the burden of your curse: the redemption of Ahasuerus—*Going under!* [*der Untergang!*][29]

With this apostrophe to the Jews, Wagner ends a text that has otherwise had only non-Jewish Germans as its implied addressee and subject, its "you" as its "we." Not only anything but dialogical, the injunction to "Go under" contained in this apostrophe is particularly unsettling as it cannot refer to mere assimilatory acculturation, or even to conversion. Wagner has already criticized these processes as leading to the mere "cultured Jew." "Going under" hence apparently refers to a literal suicide of the Jews or to their literal genocidal murder. And Wagner's use of the phrase "self-annihilating, bloody struggle [*diesem selbstvernichtenden, blutigen Kampfe*]"[30] in the first edition, even if he replaces it with the more prudent "regenerative work of deliverance through self-annulment" in 1869, seems to support such a reading. While it remains nonetheless possible to understand Wagner as recommending a *figural* self-destruction, in the sense of a more radical inner self-transformation than the "cultured Jews" have thus far achieved, such a reading is less plausible than the *literal* one (even if it was Wagner's own), given the structure of Jewish-German relations as figural-literal relations.[31] For the transformation of the figural (Jew) into the literal (German) can always be suspected, from Wagner's point of view, of being merely figural, not literal, merely apparent, not real. The only way of being certain that the figural has literally transformed itself into the literal is to destroy the figural literally. This is the antirhetorical logic that leads directly—if not without the cooperation of manifold additional factors— from Wagner's reversal of emancipation to the Holocaust. But since the figural dimension can never be eradicated, even the *literal* destruction of the figural cannot definitively accomplish its *figural* destruction. Even if it had been total with regard to the historical existence of Jews, the Holocaust would thus have been carried out *in vain*. It was necessary for the perpetrators of the Holocaust to repress this last consideration through an ever-increasing level and scope of the violence of attempted literalization.

Postscript

THROUGH MODERNISM TO—"EMANCIPATION"
FROM HOLOCAUST MEMORY?

The epoch of emancipation ends with the mid-nineteenth-century reversal that proceeds upon a certain degree of cultural and social assimilation, although it precedes the definitive (if more Pyrrhic than empirical) achievement of civil emancipation under Bismarck. When the epoch of emancipation comes to an end, so does the notion of a possible Jewish-German dialogue, even if it takes another century for the German "people" to draw the unspeakably misguided and unspeakably bloody consequences that emerge in the 1940s.[1] This book has itself come to an end—"properly speaking"—with the consideration of Marx's and Wagner's texts, in which the reversal of emancipation perhaps most strikingly and influentially makes itself felt. But the foregoing analyses no doubt raise a number of questions as to how they would be extended to cover both the many aspects of German Jewish life and thought during the first three-quarters of the nineteenth century, which we have hardly addressed, and also the period from the achievement of civil emancipation in 1871 to World War II and thence up to our own moment. What general trajectory do the Jews of Germany traverse, in their ideological development, from the time of the Enlightenment through the nineteenth century until civil emancipation? Looking in the other direction, what is the general trend of the cultural politics of religion in Germany for Germans and Jews from the unification until the end of the First World War? What historical roles do the Marxist and Wagnerian discourses play in this period, and then through the

Weimar Republic until 1933 and beyond? And more broadly, what German religio-cultural or theopolitical phenomena proceeding upon Marx's and Wagner's essays are determined by the post-Romantic discourse whose extremes these two figures articulate? Further, in terms of the rhetoric of Jewish-German dialogue, what is the structure of the German-language *modernism* that presumably at some point succeeds upon post-Romantic discourse? Finally, what light does the relationship between contemporary German culture and the memory of the Holocaust shed on the relationship between that same contemporary German culture and the modernist tradition, and vice versa? While it would require at least another book, if not more, to deal with these questions in an "adequate" manner, I will attempt to provide provisional answers here.

The Fading of Enlightenment Liberalism: Through the 'Kulturkampf' to Polarized Historicisms

First of all, as is well known, the general tendency of German Jewry across the nineteenth century, as it approaches civil emancipation, is a liberal one. Both within theology or religion per se and in the broader bourgeois sphere outside of it, German Jews overwhelmingly affirm the Enlightenment discourse, with its ethics of tolerance guided by the notion of universal humanity situated in law-governed, rational freedom, which initially enabled the Jews whose discourse it ambivalently imitates to enter into "secularized" German society. As Mosse and others have persuasively shown, to focus on the example of theological reform alone, nineteenth-century German Judaism repeatedly emphasizes Enlightenment ethico-theology in the traditions of Lessing, Kant, and Mendelssohn (although without the latter's orthodox position on the law, and sometimes without his natural religion either).[2] Since the "triumph" of Enlightenment is fleeting, liberal Judaism mixes with this ethico-theology aspects of the "Romantic" Protestantism of Schleiermacher (which however precisely resists or refuses the Neo-Catholic "Romantic" turn in the sense in which I have been using the term and is consequently either "behind" or "ahead" of its time), as well as motifs from petit bourgeois morality and patriotism. These in-mixings no doubt have as much to do, for nineteenth-century German Jewry, with the social necessities of making oneself agreeable to one's German national cultural environment as with explicit theoretical or theological considerations per se. In the incorporation of Schleiermacher's influence, however, we can already see the anticipatory shades of a partial abandonment of the Enlightenment mentality in the German Jewish community. By the latter part of the century, particularly just after the civil emancipation which would seem to have realized the hopes of German Jewry, this Enlightenment liberalism comes to grief. Since it is in the years of the *Kulturkampf* of the 1870s and 1880s that Enlightenment liberalism most glaringly reveals itself to be no longer workable within, or compatible with, the world that the German Jews confront as their alienated own, let us say a few words to characterize the period of the *Kulturkampf* from the perspective of the present study.

When the Prussian State acts to restrict the power of the Catholic Church, it clearly does so not in terms of the Enlightenment principle of tolerance and freedom of religion, which would entail the equal freedom of both state and church, but rather—and more boldly as time goes on—in terms of the Reformation version of the principle of the sovereignty of the state over the church.[3] When the state becomes sovereign, however, it will reveal a tendency to *become* a kind of church or God on its own, as the Catholics hasten to point out, even as the conflation of state with church (and in particular the implicitly Judaeo-pagan character of such a conflation) was one of the objections the Reformation raised against medieval theopolitical arrangements. Accordingly, under the guidance of the conservatives from the late 1870s until just before the First World War, the Prussian State becomes a "Christian State" in a way that equally bases itself on the cultural particularity of German national historical traditions and on Lutheranism, as the German, and more specifically, Prussian, religion. In short, the conservative Second Reich bears witness, although in a manner different from the texts of Marx and Wagner, to the late-nineteenth-century ascendancy of an oxymoronically heathen Neo-Reformation culture. In this case, the answer to both Enlightenment and Romanticism appears to be situated in the idolatrous worship of the authoritarian state as conflated with the lawless faith in Luther's God. The *Kulturkampf*, then, is a major cultural-political manifestation of the shift from the Romantic discourse to the post-Romantic one I outlined in Chapter 7.

If this is the case, then how does one explain that the *Kulturkampf* subsides by means of a *reconciliation* between Catholic and Protestant forces? As Uriel Tal shows, this is a "reconciliation" that is not one, for it boils down to an assimilation of the Catholic forces into the conservative, nationalist discourse of the Protestant, German state (85–96). Moreover, Catholics assimilate here precisely in place of the Jews; for the Jews, of course, this is already a bad sign. Only truly *Christianized* Jews, it seems, can enter into a Christian State, and the Catholics qualify for this position much more easily than recently converted Jews, as the discourse of racism begins to supplement that of religious anti-Semitism toward the end of the century. What position, then, will the Jews of Germany themselves occupy in this situation?

In the face of the *Kulturkampf*, the Jews of Germany, who are still by and large operating, in these early years of the Second Empire, as if their emancipation had been carried out in terms of Enlightenment liberalism, at first largely applaud the initiatives of the Prussian State against the Catholic Church (for the latter seems to them to stand, in a radically pre-Enlightenment manner, for the subordination of state to church). It gradually becomes clear, however, that not only the *conservative* Protestants, who are most influential in the secular yet "Christian" State, but also the *liberal* Protestants, who are relatively apolitical, function in terms of a nationalistic repetition of the Protestant discourse whose earlier resistance to Enlightenment we have already seen at work, for example, in the attack of Cranz on Mendelssohn almost a century before. Although we've already indicated the conservative position, a word about the liberal position would no doubt be helpful here.

By arguing in terms of "scientific," historical studies of the Old and New Testaments, the liberal Protestants attempt belatedly to accomplish or to repeat the counter-Enlightenment, not in an irrationalistic mode (as in the *Sturm und Drang* of Jacobi, Hamann, and others), but (perhaps more treacherously) in a *historicist* mode. More specifically, the liberal Protestants reassert or repeat the (post-)Reformation reassertion of the early Christian claim that Christianity, as religion of faith, supercedes Judaism. But this time the repetition is undergirded by modern, historical research. The Protestantism that, for the early Romantics such as Schlegel and Novalis, still needed some sort of synthesis with the law in order to prevent it from becoming completely formless, now simultaneously reasserts its independence of, and superiority to, the law, *and* gives itself the kind of structural underpinnings and situatedness that the law provides. Here, the law in this latter sense appears as history itself. Because it provides a structure for faith, history becomes, to so speak, the law without law of the overcoming of law through faith. Because this solution can now be obtained within the Protestant framework, the Neo-Catholic turn of so many of the Romantics appears, from the perspective of liberal (as well as conservative) Protestantism in the late nineteenth century, to have been as much of a mistake as the Judaizing tendencies of Enlightenment.[4]

By the end of the century, the Enlightenment liberalism of German Jewry is no longer tenable. Liberal Jews have been disappointed by both conservative and liberal Protestantism, and in turn, liberal Protestants, who were expecting the Jews to convert as a means of reconciliation, have also suffered disappointment. Finally, the worst suspicions of the conservatives concerning the impossibility of assimilation seem also to have been confirmed, if largely because they themselves have ensured this impossibility through their policies of exclusion. The failure of liberalism will have consequences for both methodology and ideology that tend to erode the political center in which, relatively speaking, all three of these groups situate themselves.

In methodological terms, first of all, the failure of Judaeo-Christian dialogue at the center reinforces the turn of all three of these cultural-ideological groups away from liberal Enlightenment models of formal reason toward historicism, a turn which, coming out of irrationalist and Neo-Catholic countercurrents to the Enlightenment from the late eighteenth century, has in part itself led to the failure. Secondly, the insistence on history as sole absolute, in methodological terms, tends to reinforce, in ideological terms, the political extremes that are most radically pseudosecularized, for these extremes associate formalism with Judaism, and they also identify Judaism with religion itself in the negative sense. Thus, on the side of the state, nationalism increasingly asserts its independence of any faith other than that in the national, cultural-historical, and, because the God of the nation is increasingly its biological "nature," racial substance. On the side of the disenfranchised, insofar as this cult of the state fails to persuade its victims of the legitimacy of its sway, communist discourse establishes itself, within the same discursive light, but at the opposite end of the spectrum, equally as a political theology of historical substantiality, here that of concrete labor. The (material and materialist) *formalism* taken to characterize Judaism and, to a lesser extent, residually Jewish Catholicism (and increasingly even religious Protestantism), will be excluded at each political extreme in the name of the realization of *history* as destiny itself. The two extreme forms of post-Romantic discourse that are exemplified by Marx and Wagner thus impose themselves increasingly in the late years of the nineteenth century and the early years of the twentieth, especially after the First World War and the Russian Revolution, as the dominant pair of cultural-political alternatives. Outside of an increasingly fragile liberalism and a multiply threatened neo-orthodoxy, Jews of Germany have little choice but to participate in the emancipation of either Humanity or Germany from *themselves* by joining either the political far left or the political far right. In the present context, a few brief remarks on the concrete contexts and prospects offered by each of these two main options will have to suffice.

As for Marx's version of the "Jew," it remains intact to different degrees within the socialist-communist worlds up until the recent past.[5] The position of the German Communist Party (KPD) in the years leading up to World War II is the least ambiguous. Lenin and Stalin follow the Marxian position (as developed further by Kautsky in the years leading up to World War I), while the KPD is obliged to follow the pattern of communism in the East. In 1919, the KPD reissues Marx's essay on the Jewish question in the attempt to counteract the drift of the Social Democrats away from Marx's position. Unfortunately, as pressure mounts from the right-wing anti-Semitic parties during the 1920s, the communists attempt to turn popular anti-Semitic sentiment to their advantage. They not only suggest that Jewish capital is supporting the Nazis and that, conversely, some of the Nazis are of Jewish background but also they decide in 1923 to compete with the right-wing parties by appealing to national aspirations. In 1930, they call upon the Nazi masses to join the KPD in a "common struggle." For non-anti-Semitic Jews as Jews, in short, life in the party is no party, even if they often denegate this fact while investing culturally transmitted messianic motifs into the "secular" messianism of Marx.

In contrast to the position of the KPD, that of the Social Democratic Party (SPD) is—not surprisingly—somewhat more flexible. Under the leadership of Karl Kautsky, as I've just indicated, Marx's view of the Jewish question maintains itself largely intact in the years leading up to World War I. But after the war, no longer under the leadership of Kautsky, and in response to the rise of right-wing anti-Semitism, the Social Democrats drift away from Marx's position on the Jewish question.

Nonetheless, some ambivalence in the attitude of the Social Democrats toward the Jews remains legible first of all in the Social Democrats' defensiveness about their potential "Jewishness" and their willingness to abandon the Jews: the Social Democrats defend themselves against right-wing attacks on the "Jewish" character of Marxism simply by insisting that Marxism is by no means Jewish. (One of their prime arguments for this point, absurdly enough, is that Engels was a Christian.) Secondly, the SPD maintains a tense relationship with its left-wing intellectual adherents, many of whom are Jewish. Despite their opposition to right-wing anti-Semitism, then, the Social Democrats during the Weimar Republic have little more capacity to accommodate Judaism in its cultural specificity than do the communists.

Finally, and therefore, many of the left-wing Jewish intellectuals of the Weimar period—as represented by the journals, the *Tagebuch* and the *Weltbühne*, for example—must remain outside the parties or on their edges. It is in the ambivalences of these left-wing intellectuals that the impossibility of entering socialist discourse without adopting a patently anti-Semitic discourse becomes perhaps most clearly manifest. These thinkers are caught not only between internationalism and nationalism but also between, on the one hand, the somewhat grayed Enlightenment ideal of respect for universal specificity and, on the other hand, the historicisms that tend to squelch either (as Marxism) cultural specificity or (as nationalism) cultural universality. Remaining close to Enlightenment ideals, combining Marxism with a Kant who has been read with idealist glasses, the predominately Jewish intellectuals of the left gravely underestimate the threat of anti-Semitism during the Weimar Republic. Even if they are clearly incapable of persuading themselves to be satisfied by the cultural politics of the left parties, and even less so by the cultural politics of the parties on the right, they nonetheless allow themselves to be misled by their optimistic faith in rationality to the point of failing to comprehend the gravity of the threat coming from the extreme right as the Weimar years wear on.

As for the development of the Wagnerian ideology, which often walks uncomfortably or ambiguously a fine (if crude and barbaric) line between Christian and anti-Christian anti-Semitism, we do not need to rehearse its entire history here nor to emphasize the—excessively obvious—exclusion of the Jews from German nationalist discourses. Rather, it is necessary to register (and it would be worthwhile to treat in detail, as cannot be done here) the alienating and unsettling fact of the (limited) degree to which German Jewry is affected by Volkish discourse in such a way as to be prompted, on some occasions, to imitate it.[6] The influence of Volkish discourse on German Jewry from around the turn of the century through the Weimar Republic goes above all, as Mosse and others have shown, by way of the youth movement. The turn toward a spiritualized nature fused with the history of the nation produces various forms of Jewish nationalism. On one end of the spectrum there is the Zionism that rightly acknowledges to itself the degree to which European "nature" is becoming uninhabitable. At the other end, there are the much more naïve and even fundamentally misguided versions of Jewish-German nationalism, those which conflate Jewish nationality with German nationality, seeing the former as "realizing" itself (according to good Protestant logic) in the latter.[7] In general terms, the partial incapacity of German Jewry to resist the nature-worshipping, belatedly Lutheran (or, in some cases, "literally" Catholic) spirituality of the youth movement, even if relatively little racism makes its way into the discourse of German Jews, bears witness to the discursive violence to which German Jewry is everywhere subject in the late nineteenth and early twentieth centuries, the nonexistence of any nonviolent dialogue in this period whatsoever.[8]

Indeed, even where perhaps the most rigorous of the Zionists and Jewish Marxists come together to produce socialist Zionism, this fusion of internationalist and nationalist ideologies generally retains the disadvantage of leaving Judaism, or at least everything Judaism has been for a long time, far behind. This occurs despite a certain "abstract" affirmation of both universality and particularity that is the vehicle of the socialist Zionists' belated attempt to save Enlightenment discourse by reabsorbing Marxism and nationalism into an ethico-theology of universal toleration. While socialist Zionism seems to harmonize nationalism with internationalism, in doing so it risks redoubling the post-Romantic negation of (diasporic) Judaism. Even if it must appear retrospectively as the most persuasive, attractive combination of realism and idealism available to German (and more generally European) Jewry in the postliberal period leading up to World War II, its failure to overcome the anti-Semitism of its two post-Romantic component ideologies remains legible in its main manifestos and manifestations from its inception until today.[9]

"Judaic" Modernism and the Affirmation of Anticipatory Repetition

If the ideological horizons of Jewish-German "dialogue" from the late nineteenth to the mid-twentieth century are bounded by the extremes of Marxist socialism-communism and Wagnerian fascism, as the conservative and liberal ideological middle becomes more and more beleaguered and so enfeebled through 1933 and beyond, then where does *modernism* fit in? The fact that the Wagnerian discourse—consequently the rejection of modernism—swept Germany away or was chosen by Germany from 1933 through the Second World War means, of course, that in a sense modernism fits in nowhere, at least until after the war. Such a remark already implies, however, that I have in "mind" a modernist discourse that did develop and propose an alternative to the Marxist-Wagnerist couple. In order to sketch out the structure of what I "mean" by German *modernist* discourse, which can (roughly and problematically) be said to begin in about the 1880s and is still no doubt partly on its way today, let us reconsider the rhetorical wheel of Judaeo-Christian (mis)fortune. The next turn of the wheel beyond post-Romantic discourse must bring about, according to the "logic" of the structure itself, and assuming the wheel is still turning, a new Judaeo-centrism. Along with this emerges a return, at least in some sense, and in some degree, to an Enlightenment sensibility. Accordingly, the paganizing Neo-Protestantism of the post-Romantic period should now appear to be a mere prefiguration of what the modernist Neo-Enlightenment achieves.[10] In turn, on the one hand, the Catholicizing move of Romanticism (and by extension later Catholicisms) must seem even more naïve and unsophisticated—more *pre*-prefigurative—than under the *Kulturkampf*, where Catholicisms were still taken by Protestant discourses to pose something of a threat. On the other hand, the Catholicizing move must now seem as if it might once again supercede Enlightenment modernism in the future as its "realization, either in a positive or in a negative sense. (See Figure 8.)

If this turns out to be the most general structure of modernism, as I wish here hypothetically to maintain, then how is this structure more specifically spelled out in its main texts or movements? In the sketch that follows, I consider first how modernist texts relate to the Enlightenment critique of positive religion, then how they relate to Judaism, Marxism/

Wagnerism, and Catholicism. My two main examples of modernist discourse here are Nietzsche and Freud.

Insofar as it repeats (even as it displaces) the Enlightenment, modernism encounters—as did Enlightenment in its natural-religious and atheistic forms—the possibility of getting off the positive-religious merry-go-round. Modernism entertains anew the possibility of putting an end to the repetition of the letter of the positive-religious attempt to go beyond the letter, i.e., beyond materiality, death, or temporality as unseizability of the fleeing present. But modernism will get further from the project of positive religion than did the Enlightenment. It will hence take its distance, in a new way, from the hope of going beyond the repetition of the letter. It will make progress beyond the hope of progress, and acknowledge itself, beyond anything of which the Enlightenment was capable, to be still inevitably caught up in the repetition of the letters of positive religion, but "now" as the repetition of all of these letters "at once." But this acknowledgment will entail neither a renunciation of the Enlightenment project nor the return to one or another revealed tradition. For only the antidogmatic Enlightenment project allows self-interrogation, which incessantly gives rise to the acknowledgment of repetition, to become an infinite process. Rather than rejecting Enlightenment, then, modernism will repeat Enlightenment in a slightly new way as the affirmation of the necessity of repetition as such, an affirmation that knows itself to be—and affirms itself as—a new departure from, or more precisely, a significantly insignificant displacement of, the resistance to repetition it repeats. Of course the letter (of "pagan" materiality) that Western positive religion has attempted to overcome, as well as the letter (of positive religion) that Enlightenment has tried to reduce to rational spirit—two letters that are finally the one letter of materiality, death, or time—are not simply graspable, in temporal terms, as repetition. As we have constantly seen above, the letter spells also anticipation, or prefiguration, and not just repetition. Indeed, every repetition, as failure to return to the origin it repeats, also anticipates the successful return to that origin; every anticipation also repeats, or functions structurally as an after-image of, the fulfillment it awaits. Thus, the modernist affirmation of *repetition* will be accompanied by an affirmation of *anticipation*. If temporality means the incessant retreat of the present into its before and after, then the affirmation of before and after, the affirmation of the self-preceding and self-successive character of "presence," will be the

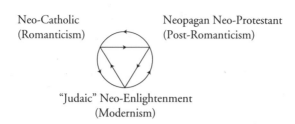

Neo-Catholic (Romanticism)

Neopagan Neo-Protestant (Post-Romanticism)

"Judaic" Neo-Enlightenment (Modernism)

FIGURE 8. The Judaeo-Christian Triangle in the Modernist Context

form in which modernism affirms temporality as such, rather than its overcoming in an always eternal or eternalized (because it is time interrupting) present.

The point can be illustrated by the discourses of Nietzsche, especially after the break with Wagner that is signaled by *Human, All Too Human* (1878), and Freud, especially from 1920 on (the date of publication of *Beyond the Pleasure Principle*), although there can be no question of doing justice here to the complexity of this topic in their texts. To start with Nietzsche, and concerning the problem of *repetition* first of all: Nietzsche's doctrine of the eternal recurrence of the same affirms repetition precisely as the way of going beyond the resentment of the will against time, not by sublating time, but by asserting its ubiquity. If everything recurs, then this is because there is no such thing as being, only endless becoming.[11] Second, concerning *anticipation*: in conjunction with the theme of the eternal return, the affirmation of the world of *appearances* as entirely lacking essential substratum, or *Ding An Sich*, is tantamount to an affirmation of the *anticipatory* character of all things. Reality presents itself as the not-yet of an essence or presence that will never arrive. According to each of these motifs, the anticipatory appearance and the recurrent "same" (or "the similar," "des Gleichen") are one "thing": what recurs is anticipation, and what is anticipated is recurrence, the repetitive nonoccurrence of the self-identical presence of any *Ding An Sich*.

In Freud, too, of course, the repetitively prefigurative character of things is underlined in important ways. First, the impossibility of excluding meaningless *repetition*, or the life of death, the self-affirmation of negativity, from presence, or life itself, pure affirmation, is the thesis of *Beyond the Pleasure Principle* (1920). The notion that there is no *fulfillment* (and this in "Kultur," and not merely in "Zivilisation") and that all experience is

therefore *prefigurative* or *anticipatory*, is asserted with particular explicitness in *Das Unbehagen in der Kultur* (1930). (The translation of this title
into English as *Civilization and its Discontents* unfortunately effaces the
sense in which it was directed against Volkish distinctions between *Kultur*,
as [Germanic] homogeneous community, and *Zivilisation*, as embodying
[non-Germanic] alienated society.[12])

This necessarily hasty characterization of the relation between modernism and the critique of positive religion that the radical Enlightenment
had desired to achieve (in accomplishing the prefiguration of the
Reformation) already allows us to surmise that the modified repetition of
Enlightenment that is modernism will still identify itself, if in a newly
qualified manner, with the *Judaism* with which Enlightenment was tendentially identified the first time around.[13] Indeed, the virulent rise of anti-
Semitism all over Europe East and West beginning in the late nineteenth
century testifies to this identification in negative form. The Jews become
particularly threatening for European non-Jews when modernism starts
coming into being as "Jewish" Neo-Enlightenment. Whereas this "Jewish"
Neo-Enlightenment makes a disconcertingly concerted effort to come to
terms with death, moreover, the Nazis attempt both to deny death by
means of its glorification and to negate it by extinguishing the Jews.[14]

How, then, does modernism position itself with respect to the Jews in
the two figures we are using as illustrations, Nietzsche and Freud? The dis-
cernment and acknowledgment of the affirmation of Jewish motifs in
Nietzsche's texts is impeded not only by the abusive appropriation of his
texts by the Wagnerian right from Elisabeth Förster-Nietzsche through
Hitler but also by the fact that, in his early years, Nietzsche repeatedly
expresses—especially in his correspondence—grossly anti-Semitic sentiments in accord with those of his family, his general milieu, and his chosen
masters at the time, Schopenhauer and Wagner.[15] Nonetheless, the rapid
development of Nietzsche's thought increasingly distances him from his
early mentors on many levels, and the development of the anti-Semitic
movement gradually reveals to Nietzsche the extraordinarily small-minded
and petty character of the anti-Semitic ideology. He thus comes to see with
increasing clarity that his own sensibility, position, and ideals coincide to a
great extent with those that have been adopted by Jews or characterized as
Jewish (if in a negative sense, which Nietzsche wishes to reverse) by Western
Christian discourses. The more Nietzsche comes to hate and despise the

"Germans," the more he tends to identify with, and so—if with a certain ironic or perverse glee—to idealize, the "Jews." The mimeticism, the carnality, and the intellectuality of the "Jews," all become positive traits. Even their legalism is viewed as the expression of a strong will to power, rather than as the expression of a decadent reaction. But it is not, of course, above all in a "literal" sense that the later Nietzsche uses the term, "Jews," since in the absence of essence the "literal," too, subsides. Rather, "Jews" in the positive sense in Nietzsche's later works mean all of those who have the capacity to affirm existence as anticipatory repetition, as nonidentity, as life in the context of the letter, life inscribed in the surround of death or otherness it also is. Thus, in *The Case of Wagner*, for example, and of course this is not just any example, Nietzsche avows in the most striking manner an identification of himself and of his own "ideal" (i.e., postideal) modernity, by way of the artist, with the Jews. Here, the thinker as artist, who means to inaugurate, prefiguratively, a renaissance or repetition of artistry, at once attempts to annihilate Wagner the anti-Semitic, pseudo-Christian, and pseudo-Romantic Nationalist, and to build positively on Wagner's own use of Heine's text on the "Flying Dutchman" for his opera of that name. Toward both of these ends, he argues that the artist is nothing other than "the wandering Jew," the one without natal or natural bearings, the one who, lacking salvation, can only repeat the alien as his or her own and prefigure the self in the language of another.[16] Nietzsche criticizes Wagner's desire for redemption (*Erlösung*) as unbefitting the "nature" of the artist, as the one who wanders "endlessly" unsaved, i.e., in time. The (dis)orientation of a postidealist modernity—the age in which a decadent theology of spirit is to be "overcome" by the artistic affirmation of prefigurative repetition—will have been for Nietzsche, in theopolitical terms, "Jewish" more than anything else, inscribed in the eternal repetition of its own displacement.

In Freud, the vexed relationship between, on the one hand, a modernism that ambiguously extends Enlightenment into the domain of the irrational and, on the other hand, the Jewish tradition (to which many of the practitioners and, as many interpreters have feared or hoped, also the "essence" of the "science" of psychoanalysis might also be said to "belong"), has been recently and richly treated by Gay, Yerushalmi, Derrida, and others.[17] Gay has emphasized the *godlessness* of Freud, the self-described "godless Jew," and so the secular universality of the claims of psychoanalysis, while Yerushalmi has countered by emphasizing Freud's *Jewishness*. Perhaps neither, however, has quite sufficiently reflected upon the *connection* between the two aspects. Through an ironic assumption of the Christian caricature of Judaism as "godless," but also hereby echoing the Mendelssohnian view of Judaism as devoid of dogmatic articles of faith, Freud proposes himself as "godless" precisely *insofar* as he is Jewish, and as a "Jew" *insofar* as he is godless, that is, beyond the need of faith as a weapon against the acknowledgment of mortality.[18] Furthermore, as has not yet been adequately underlined, the reason why it is possible for Freud and other modernists to play out this position is that they occupy a discursive "space" where the repetition of a Judaic Enlightenment makes Enlightenment both more godless than ever before, because by now reason, nature, and artifice have all been demystified, and consequently more "Jewish," in the sense of dispersed, exiled, and openly affirmative of the culture of the letter.

How, then, does this "godless Jew" articulate psychoanalysis with Judaism in such a way as to argue, nonetheless, for its universal legitimacy as a modern discourse? After having gradually given up, in the course of his life, and as Yerushalmi shows, the hope to become a German and to persuade the world that psychoanalysis is *not* a "Jewish science," in *Moses and Monotheism* Freud changes tactics. Becoming fully "modernist" in the sense I am sketching here, he now tries to argue for the relative universality of "godless Judaism" by demonstrating that Christian anti-Semitism (or Christianity as an anti-Semitism), as which he is sufficiently savvy to recognize even its explicitly anti-Christian and racist avatars, repeats the partial particularism/paganism it sees in Judaism. This is the case because Christianity evades the one universal truth—which Judaism confronts—of universal involvement in death, that is, in the materiality that *limits* universality. The argument goes briefly as follows. First of all, the murder of God is (or repeats, returns to) the murder of the *Urvater*, while the murder of the *Urvater* means ultimately simply the repetition of violence (i.e., the repetition of the violence of the *Urvater* who, the story goes, had attempted, by means of nascently social violence, to tame the violence of nature) in the attempt to put a stop to violence. The question of whether or not one has killed God reduces, in other words, to that of whether or not one participates in the repetition of violence, the violence of repetition: death itself. But as Freud suggests, if Christianity indirectly "recognizes," through the story of Christ's redemptive death, that it has murdered God, then it also denies its responsibility for that murder in at least three ways.

It blames the murder on the Jews as "murderers of Christ"; it denies that as a religion of the Son it repeats the murder of the Father; and it imagines that its adherents are redeemed. Judaism, on the other hand, also indirectly recognizes its share in the murder of God, through hyperbolic praise of God, moralistic-legalistic rigorism, and so on. Judaism does not, however, according to Freud, blame the murder of God on some other religious group, nor does it consider its adherents to be "saved." Rather, once again, it assumes its own culpability in the form of an ever intensifying "intoxication of moral asceticism [*Rausch moralischer Askese*]."[19] Because Christianity fails, relatively speaking, to assume its "guilt," which is again simply the participation in violence, repetition, or death, it ultimately recognizes the murder of the Father to an even lesser extent than Judaism. For these reasons, Freud feels he can characterize Jewish monotheism as "Progress in Spirituality" (557–61), in contrast to which the Christianity of St. Paul appears as a regressive compromise with the materiality of Egyptian polytheism (580). Because it denies the letter, Christianity fails to accede to spirit, but instead falls back into the position of the letter that usurps the position of the spirit; by acknowledging the letter, Judaism accedes to the position of spirit.[20]

If these remarks suffice to illustrate quickly the sense in which modernism repeats Neo-Judaic Enlightenment, one will still want to know how and to what extent modernism places post-Romantic discourse into the position of a prefigurative pre- or protomodernism, even as it places the entire notion of prefiguration within the quotation marks of irony. Since it itself attempts to affirm the letter of prefigural repetition, modernism must understand the post-Romantic discourse as a failure to accomplish this affirmation. To see how it does so, we have to begin by summarizing the most basic operations of that discourse. In Marxism and Wagnerism, a particular class and nation, respectively, are at once turned into absolutes and transcended. The telos of history is in the former case the self-establishment of a metaclass and in the latter the self-realization of a metanation (or metarace). Further, we have argued that Marxism and Wagnerism are the two extreme forms of natural supernaturalism or paganized Protestantism. Class and nation therefore are concrete universals or absolutes in these discourses only insofar as they are—in Marx's case, surreptitiously—at once *spiritualized* (or supernaturalized) and (still spiritually) *naturalized*. The response of the modernist discourses, accordingly, will be to "realize" that class and nation are at once *nonspiritual,* or purely material, and *nonnatural,* or purely artificial/constructed, and not just in their "present" forms, as Marxism and Wagnerism already show (in this resides the sense in which they "prefigure" modernism), but inescapably. As artifice, class and nation are always either in advance of, or in pursuit of, "themselves" (in the sense of their natural truth or essence). As matter, too, they either constitute the mere repetitive remainder or the not-yet-spiritualized anticipation of "themselves." Modernism, in short, denies that there can be any overcoming of the "Jewish" abstract formalism that Marx bemoans or of the "Jewish" alienation from the mother-tongue that Wagner execrates, even as it acknowledges the materiality and artificiality of class society and of national identity that Marx and Wagner respectively sensed. In accordance with this structural necessity, modernists such as Nietzsche and Freud are critical of the utopias of both classless society and the purification of national identity. Instead, they insist *both* on the ultimate non-self-identity of all national and class categories *and* on the impossibility of completely doing away with them.

Finally, if modernism seems to have left the Catholicizing discourse of late Romanticism far behind, in the now-nonthreatening distance of that which the immediate opponents of the modernists have already overcome, then this Catholicizing discourse also represents for modernism a kind of implicit danger or threat. Insofar as European discourse sees modernism as "Jewish," it will be tempted to make sense out of its situation by attributing the inevitable "failure" of modernism, that is, its failure to solve all problems and to transcend all generational conflict (and thus, in a sense, to stop time), to traits traditionally associated with Judaism. These traits will be gathered under the heading of the splitting of abstraction from concretion: the merely promising attainment of a still-limited universality and an insubstantial materiality. The next step will appear to require a broader universality and a deeper concreteness, along the lines, in short, of Pauline Christianity and its faith, even if these lines appear in the language of the secular. If Nietzsche's text perhaps provides little direct evidence of such a tendency, due to the extreme intensity of his anti-Christian *animus,* then a number of other late-nineteenth- and early-twentieth-century literary, philosophical, and artistic texts and destinies provide more.[21] For example, there is a level on which, in some of the works of Rainer Maria Rilke (*The Book of Hours, The Notebooks of Malte Laurids Brigge,* and so forth) and

Stefan George, a certain Romantic medievalism, along with its Catholic symbolic accoutrements, plays an important role in the determination of setting, imagery, and thematic concerns. Further, beyond these figures, the entire European decadence from Huysmans to the various literary and painterly formations of the 1890s could be seen as a precocious form of virtually Catholicizing postmodernism. Programmatic decadence both broaches the transition to modernism and resists or already proleptically supercedes it. The decadents do, of course, assert the claims of artificiality against those of naturalness, but they still (or already) supernaturalize and spiritualize the artificial in order to prevent "dead" materiality from asserting itself in an unadulterated form. Because they spiritualize the dead letter of artifice, we can see them as being always on the verge of becoming Catholics, as is often borne out biographically: to name just a few, Huysmans converts after writing *A Rebours*; Wilde toys with conversion; and Hofmannsthal rejects the modern Jew within himself in favor of the Austrian Catholic.[22] Especially in a Christian Europe, "progressive" modernism is always susceptible of being reduced to an infinitesimal moment, so that one seems to pass directly from the pagan spirit of the late-nineteenth-century utopias of class and nation to a renewal of Romantic Catholicism (or Anglicanism or medievalism) that is proleptically postmodern, in the sense of that which the modern structurally anticipates.[23]

In the case of Freud, the prominence of the confessional ritual—in which the lawlessness of free association is the only law, so that law is maintained while being subverted, as in Schlegel's definition of Romantic poetry—already betrays a mimetic, imaginary rivalry. Freud, the Austrian Jew, clearly wishes, among other things, to sublate Catholic discourse and so always risks reducing his own discourse to a version of what it hopes to exceed. More particularly, to cite just one passage as an example, in *Moses and Monotheism*, after granting Christianity the privilege of having acknowledged the murder of God, he interprets the Christian claim that Jews are murderers of God as the accusation: "They [the Jews] don't want to believe that they have truly murdered God, whereas we [Christians] admit it and have been cleansed of this guilt."[24] To the extent that Freudian analysis wants to cure by occasioning the extended therapeutic confession of oedipal entanglements, it clearly wants first to go "beyond" Jewish repression and to achieve Christian "cleansing." But then it aims to go beyond Christian "cleansing," since the Christian "cleansing" is not achieved merely by means of confession of the murder of God—a confession which, of course, Christian anti-Semitism essentially revokes—but by way of "the death of the Son." However, if Freud's analysis achieves, in some sense (for example, through the dissolution of the narcissistic ego) a "death of the Son," or even if it replaces this death with a more effective cathartic procedure, then the Freudian institution becomes, in a more than trivial if not quite "literal" sense, and despite Freud's attempt to demystify the church from *Group Psychology and the Analysis of the Ego* onward, a kind of "church" of its own.[25] In short, Judaic modernism is always structurally on the verge of turning out to be a "Catholicizing" postmodernism. The complicated question of whether any contemporary postmodernisms "realize"—perhaps in displaced and secularized terms—this potential repetition of "Catholic" anti-Judaism that modernism contains will have to remain a question beyond the limits of the present study.[26]

Desire for Emancipation from Holocaust Memory in Contemporary Germany as Repetition of the Rejection of Modernism

Assuming as I have suggested above that the Holocaust was conditioned, if not produced, by the desperate and panicked right-wing rejection of modernism, coupled with the sacrificial identification of this modernism with the Jews (whereas modernism was "Jewish" only in the "figural" sense that it identified its own condition and values as similar to those traditionally attributed to the Jews), it is necessary to close by raising the following question: What implications does the relationship of contemporary German culture to Holocaust memory have for the relationship of that culture to the modernist tradition? No doubt not fully understood or explained, even if well known, the encounter between postwar Germans and the Holocaust, as organized within both the Federal Republic of Germany and the German Democratic Republic, has from the beginning always involved, in one form or another, a significant degree of evasion of, and/or incapacity to confront, this unspeakable legacy. In *The Jews and Germany: from the 'Judeo-German Symbiosis' to the Memory of Auschwitz*, Enzo Traverso has summarized with unusual succinctness and precision the vicissitudes of this encounter, from the myth of an essentially Good Germany of antifascist resistance-fighters propagated within the German Democratic Republic to (in the Federal

Republic) the Adenauer years of relative silence and self-exculpating "compensation [*Wiedergutmachung*]," to the return of a kind of memory in the 1960s, which nonetheless remained marked by a certain degree of "oblivion" of "the Jewish question," and up through the 1980s, when we were treated to the spectacle of intermittent eruptions of a precipitous desire for "normalization" (e.g., Kohl meeting with Reagan in Bitburg, and the "historians' debate" from 1986 on), culminating in the "flight from the past"[27] of "reunification." Since that time, the encounter has continued through, among many things, debates of the 1990s around Neo-Nazism in the new *Bundesländer*, Daniel Goldhagen's book, *Hitler's Willing Executioners*, the Holocaust monument proposed for construction in Berlin, and most recently Martin Walser's acceptance speech for the Peace Prize of Bremen in fall, 1998. In a variety of ways, in all of these situations, the German encounter with the Nazi past and the Holocaust has been characterized, and not just for the younger generations, by a simultaneous "impossibility of *remembering* and . . . impossibility of *forgetting*."[28] While it is neither necessary nor possible to treat here this entire history of postwar German Holocaust reception, it is possible, and of some importance, to comment on the most recent tendencies and expressions of the desire for a "normalization" of Germany, that is, for a suspension of or, as my perspective here prompts me to put it, "emancipation" from the memory of the Holocaust in Germany: for a liberation of the younger generations, at least, from their sense of having inherited a legacy of unbearable guilt, shame, and culturally delegitimating trauma. In light of what I have suggested above about the importance of the rejection of what I am calling *modernism* in the creation of Nazi Germany, and in light of the implication that the main next ideological-discursive task for postwar Germany would be to affirm or to assimilate the modernist discourse, the question to be asked about the most recent expressions of a desire to be liberated from Holocaust memory, the question in terms of which such expressions can be perhaps best evaluated or measured, would be this: What attitude do they presuppose toward the modernist legacy? Assuming that it might be appropriate and legitimate for Germans, especially those born since the war or their children (who are already adults), to seek a new way of relating to the Holocaust and the Nazi past, the question would be: Is it possible to seek "normalization" of Germany and at the same time to finish the work of catching up with modernism? And if so, in what sense is "normalization" to be understood?

Before answering this question with illustrative reference to the debate most recently prompted by Martin Walser's expression of impatience under the burden of the Holocaust legacy, it is necessary to clarify or (more modestly) to suggest that, from the perspective of the current study, the fact of "reunification" provides two disjunct opportunities. On the one hand, it provides an opportunity for, or temptation toward, the effacement (or relativization) of the horrors of the German past. On the other, it provides the opportunity for a new opening toward modernism beyond what was possible before the fall of the wall and the consequent end of the occupation of Germany by Soviet and American, as well as French and British forces. As for the states of Germany that were formerly part of the German Democratic Republic, one does not have to embrace Neo-Conservative ideology to acknowledge that it is conducive to the possibility of a new encounter with modernism for their inhabitants no longer to be dominated from without by the largely pre- and antimodernist discourse of Marxism-Leninism. With "reunification," the former citizens of the GDR become, politically speaking, relatively "free" to accept in a new way the burden of responsibility for their own ideological-discursive orientations and to examine the fascist period in terms of an understanding other than the massively oversimplified one, blind to the workings of the theopolitical "superstructure," that reduces fascism to the capitalist rejection of communism. On the other side of the equation, those who were part of the Federal Republic prior to the anniversary of *Kristallnacht*, 1989, and who fundamentally belonged to West Germany's Americanizing defense of itself against its own history, are perhaps in a good position to reconsider this history and the modernism that this history has hitherto largely resisted. For if the American cultural worldview is more hospitable to modernism than were Soviet-style communism or the Nazi regime, then the American tutelage has doubtless nonetheless tended to prevent the West Germans from *choosing* modernism by means of the sheer *force* of the American influence. This is true by virtue of the fact that West Germany has had little *choice* but to adopt the veneer, and perhaps also the "depths," assuming that it has some, of the American style. Moreover, Americanization prevents the BRD from assimilating modernism to the extent that the "American," that is, free-market capitalist ideology, itself constitutes a version of the metaphysics of presence. This metaphysics, as I cannot demonstrate here and therefore will simply posit for the sake of the current argument, continues to assert itself in the pragmatic and individualist-actionist combination of antiformalism with antihistoricism that constitutes the "American" ideology. To assume that the value of things and people can be situated in what they do—what functions they have, what they are good for—is to assume that what they do *now* can be isolated. It presupposes that other modalities of value, the material *forms* of things as well as *meanings*, in their historically transmitted inertia and their arbitrariness from the standpoint of "today," could be simply prevented from repeating themselves in the present in a manner that would be disruptive of the pure presence of functionality, that is, disruptive of the pure freedom to posit the functionality of the "new" as sole site of value. Anticipatory repetition, radical temporality, and finitude, in short, are not reconcilable with the notion of the land of endless opportunity, the culture of immediate gratification, satisfaction, or fulfillment, the limitless freedom of the individual, and the rejection of the nonfunctional—non-freedom-serving—aspects of the past, the occasional enthusiasms of certain French poststructuralist intellectuals for the delirium of America notwithstanding. If therefore the current situation of Germany, its newfound freedom from not only fascism and state socialism but also (potentially, or "ideally") capitalism as a way of life, conduces potentially to a renewed and "deepened" encounter with the modernist tradition, then to what degree are the recent calls for "normalization" of Germany, of its past and so of its present and future, consistent with such an encounter?[29] Since it is impossible to answer the question here in any breadth, I will content myself with suggesting how the answer looks in the case of just one text, a speech by Martin Walser entitled "Experiences During the Composition of a Sunday Sermon [*Erfahrungen beim Verfassen einer Sonntagsrede*]," delivered in acceptance of the Peace Prize of the German Book Trade, in the fall of 1998, and thereby occasioning a storm of controversy in the journals that did not abate for some time.

In this "sermon," the main irony contained in its title being that it is a *sermon* no doubt in a more traditional and problematic sense than its author would like, the prominent fiction writer Martin Walser protests in a number of ways against what he takes to be the inappropriate public presentation of the Holocaust in contemporary German society. His protest is initially confusing, perhaps, because it emphasizes two opposed aspects of this inappropriateness, but when one takes these two aspects together the general import of Walser's concerns comes clearly into focus. On the one hand, the constant reminders of the Holocaust desensitize those who are constantly confronted with them, he argues, so that these people begin to take the Holocaust less seriously than they otherwise would. Thus, Walser worries that, if he "looks away" when scenes of the Holocaust come up on the screen, the reminders are proving counterproductive. On the other hand—and as if in a kind of unwitting expression of what the overexposure has produced in him—Walser also argues that exposure to the Holocaust overwhelms German society to such an extent that it is no longer possible for Germans to realize, or consequently for the German public sphere to acknowledge, that Germany has now returned to "normalcy." From this perspective, Walser is arguing not that Germans should be able to be *more* deeply concerned about the Holocaust than the media allow them to be, but rather that they should be able to be *less* concerned. The Holocaust is thus *not sufficiently* present in German society because it is *too* present. And it is *too* present because it is *not really* as present as it is made to seem. The Holocaust only returns as an overwhelming nonpresence: it is always too much or too little to return as itself, to return appropriately, or in a fitting manner, in its literal, proper truth.

Now, as everything I've said above makes clear, my own response to Walser will not be to contest his sense that there is something *inappropriate* about the way in which the past returns in the present in the case of Holocaust memory. If presence is always self-anticipatory and self-repetitive, then this will certainly apply also to the presence of whatever acts constitute the denegation of this ontological-temporal condition, even when these acts make use, as did those of fascist Germany, of all the technological capacities at the disposal of mid-twentieth-century Europe in order to demonstrate their own immunity to that condition. Rather than contest Walser's constatation of inappropriateness, therefore, I will simply contest his suggestion that this inappropriateness would be as such either undesirable or, especially, *avoidable*. I also briefly examine critically—with an interest in what is repeated there—the *terms* in which Walser specifies his objection, the causes to which he attributes this inadequacy of the current treatment in Germany of the Holocaust, the Nazi past, and so forth, and how he thinks this inadequacy is to be corrected.

The terms in which Walser states his protest strikingly reveal his commitment not only to a premodernist metaphysics of presence but more specifically to a secularized and "aestheticized" Protestantism that privileges, first in the name of private conscience and then in the name of literary monologue, the value of absolute inwardness over the impurities of the external. Not only does he open his discourse with a plea to the state for "mercy before justice" in the treatment of a former East German spy, a plea whose genealogical background in a certain Christian anti-Judaism is all too familiar, but—and more importantly—he goes on to criticize the current representations of the Holocaust in terms that repeat those traditionally used by Christianity to contest Judaism, as religion of ritual, letter, dead works, and so on. For example, the problem with the public presentation of the history of the Holocaust "in the media" is for Walser that it has become "a routine of inculpation," which also means indirectly or subliminally that it has become a routine of "rendering us indebted," since the word "Beschuldigen" for "inculpation" also contains the word "Schuld" for "debt."[30] Like the Jews, the mediatic presentation of the Holocaust puts the Germans into "debt," and this presentation is also a "routine," a ritualization of the dead letter. Similarly, although the Holocaust is used by those who represent it for "good purposes, honorable ones" (18), the problem is that it is used for any purposes at all, that it is the "instrumentalization of our shame" (18). While one can grant that Walser is no doubt right to object to certain abusive applications of the Holocaust, one wonders why it would be wrong to use it to "good purposes," assuming he is not entirely sarcastic here, e.g., for teaching the young about their history and the dangers posed by the inevitable inertial tendencies of history itself, and so forth. According to Walser, the problem is that the Holocaust should be treated as something beyond "use," as a sacred sacrifice perhaps, or as an aesthetic object, beyond social inscription. But whatever Walser's reasons for a blanket condemnation of "instrumentalization," one cannot help but hear echoing through Walser's text the nineteenth-century view of the Jews as instrumentalizing egoists, a view that itself repeats the theological opposition to works in the name of faith. Or again, Walser says:

Auschwitz is not appropriate as a threatening-routine, a means of intimidation, moral bludgeon, or exercise in duty, to be used on all occasions. Whatever comes about through such ritualization is of the quality of lip-service [*Lippengebet*]. But under what suspicion does one come, when one says that the Germans are now a normal people, a usual society? (20)

Ritualization, the violence of an externally imposed moral law: Walser's impatience sounds uncannily familiar.

But what causes the ritualization and the instrumentalization of Holocaust memory? The cause of the problem is, for Walser, the public, mediatic imposition on private conscience, the externalization of the religiosity of the sphere of individual inwardness, which also happens to be where the normal *Volk* is to be found. The media—and "we" all (at least used to) know who runs the media—are responsible for the falsification of conscience by means of its external representation. "Everyone is alone with his conscience. Public acts of conscience are therefore in danger of becoming symbolic. And nothing is more foreign to the conscience than symbolism" (22). While "the conscience, left to itself, produces enough illusion" (23), when "publicly required, only illusion reigns" (23). While everyone possesses his or her own "inner chamber of mirrors [*Spiegelkabinett*]" meant for "the production of self-respect" (23), still the public production of conscience only makes things worse. In response to these claims one may respond that although Walser is not wrong, of course, to suggest that externality compromises inwardness, first of all he seems grossly unaware of the anti-Semitic history to which this suggestion has belonged. Secondly he seems blithely ignorant of the complexity and difficulty of any attempt to limit the public character of private conscience. Whatever happy illusions Walser and his sympathetic readers may entertain about the possible purity of inwardness: historically given (which is not to say merely *punctually* given) representations and semiological material condition even the most private experience any subject can imagine having within him- or herself. The only way to avoid this would be to arrange for such a self-experience in the absence of all language. Not suprisingly, therefore, while Walser manages to seem to distance himself from the illusion of a possible extralinguistic self, at the same time (at once openly and surreptitiously), he maintains it in its most classical form.

There is, in Walser's view, one possible retreat from the public, mediatized realm of the disfiguration of conscience: the aesthetic retreat of the literary writer-reader couple, where pure inwardness can finally be constituted. The writer who consents to being forced into the "service of opinion" (25) run by the media is therefore "guilty" (25)—it is his or her own fault—for getting involved with "this borrowed language" (25). The language of mediatic/public opinion—opinion as such—is the "borrowed" language that makes one "guilty" or "in debt." (Again, one hears the profound indebtedness of Walser's own language here to anti-Semitic discourse, which is precisely more, and not less, disturbing if Walser is unaware of it and refers explicitly not to "Jews" but to those who—somehow too "Jewishly," he seems inchoately to feel—won't let "us" Germans forget murdering the Jews.[31]) There is, however, one language that is not borrowed, and this is the literary language, in which the writer, although only responsible "for himself" (25), nonetheless becomes "useful for others" (25). Not only does he become useful in retreat, such that the individual and the collective are reconciled there, but also he does so "in the most guiltlessly beautiful cooperative work in the world [*unschuldig schönsten Zusammenarbeit der Welt*]: that is, the work between author and reader" (26). Although Walser has above criticized those who speak publicly of the Holocaust for trying to make themselves "a little bit exculpated" (17) and said that in contrast, "I have never held it to be possible to leave the side of the inculpated" (17), and although he has based much of the force of his discourse on the premise that "a good conscience is none" (22), he now posits that literary writing—in unity with its reading, lest his readers should not themselves feel exculpated simply by reading him—is the most "guilt-less" thing one could possibly do. Fiction indeed—and no doubt a beautiful one. Further:

> This [cooperative work] arises through a single condition: the same reasons that bring us to reading and writing. The having-to-spell-out our existence [*Das Buchstabierenmüssen unserer Existenz.*]. . . . The novel and poem address themselves never first of all to another; they are only addressed to the other when they awaken his interest; then the interested one becomes active and produces sense where an uninterested one only sees thickets of letters [*Buchstabendickichte*]. . . . My faith in language has been formed through the experience that it [*sie*, or she] helps me when I don't believe that I already know something. It (she) holds back, doesn't so to speak awaken, when I opine that I know something that I only have to formulate with the help of language. (25–26)

Not only does Walser posit the guiltless beauty of literary writing-reading as the active-passive place of (quasi-Schillerian) grace, in which the pure inwardness of Protestant conscience is realized as *good* conscience, but also he does so by simultaneously characterizing writing in terms of the letter *and* conjuring the de-subjectifying, de-spiritualizing effects of the letter out of existence by speaking of language as a subject, indeed an absolute subject. It is what "helps" us when we, through a kind of guiltless modesty and faith, let it tell us what it has to say, granting us a kind of grace. Walser can know this grace directly and we can share in it, no doubt, by buying and reading his novels, composed as they are in the "literary language," the only one "that doesn't want to sell me anything" (26). Thus, the oratorical-rhetorical function of language can be undone, Walser tells us in this oration, by the language of literature. Walser hopes that this language, being used in the exceptional case of the "sermon" in question, will make it possible for him to touch our "Dasein"—our existence—"in a way that cannot be calculated but perhaps can be experienced [*erlebbare Art*]" (28). In the end—at least this is Walser's hope—literary colloquy allows for "Erlebnis": we are returned by aesthetic representation to the presence of felt life itself. The dead letter of rhetorical language is transformed into living experience by literary spirituality. And in this living, inner experience the guiltless conscience finds respite from the external, mediatic representations of a debt owed to the Jews.

The belated rejection of the modernist affirmation of the letter qua anticipatory repetition could, I think, be no more strikingly illustrated than in Walser's text. His text is as apparently "reasonable," "literary," and "non-anti-Semitic" as one—at least, if one were one of the younger contemporary Germans impatient to shed an admittedly unenviable historical burden—might want, and yet this text is filled with echoes of the epistemologically and ethically questionable discourses that led to the Holocaust. Such echoes are, of course, in one way or another inevitable. But the question remains as to whether one attempts to gain at least maximal clarity on the ways in which such echoes persist in one's own discourse, not just in the German context, or merely with respect to the Christian-Jewish relation. On this point, Walser does, one must acknowledge, a singularly unimpressive job. The attempt to escape the traumatic memory of the Holocaust by insisting on a possible normalization of the German past, present, and future, even if it takes place in Walser ultimately in a literary retreat from the social sphere, repeats the rejection of modernism (without which there would have been no Holocaust). For modernism prescribes the necessity of anticipatory repetition, and so the impossibility of any total escape from *any* event that has occurred, including the worldwide trauma of the German (and more broadly European) fascist denial of modernism in this century. There will be no total escape, except through denial—for the Germans, and differently for the Jews, and differently again for the rest of the world—from the haunting of the Holocaust. On the other hand, the modernist notion of radical temporality also forbids reading any spatiotemporal point in history solely in terms of another such point. Clearly contemporary German culture—and also Jewish culture, and other cultures in the world—should not be entirely determined, *are* not entirely determined, by the sole trauma of the Holocaust, even if in turn the Holocaust precedes itself throughout the prior history of Germany (and Christian Europe) and will continue to succeed itself and survive its death in the future for Germans, Jews, and others, always differently, for as far as the eye can see and beyond.[32]

What, in a (provisionally final) word, does the modernist legacy imply for the theory of reading or the everyday hermeneutics we have been considering under the title of the "rhetoric of cultural dialogue"? The repetition of a past and the anticipation of a future, both without horizon, in the speech-acts and other acts of the "present" make these acts at once belong to the past moments they extend and to the future moments that extend them in turn, even as these acts also exceed complete situatedness in any moment—past, present, or future. The reading of the other—including oneself—in terms of such a notion of anticipatory repetition would begin where the rhetoric of dialogue ends (and so begins to repeat itself, put somewhat differently), whether between cultures or between individuals (and here the rigid distinction between cultures and individuals itself would end). A different rhetoric would begin there, the same differently, in which the reading of the other would always have been taken to comprise the (in principle) infinite and (in fact) finite search for a meaning that will never fully have arrived.

Notes

PREFACE

1. Gershom Scholem, "Wider den Mythos vom deutsch-jüdischen «Gespräch»," in *Judaica 2*, 7–11. Published in English as "Against the Myth of the German-Jewish Dialogue," in *On Jews and Judaism in Crisis*, 61–64; emphasis added. Translation slightly altered in the case of the word "Selbstaufgabe" in order to highlight the repetition of the word in German and to give it a more literal translation. This passage comes from Scholem's famous refusal in 1962 of an invitation to contribute to a Festschrift in honor of the "German-Jewish dialogue, the core of which is indestructible" (Scholem, "Against the Myth," 61). The woman to whom the Festschrift was dedicated was Margarete Susman, whose work on Dorothea Schlegel we will encounter in Chapter 5. Throughout what follows, unless otherwise indicated, translations are my own.

2. Erich Auerbach, "Figura," in *Gesammelte Aufsätze*, 55–92. In English: "Figura," *Scenes*, 11–78. Citations given hereafter with the English pagination first, then a semicolon, then the German pagination.

3. One indication of the extraordinary degree to which the hermeneutical notion of dialogue belongs to common sense is the fact that Hans-Georg Gadamer on occasion attempts to justify his own theory of dialogue by reference to the self-evidence of what "everybody" experiences and knows. See Hans-Georg Gadamer, "Text and Interpretation," in Michelfelder and Palmer, *Dialogue*, 21–52; and the comments on this tendency in Gadamer as rooted in metaphysics and unsuccessfully legitimized prejudice, respectively, in Jacques Derrida's contribution to the same collection, "Three Questions to Hans-Georg Gadamer," 52–55; and Philippe Forget's commentary there on the Gadamer-Derrida exchange, "Argument(s)," 129–50.

4. For sociohistorically oriented overviews of part or all of the emancipatory epoch, see Kampmann; Grab, especially 9–108; Katz, *Out of the Ghetto*; Sorkin, *Transformation*; Lowenstein; and Meyer, *German-Jewish History* and "Reform Jewish Thinkers." For a richly informative and illuminatingly argued study on German anti-Semitism in relation to the fear that the Jews have a "hidden lan-

guage"—in fact, they had two, Yiddish and Hebrew—see Sander L. Gilman, *Jewish Self-Hatred*, especially 68–243, for the period with which I am most specifically concerned here. While I have taken much inspiration from this work, the most important difference between Gilman's approach there and my own, in terms of *theme*, can perhaps be put like this: whereas he is interested in the fear that Jews possess a specific hidden language, I am interested in the identification of the Jews, by way of Christian typological presuppositions, with the materiality of language in general. Beyond this, of course, methodological influences and authorial and textual foci differentiate these studies as well, but not in terms that any binary oppositions would suffice to determine.

5. Thus, even if Scholem's thesis on the absence of Jewish-German dialogue cannot be taken "literally," but rather needs to be developed in terms of the rhetorical foundation of its sense, it is inadequate to suggest, as Klaus Berghahn has done recently in referring in turn to George Mosse, that the denial of Jewish-German dialogue simply results from a pessimistic post-Holocaust mood (see Berghahn, 2). Even if what motivates such a suggestion is the generous desire to include the Jewish Germans within the German canon, and so to refuse to capitulate to their former exclusion, still such a gesture risks obscuring the impossibilities of the past. When in this same introduction, the editor suggests that "it is out of the question to take comfortable refuge in a distant past, when Mendelssohn and Lessing started a German-Jewish dialogue" (1), again the wish to refuse comfortable platitudes is commendable, but the assumption that there was in fact a time when "German-Jewish" dialogue took place seems to remain intact here. It is precisely this assumption that my study places in question.

INTRODUCTION

1. Jacques Derrida's exposition of the history of the ideological privilege granted to ostensibly spiritual speech over supposedly material writing in Western metaphysics began in the sixties with *De la grammatologie* and *L'écriture et la différence* and has been pursued in his many writings since. The rhetoric-philosophy opposition, as well as the two dimensions of rhetoric (figure and performance), and more particularly the incapacity of philosophy to master rhetoric, even by means of the ruse of identifying with it or subordinating itself to it completely, as well as the incapacity of figurative transformation to harmonize itself with the performative power it carries, were explored with particular tenacity and acuity in the works of Paul de Man, from *Blindness and Insight* to *Allegories of Reading*, to *Rhetoric of Romanticism*, to *Resistance to Theory*, to *Aesthetic Ideology*.

2. While he has not attempted any historiographical schematization of the type I will attempt here, Derrida has explicitly and critically addressed the ways in which the binary opposition between writing and speech (along with those metaphysical oppositions with which it is homologous) has been historically invoked in order to structure ideologically, among other things, the distinction between the

Jewish and Greco-Christian discourses. Indeed, the "Jewish" question is one of his enduring concerns. See, among other texts, in *L'écriture et la différence*, "Edmond Jabès et la question du livre" (99–116) and "Violence et métaphysique: Essai sur la pensée d'Emmanuel Levinas" (117–228); *Glas*; *Schibboleth, pour Paul Celan*; in *Psyché*, the essay on Emmanuel Levinas, entitled "En ce moment même dans cet ouvrage me voici (1980)," 159–202; and among the more recent works, "Circonfession," in Derrida and Bennington, *Jacques Derrida*, 7–291; *Spectres de Marx*; *Mal d'archive*; Derrida et al., *Moscou aller-retour*, 28–60; "Foi et savoir"; *Le monolinguisme de l'autre*; *Adieu, à Emmanuel Levinas*; and "Un ver à soie," in Derrida and Cixous, *Voiles*. In all of this work, however, there is little or no mention of Moses Mendelssohn, the Schlegels, Lessing, and Wagner. And he writes very little of an explicit textual-historical character about Marx on the Jewish question in the Marx book, even if the entire problematization of "spirit" there is related to this question. As for Paul de Man, who certainly seems to have begun his career during World War II as a petty collaborator in occupied Belgium, his later critical work on rhetoric, while it remains evasive in various ways and always tries to avoid discussions of Jewish-Christian relations, nonetheless seems to me to work to undo the philosophical foundations of the nationalist, racist, and anti-Semitic ideologies with which de Man evidently sympathized at one moment in his youth.

3. Scholem, "Against the Myth of the German-Jewish Dialogue," in *On Jews and Judaism in Crisis*, 61–62.

4. In *Ich und Du* Martin Buber attempts to conceive of the fusion of understanding and response, as well as self and other, as the immediate "being-in-relation" of the I-Thou, whereas he characterizes the fission or separation of understanding from response, self from other, in terms of the mediated "experience" of the I-It. The latter is for him a fallen and secondary version of the former. By displacing the split internal to dialogue onto the border between dialogue and its other, Buber means to rid dialogue of its double internal violence, but the I-Thou relation (or identity) nonetheless remains dependent on, and thus partially both contains and remains inscribed within, the I-It world (of difference) from which it must differentiate itself in order to come into being. The notion of dialogue we are considering here in Scholem's text differentiates itself from Buber's insofar as Scholem seems to situate the totalization of understanding and response in a linear sequence of steps, across the give and take of a dialogical conversation, rather than in the eternal moment of an effacement of difference, as envisioned by Buber's mysticism. While Scholem preserves the values of distance, clarity, and respect for the interlocutor within dialogical communication, he nonetheless seems to underestimate in theory the difficulty of achieving understanding without doing violence to the other and so producing understanding as misunderstanding. For Scholem's critique of Buber, see Gershom Scholem, "Martin Bubers Deutung des Chassidismus," in *Judaica 1*, 165–206; published in English as "Martin Buber's Interpretation of Hasidism," in *The Messianic Idea*, 227–50; and "Mar-

tin Bubers Auffaßung des Judentums," in *Judaica 2*, 133–92; published in English as "Martin Buber's Conception of Judaism," in On *Jews and Judaism in Crisis*, 126–71. Scholem criticizes Buber's concept of dialogicity more by criticizing his interpretation of Jewish traditions than by directly attacking the concept itself. He shows how Buber's own modern—and in various respects Christian and Romantic—subjectivism and spiritualism, as well as the cult of immediacy bound up with these, violently misread the (Jewish) tradition into which he projects them. Buber thus provides us, in Scholem's account, with an *example* of how an emphatic notion of dialogue can mask an effacement of the interlocutor. Here, the Jewish tradition threatens to disappear into a Buberian discourse already in large degree assimilated to Protestant spiritualism. On the backgrounds of Buber's thought in German hermeneutics from Schleiermacher through Dilthey, see Gilya Gerda Schmidt, *Martin Buber's Formative Years*, 35, 44ff. For a useful overview of modern dialogical philosophies, see Bergman.

5. A good example of the denegation or—to be more "generous"—ignorance of this violence is provided by Hans-Georg Gadamer's position in the following response to Jacques Derrida during their exchange. When Derrida suggests that the "good will" which Gadamer makes into a precondition of hermeneutic dialogue might be a repetition not only of the metaphysics of the will but in particular of the will-to-power, Gadamer attempts to clarify what he means by "good will": "One does not go about identifying the weaknesses of what another person says in order to prove that one is always right, but one seeks instead as far as possible to strengthen the other's viewpoint so that what the other person has to say becomes illuminating. Such an attitude seems essential to me for any understanding at all to come about" (Gadamer, "Reply to Jacques Derrida," in Michelfelder and Palmer, *Dialogue and Deconstruction*, 55). While it is evidently important not to want to prove simply that one is always right, it is certainly possible to wonder whether the attempt to strengthen the other's viewpoint in the interests of making the other person's utterances "illuminating" can ever escape being the surreptitious and violently manipulative attempt to make the other person say what one believes *ought* to be said on the particular occasion, in other words, to persuade the other person to accept one's views, while pretending to be simply helping the other person arrive at the successful utterance of his or her own views.

6. As is well known, to some degree in the wake of Melanie Klein Jacques Lacan produced an important analysis of this violence of the dialogical dyad under the name of the "imaginary" dimension. See "Le stade du miroir comme formateur de la fonction du Je" and "L'agressivité en psychanalyse," in Lacan, *Écrits*, 93–100 and 101–24, respectively. The interpretation of his oeuvre turns still to a great degree around whether or not one wishes to read him as having principally argued that the intervention of language, the assumption of the symbolic order, makes it possible to mitigate or possibly even to overcome the violent instability of the imaginary, dyadic structure.

7. The one who has probably gone the furthest in the development of a theory of dialogue that is adequate to this impossibility-necessity and who accordingly no longer even speaks in terms of dialogical ambitions nor privileges a hermeneutic approach, is Emmanuel Levinas. In Levinas, to whose subtle and complex thought I cannot hope to do justice here, the privileged attitude of hospitality is based on the affirmation of radical separation, absolute distance, and infinite difference or otherness, as opposed to the I-Thou fusion of Buber, and the passage from this ethical face-to-face encounter to the triadic realm of justice, or the political (where there is not only I and Thou but also the third person, or the "He") involves the establishment of comparisons between incommensurable singularities, and so a kind of false, if also necessary, identification. Levinasian ethics is in this sense the very opposite of Buberian dialogue. Moreover, Levinas doesn't simply reverse the terms of identity and difference, seeing the former as a fallen form of the latter, for he also sees the movement from ethics to politics, or from infinite differences to the consideration of finite identities, as necessary in order to safeguard or realize the ethics of the other. In Levinas, that is, something like comparative understanding, the means to decisions on the level of justice, or the political, is necessary to the preservation of ethical responsibility, insofar as, without understanding, nonunderstanding—or separation, as the opposite and remainder of understanding—cannot be maintained. See, among Levinas's many writings, above all, *Totalité et infini*; *Autrement qu'être*; and "Martin Buber et la théorie de la connaissance, in *Noms Propres*, 23–43. On the complex relation between ethics and politics in Lévinas, see Derrida, *Adieu*.

8. On the question of necessity, see Librett, "Interruptions of Necessity."

9. When Scholem says that we must perceive the other as "what he is and represents," he registers in his way the two options for the modal determination of the literal. For the other is the literal here, insofar as he is that which I am to understand, and the literal thus appears here under the category of existence or reality ("what he is") and under that of essential possibility ("what he . . . represents"). Indeed, Scholem is right thereby to suggest that dialogue attempts to unify the two ontorhetorical configurations we have just sketched out.

10. For a much more detailed consideration of the ontorhetorical configurations of empiricism and rationalism, see Chapter 2 below.

11. In aestheticism, or in poetic or irrationalist discourses, there is a reversal of these polarities, linking figure (or rhetoric or aesthetics) to necessity, literal speech (or philosophy or science) to impossibility, and thus making figure more literal than the literal, while making the literal more figural than the figural. This reversal has been shown—notably by Paul de Man in his late essays on the topic of "aesthetic ideology" (despite the fact that de Man's work is often wrongly characterized as having attempted such a reversal), to be an only trivially displaced repetition of the Platonism it reverses. See "Anthropomorphism and Trope in the Lyric" and "Aesthetic Formalization: Kleist's *Über das Marionettentheater*," in *Rhetoric of*

Romanticism; and the essays on Kant, Schiller, and Hegel in *Aesthetic Ideology*. On de Man's critique of aestheticisms, see Librett, "Vom Spiegelbild zur Unterschrift."

12. "Noch einmal: das deutsch-jüdische Gespräch" and "Juden und Deutsche," in *Judaica 2*, 12–19, 20–46, in English as "Once More: The German-Jewish Dialogue" and "Jews and Germans" in *Jews and Judaism in Crisis*, 65–70, 71–92.

13. See Scholem, "Juden und Deutsche," in *Judaica 2*, 26–27.

14. Cf. the development of the motif of the hermeneutic "restitution" of sense in Derrida, "Restitutions de la vérité en peinture," *La vérité en peinture*, 291–436.

15. Auerbach, "Figura," in *Scenes*, 11–78. For a reading of the connections between Auerbach's *Mimesis* and his own situation of exile during the war, see Damrosch. On Auerbach's attempt to rehabilitate Judaeo-Christian culture as against Nazi nationalism, see Green. For a deconstructive reading of Auerbach with which my own intersects, although the emphasis there is on the rhetorical structures of historiography, especially Hegelian historiography, and the focus is largely on *Mimesis*, see Bahti, *Allegories of History*, 137–55, especially 142–45.

16. It is not by chance that Auerbach (80; 57–58) characterizes symbol as young and allegory as old, when he is defining figural interpretation at one point as situated between the two: allegory is tilted by the realist/symbolist aesthetic Auerbach adopts in the direction of Judaism, or Old Testament culture, while symbol is associated with Christianity, or the New Testament. We will return to this alignment below.

17. In the Holocaust, the Nazis referred to the dehumanized bodies of their (Jewish) victims as "Figuren."

18. Auerbach no doubt rightly situates the persuasiveness of figural interpretation in its way of combining the abstract with the concrete in a teleological narrative, 51–52; 55–56.

19. Cf. Derrida's analysis of the structure of the "supplement" in *Grammatologie*, 207ff. The substitutive supplement replaces all too completely what it stands for, the figure becoming the literal replacement of the literal, as the literal becomes the mere figure of the figural.

20. I omit the first part of the article, in which Auerbach traces the semantic development of *figura* in the pagan Latin authors ("From Terence to Quintilian") as a translation of the Greek terms, *skema* and *typos*, the vicissitudes of its sense moving from form to outline and on to rhetorical figures by way of subtle gradations and wandering variations of qualitative coloration.

21. The reason why realism and symbolism overlap, as we will see below, is that each embraces the ontorhetoric of empiricism, or materialism. For crucial recent discussions of the opposition between allegory and symbol, discussions which usefully place in question the privilege of symbol that was installed so strongly by the nineteenth century, see Benjamin, *Ursprung des deutschen Trauerspiels*; and de Man, "The Rhetoric of Temporality," in *Blindness and Insight*, as well as *Allegories of Reading*; and the essays on "Sign and Symbol in Hegel's Aesthetics" and "Hegel on the Sublime," in *Aesthetic Ideology*, 91–104, 105–18.

22. Auerbach, "Figura," 29–30; 65–66.

23. "Figural interpretation establishes a connection between two events or persons, the first of which signifies not only itself but also the second, while the second encompasses or fulfills the first. The two poles of the figure are separate in time, but both, being real events or figures, are within time, within the stream of historical life. Only the understanding of the two persons or events is a spiritual act, but this spiritual act deals with concrete events whether past, present, or future, and not with concepts or abstractions. These are quite secondary, since promise and fulfillment are real historical events, which have either happened in the incarnation of the Word, or will happen in the Second Coming. Of course, purely spiritual elements enter into the conceptions of the ultimate fulfillment, since 'my kingdom is not of this world'; yet it will be a real kingdom, not an immaterial abstraction, only the figura, not the natura of this world will pass away, . . . and the flesh will rise again" (53).

24. Here the pagans replace the Jews in Paul's (i.e., in the original) version of figural interpretation, as if Auerbach were repressing in this passage the fact that the Jewish-Christian conflict is behind the allegory-symbol debate, a fact he elsewhere acknowledges. But as I will spell out below, in the post-Reformation period, the Jewish and pagan become particularly close from the standpoint of Lutheran Christianity. As a result, it makes a kind of sense for Auerbach to conflate the Jewish and pagan here, yet a sense that is dictated by the history of religious ideology.

25. On Pauline Christianity, see Leo Baeck, "The Faith of Paul" and "Romantic Religion," in *Judaism and Christianity*, 139–70 and 189–292. On Paul and his influence on modernity, see Taubes, *Politische Theologie des Paulus*; for an attempt to rehabilitate Paul as a Jew, see Boyarin, *A Radical Jew*, especially 86–105 on letter and spirit.

26. Auerbach, "Figura," 29; 65.

27. Auerbach writes, "Insofar as in figural interpretation one thing stands for another, since one thing represents and signifies another, figural interpretation is 'allegorical' in the broadest sense. But it differs from most of the allegorical forms known to us by the historicity both of the sign and what it signifies. . . . The symbolic or mythical forms have certain points of contact with the figural interpretation; both aspire to interpret and order life as a whole; both are conceivable only in religious or related spheres. But the differences are self-evident. . . . These two comparisons, with allegory on the one hand and with the symbolical, mythical forms on the other, disclose figural prophecy in a twofold light" (54–58; 79–80).

28. On chiasmus as a figure of totalization in hermeneutic discourse, see de Man, "Reading and History," in *Resistance to Theory*, 60.

29. Once we have recognized, as we have above, that the reference to the fulfillment of the Christian fulfillment at the end of the world and the Last Judgment is a *supplement* of figural interpretation, and once we have seen that figural inter-

pretation combines the allegorical with the symbolic, we need only recognize that symbolic modes of representation coincide ontorhetorically with the literal level of interpretation (insofar as symbol and literalism—or realism—both privilege the real as the literal and see the possible or conceptual as the figural) in order to be in a position to make ontorhetorical sense rather easily of the unity of the fourfold interpretation of scripture. The allegorical level of meaning, the opposite of the literal level, would privilege the possible (or abstract) as literal. The literal interpretation privileges the real (or concrete) as literal. The figural interpretation, then, as we have seen, combines these two levels, literal and allegorical, into a neat whole. But again, since the New Testament fulfillment is not quite a fulfillment, but rather remains marked by a certain degree of prefigurative nonliterality, because it remains both a bit too real and a bit too unreal (or merely possible), the anagogical fulfillment of this fulfillment must be called upon to supplement this lack with what it lacks. The end of the world—the topic of anagogical interpretation—is both part of the world and beyond the world. It is on the border between the world and what transcends it absolutely, precisely in the position the figural fulfillment was supposed to occupy insofar as it, too, mediated between literal and allegorical meanings, concrete and abstract terms, or realist and idealist ontorhetorical configurations. The mere fact of the anagogical level of interpretation testifies, then, to the residually prefigurative character of the (Christian) fulfillment of the original (Jewish) prefiguration, threatening to undo our faith in the prefiguration-fulfillment model precisely by repeating its structure.

30. Luther, 9.

31. For the sake of this discussion, I mean by "Protestantism" the Lutheran Church per se. The situation in the case of the other (post-)Reformation denominations would have to be qualified in various ways, but it is with the Lutheran center of the German Protestant movement that we are concerned here.

32. Similarly, the Jewish prefiguration led to a Christian fulfillment that had to be fulfilled in its turn at the end of the world. This would imply that with Protestantism the world comes to an end: Protestantism is the institutional realization of the end of the world, the third term. The world ends, then, when it is absorbed into radical Lutheran inwardness. This is what the young Friedrich Schlegel experiences, for example, in its dialectical doubling also as a loss of God in a pure worldliness or chaos (which is why pantheism becomes a privileged possibility in this age). But Schlegel solves the problem of this world-loss with Catholicism, as I discuss in Part II.

33. Typological interpretation also plays a role within medieval Judaism, but a minor one, and one that may have developed under the influence of Christianity. On this topic within the more general topic of *pardes*, the Jewish "equivalent" of the Christian medieval fourfold sense of scripture, see Talmage, "Apples of Gold: The Inner Meaning of Sacred Texts in Medieval Judaism"; for a recent reconceptualization of *pardes*, through which it becomes clear that *drash*—the (non)equiv-

alent of the "tropological" level—bears the burden of distinguishing Jewish from Christian scriptural interpretation, see Fishbane, "The Teacher and the Hermeneutical Task: A Reinterpretation of Medieval Exegesis," in his *Garments of Torah*, 112–20; and in the same collection, see Fishbane's "Inner-Biblical Exegesis: Types and Strategies of Interpretation in Ancient Israel" (3–18), in which one Jewish "equivalent" of tropological interpretation is briefly characterized; on the Kabbalistic hermeneutic of the letter as distinguished from the Christian doctrine of the fourfold sense of scripture, see Scholem, "Der Sinn der Tora in der jüdischen Mystik," in Scholem, *Kabbala*; for a classical reading of medieval Jewish hermeneutics in the style of the "Science of Judaism," see Heinemann.

34. The ambivalence of medieval thinkers toward the "pagan" rhetorical traditions of ancient Greece and Rome overdetermines, and is overdetermined by, their ambivalence toward the "Jewish" prefiguration, such that the view of Jews as residually pagan is reinforced by the association of both Jews and pagans with the rhetorical materiality of language. On the ambivalence of the church fathers, Augustine, and Boethius toward "pagan" rhetoric with respect to Christian "truth," and on the tensions between dialectic and rhetoric that registered this ambivalence, see Conley, 62ff., 74–82.

35. On the practice, particularly prevalent in the seventeenth century, of drawing analogies between Jews and pagans, see Manuel, 168–72.

36. On Luther's attitude toward the Jews, see Oberman, *Wurzeln des Antisemitismus* (published in English as *Roots of Anti-Semitism*), especially Part Three; Gilman, *Jewish Self-Hatred*, 57–68. Gilman points out that the Jews are likened to Catholics in Luther's discourse, but he doesn't explicitly indicate that if this is the case, it is because the Catholics are, for (and since) Luther, (pseudo)Christian Jews.

37. The philo-Semitism of certain prominent French Catholics in the eighteenth and nineteenth centuries testifies indirectly to the attempt of the Catholics to insist that the Jews, and not they themselves, are in the position of the prefiguration and thereby to reinstall themselves in the position of the fulfillment. See the chapter on "Catholic Vindications of Israel" in Manuel, 222–48.

38. Cf. the slightly different way of connecting the fourfold sense of scripture to the four causes in Fletcher, 313n: "It is not often noticed that the fourfold scheme of levels, which becomes a semantic puzzle for students of medieval exegesis, and for students of Dante especially, is a translation into semantic terms of the fourfold Aristotelian scheme of causes. Yet we get the correspondence: literal—material; allegorical—formal; tropological—efficient; anagogical—final." While this schematization strikes me as at once plausible and suggestive, my proposal would be that the literal and allegorical levels are both to be associated with efficient causality as overdetermined by material and formal causality, respectively, while the tropological and anagogical levels are both versions of final causality, but the first on a material level, the second on a formal/spiritual level. So that one

would end up with: literal—materially efficient; allegorical—formally efficient; tropological—materially final; and anagogical—formally final.

39. In terms of the Lacanian reformulation of Freudian metapsychology, what is psychoanalytically at stake in the triangular structure of typology is the attempt to establish the passage from the (pagan) imaginary (i.e., the body image always threatened by immanent dissolution) to the (Jewish) symbolic and from there (once the symbolic has revealed itself to be imaginary in turn) to the (Christian) real (as *Aufhebung* of imaginary and symbolic). In each case, however, the real turns out to split into its imaginary and symbolic representations, that which would be life splits into two forms of death, to the degree or for the "reason" that the real is never securable as such, as impossible as forbidden. But no doubt the attempt to characterize the dynamics of typology in Lacanian terms would have to be completed by an attempt to situate Lacan's own thought with respect to the history of typology, a task which evidently cannot be undertaken here.

40. It seems to me that this strange Enlightenment turn from Protestantism to its Jewish "essence" accounts, for example, for what Jürgen Habermas—without ever really explaining its origins—calls "The German Idealism of the Jewish Philosophers" in an essay of that title in *Philosophical-Political Profiles*, 21–44.

41. Holborn, 128–35.

42. On the intermediate position of Pietism between Lutheran orthodoxy and Enlightenment, see Holborn, 137–44, 164.

43. On the discourses of tolerance and natural religion in the seventeenth and eighteenth centuries, see the chapter on "Historical Background" in Allison, *Lessing and Enlightenment*, 1–49.

44. When "Catholic propaganda" spread rumors in the sixteenth century that "Luther's heresy was a Jewish conspiracy to destroy Christianity" (Manuel, 47–48), it at once ("prophetically") bore witness to the becoming-Jewish of Protestantism and defended itself against the Judaization of Catholicism that Protestantism implied—how else but by calling the kettle black?

45. Allison, *Lessing and the Enlightenment*, 3–15; Poliakov, 3:59–69; Manuel, 175–91.

46. Manuel, 181ff.

47. Allison, 16–24; Poliakov, 70–156; Manuel, 192–221.

48. Allison, 24–49, 8–120; Poliakov, 157–212; Manuel, 250–92.

49. Manuel, 263–72; the Herder texts we are referring to here are: *Über die ersten Urkunden des Menschlichen Geschlechts*; *Älteste Urkunde des Menschengeschlechts*; and *Vom Geist der Ebräischen Poesie*, in Herder, 9–178, 179–660, and 661–1308, respectively.

50. Cf. Librett, "Humanist Antiformalism as a Theopolitics of Race: F. H. Jacobi."

51. When the three sons of the dead king claim each to have received from him his sole ring, where the ring is a figure for the true revelation or letter, and its power

is "die Wunderkraft beliebt zu machen" ("to make its wearer beloved"), the judge gives the sons this advice: "Es eifre jeder seiner unbestochnen/Von Vorurteilen freien Liebe nach!/Es strebe von euch jeder um die Wette,/Die Kraft des Steins in seinem Ring' an Tag/Zu legen! komme dieser Kraft mit Sanftmut,/Mit herzlicher Verträglichkeit, mit Wohltun,/Mit innigster Ergebenheit in Gott,/Zu Hülf'!" ("Let each aspire/To emulate his father's unbeguiled,/Unprejudiced affection! Let each strive/To match the rest in bringing to the fore/The magic of the opal in his ring!/Assist that power with all humility,/With benefaction, hearty peacefulness,/And with profound submission to God's will!" (Act III, Scene 7, lines 113, 134–41; pages 79–80 in English edition; 667–68 in German edition, vol. 1). To make one-self beloved of others by struggling to express more love through good deeds than anyone else is to place the essence of one's religion in a practical, ethical dimension for which works are the very touchstone of spiritual content.

52. In "Interpretations at War," Derrida has pursued the implications of Kant as quasi-Jewish thinker in the work of Cohen and Rosenzweig.

53. Poliakov, 178–80; Manuel, 285–90.

54. On Kant's response to Mendelssohn's theory of writing in *Jerusalem*, see Hamacher, *"Pleroma,"* 32–41. For suggestive indications as to the subterranean importance of Mendelssohn to Kant's essay from the *Conflict of the Faculties* on the "Renewed Question: Whether the human race is continuously progressing toward that which is better," see Fenves, *Peculiar Fate*, 185–86, 192n, 242n.

55. The main texts between which one would have to arrange confrontations in any extended reading of the Mendelssohn-Kant relationship begin with the two prize-competition essays on the crisis of rationalism, Mendelssohn's *Abhandlung über die Evidenz* and Kant's *Über die Deutlichkeit der Grundsätze der natürlichen Theologie und der Moral* of 1763, and include Mendelssohn's *Über die Empfindungen* and Kant's *Kritik der Urteilskraft*, Mendelssohn's *Phädon* and Kant's critique thereof in the second edition of the *Kritik der reinen Vernunft*, Mendelssohn's *Jerusalem*, on the one hand, and Kant's writings on religion and reason, on the other hand, both authors' essays on the question of Enlightenment, and Kant's contributions to the pantheism-discussion in the few brief texts in which he responds to Mendelssohn's *Morning Hours*. While this comparative reading has already been worked out in piecemeal fashion in essays by various scholars, an extended, close reading—preferably one informed by a deconstructive conception of metaphysics—remains to be done. From this list of texts, it can readily be seen that to have addressed the Kant-Mendelssohn relationship here in a serious way might have prevented me from giving Mendelssohn his due as an independent thinker and certainly would have made it impossible to include extended readings of Friedrich and Dorothea Schlegel, as well as Marx and Wagner, in this study.

56. Those who see Mendelssohn as contributing to a "Reform" of Judaism—both those who celebrate such a contribution and those who bemoan it—read Mendelssohn as a Protestantizer, but in this sense as progressive (whether they

affirm or negate the value of progressivism); those who emphasize Mendelssohn's preservation of his Judaism see him as a Judaizer, but in this they tend to see regression, or at least conservatism, in the sense of a conserving attitude toward Rabbinic Judaism. The perspective of the present study displaces this alternative in two ways. First, it considers the Protestantizing dimension in the context of German Enlightenment to be a *regressive* or conservative tendency, while it sees in the Judaizing dimension a *progressive* or radical tendency. Second, given that the Judaizing moment of German Enlightenment develops out of the very logic of the (post-)Reformation, this distinction between regressive and progressive, or even between Protestantizing and Judaizing tendencies, is relativized. For the reading of Mendelssohn, the main point is that there is just this one historical moment when to be a Jew and to fit oneself into the unfolding of (post-)Reformation spirit are gestures that, on the level we have been considering, are absolutely compatible, seamlessly articulable with one another. Subsequently, in the generations that follow upon that of Mendelssohn, this is no longer the case. Hence, for example, the rush of Mendelssohn's children to convert. I consider one example of these conversions in textual detail in Part II, that of his eldest daughter, Brendel/Dorothea.

57. Librett, "Can a Jew Have Feelings?"

58. On the way in which Judaism presented itself to Renaissance Christian Hebraists as containing two traditions, one of which (the Halachic) was literalist, while the other (the Kabbalistic) was allegorical, see Manuel, 38ff.

59. As we have seen, the structure of the Jewish-Christian relation, as a letter-spirit relation, is repeated within Christianity as the Catholic-Protestant relation. As a result, on the one hand, the potential compatibility of Jewish and Christian with rationalist and empiricist ideologies, respectively, is illustrated or realized by the existence of a Catholic rationalism, as in Descartes or Malebranche, and a Protestant empiricism, as in Locke or some of the later German Lockeans. And on the other hand, the inversion of this pattern, the compatibility of Jewish and Christian with empiricist and rationalist ideologies, respectively, is illustrated by the existence of a Catholic empiricism, as in some of the French sensualists such as Condillac, and a Protestant rationalism, as exemplified by Leibniz, whose own efforts to reconcile Protestant and Catholic would no doubt merit a close reading from this perspective (see Hazard, 199–217, for a summary of Leibniz's debates with Bossuet). Spinoza—as a rationalist who however identifies the most rational (God) with the most material (creation), and a Jewish Protestant, i.e., a letter who is simultaneously pure spirit—is in all respects on the edge. And this is where Mendelssohn picks up the relay.

60. When Kant "overcomes" this opposition, however, he will also reinstate it on the level of the opposition between the (rationalist) faculty of reason and the (empiricist) faculty of the understanding, an opposition the tension of which in turn constitutes the (aesthetico-teleological) reflexive judgment. And it is in the struggle to overcome this tension that German Idealism will, to a very great extent, consist.

61. For a relatively reliable, if also excessively psychologistic or personalistic, Protestant perspective on German Romantic conversions, see, in Huch, *Romantik*, the chapters on "Die neue Religion" (167–84); "Die alte Religion" (317–33); and "Romantischer Katholizismus" (561–77). Huch understands that the attempt to overcome Protestantism has to do with a desire to overcome its literalism (324), and she is well aware that Schlegel and his colleagues envisioned, early on, a synthesis of Protestant and Catholic, but she does not attend to the importance of Judaism nor to the triangular structure of the "Judaeo-Christian" religion(s). For a fascinatingly self-persuaded German Catholic perspective on the Protestant Romantic Catholicizers, within a general appreciation of Catholicism as "complexio oppositorum" (11 passim), see Schmitt, 15 passim. For a useful overview of Romantic Catholicism, see Walzel, 91–102.

62. See Hertz's excellent, sociohistorically oriented treatment of the salon culture in *Jewish High Society in Old Regime Berlin*. My own, more narrowly textual, treatment of the philosophico-ideological determinations of these interactions by no means intends to deny the kinds of social, ideological, and personal forces Hertz traces. Rather, as I have indicated above, it attempts to clarify one important level of these (overdetermined) events, the way in which they are pushed toward their realization by the philosophico-ideological or discursive demand for a letter-spirit synthesis (and for all that this synthesis entails).

63. Even Philippe Lacoue-Labarthe and Jean-Luc Nancy, in their excellent book, *L'absolu littéraire*, still underestimate the importance of the Jewish-Christian connections, to some extent misled perhaps by Heidegger's Greco-centrism. Thus they overestimate the daunting character, for the German moderns, of Greek originality, failing to appreciate the degree to which Protestant German intellectuals are haunted by the indebting originality of the Jews (and Catholics). Schlegel prescribes this oversight in the subsequent scholarship in two fragments ("Lyceum" fragments 91 and 93, respectively), the first of which denegates the importance of the Jewish-Christian opposition for the understanding of the relations between ancient and modern, while the second posits the Jewish-Christian opposition, in the form of the letter-spirit opposition, as precisely the model for the understanding of the ancient-modern opposition and so as what is, in a veiled way, at stake in that ancient-modern opposition.

64. It is instructive that the most prominent representative of a resolutely Protestant early German Romanticism—Friedrich Schleiermacher—responds, in the face of the proposals of a kind of mass conversion submitted to Pastor Wilhelm Teller by David Friedländer and a number of prominent enlightened Jews in 1799, that he fears a resultant "judaizing Christianity" (Quoted in Poliakov, 3:209). From the perspective of the present study, this Judaization was, in any case, implied by Enlightenment, requiring from an anti-Jewish Christian German intellectual community either the move to a Catholicism or a (regressive) reconstitution of Protestant inwardness, as Schleiermacher attempts in *Über die Reli-*

gion. For the quotation and discussion of a crucial anti-Jewish passage in *Uber die Religion,* which follows the pattern of the English deists in refusing to grant Judaism a prefigural (and so also an ultimately fulfilling) function with respect to Christianity, see Poliakov, 186.

65. This logic is spelled out quite explicitly in the seminal text of Romantic Neo-Catholicism, Novalis's "Die Christenheit oder Europa" (in Friedrich von Hardenberg, *Schriften,* 2:507–24). Even before the idealized medieval church enters into a state of decay, it is characterized as becoming Jewish: "Rom selbst war Jerusalem . . . geworden" ("Rome itself had become . . . Jerusalem," 509; my translation), and thus when it falls into decay it is not surprising that it takes on the negative characteristics of the Jewish letter, becoming "Ruine, Buchstabe" ("ruin, letter," 510). Consequently, the Protestant Reformation appears as an "Aufstand gegen den despotischen Buchstaben" ("an uprising against the despotic letter," 511). But the paradoxical problem with Luther's Reformation is that, not only is it excessively spiritual in the sense of structureless—"etwas durchaus Widersprechendes—eine Revolutionsregierung permanent erklärt" ("something thoroughly contradictory—a revolutionary government declared to be permanent," 512)—but also excessively material—Luther "führte einen anderen Buchstaben . . . ein . . . Bibel . . . Philologie" ("introduced another letter . . . Bible . . . philology," 512). The letter undoes the religious spirit: "Dem religiösen Sinn war diese Wahl" of Luther's Bible "höchst verderblich, da nichts seine Irritabilität so vernichtet wie der Buchstabe" ("For the religious sense this choice" of Luther's Bible "was highly ruinous, since nothing annihilates its irritability like the letter," 512). The excessive spirituality of Protestantism fixes itself in a new letter. The only way out, then, will be to take the letter back up into the spirit in order precisely to respiritualize the spirit. This movement Novalis sees as announced in Schleiermacher's *Über die Religion.* Of Schleiermacher, he writes, playing on his name: "Er hat einen neuen Schleier für die Heilige gemacht, der ihren himmlischen Gliederbau anschmiegend verrät und doch sie züchtiger als ein andrer verhüllt.—Der Schleier ist für die Jungfrau, was der Geist für den Leib ist, ihr unentbehrliches Organ, dessen Falten die Buchstaben ihrer süßen Verkündigung sind; das unendliche Faltenspiel ist eine Chiffernmusik, denn die Sprache ist der Jungfrau zu hölzern und zu frech, nur zum Gesang öffnen sich ihre Lippen" ("He made a new veil for the sacred one, which betrays the heavenly architecture of her members by clinging to them, but nonetheless hides her more chastely than another. The veil is for the virgin what the spirit is for the body, its indispensable organ, whose folds are the letters of her sweet annunciation. The endless play of folds is a music of ciphers, for language is for the virgin too wooden and impertinent: her lips open themselves up only in order to sing," 521). Here, the letter is incorporated into the spirit as folds into a veil, and the play of the letters is totalized as an infinite music and so it enters the domain of the voice as image of presence. Novalis then goes on to figure this assimilation of the letter into the spirit as the renewed visibility of the

church that he prophesies toward the end of his text: "Die Christenheit muß wieder lebendig und wirksam werden und sich wieder eine sichtbare Kirche ohne Rücksicht auf Landesgrenzen bilden, die alle nach dem Überirdischen durstige Seelen in ihren Schoß aufnimmt und gern Vermittlerin der alten und neuen Welt wird" ("Christianity must become once again living and effective, and constitute for itself once again a visible church without concern for national borders, to take up into its womb all souls that thirst after the unearthly, and to become happily a mediator between the old and the new world," 524).

CHAPTER I

1. Librett, "Can a Jew Have Feelings?"

2. Mendelssohn, "Phädon," in *Gesammelte Schriften, Jubiläumsausgabe* (here-after cited as *JubA*), 3, 1:5–161; and "Die Seele," in *JubA*, 3, 1:201–34.

3. I spell out this argument in the article cited in note 1 above.

4. Lowenstein, 43–54, 104–33 passim.

5. Cf. Shell for an excellent analysis of the universalism of the Christian "spirit" as based on the absence of any principle of the nonsibling human being. In this analysis, the sibling, as that which shares the same body, or ego-ideal, would amount to an absence of body, or letter, in my terms, since the body is only a body when it is another body, not "my own." See especially 35–36, 38 passim for Shell's characterization of Mendelssohn's awareness of, and response to, this denegation of (non)sibling rivalry in *Jerusalem*.

6. In *JubA*, 8, *Schriften zum Judentum* II:99–204. The excellent English edition to which I refer here is the translation by Arkush, *Jerusalem, or on Religious Power and Judaism*. I cite first page numbers from this edition, then after a semi-colon page numbers from the German edition, although I sometimes translate for myself or alter Arkush's version here and there in accordance with my way of working in English with Mendelssohn's German.

7. A telling illustration of Mendelssohn's intention to make this argument is his note in the outline of *Jerusalem*: "Christianity is a yoke in spirit and truth" (248; 96). Since Christianity traditionally polemicizes against the "yoke" of the Jewish law as dead letter, Mendelssohn is clearly suggesting that Christianity becomes the actual religion of the "letter" by trying to fix doctrine to specific formulations.

8. I do not attempt to determine here the extent to which Mendelssohn's claim that Judaism has no dogmas is true or false. For classical essays on the subject by leading members of the *Wissenschaft des Judentums* group, see Wiener; Baeck, "Besitzt das alte Judentum Dogmen?"; and Guttmann, "Die Normierung des Glaubensinhalts." Baeck's defense of Mendelssohn's claims strikes me as generally persuasive, including his demonstration that the modern defenses of dogma in Judaism tend to be conducted by those thinkers who are in the process of estab-lishing Reform Judaism relatively independently of *halachah*.

9. "Manasseh Ben Israel Rettung der Juden nebst einer Vorrede," *JubA*, 8:1–72.

10. Altmann in Introduction to "Salvation of the Jews," *JubA*, 8:xiii–xvi.

11. "Das Forschen nach Licht und Recht," *JubA*, 8:73–88. As Mendelssohn is suspected of implicitly converting to Protestantism by shedding the legalism of Judaism, so conversely, as we will see in Part II below, Friedrich and Dorothea Schlegel retrospectively interpret themselves as having become Catholic merely by submitting to the ceremoniality that even a Protestant marriage ceremony involves.

12. Cranz, "Forschen," *JubA*, 8:75.

13. Astonishingly, Cranz is not troubled here by the fact that the early Christians use figural expressions to express their claim to be beyond figural expressions.

14. As one particularly explicit example of Cranz's awareness of, and indebtedness to, the prefiguration-fulfillment model of Jewish-Christian relations, let the following suffice: "The essence of the Christian religion too is the faith of your fathers, carried up and over, purified from the laws [*Sazungen*] of oppressive Rabbis, and multiplied by new additions which nonetheless are derived from the faith of your fathers and explained as the fulfillment [*Erfüllung*] of Old-Testamentary prophecies" (77). And as an example of how Cranz associates the Christian fulfillment with reason: "Perhaps you have now stepped closer to the faith of the Christians, in that you are tearing yourself away from the servitude of iron Churchbonds and now yourself teach the system of freedom represented by the more rational form of worship, which is the actual type [*Gepräge*] of the Christian way of honoring God, in accordance with which we have escaped compulsion and burdensome ceremony, and tie the true divine service neither to Jerusalem nor to Samaria, but posit the essence of religion herein: that in accordance with the words of our teacher the true worshipers pray to God in the spirit and in truth" (81).

15. The rhetorical problematic figures further, of course, the psychosexual problematic (that is, the problematic of circumcision qua castration), but in a paradoxical manner. Cranz's desire to see Mendelssohn wholly unveiled—"sie ganz zu sehen"—implies a desire to see him circumcised. Yet his desire to see Mendelssohn whole and as a Christian—another possible reading of "sie ganz zu sehen"—in the literal light of spiritual truth, implies a desire to see him uncircumcised.

16. While Sander Gilman, in "'Hebrew and Jew': Moses Mendelssohn and the Sense of Jewish Identity," convincingly shows Mendelssohn to be, in part, passively subject to the pressures of his anti-Semitic milieu, still it is my sense that Mendelssohn also actively resists these pressures in various, strategically calculated ways. Certainly, the Hebrew rabbinic and Yiddish linguistic and cultural traditions tend to be assimilated, by the discursive milieu around Mendelssohn, to the Christian-philosophical notion of the "bad" rhetorical letter, but Mendelssohn doesn't entirely abandon the rabbinic tradition of Jewish law, at least, and his work within the German philosophical discourse not only supports Leibniz-Wolffian metaphysics but also attempts to displace, at times, the most insidious denegations of the prefigural letter that organize this metaphysics.

17. Mendelssohn, "Vorrede" to "Rettung der Juden," *JubA*, 8:7.

18. Not only is figural language tendentially like poison in that it claims to provide the nourishment of meaning yet withholds that nourishment, undermining meaning by multiplying it uncontrollably, but further Jews were thought to poison not just anything but wells. Since wells are figures of pure origination, this fear that the Jews were poisoners of wells signified the fear that the Jews were undoing the purity of the *origin* for Christianity.

19. Mendelssohn, *JubA*, 8:11–16. On the backgrounds, historical and textual, of economic considerations in Manasseh Ben Israel's petitions to the English government, see Ravid.

20. While Mendelssohn goes on to acknowledge that there can be an "abuse" ("Misbrauch") of the position of the middleman (15–16), where the middleman lowers the prices for the producer and raises them for the consumer, exploiting their need of his mediation in order to maximize his profits, he argues that such abuse can be avoided if the government controls monopolies in order to maximize competition between middlemen. The "unlimited freedom and equality in the rights to buy and sell" (15) is the means to the avoidance of the abuse of mediation in the economic sphere. If mediation corresponds on the economic level to figurality, the play of the letter, on the level of language, then Mendelssohn's argument here would be the equivalent of the suggestion that *unlimited* figurality, an endless play of the letter, the endless deferral of meaning through a limitless process of interpretation, would be the way to prevent the letter from hardening into a dogmatically fixed form whose implication would be violence.

21. In response to Cranz's suggestion that he might be in the process of converting from Judaism to Christianity, Mendelssohn responds, with caustic irony, in terms that translate the prefiguration-fulfillment model into an architectonic image: "This suggestion is advanced with sufficient solemnity and pathos. But, my dear sir, shall I take this step without first deliberating whether it will indeed extricate me from the confusion in which you think I find myself? If it be true that the cornerstones of my house are dislodged, and the structure threatens to collapse, do I act wisely if I remove my belongings from the lower to the upper floor for safety? Am I more secure there? Now Christianity, as you know, is built upon Judaism, and if the latter falls, it must necessarily collapse with it into one heap of ruins. You say that my conclusions undermine the foundation of Judaism, and you offer me the safety of your upper floor; must I not suppose that you mock me? Surely!" (87). By reading the prefiguration-fulfillment metaphor as a figure of foundation, Mendelssohn makes explicit the potential for inversion that this metaphor always contains, a potential to which the hostility of Christianity and Christians for Judaism and Jews can in large part be attributed.

22. Thus, the state becomes the (formerly Jewish) letter here, while (natural) religion in its independence from the state, and including the Jewish religion, becomes the (formerly Christian) spirit. "The state, then, is indeed satisfied with

dead actions, with works without spirit [*Werken ohne Geist*], with agreement in the doing, without agreement in thoughts. . . . Not thus religion! The latter knows no action without reflexion, no work without spirit, no agreement in the doing, without agreement in sense. Religious actions without religious thoughts are empty puppet-show, no divine service [*Gottesdienst*]" (44; 113).

23. On Mendelssohn's distance from his friend Lessing's faith in the progress of humanity, see Cassirer; and Mendelssohn, *Jerusalem* (160–64). Peter Fenves has illuminatingly developed the comparison between Mendelssohn's disbelief in progress, as articulated in *Jerusalem*, and Kant's progressivist notion of history in an unpublished essay entitled "The Renunciation of Progress in Mendelssohn's *Jerusalem*."

24. For a reading, in terms of recent political theory, of the tension between the universalism and the particularism, or the liberalism and the communalism, in Mendelssohn's account, see Morgan, "Liberalism in Mendelssohn's *Jerusalem*." For a further reflection by the same author, in which this tension is attributed to Mendelssohn's excessive rationalism, see his "Mendelssohn's Defense of Reason."

25. Today's discussions of knowledge-power relations are late avatars of the eighteenth-century debate on church-state relations. See Foucault.

26. Mendelssohn, *Jerusalem*, 33; 103.

27. The terms Mendelssohn uses for the separation of the different realms of religion and state into "Gebiete" (33; 103) and the attempt to determine the common domain or "Bezirk" (33; 103) they divide up are approximately the same terms Kant subsequently uses, hereby alluding and responding to Mendelssohn, in the second version of the "Einleitung" to the *Kritik der Urteilskraft*, where he distinguishes between "Feld," "Boden," and "Gebiet."

28. Alexander Altmann has usefully reconstructed the ecclesiastical legal traditions with which Mendelssohn is working, not only in *Moses Mendelssohn* (518–20) but also in much greater detail in "Gewissensfreiheit und Toleranz" and in "Moses Mendelssohn on Excommunication: the Ecclesiastical Law Background," in Altmann, *Essays in Jewish Intellectual History*, 170–90. While he rightly emphasizes in the latter essay that Mendelssohn opposes even the minor ban because it cannot fail to result in civil injury (171, 185–86), and while he rightly attempts to place this opposition within the context of Protestant ecclesiastial law theories, Altmann fails to appreciate adequately the sense in which Mendelssohn's opposition to even the minor ban implies and/or results from the consideration that knowledge (for in Mendelssohn's text religion as such, or natural religion, is knowledge) produces effects on the level of power (for the civil status of the individual exists within the political world, the world of the state qua world of power).

29. Cf. Guttmann, "Mendelssohn's *Jerusalem*," where Guttmann clarifies usefully that, whereas according to the traditional, medieval conception, the state was seen as a servant of the church (58), in the seventeenth century there arose the tendency (and the task) to assert the sovereignty of the state vis-à-vis the church, while in the eighteenth century, this having been accomplished, it was necessary to

assert, conversely, the independence of religious conviction from the state (54). On the law of separation of church and state in Judaism, see Graff, 30–54, where he explores the gradual encroachment of the absolutist state on the self-governance of the Jewish communities and so the gradual erosion of the political character of the Jewish law during the Enlightenment.

30. Mendelssohn, *Jerusalem*, 40; 110.

31. The core of the argument is stated very succinctly in the "Preface" to "Salvation of the Jews": "And now especially a right over opinions, over judgments of our human neighbors, with respect to eternal, necessary truths: what human being, what society of human beings is permitted to lay claim to such a thing? since they do not immediately depend on our will; therefore, the only right we have is that to investigate them, to submit them to the strict examination of reason, and to delay our judgment until we have received the agreement of reason, etc./But this right is inseparable from the person: can, in accordance with the nature of the matter at hand, be as little alienated, externalized, transferred to others, as the right to still our hunger, or to draw free breath. Contracts about this are incoherent. . . . It is one thing to renounce one's opinion with respect to an action; another thing to renounce one's opinion itself. Actions stand immediately within our will-power; opinions do not" (20).

32. For the natural law backgrounds, see Altmann, "The Philosophical Roots of Moses Mendelssohn's Plea for Emancipation," in *Essays in Jewish Intellectual History*, 154–69, where Altmann overlooks the paradoxical fact, heavy with rhetorical and theological consequences, that one's "innermost and private sentiments and convictions" (158) cannot be relinquished only because they are so properly our own that they are *not* our own from the start. See also Altmann, "Moses Mendelssohn über Naturrecht und Naturzustand."

33. David Sorkin, in his highly informative recent book, *Moses Mendelssohn and the Religious Enlightenment*, perspicaciously recognizes that Mendelssohn rejects oaths because "language is too imprecise and suceptible of change over time for oaths to have any meaning" (124). He does not go on, however, to reflect on how Mendelssohn's appreciation of the instability of language relates to the tradition of the anti-Semitic use of the phonologocentric opposition between prefigural letter and literal spirit, which Mendelssohn must contest.

On the other hand, Sorkin's contribution, in this book, to the understanding of Mendelssohn's work in translation and exegesis is considerable to say the least (35–89 passim). Mendelssohn's work in the "literalist" tradition, which Sorkin explains with extraordinary learnedness and clarity (65–78), can be understood, in terms of the Jewish-Christian, letter-spirit polemic, as an attempt to establish the self-adequacy of what counts, in the Christian discourse, as the merely prefigural letter. "Literalism" in this sense would be understandable as the "literalism" of the prefigural letter, the attempt to establish the literal reality of figures. As Sorkin points out, Mendelssohn undertakes this "literalism" in opposition to "erroneous christological interpretations" (54), and within a tradition where, moreover, the notion of "literal meaning" is itself multiply overdetermined (65ff.). If to translate a verse literally is to fabricate, as Sorkin quotes Mendelssohn as quoting the Talmud to say (67), then to translate figurally is to translate literally. In short, the distinction between figural and literal is relativized within the Jewish tradition on which Mendelssohn draws.

34. Another example, and this time one which illustrates not only how the state enters, somewhat against Mendelssohn's will, into religion but at the same time how religion enters into the state, occurs when Mendelssohn posits, on the one hand, that the operations of the state determine one's duties toward one's fellow man, while, on the other hand, the operations of religion determine one's duties toward God (50; 119). (Cf. also 56–57; 125ff.) For the fulfillment of *each* of these sorts of duties involves *both* the components of action *and* thought. Thus, the distinction between action and thought does double duty here: first, it functions to distinguish between state and religion; and then it functions to distinguish between the two aspects of the state and the two aspects of religion. *The difference between state and religion is a difference within each term.* The linear, sublationary development, then, that Cranz very traditionally conceived as passing from figural to literal, from matter to spirit, from state to church, has been replaced in Mendelssohn by a structural distinction between these terms, a distinction marked by its proper undecidability.

35. On the way in which only the desire for a *separation* of church and state (and not the desire for their unification), and along with this only the notion of Judaism as essentially apolitical and in this sense passive, became in the post-Enlightenment period the predominant legacy of the Enlightenment ideology formed under the pressure of the absolutist state, see Biale, 87–117.

36. Heinrich Heine, in *Zur Geschichte der Religion und Philosophie in Deutschland*, in fact wrongly takes Mendelssohn to be doing just this: functioning as the Jewish Luther and destroying Jewish "Catholicism." He writes, "As Luther overthrew the Papacy, so Mendelssohn overthrew the Talmud, and in the same way: in that he rejected the tradition, declared the Bible to be the source of religion, and translated the most important part of it. He destroyed thereby Jewish Catholicism, as Luther had destroyed Christian Catholicism. In fact, the Talmud is the Catholicism of the Jews. It is a Gothic cathedral . . . a hierarchy of religious laws" (86). Since of course the law for Mendelssohn included the rabbinic tradition, in fact Mendelssohn was not destroying Talmudism, but rather making it safe for natural religion and the secular state. But Heine's remarks have the virtue of making explicit the analogy between Catholicism and Judaism from a Protestant point of view, for if Talmudism is the Catholicism of Judaism, then this is because Catholicism is the Talmudism, i.e., the Judaism, of Christianity. On Mendelssohn's refusal of the politics of *Glaubensvereinigung*, see, for example, Bamberger, 17–18.

37. In the indispensable chapter on *Jerusalem* in *Moses Mendelssohn*, Altmann discusses the combination of separateness and unity of state and church in this text

(543ff.), but in a manner that is apparently intended to soften to some extent the contradictory or dialectical character of Mendelssohn's conception. Altmann also fails to note that the combination of unity and separation of church and state in Judaism makes Judaism into a kind of synthesis of Catholic and Protestant solutions to the religious power question.

38. On the medieval tradition of the formulation of dogma for Judaism, a tradition Mendelssohn is manifestly opposing here, see Kellner. For useful historical analyses of Mendelssohn's defense of rabbinic law as a basis of spirituality in *Jerusalem*, see Breuer, "Politics, Tradition, History," and "Rabbinic Law and Spirituality."

39. Mendelssohn, *Jerusalem*, 156–57.

40. On the difference between the conception of the Jewish law as a political law in Spinoza and the thought of this law as nonpolitical in Mendelssohn, see Guttmann, "Mendelssohn's *Jerusalem*," especially 49.

41. It is not clear to me that Arkush translates "Stab gelinde" correctly here by interpolating "called" in "staff [called] gentleness," thus turning the adverb "gelinde" into the name of the staff used. There is no doubt, however, that the passage is difficult to translate, simply because Mendelssohn should be saying here, in accordance with his argument, that the Jewish religion uses no "Stab" whatsoever, being noncoercive. One path toward an understanding of this strange passage proceeds by way of the recognition that the German word, "Stab," is half of the German word, "Buchstab," or "letter." The "letter" intrudes here with a residual violence, but a violence that is "mild" (*gelinde*), and accordingly the "letter" has been broken in half. After the destruction of the temple, only the fragment of the letter remains to do its nonviolent violence.

42. The first time he mentions this saying, he uses it as evidence of the sundrance of the state-church unity that characterized the ancient Hebrew empire, commenting upon it in these terms: "Obvious contradiction, collision of duties!" (132; 197), yet he is aware that, although he wants to argue that Judaism is not a political law, still it is necessary to make do with this saying: "And even still no wiser advice than this can be given to the house of Jacob. Accommodate yourselves to the customs and the constitution of the land in which you have been displaced; but hold steadfastly also to the religion of your fathers" (133; 198). And in the very last lines of the text, Mendelssohn returns to this line, addressing the rulers of his day and enjoining them: "If we give to Caesar what is Caesar's, then give to God what is God's!" (139; 204). Thus he apparently places religious law again purely on the side of the powerless goodness of religion, even though he is continuing to differentiate it (with apparent reluctance) from doctrine or knowledge as such.

CHAPTER 2

1. Moses Mendelssohn, "Morgenstunden, oder Vorlesungen über das Daseyn Gottes," in *JubA*, 3, 2:1–175. Page references parenthetically in text. Quote from 61.

2. When Mendelssohn uses the metaphor of "Schattenriß" or "silhouette" repeatedly, in *Morning Hours*, to refer to "words" (10, 104–5), he likens one of the main elements of Lavater's physiognomic imaginary to the linguistic letter: words are like silhouettes. He thus places in question the distance between work with images and work with words, the distance Lavater wants to place between his own domain and the domain of the (Jewish) letter. Further, in the figure of the Swiss man—"a young rough Swiss man, of strong bodily members, but not of the finest understanding" (81)—who embodies "common sense," in Chapter X, Mendelssohn at once alludes, obliquely and somewhat disparagingly, to Lavater ("not of the finest understanding") and ironizes, or takes his distance from, his own notion of "common sense," which is in the end subject to the approval of reason.

3. On Lavater's activities and commitments leading up to his provocation of Mendelssohn, see Altmann, *Moses Mendelssohn*, 201–9; and on the Lavater affair more generally, see 194–264.

4. See Jacobi; on the priority of (inner) experience, see Jacobi, 90, 183, 185, 191, 194, 197 passim; and on the critique of rationalism and Enlightenment more generally, see Jacobi, 183–201. For informative readings of Jacobi that are, in terms of their general orientation and presuppositions, generally much more sympathetic to his philosophical position than my own reading, see Hammacher, *Die Philosophie Jacobis*; and "Über Friedrich Heinrich Jacobis Beziehungen zu Lessing." On the influence of Jacobi's precipitation of the pantheism debate on the development of immediately post-Kantian philosophy, see Snow.

5. Altmann, *Moses Mendelssohn*, 748.

6. In other words, Jacobi is a kind of exaggerated reincarnation of Mendelssohn's character, Euphranor, in *Letters on Sentiments*, but now as applied to theological questions rather than "merely" aesthetic ones.

7. In the case of Friedrich Schlegel and Dorothea Schlegel (who was present in the form of Brendel Mendelssohn at the philosophical discussions that comprise the biographical background of the *Morning Hours*), as we shall see in Part II, the inference they draw from what they see as the disaster of the dialectical becoming-letter of Protestant spirit—both in the rationalist and the irrationalist forms of spirit—is the (equally phantasmatic) notion of a return to Catholicism as synthesis of (Jewish) letter and (Protestant) spirit.

8. On the reception of Spinoza in the German Enlightenment, see Patzold. On Spinoza in the context of marrano culture, see Yovel, *Spinoza and Other Heretics: The Marrano of Reason*; and on the reception of Spinoza from Kant through Freud, see the continuation of this study, Yovel, *Spinoza and Other Heretics: The Adventures of Immanence*. For the relevance of Spinoza to today's debates in critical theory, see Norris.

9. In a letter from April 26, 1785, to Mendelssohn, Jacobi writes, "Perhaps we will live to see the day when a dispute will arise over the corpse of Spinoza like that over the corpse of Moses between the archangel and satan" (quoted in Beiser, 70).

For Jacobi, then, Spinoza is evidently Moses, while Mendelssohn, a double of "Moses," is satan, and Jacobi is the archangel.

10. On Jacobi's "equation of the Enlightenment and Judaism," see Altmann, *Moses Mendelssohn*, 604. For evidence of the way in which the "Judaism" of Enlightenment reason becomes linked, by way of a common association with the letter, with Catholicism (and also more specifically with Jesuitism, itself popularly known for its "sophistical" casuistry), in Protestant Germany, and especially by Jacobi and his other *Sturm und Drang* colleagues such as Hamann, see Altmann (604–5 passim) and also Beiser, 75.

11. For a discussion of *Morning Hours* in the context of the pantheism debate, see Beiser, 44–126, especially 92–109 on *Morning Hours* itself. One weakness in Beiser's account of the pantheism controversy is that he does not do justice, when discussing Jacobi, Mendelssohn, and Wizenmann, to the sense in which the crisis of reason was not only a matter of the opposition between reason and faith, or rationality and irrationality, but of this opposition as *overdetermined* by the opposition between *rationalism* and *empiricism*, which had already begun to call forth a crisis in the German Enlightenment as early as the 1750s. A second way in which I would differentiate myself from Beiser's account is by suggesting that Beiser does not sufficiently emphasize the dangerously *reactionary* character of Jacobi's irrationalist empiricism of inward feeling. Third, while Beiser usefully clarifies the connection between pantheism and a certain Pietist stream of Lutheranism, it is necessary to add: (1) that the Spinoza who appealed to this Lutheranism was the Spinoza of pure "spirit," the opposite of the Spinoza of the "letter" Jacobi detested and feared; (2) that this Lutheranism was always in principle both radically anti-Semitic and, in more general cultural-political terms, quite dangerous insofar as it was an ideology of radical immediacy; and (3) that Lessing's belonging to Lutheranism was one "in spirit" (Beiser, 56) only in the sense that he reread "spirit" as "letter" of "works" (see Chapter 3 below). For an examination of the place of *Morning Hours* in Mendelssohn's life and career, an examination which provides useful epistolary evidence of the generally anti-Semitic atmosphere in which Mendelssohn is operating, see Altmann, *Moses Mendelssohn*, 638–759, especially 742–43 passim. For Altmann's less biographically focused treatment of the Mendelssohn-Jacobi debate, see his "Lessing und Jacobi: Das Gespräch über den Spinozismus." See also Allan Arkush, *Moses Mendelssohn*, 69–98 and also 134–66. While I agree with much of what Arkush says in this tenaciously thoughtful book, he more or less ignores, like Beiser, the role of the rationalist-empiricist divide in the tension between Jacobi and Mendelssohn. Further, when Arkush writes on two occasions, at the beginning and end of his book, that Mendelssohn's "defense of Judaism was . . . more rhetorical than real" (xiv, 291), he commits himself to the kind of traditional distinction between "rhetoric" and "reality" that, as I am attempting to show, Mendelssohn begins to interrogate, if intermittently, in a significant way.

12. Mendelssohn's discussion of the proofs of God's existence will not comprise one of our principal foci here. On the background, structure, and limits of Mendelssohn's proofs, see Altmann, "Mendelssohn's Proofs for the Existence of God," in his *Essays in Jewish Intellectual History*, 119–41.

13. One can also see *Morning Hours*—in light of both its title and its thematization of the undecidability of the border between creation and its anticipation— as an indirect answer to Herder's *Älteste Urkunde des Menschengeschlechts* (in *Schriften zum Alten Testament*, 179–660), in which Herder claims to be able to perceive immediately the creation narrative from Genesis as a primitive dawn-song in praise of God (I, 1, iv, "Unterricht unter der Morgenröte," 246ff.), the sun rising to reveal the world of creation. In this striking anticipation and prefiguration of modern phenomenology, Herder privileges intuition over rationality because the former enables an (anti)hermeneutics of immediacy. In *Morning Hours*, Mendelssohn can be seen to reclaim sunrise for a modified rationalism that insists on the mediated character of all experience, whether it be that of God, the creation, or the self. From this perspective, Mendelssohn's defense of the Enlightenment is a defense of mediation.

14. One should note that the pantheism debates begin around the question of whether or not, when Lessing told Jacobi he supported Spinozism, he was being *ironic*, as Mendelssohn claimed. In other words, the question is that of the presence or absence of a figure, *the figure of irony*. Moreover, if Spinoza's denial both of substantial subjectivity and of the existence of a personal God turned out to be true, then *intentionalist hermeneutics* would suffer a severe blow, for how can one know what someone means when that someone isn't really there at all? Thus, if Spinoza's philosophy turned out to be true, it was not clear how one would ever know for example either what he meant by it, or what Lessing might have meant when he said that he supported Spinoza. From this perspective, then, the pantheism debates appear to concern hermeneutics and rhetoric even more centrally or pressingly than they concern the tension between reason and faith, as for example Beiser argues they do in *The Fate of Reason*, 75–83.

15. Mendelssohn, *JubA*, 3, 2:3.

16. Cf. Mendelssohn's discussions of the "tone" of the nerves and also of the status of music as an art of "tone," in his attempt to elaborate the mind-body unity, in *Letters on Sentiments*, *JubA*, 1:81–88.

17. Altmann, *Moses Mendelssohn*, 264–70; and on the eighteenth-century backgrounds and nineteenth- and twentieth-century manifestations of clichés about Jews as marked by mental illness, see Gilman, *Difference and Pathology*, 150– 62 passim; *Jew's Body*, especially 60–103; and *Case of Freud*, especially 20–26 on pre–fin de siècle backgrounds.

18. Mendelssohn, *JubA*, 3, 2:3.

19. Of course, to the extent that femininity is sometimes also associated with spirituality, while masculinity is aligned with materiality, we should also consider

the passage from the opposite point of view. In this case, Mendelssohn would have to be read as alluding to the alignment of Christian by means of spirit with femininity, and the corresponding alignment of the Jewish by means of matter with masculinity. The fact that the feminine figure of philosophy appears in Mendelssohn's text as a diseased woman endangering the masculine figure of Mendelssohn himself would imply that here the "Christian" discourse of philosophy takes on the characteristics of the "Jewish" discourse of rhetoric, with respect to which the "Jewish" discourse of rhetoric appears as the pure, endangered discourse of philosophy itself, in the sense of the philosophy that is not tainted by the diseased "letter" of the schools, intellectualist debates, academicism, and so on. Neither this reading of the passage nor the one given in the body of the text can be excluded from its interpretation. Indeed, they amount to very much the same gesture, even if they displace opposite gender stereotypes, as well as opposite ways of constellating religious identity (Jewish and Christian) with gender identity (masculine and feminine).

20. In the moment when Mendelssohn writes *Morning Hours*, the opposition between philosophy and sophistry is with particular obviousness in disarray. Kant has recently argued in the transcendental dialectic of the first *Critique* that dogmatic rationalist metaphysics represents a kind of "sophistry" inherent to human reason itself. And Jacobi has begun to produce a counter-Enlightenment distortion of this critique of reason, arguing that *all* philosophy is a kind of sophistry that must be replaced by the leap of faith in the true beyond all knowledge and thought. In such a context, the figuration of metaphysics as a kind of virtuous *femme fatale* is immediately legible as the conflation of philosophy and sophistry.

21. This remains the case even if he hedges his bets—as Beiser argues (100–101), following Wizenmann—by giving "common sense" a provisional and practical privilege over "contemplation" in their rivalry for the approval of "reason." On this point and its reception, see also Arkush, 83–93. It seems to me clear that in "What Does It Mean to Orient Oneself in Thought?" Kant rightly recognizes Mendelssohn's commitment to reason, even though he points out that a defense of rationalist, Leibnizian-Wolffian reason is itself, from the standpoint of his own critical philosophy, unreasonable. Concerning the topic of Kant's response to the conflict between faith and reason as formulated in the pantheism controversy, the most interesting question, to my mind, which neither Beiser nor Arkush nor Altmann raise, is the question of what happens to "common sense" in Kant's text *subsequent to* the first phase of the pantheism controversy, that is, in Kant's last works. Clearly, the beginning of the answer, which we cannot pursue in detail here, is this: Kant repeatedly argues that "common sense," or *sensus communis*, is finally nothing other than the aesthetico-teleological reflexive judgment. Here, an overdetermined composite of Jacobi's irrational "faith" and Mendelssohn's "common sense" is situated between understanding and reason, the speculative and practical forms of reason, in the space of their aesthetico-teleological interruption. See *Kritik der*

Urteilskraft, § 20–21, 40; and compare this text, published in 1790, with the account given of the common understanding in the *Prolegomena zu einer jeden künftigen Metaphysik, die als Wissenschaft wird auftreten können*, in *Werkausgabe*, V:117ff., and 247ff. In the *Prolegomena*, published in 1783, two years before the publication of *Morning Hours*, the notion of "common understanding" as an aesthetico-teleological faculty has not yet crystallized, which indicates that it was the pantheism controversy that led Kant to rethink the position and status of the *sensus communis* as aesthetico-teleological faculty, or what Mendelssohn calls, in the first part of *Morning Hours*, the *Billigungsvermögen*. For a valuable recent attempt to sort out these matters, see Zammito, 228–62.

22. Mendelssohn, *JubA*, 3, 2:5.

23. "Everyone admits to themselves that the ailment is becoming too destructive, that it is time to give the wheel another turn, in order to elevate that which, through the circular course of things, has for too long been brought under our feet. But I am too well aware of my weakness to even have the intention of effecting such a general reversal. Let the task be entrusted to better forces, to the deep mind of a Kant, who will hopefully build up with the same spirit with which he has torn down" (5).

24. Mendelssohn actually poses two questions about truth in this text: "1) What is truth 2) In what characteristics shall we recognize it and distinguish it from illusion and error?" (10). But when he rejects the correspondence model for the force model, to which we will come in a moment, he does so because the former does not provide a criterion for the identification of truth. That is, he does not always hold the two questions apart, which creates a certain amount of confusion in his argument.

25. One of the main ways in which Mendelssohn tries to make the unification of rationalist with empiricist aspects of knowledge plausible is by arguing, in a Leibnizian-Wolffian mode, that all mistakes of perception are actually mistakes of thought. While he first divides the powerlessness of thought, or untruth, into deception (*Täuschung oder Sinnenbetrug*), or the weakness of the "so-called lower capacities of the soul" (29), on the one hand, and error (*Irrthum*), or the weakness of the "upper capacities of the soul" (29), on the other hand, he immediately goes on to show that, in the final analysis, deception and error have the same source. In both cases, this source is false inference, positing the presence of an object where none is present, or positing the presence of certain characteristics in an object where other characteristics are actually given. Both flow from the same source: "incapacity of knowledge, . . . the limitations of our powers of representation" (34), either on the level of "sensuous knowledge" ("in der sinnlichen Erkenntnis" [34]) or on the level of "reasoning" ("in der Vernunfterkenntnis" [34]). The mistaken inference is understood here as the result of an "insufficient analogy" ("unzulänglichen Analogie" [34]), moreover, and so as the result of a figurality that has gone out of control.

26. This definition of truth as force, which Mendelssohn takes to be the definition he is proposing, is repeated a few pages later, at the end of Chapter 3 of *Morning Hours* in italics (34).

27. First of all, this model ends up depending, in a problematic way, on the correspondence model. For as it turns out the only way in which we can determine the degree to which our knowledge is true, the degree to which it is a manifestation of the *force* of our own understanding, is to determine whether or not our representations *correspond* to their objects. Secondly, even if we *could* determine the extent of correspondence, this extent would not actually provide an adequate criterion for the degree of force manifested by our understanding in the operation of knowing. To be sure, to know rationally, i.e., in terms of the rationalist notion of knowledge as the reduction of objects to substantial essences, is indeed *to exercise force over the object*, to make the object correspond to our knowledge, or to reduce its *figural appearance* (on the level of material reality) to its *literal essence* (on the level of spiritual ideality or possibility). To know empirically or in accordance with empiricist presuppositions, however, is to reduce the *figural essence* of the object, which "exists" only on the level of spiritual ideality or possibility, to the *literal appearance* of the object, which actually exists on the level of material reality, and so *to yield to the force of the object*. Insofar as knowledge must mediate between things and ideas, it must pass in both of these directions at once. It must operate at once rationally and empirically. But this means that, in order to correspond to the object, knowledge has to be *at once forceful and forced*, active and passive, or it has to exercise force against the object and against itself.

Further problems one might consider are: (1) that "force" is itself always dual, as possible and actual, as comes out in various ways in the text (e.g., 143ff.); and (2) that the distinction between what comes from force and what comes from the limitation of force cannot be drawn insofar as the limit is double, inside and outside the thing it (de)limits, or insofar as force depends on its own limitation.

28. I ignore in my account Mendelssohn's introduction of a third faculty, the faculty of "Billigung," between the faculties of "Erkenntniß" and "Begehrung." While its introduction is philosophico-historically of great importance (as one of the main predecessors of Kant's *Urteilskraft*, and so forth), and while its introduction here functions as an acknowledgment on Mendelssohn's part that some sort of unification of knowing and desiring is still necessary, Mendelssohn's account here quickly, and inconsistently, assimilates this new faculty to the position of desire. Hence, the main outlines of his thought here are best represented by the binary structure of faculties of knowledge and desire.

29. The aporias of hermeneutic understanding I have sketched in the Introduction are here provided with a kind of pseudoresolution, as the effacement of the reading before the text takes on the name of the "faculty of knowledge," while the effacement of the text before the reading takes on the name of the "faculty of desire." Desiring knowledge, or knowing desire, combines the operation of these

two "faculties" or "capacities" in a synthesis that marks the necessity of understanding with its proper impossibility.

30. The distinction between knowledge and desire establishes the basis on which Mendelssohn will generate, in the second part of *Morning Hours*, his new psychocosmological proof of the existence of God (138–47), where God's thought and desire step in to ensure the existence of the possibilities and realities of the world we know in our severely limited way. However, this proof will still not solve the problem of the unity of knowledge and desire, but just defer it in principle until it becomes the problem of that unity in the infinite mind of God, a problem whose solution Mendelssohn simply presupposes in the notion of God's unity.

31. Kant takes him to task for this in his "Bemerkungen" appended to *Ludwig Heinrich Jacob's Prüfung der Mendelssohnschen Morgenstunden oder aller spekulativen Beweise für das Dasein Gottes* (*Werkausgabe*, 287–91, especially 288–89), yet in a way which violently trivializes Mendelssohn's attempts to show that certain questions are undecidable not merely because of a dialectical tendency of the "mind" but also because of a rhetorical tendency of "language."

32. See, for example, *JubA*, 3, 2:37–38, 44, 89ff., 138ff.

33. For an extended reading of the Jacobi-Mendelssohn debate, which usefully compares and contrasts what Jacobi and Mendelssohn say about Spinoza's doctrines with Spinoza's texts themselves, see Zac, especially 92–185.

34. Mendelssohn has developed this view already in his first German-language text, "Philosophische Gespräche" (*JubA*, 1:1–39, especially 17ff.), and he is essentially restating that argument in *Morning Hours*. On Mendelssohn's early reading of Spinoza in the "Philosophische Gespräche," see Altmann, "Moses Mendelssohn on Leibniz and Spinoza," in his *Die trostvolle Aufklärung*, 28–49. On Lessing's answer to Mendelssohn's early remarks on Spinozan and Leibnizian ontology, as Lessing worked this out in the posthumously published fragment, "Über die Wirklichkeit der Dinge ausser Gott," see Allison, "Lessing's Spinozistic Exercises."

35. The arguments he makes, into which we will not enter in detail here, are the following. First, he introduces the distinction between that which is independent (*das Selbständige*) and that which exists for itself (*das Fürsichbestehende*), suggesting that the monadic souls of Leibnizian provenance are thought of as substantial only in the sense of "das Fürsichbestehende," and thus relativizing the distinction between the Leibnizian and the Spinozan concepts of "substance." Second, he argues that Spinoza accounts only for the "matter," but not for the "form" of the dimensions of both extension and thought. The "form" of the extended is its motion, while the "form" of thought is desire. Since only the independent existence of individual, substantial parts of the whole, can account for the origin of form, figure, and motion (the whole being unmoved and unmoving), while only the independent soul can desire (the whole being again without desire), the parts of the whole must be independent on the levels of both bodies and souls (107–8). Here, incidentally, Mendelssohn connects the reality of the world with the figural

("Figur" [108]), and so in this respect his qualified opposition to Spinoza is to be understood as opposition to the denial of the letter. Here too, Mendelssohn's interpretation of Spinoza begins by reversing the Jacobian perspective. Third, and finally, Mendelssohn reproduces Wolff's suggestion that Spinoza only accounts for the extensive, not the intensive infinity of the world: an infinitude of finite beings yields only extensive infinity, not intensive or totalized infinity. The world needs a mind behind it in order to cohere systematically. This mind, separate from the world, would be a God that is not identical with that world. With this last argument, Mendelssohn does edge onto the terrain of the reading of Spinoza as atheist, yet here too the emphasis is on whether one has to think of the world and God as separate or as unified.

36. First, to the claim that Spinoza doesn't account for the "formal" dimension of extension, "Lessing" argues that the Leibnizian-Wolffian system does not do much better; while to the question of the "formal" dimension of the mind, that is, the faculty of desire, he argues that the pantheist can, in principle or in all likelihood, make room for such a faculty in his one substance. Second, to the question of extensive versus intensive infinity, "Lessing" claims that the pantheist could allow of a separate dimension of substance that would be the origin of the intensive infinity. Moreover, since the first objection raised by Mendelssohn, the distinction between "das Selbständige" and "das Fürsichbestehende," is more a clarification of what Leibniz and Spinoza mean by "substance" than a critique of Spinoza, "Lessing" is not compelled to answer this objection. The result of "Lessing's" intervention, then, is to establish that the essential and only difference between Spinoza and Leibniz is that the former leaves the world in a state of possibility or virtuality in God, whereas the latter places the world outside of God on its own, giving it the status of its own reality: "This the pantheist can admit without compromising his system. But he does not go further than this ideal existence, and when the theist goes further and adds to this claim: God has imparted to this real series of things also an objective existence outside of him, then the pantheist pulls himself back modestly and sees no reason to grant this. How are you going to persuade him of this objective existence also outside the divine understanding" (115–16). Mendelssohn answers, "'If I understand you properly, . . . you admit, in the name of your pantheist, an extra-worldly God, but you deny an extra-divine world . . .'" (116). And beyond this point, despite one or two attempts on Mendelssohn's part to persuade "Lessing" to abandon his Spinozism, the argument does not advance until the chapter ends with the passage we will quote in just a moment.

37. Indeed, at the very outset of the discussion of Spinozism, Mendelssohn expresses his sense that it might just be a matter of merely "verbal disputes [*Wortstreitigkeiten*]" (104), and so it is not surprising that the discussion ends where it does.

38. Mendelssohn, *JubA*, 3, 2:123–24. Note that on the one hand, Mendelssohn

suggests that one "renounce words," while on the other hand, he has said in the passage that functions as an epigraph to this chapter that we cannot get away from words. He therefore apparently does not mean that we can simply get beyond the different words to a common understanding. Rather, he acknowledges that, since to be "in" God is to be "outside" God, excluded as absent center, while what is "outside" of God belongs to God's determination as its external border and so is precisely *part* of God, we have to do here with an *undecidability*: neither inside nor outside has any meaning that can be decisively distinguished from the other.

39. In light of the rather low (and reactionary) blow by means of which Jacobi tries to usurp the public position of "friend" which Mendelssohn the Jew has occupied with respect to Lessing the Christian (Jacobi claims that Lessing confided his Spinozism to him, while never mentioning it to Mendelssohn) it is useful to read the reconstruction of the Mendelssohn-Lessing friendship in the 1770s that is carried out in Strohschneider-Kohrs, "Lessing und Mendelssohn im Dialog." And in even more direct proximity to the pantheism debates, see Strohschneider-Kohrs, "Lessings letzter Brief an Moses Mendelssohn."

40. By taking responsibility for putting Spinozism in Lessing's mouth, Mendelssohn here puts himself in the place which will soon, he expects, be publicly occupied by Jacobi. Thus he attempts to situate or frame Jacobi's accusations in advance. By making the defender of Lessing appear as "D," Mendelssohn distances himself from the defense of Lessing, in order to make that defense appear less self-interested than it would if Mendelssohn carried it out in his own name. (Altmann, *Moses Mendelssohn*, 695, suggests that "D" is Doctor Reimarus, although his argument for this hypothesis is so thin as to be almost nonexistent.) As a compositional strategy, this play and displacement of positions disconnects points of view from those who hold them, and so facilitates disinterested consideration of the matters at hand. The rhetoric of dialogue is slightly unsettled when persons are separated from the opinions we otherwise imagine they hold. Further, "D" appears here both as defender of Lessing and as a German national-linguistic patriot. Speaking of the connection in Lessing between philosophical spirit and poetic letter, he says, "A connection that would only have been possible for a Lessing, but also perhaps even for him only in our mother tongue. Only our mother tongue seems to have achieved the sort of formation, that allows it to combine the language of reason with the most lively presentation" (129). Thus, the defense of Lessing, despite his purified pantheism, is placed at a distance from any taint of the non-German, of the Judaism of Spinoza, Mendelssohn, and company.

41. For a relatively recent Marxist reading of Lessing's pantheism as a historico-philosophical anticipation of dialectical materialism, see Liepert. The preference for concretion or "reality" over abstraction or "possibility" in such a reading is itself not only complicitous with but also a direct descendant of the anti-Jewish Christian preference for the humanization of the divinity, as opposed to the perceived excessive abstraction of Jewish radical monotheism. See Chapter 7 below.

42. Mendelssohn's word is "verfeinert" (136) in addition to "geläutert" or "purified," as in the title of Chapter XV, "Lessing.—Dessen Verdienst um die Religion der Vernunft.—Seine Gedanken vom geläuterten Pantheismus" (125).

43. That is, Mendelssohn's "philosophers" begin as "figuralists" in the sense of those who make a radical distinction between the figural and the literal, or world and God, and so they end as "literalists," in the sense of those who efface the distinction between world and God. Conversely, his "poets and priests" begin as "literalists," fusing figural and literal as one must on the level of the "literal" spirit of ethics, and so they end as "figuralists," making a radical distinction between the world and God.

44. The passage is given in Altmann, *Moses Mendelssohn*, 867, n 46, as Rabbi Yohanan in *Megilla*, 31a. It is explicitly attributed to Rabbi Yohanan, as Altmann also points out, in Mendelssohn's *Sache Gottes*.

45. See Altmann, *Moses Mendelssohn*, 741ff., on the controversy concerning whether or not Jacobi had led to Mendelssohn's death. Beiser remarks, "If Jacobi did not literally kill Mendelssohn, he did so figuratively" (75).

CHAPTER 3

1. "Abschluß des Lessing-Aufsatzes," in *Kritische Friedrich Schlegel Ausgabe* (hereafter *KA*), vol. 2, *Charakteristiken und Kritiken I (1796–1801)*, ed. Hans Eichner, 397–419. Quote from 400; "Eisenfeile" 21, A99. Fragments appearing in the "Abschluss" essay that appear elsewhere in Schlegel's fragment-collections will appear first under the page number of this edition, then under the subheading Schlegel gives them in the "Abschluss" text, "Eisenfeile," followed by the number in that collection, then under the letter indicating the collection in which they originally appeared, followed by the number in that collection, where L=Lyceum, A=Athenäum, I=Ideen. All of these fragment-collections can also be found in the volume in which the "Abschluß" also appears. The "Abschluß" text will simply be referred to here as the "Conclusion" to the Lessing essay. Other fragments will be also cited with the page number, letter indicating the fragment-collection, and fragment number.

2. "Ideen," *KA*, 2:256–72, quote from 263, I 74.

3. "Über Lessing," in *KA*, 2:100–25, citations given below parenthetically in text.

4. On language in Friedrich Schlegel, see Nüsse, especially the chapters on "Gespräch und Buchstabe" (83–87), "Geist und Buchstabe" (88–97), and "Philosophie und Philologie" (98–108). Nüsse's discussion does not address the theopolitical and the personal dimensions of Schlegel's involvement with the spirit-letter relation that interest me here, however, nor does he take the Lessing relationship particularly seriously.

5. F. Schlegel, "Über Lessing," 100.

6. For one of Schlegel's more suggestively clear formulations of the parity between author and critic, consider the following fragment, from the "Abschluß": "When the author knows of no other answer to the critic, he likes to say to him: you can't do it any better. This is as if a dogmatic philosopher wanted to accuse the sceptic of not being able to invent a system" ("Eisenfeile" 61, A 66, 404).

This fragment has important ramifications for the Jewish-Christian opposition. On the one hand, since the critic is here the sceptic, i.e., the one without faith (but rather governed by the laws of the understanding and reason), while the writer is the dogmatist, or the one who relies on faith, the opposition between critic and author here clearly runs parallel to the opposition between Jew and Christian, insofar as Luther opposes law to faith. On the other hand, since the Jew makes works while the Lutheran Christian has a purely spiritual or theoretical relation to God, and since the Jew comes first while the Christian comes after, the critic here is more like the Christian, while the author is more like the Jew. The author-critic opposition, as understood in terms of the dogmatic-sceptic opposition from Kant's transcendental dialectic, replays and doubly inverts the Jewish-Christian one. The parity thus wittily operated between author and critic—the point being that their functions are different ones within an inevitable and nonsublatable dialectic or undecidability that includes both functions—implies also an undecidable dialectical parity between Jew and Christian as well.

7. Krüger, 43–80, who has done research in the early reception history of Lessing in order to evaluate the originality of Schlegel's Lessing reading, makes it clear that others had publicly criticized Lessing as a poet and had admired his wit and prose style. Schlegel's reading was truly original where it emphasized in positive terms both the polemical and the fragmentary dimensions of Lessing's œuvre.

8. Moreover, since Schlegel also identifies, as is well known, with the traits he praises in Lessing's work, we must infer, as is not generally done, that he identifies himself at this phase—despite the fact that he is also drowning in Protestant spirit—with the "Judaic" position, an identification no doubt at work in the "prophetic" ambitions and rhetoric Schlegel often adopts, whether in a backward-turned direction or not.

9. Cf. Benjamin on "prose" in early Romanticism and in Hölderlin, in *Begriff der Kunstkritik*, 100–109. While Benjamin speaks neither of the letter nor of Jewish-Christian equivalents of the poetry-prose relation, his explication of prose reads like an explication of the notion of the letter.

10. F. Schlegel, "Über Lessing," 105.

11. When Schlegel writes in "Athenäum" fragment 366, "The understanding is mechanical, wit is chemical, genius is organic spirit" (232), he places wit—the early Romantic modality par excellence—midway between the mechanical and the organic, and thus between letter and spirit. Yet he characterizes that which is in this middle position of the chemical also as a mode of *Geist*. Schlegel's reading of Lessing is very much in accord with the ambivalence of this fragment, for it too in its

way formulates a place beyond both spirit and letter, but does so in the name of spirit.

12. Schlegel's use of the term, "zermalmende Kraft der Beredsamkeit" here alludes to Mendelssohn's phrase "die Werke . . . des alles zermalmenden Kants" (*JubA*, 3, 2:3), from the Preface to *Morning Hours*. As Kant had undone for Mendelssohn the opposition between rationalism and empiricism, so Lessing has undone for Schlegel the opposition between spirit and letter. And just as Kant became unreadable therefore for Mendelssohn, so there is a certain blinding unreadability for Schlegel in Lessing's text. By quoting Mendelssohn here, Schlegel identifies himself with Mendelssohn, even as he is rivaling Mendelssohn for possession of the "real" or "true" Lessing. Unfortunately, Schlegel indicates his rivalry with the man who will soon be his late father-in-law only in a defensively haughty tone: he mentions that some people have been silly enough to read Lessing through the eyes of Mendelssohn. "One seems to know Lessing's philosophy only as the occasion of Jacobi's, or even merely as an appendix to Mendelssohn's!" (107), whereas evidently they should read Lessing through the eyes of Schlegel.

13. The "explosions" of Lessing's polemic recall one of Schlegel's most striking definitions of wit: ""Wit is an explosion of bound spirit" (158, L 90). Since what binds the spirit is the letter, the explosion of bound spirit is the unlettering of the letter, but since the unlettering depends on the lettering, and since in fact the fragment does not claim that the explosion puts an end to the being-bound of spirit, the explosion of bound spirit is here the unlettering of a lettering. Wit is the interplay of letter and spirit. Further, in the passage quoted above, the "heat" of struggle that tears these explosions out of Lessing rhymes literally with the German for witticisms—"Hitze" with "Witze"—such that, on what may well be a less than conscious level, the textual letter of Schlegel's praise of Lessing's polemicism binds its sense to that of wit.

14. While the apparent lovelessness and scepticism of the polemical critic obviously connects him or her to the traditional figure of the "Pharisaic" Jew, Schlegel will also make it into something like the essence of the Protestant spirit, not only in his comparison of Lessing to Luther (which we will discuss in a moment) but also, more tentatively perhaps, in the "Conclusion," which we discuss below in this chapter, and even more explicitly in his characterization of the Protestant spirit in *Lessings Gedanken und Meinungen*, which we examine in Chapter 6 below. That the essence of Protestantism is such an obviously un-Christian trait is the dilemma or dialectic within which Schlegel is trying to make his way.

15. He speaks, for example, of the "dignified, manly principles, . . . the great free style of his life . . . bold independence, . . . solidity . . . aristocratic cynicism . . . liberality . . . heartfelt warmth . . . [concerning] . . . the primary bonds of nature and the most intimate social relations . . . the virtuous hatred of half-truths and lies . . . sensitive avoidance of any wound to the rights and freedoms of every

independent thinker . . . respect for what he saw as the means to the extension of knowledge . . . zeal . . . divine impatience. . ." (105).

16. In addition, Schlegel is evidently arguing against his own lingering fears here, for as his early correspondence reveals, especially around 1791, but still also in the late 1790s, he was worried that he himself was a loveless man. On this topic, see Eichner, 15. Further, on the question of "Gemüt," Henriette Herz strikingly confirms Schlegel's early fears about himself: "I admit that I was not without fears for her future happiness after my friend got involved with Schlegel. Indeed, I soon believed myself to have arrived at the conviction that he lacked heart [*Gemüt*]. I had come to this conclusion on the basis of my observations of his relationship with Schleiermacher, who was so thoroughly generous and heartfelt [*gemütvollen*] toward his friends, and I had expressed myself to Schleiermacher on this point both orally and in writing. Schleiermacher, infinitely mild in his judgments of his friends, did not want to believe it was true. In the sequel, I was proven not to have deceived myself," Herz, 62. On the notion of *Gemüt*, which remains one of the obsessional motifs of the early fragments, see "Athenäum," fragments 339 (225) and 350 (227), "Ideen," fragments 116 (267), 152 (272), 153 (272).

17. The triangular identification between Lessing, Mendelssohn, and Schlegel in Schlegel's text here is both extremely strong and fraught with a certain instability. And both aspects of this triangular identification are crucial to our reading. The fact that Schlegel praises Lessing for the power of his criticism and the importance of his fragmentary mode of writing already makes fairly clear that Schlegel identifies his own work and spirit strongly with those of Lessing. In painting a portrait of Lessing, he is painting a portrait of himself in a somewhat idealized form, and criticism and autobiography therefore here overlap. While such a gesture may seem to place the adequacy of Schlegel's portrait in question, Schlegel legitimates it implicitly later on in his essay by mentioning that Lessing himself was one of those writers who paint their best portraits when they are painting people who look very much like themselves. Schlegel "justifies" the self-portraying character of his portrait of Lessing, that is, by way of the argument that Lessing himself was a self-portraying portrait-painter. But further, Schlegel's authority for this view of Lessing, i.e., the mediation between himself and Lessing on this crucial point, *is Mendelssohn himself*, for in the context of the discussion of Lessing's bourgeois tragedy *Emilia Galotti*, which Schlegel sees as a particularly non-self-portraying and objective work, Schlegel writes that Lessing "belongs, according to Mendelssohn's remark, to the portrait-painters who are all the more successful in painting a character the more similar that character is to themselves, and who can form only a number of variations on favorite characters who share a decided, striking family-resemblance" (116). Mendelssohn, himself both strongly, effectively portrayed by Lessing (and thus according to Mendelssohn's remark a *likeness* of Lessing) and in turn a (presumably successful, perhaps even for Schlegel dauntingly successful) portrayer of Lessing, stands here as an authority on who Lessing is, and

thus at once as a guarantee of the link between Schlegel and Lessing and also as an obstacle standing in the way of Schlegel's attempt to claim Lessing as his own.

18. This would be the epistemological-hermeneutic dimension of the attractiveness of this principle. It also possesses an ethical attractiveness, of course, since it recommends that one use force only against those who possess sufficient force to defend themselves, and so forth. The epistemological-hermeneutic dimension coheres with the ethical one insofar as the desire not to read inappropriately is also clearly a desire not to do violence. Unfortunately, the ethical productivity of the principle is undermined by the circularity of the epistemological dimension: one would have to know what kind of writer one is dealing with in order to know how to read the given writer, but one would have to read him or her in a certain way in order to know what kind of writer one is dealing with.

19. Cf. Nüsse's summary of Schlegel's hermeneutical attitude with respect to letter and spirit: "The penetration of a work can only occur in that the one who wishes to understand attends at once to letter and to spirit. And one presupposes the other. . ." (95).

20. Lessing's law prescribes that one must be gentle with the weak and stringent with the strong, where such stringency consists—Schlegel has this printed in italics—in the combination of admiration with doubt ("*mit Bewunderung zweifelnd, mit Zweifel bewundernd gegen den Meister*" [109]). This paradoxical simultaneity of admiration and doubt already implies the paradoxical simultaneity of reading for the *letter* and reading for the *spirit* that emerges out of Lessing's radicalization of Luther as I will trace it in a moment: to admire while doubting requires at once following to the letter and applying an intense interpretive energy to the text.

21. Schlegel has said near the outset of his text (101) that Lessing called forth a permanent revolution in theology, as well as in drama and criticism.

22. Cf. Allison on Lessing's theological works in context in *Lessing and the Enlightenment*, especially "Goeze's Attack" (107–10), where the literalism of Goeze ("The letter is the spirit") is contrasted with the *distinction* Lessing draws between letter and spirit. It only needs to be added that Lessing did not merely deny the identity of letter and spirit but simultaneously affirmed and denied it. This is what Schlegel perspicaciously discovers in Lessing's text.

23. Heinrich Heine, who is no doubt aware of Schlegel's reception of Lessing, strikingly confirms Schlegel's reading of Lessing's significance, although without mentioning Schlegel, in *Zur Geschichte der Religion und Philosophie in Deutschland*: "Lessing had an effect similar to Luther . . . in that he brought forth a healthy movement of the spirit, through his critique, through his polemic. He was the living critique of his time, and his entire life was polemic. . . . Lessing was only the prophet who pointed from the second Testament to the third . . . the continuator of Luther. . . . After Luther had freed us from the tradition, and had raised the Bible to the sole source of Christianity, there arose . . . a fixed service of the word,

and the letter of the Bible ruled quite as tyrannically as once the tradition had. Lessing, however, contributed most of all to the emancipation from this tyrannical letter. . . . Indeed, the letter, Lessing said, is the last shell of Christianity, and only after the annihilation of this shell will the spirit step forth" (88–93). The play of letter and spirit in this extraordinary text by Heine would, of course, merit a much longer discussion, especially since in his second edition Heine takes his distance from the entire theological content of the book in the direction of a renewed appreciation of biblical theism.

24. Cf. note 51 in the Introduction above.

25. On the backgrounds of such a position in rational theology and deism, see Allison, *Lessing and the Enlightenment*, especially 3–15.

26. In support of such a reading of "character," one might quote this Schlegel fragment from "Ideen": "All thought of the religious person is etymological, a derivation of all concepts from the original intuition, from the characteristic [das Eigentümliche]" (I 78, 263). For a richly suggestive discussion of the tension between the specificity of "characterization," as an activity of the critic, and the generality of the speculatively deductive procedures of the idealist philosophers, see Lacoue-Labarthe and Nancy, *L'absolu littéraire*, 386–92 passim.

27. In *Begriff der Kunstkritik*, especially in the chapter on "Das Kunstwerk" (72–87), Benjamin emphasizes the importance of form, in Schlegel and the other early Romantics, as the objective expression of the reflexion that is immanent to the work (73). Since reflexion is the work's essence ("Wesen," 73) and the privileged modality of spirit ("Geist," 66), what Benjamin calls form may be understood here as *letter*. While Benjamin barely mentions anything related to the German-Jewish "dialogue" (one partial exception would be the fleeting mention of "romantic Messianism" in a cryptic note [92]), and does not discuss explicitly Schlegel's relation to Lessing (although he quotes the essays on Lessing repeatedly), his opposition to the reception of Romanticism as a subjectivism does indeed involve a pathbreaking appreciation of Schlegel's commitment to the "objective lawfulness" (83) of the artwork's form, in other words, of Schlegel's commitment to the letter in the name of the spirituality of reflexion. Benjamin does not, however, to any great degree problematize—certainly not in terms of the history of the rhetoric of religious cultures—the idealism of the early Romantics, their "metaphysical intuition of all that is real as a thinking being" (62). Still, he does (62) acknowledge that he is not dealing here with Romantic metaphysics, which he determines more narrowly as the Romantic concept of history. The present study intersects with Benjamin's study by addressing the Romantic concept of history insofar as the prefiguration-fulfillment model is a model for historical narrative: it gives Romantic history its endless (and impossible) horizon.

28. F. Schlegel, "Über Lessing," 112.

29. Cf. the important discussion of the early Romantic fragment in Lacoue-Labarthe and Nancy, *L'absolu littéraire*, especially 57–80, 181–205. Lacoue-Labarthe

and Nancy read the Romantic fragment in terms of a notion of the waiting for the work (or absence of the work) that is inspired largely by Maurice Blanchot's "works" on that "subject," in particular "The Athenaeum" (in *The Infinite Conversation*, 351–59), but that in turn takes its place for them in a genealogy of metaphysics they inherit above all from Heidegger. Perhaps because Lacoue-Labarthe and Nancy think of "work" here in these more or less Heideggerian (i.e., ontological and psychocosmological, but not strictly speaking theological or theopolitical) terms, and thus as a modern vernacular translation of the Latin "opera" which in turn translates the Greek "energeia" as a kind of "realization" of "dynamis" (for example, 79), they fail to take seriously the importance, for the early German Romantics' discursive context, of the Lutheran radicalization of the Christian displacement of Jewish works by faith. This oversight, or in any case this de-emphasis, facilitates their efforts to demonstrate the contemporary relevance of the early Romantics, i.e., to demonstrate the sense in which the Romantics "anticipate" our modernity. In this manner, the Romantics become, as it were, the ("Jewish") prefiguration of which our own post-Romantic modernity, with its dissolution of the borders between philosophy and literature or science and art, would be the (structurally, if not theologically "Christian") fulfillment. This Heideggerian approach nonetheless renders their presentation of Romanticism to some degree historically inaccurate. This weakness of Lacoue-Labarthe's and Nancy's account becomes particularly clear at moments when the (always somehow embarrassing) question of *religion* comes up, such as in the chapter on "Religion within the Limits of Art" (181–205), in which they discuss Schlegel's "Ideen" fragments and "On Philosophy." Here, in the midst of what is in many respects a learned and attentive reading, they nonetheless allow themselves the patently denegational: "religion, here the religion of the *Ideas* or of the letter *On Philosophy*, is not religion, and especially not Christianity" (201), a remark which almost immediately gets toned down into "a complex relation" (201) to religion, or "art as religion" (201). This argument ultimately reduces Schlegel's interest in religion to the apparently totally secular and therefore socially acceptable motif of the "subject-work" (203). To this reduction one can have in many respects no objection, except that, from the perspective of an interest in the theopolitical overdeterminations of early Romanticism, the "subject-work" must be understood as a version of the "faith-work," since subjectivity for Luther is faith, while the work is for Luther above all the work of the Jewish law. The fragmentary exigency, then, as the Romantic demand for the subject-work, is what translates for Schlegel in turn the Judaeo-Protestant exigency of a middle ground between faith and law. Indeed, consider the purely "philosophical" determinations of the Romantic fragment: even if (as one could well argue) Kantian philosophy already essentially introduces the fragmentary exigency through the notion of reflexive judgment, where the work is already not quite a work, but the endless reflexion upon it that (never) completes it, then one might still say that Kant's attempted transcendental overcoming of the opposition between rationalism and empiricism (which culminates in the notion of reflexive judgment introduced by the third *Critique*) is already readable, in terms of the history of Protestantism, as an attempt to overcome the opposition between Protestant spirit and Jewish letter, as I suggested in the Introduction above. If neither mind nor matter is the starting point, then the "absolute," which would here be more a "critical" than a "literary" absolute, must be situated between possibility and reality, subject and work, spirit and letter. The work that still strives to be a work, the work that is not yet the work it is—the fragment—would be what occupies this position of absolute starting point. In sum, if one considers the horrendous, theopolitically motivated abuses of the Romantic tradition in twentieth-century Germany (even if the theopolitics was at times that of Christianity intermingled with a Germanic pagan mythologism), then one should also recognize the necessity of taking into account with maximal attentiveness the *theopolitical overdeterminations* of early Romanticism, rather than risking the denegation of these overdeterminations by exclusively or almost exclusively attending to the philosophico-poetic border and its various transformations, such as that into the notion of the subject-work. For a treatment of Romantic fragmentation that is both profoundly sympathetic with Lacoue-Labarthe and Nancy's book and gently critical of its tendency to exaggerate the proximity of Romantic fragmentation to the work of certain (post)modernist writers such as Blanchot and Derrida, see Gasché. For a review article on *L'absolu littéraire* that questions its philosophical bias, see Newmark.

30. Moreover, Schlegel's affirmation of fragmentariness in this context explicitly privileges speech in a traditional way, to the degree that it seems to presuppose that the telos of writing is to become as "lively and dialogical"—as speechlike—as it possibly can. In the part of the passage that I have cut away in the quotation above, Schlegel writes: "Not merely from the reports of his dialogues [or conversations], not merely from the *letters*, which it seems have been, thus far, largely neglected . . . [but] also from his writings themselves one would almost want to imagine that he had even more control of *living dialogue* than of written expression, that here he had been able, even more clearly and boldly to communicate his innermost and deepest, most proper self. How lively and dialogical his prose is requires no explanation" (112).

31. Cf. Schlegel's remark, "His angry polemics are almost unanimously sorely regretted, just like the fact that the man even wrote in a fragmentary vein and despite all admonishments didn't want to complete a series of masterpieces" (106). The suggestion here is that fragments are the product of an *act* of the will, rather than a mere *failure* of the will to realize itself in complete expression. Further, when Schlegel elsewhere speaks of Lessing's philosophy (197), he stresses the fragmentary character of Lessing's philosophical works within a more generalized fragmentariness, a fragmentariness Schlegel dignifies by erecting it into a model, comparing it with the fragmentariness of the torso which sculptors are conventionally required, in his day, to copy and emulate.

32. Of course, Lessing was particularly well known for having published the scandalous fragments of Samuel Reimarus, and so the fragmentary character of his work, which makes him the "author" of the age, implies also, paradoxically, the performative disauthorization, displacement, or strewing, of his own inwardness: he speaks of the spirit of another through the letters of another for which he nonetheless assumes an anonymous responsibility.

33. Cf. de Man, "The Concept of Irony," in *Aesthetic Ideology*, 163–84. While the rhetorical focus of my approach to Schlegel obviously owes much to de Man, I do not follow him in the specifics of his reading of Schlegel, which I find flawed to the extent that he is apparently indifferent to the theological overdeterminations of Schlegel's text. When, for example, de Man emphasizes in Schlegel's notion of irony the parabasis as a continuous movement toward "detachment in relation to everything, and also in relation to the self and to the writer's own work, the radical distance (the radical negation of himself) in relation to his own work" (177), he fails to reflect in any explicit way upon the complex political and historical implications of the proximity of such a distance from the "work" to one particular œuvre, namely, that of Luther, and its rejection of works in favor of faith.

34. Cf. Bolz. Not suprisingly, given that Bolz was working in the 1980s under Jakob Taubes on Carl Schmitt, Bolz provides here one of the relatively few significant recent essays on *Frühromantik* dealing with its theopolitical dimension.

35. Cf. the discussion of the fragmentariness of Dorothea Veit's novel, *Florentin*, in Chapter 5 below, in the section entitled "The End of the Novel, the End of the World."

36. In turn, by representing Lessing's totality in a fragmentary critical work, Schlegel can perhaps hope to be seen as the performative realization of Lessing's exemplary prefiguration.

37. Indeed, before becoming involved with Lessing's theological writings while working on the Jacobi essay, Schlegel had generally tended to dismiss Lessing as an artist of the mere mechanical understanding, along with other Enlighteners such as Garve. See Krüger, especially 2–28, for the years 1791–1794. Krüger points out that, in these years, Schlegel characterized Lessing several times as "spiritless [*geistlos*]" (28), and she persuasively argues that, among other things, Schlegel's fears concerning his own excessive intellectuality were tied up with his rejection of Lessing in this phase.

38. F. Schlegel, "Über Lessing," 118. This sense of the spirituality of *Nathan* is emphasized again a bit further on when it is a question of the swiftness and ease with which Lessing developed his conception of the play: "The *Idea of Nathan* stood thus all at once before his spirit" (119).

39. F. Schlegel, "Über Lessing," 123. Note that Schlegel's word, "schwebt," ties him to Luther's translation of what "spirit" ("ruach") is doing over the waters at the outset of the creation myth in Genesis. On the shifting fortunes of this relatively flawed translation in the German tradition, a translation to which Rosenzweig and

Buber prefer the equivalent of the English "brooded," see Rosenzweig, "The Hebrew Bible's Direct Influence on Goethe's Language," and Buber and Rosenzweig, "The Bible in German: in Reply," both in their *Scripture and Translation*, 70–72, and 151–60, respectively, and in the latter article, see especially 153–55.

40. Hans Eichner's otherwise excellent scholarship, for example, is nonetheless marked by this limitation, which is characteristic of the historical moment in which that scholarship emerges. See his *Friedrich Schlegel*, 29–34.

41. F. Schlegel, "Über Lessing," 118.

42. Cf. Chapter 6 below on the way in which Schlegel's text, *Lessings Gedanken und Meinungen* (1804), characterizes the interplay between determinacy and indeterminacy in "dialogue" as an interplay between prose and poetry.

43. This structure is (a)systematically related to the structure of the following fragment: "It is equally deadly for the spirit to have a system and to have none. It will thus evidently have to decide to combine both" (A 53, 173). Since whatever kills the spirit is always understandable as letter: the spirit killed by letter as system flees into nonsystematicity, chaos, materiality, in short, poetry for example; and the spirit killed by letter as chaos or materiality flees into system, philosophy for example. This interplay takes us beyond the privilege of spirit, since each term—system and nonsystem—appears as both letter and spirit, yet it takes us beyond the privilege of spirit in the name of spirit itself.

44. Not only does Schlegel's discussion of *Nathan der Weise* comprise the conclusion of his essay but furthermore the characterization of this play is the characterization of Lessing's essence: "He who understands NATHAN properly, knows Lessing" (118); and "NATHAN . . . is incontrovertibly the most proper, most self-willed, and strangest amongst all of Lessing's products" (118).

45. In terms of the Spinoza controversy, Mendelssohn's contribution to which some twelve years earlier (1785) has been discussed in detail in Chapter 2 above, Schlegel's position evidently comes quite close to Mendelssohn's. Lessing's polemic against illiberal theology is situated in the tradition of rational theology and its extension into deism (thus in the Leibniz-Wolffian tradition), while his defense of nature as an ethically legitimate force is akin to pantheism (thus in the Spinozist tradition). Mendelssohn had argued that Lessing was on the undecidable border between theism and pantheism, as the limit of an inside/outside, potential/actual distinction whose status exceeded the alternative between figural and literal uses of language; Schlegel is arguing that Lessing was on the undecidable border between spiritual content and material form, figural and literal, as the limit between the supernatural that is natural and the natural that transcends itself. In contrast to Mendelssohn, Schlegel puts "cynicism" in the place of "pantheism." But given both the ethical horizon of Spinoza's pantheism and the self-limiting, ascetic character of Spinoza's ethics, there is not such a great distance as might at first appear between Spinozism and the ancient cynicism with which Schlegel associates Lessing. In each case, the turn of spirit back toward natural simplicity and clarity is

aligned with a turn of the spirit back toward the acknowledgment of the ineluctable materiality of the letter it also is.

46. The hyperbolically *Protestant* character of this tendency is made evident in the passage just cited by Schlegel's suggestion that even Lessing was perhaps still nostalgically attached to the desire for an "objective and dominant" religion, followed by the remark that, in view of the infinite variety of subjectivities, an infinity of religions is necessary. This notion radicalizes the Lutheran notion that everyone (and hence no one) is a priest. On the Bible as an infinity of books, see I 95, 265; on the decentralization of the artist, see I 114, 267; and on pedagogy as multiple Reformation, see I 115, 267.

47. Cf. the "Ideen" fragments, which comprise a sustained attempt to determine the mutual relations between *philosophy, poetry, religion, and morals.* That the opposites, *religion and morals,* belong together, and that they are in some sense in turn the dialectical opposite of the opposition between *philosophy and poetry,* is suggested by the following: "Religion and morals are symmetrically opposed to one another, like poetry and philosophy" (I 67, 262). Cf. also I 90, 264; I 96, 265; and I 105, 266; and I 123, 268.

48. "The difference between religion and morals lies quite simply in the old division of all things into divine and human, if one only understands this division correctly" (I 110, 267).

49. Indeed, in some of the "Ideen" fragments that treat the relation between religion and morality, religion as a polemical spirit is said to have need of the guiding letter of morals, as Protestant spirit cannot do without Judaic letter, in order to protect itself from becoming an uncontrollably destructive rage: "Divide religion completely from morals, and you will have the actual energy of the evil in the human being, the terrible, cruel, raging, and inhuman principle, which originally lies in his spirit. Here is where the division of that which is indivisible is punished in the most horrible way" (I 132, 269). This passage strongly illustrates Schlegel's desire to mediate between Protestant spirit and Jewish letter, which will ultimately culminate in his conversion to Catholicism. In the following, the violent commitment of "spirit" on its own to the destruction of the "letter," a commitment that will emerge quite literally some 135 years later in the German lands, is stated with frightening explicitness: "The secret sense of sacrifice is the annihilation of the finite because it is finite . . . to become an artist means nothing other than to devote oneself to the divinities of the underworld. In the enthusiasm of annihilation the sense of the divine creation first reveals itself. Only in the midst of death is the lightning bolt of eternal life ignited" (I 131, 269).

50. One of the "Ideen" fragments in which Schlegel expresses with striking clarity his ambivalence about the need of Protestant spirit to embrace its undecidable identity with the Jewish letter in order to go beyond the fixation, in the form of the letter, of the distinction between spirit and letter, is this: "One has already spoken for a long time about an omnipotence of the letter"—this motif of "All-

macht" of course anticipates late-nineteenth- and twentieth-century European anti-Semitic fears—"without really knowing what one was saying. It is time that this be taken seriously, that the spirit should awaken and grasp hold again of the lost magic wand" (I 61, 262). The ambivalence of this passage consists in the fact that to take hold of the lost magic wand is here both to deal with it and to deny it by appropriating it. The Jewish-German "dialogue" here gains expression in perhaps its most appropriately derisory form. Or again, "The original Protestants wanted to live in accordance with the scriptures with loyal hearts and to be serious, and to annihilate everything else" (I 66, 262).

51. For some of the details of this publication history, see Eichner's account, *KA*, 2:XXVII–XXXV.

52. F. Schlegel, "Conclusion," 398.

53. In "The Education of the Human Race," the "New Gospel" refers to a new age that will succeed upon the Christian age that succeeded upon the Jewish age. In terms of the assumption that reincarnation is part of this divine plan, in order for each human being to have the chance to progress through each of the three ages individually so that in turn the arrival of the universal collectivity at the third age should be possible, Lessing raises the rhetorical question, "Can every man have been, in one and the same life, a sensuous Jew and a spiritual Christian? Can he have surpassed both of them in that same life?" (*Werke in drei Bänden*, III:658). This formulation illustrates Lessing's partial acceptance of the notion that Judaism is the material prefiguration of the Christian spiritual fulfillment, but it makes clear also that his acceptance comes with the all-important qualification that the Christian fulfillment in turn prefigures a move beyond the figural literal, letter-spirit opposition, as well as beyond the Protestant "literalist" notion of the assimilation of letter to spirit.

54. Cf. Behler, "Friedrich Schlegels Theorie des Verstehens." Tracing the ambiguity of Schlegel's position on "understanding," Behler judiciously shows how Schlegel can be assimilated neither to traditional hermeneutics nor to deconstruction.

55. F. Schlegel, "Conclusion," 410.

56. Something very much like this view is also registered in the following notation: "But actually, everything that is work in a work is poetry: letter; the spirit is philosophy" (cited in Nüsse, 104).

57. F. Schlegel, "Conclusion," 410.

58. In this context, it is suggestive that Schlegel introduces the "Eisenfeile" fragments in the "Conclusion" by saying, "Let this be a pleasing sacrifice to the dead for the immortal one whom I early chose as my guiding star" (398). The fragments are hereby dignified, even if somewhat playfully, as a "sacrifice" of the self to Lessing as quasi-divine figure or ancestor who must be propitiated and appeased. If "sacrifice" is the annihilation of the finite for the sake of the infinite, as Schlegel suggests in "Ideen" fragment 131 cited above, then "sacrifice" precisely runs counter to the notion of the fragmentary (non)work: the work of sacrifice

(and "Opfer" is etymologically related to the Latin *opera* or work) is the annihilation of the work as a means to faith, as opposed to the simultaneous affirmation and negation of both work and faith (or theory of the work) that occurs in the fragmentary (non)work.

59. As Schlegel writes, in commenting on the "symbolic form" of Lessing's works: "The essence of the higher art and form consists in the relation to the whole. . . . Therefore all works are One work, all arts One art, all poems One poem. For all want, of course, the same thing, that which is everywhere One, and in its undivided unity. But for this very reason each member in this highest form of the human spirit wants at once to be the whole, and this wish . . . is attainable, for it has already often been attained, through the same thing through which everywhere the illusion of the finite is placed in relation with the truth of the eternal and by thus being placed in relation, is dissolved into this truth: through allegory, through symbol . . ." (414).

60. Cf. Benjamin, *Begriff der Kunstkritik*, whose more generous interpretation of Schlegel's dissolution of the individual work into the totality of art seems to me perhaps too generous. While Benjamin wants to see the totality of art in Schlegel as a form of order rather than as a creative geniality (86), he is nonetheless forced to acknowledge quite explicitly that symbolic form in Schlegel is the mere expression of the self-limitation of reflexion (97), yet he fails to balk at the credulous (and in its Christian and more specifically Lutheran tradition anti-Semitic) idealism of such a notion of the formal letter. Since in the Romantics criticism becomes, on the one hand, the (always Christian) fulfillment of the (always Jewish) work (77–78 passim), and since Benjamin is at this time a "budding" critic, it is no doubt difficult for him to question the privilege of criticism established by Romanticism and with which he has chosen, pursuing his own ambivalently assimilated route, to identify. Further, it is no doubt all the more difficult for him to question this privilege as this privilege seems, on the other hand, to coincide with a privilege of (Jewish) formal cerebrality over (Christian) affective content, and since the Romantic gesture that privileges criticism is also allied (paradoxically) with a hyperbolic notion of the absolute work, whereas the Goethean devaluation of criticism implies (equally paradoxically) a devaluation of the work insofar as the work is not considered capable of connecting immediately with the *Urbilder* it is supposed to imitate. A more thorough reading of the problematic of Jewish-Christian relations in Benjamin's writings on the Romantics and Goethe lies, however, beyond the scope of the present study.

CHAPTER 4

1. Friedrich Schlegel, *Lucinde*, in *KA*, 5, *Dichtungen*, 1–82, quote from 3. References in this chapter to "Über die Philosophie. An Dorothea," are from *KA*, 8, *Studien zur Philosophie und Theologie*, ed. Ernst Behler and Ursula Struc-Oppenberg, 41–62.

2. From the point of view I am developing here, an analysis such as that of Menninghaus (in *Unendliche Verdopplung*, 81–85, 115–31 passim), to the effect that Schlegel and Novalis would have achieved the "semiological deconstruction of a transcendental signified" (84), somewhat credulously—as if driven by wishful thinking—and one-sidedly credits the early Romantics for having gone much further than they were actually able to go in their interrogation of the privilege of spirit over letter.

3. For critical perspectives on Schlegel's theory and literary practice of androgyny, see Friedrichsmeyer; and Weil. The former traces the shift of Schlegel's interest in androgyny away from a political interest toward an aesthetic concern. The latter focuses usefully on the intimate relations between androgyny and irony. Neither gives particular attention to the question of Jewish-Christian relations insofar as these relations importantly determine those between letter and spirit. Weil, in particular, provides a critical perspective on Schlegel's reappropriation of the feminine letter (58–68 passim) with which I am essentially in accord. A more recent critical perspective that summarizes usefully and builds on these prior efforts is Roetzel.

4. Schlegel speaks, for example, in "On Lessing" of regretting having failed to make the "*living acquaintance of Lessing*" (*KA*, 2:111).

5. One could also speak of the daughter in *The Jews* here, but I will restrict myself to the echoes from *Nathan the Wise*, since that particular version was important to Schlegel, as we've seen, in "On Lessing."

6. For useful portraits of Dorothea within the family, see Körner; and Geiger.

7. For a suggestive essay on *Lucinde* that considers the philosophical resonances of this lack of children, see Lacoue-Labarthe, "L'avortement." Lacoue-Labarthe reads *Lucinde* as demonstrating that the birth of literature is contemporaneous with the birth of the philosophical concept of birth (as crossing of chronological and transcendental notions of origination), but he sees this birth of literature in *Lucinde* as ending in a kind of spontaneous abortion, suggesting that such a concept of birth is deeply problematic. Lacoue-Labarthe considers the obsession with dead babies in *Lucinde*—as hauntingly "confirmed" by the fact that Schlegel had no children—"as the avowal that literature could not be born, at least according to this concept of birth, which is at bottom the conception of self-conception" (18). While Lacoue-Labarthe rightly reads the Lucinde-Julius relation in terms of the *phusis-techne* relation, because of his exclusive emphasis on the Greek origins of Romantic conceptuality, he ignores the important overdeterminations that concern the Jewish-Catholic-Protestant triangle.

8. F. Schlegel, *KA*, 8:41.

9. One example of the complexity would be this: he emphasizes that he is coming to keep his promise ("mein Versprechen zu halten"), which appears, on the one hand, to be a "Jewish" or law-governed thing to do (one must keep one's promises), an ethical act, and on the other hand, as a "Christian" thing to do, since Chris-

tianity is precisely the realization of a promise. When he goes on to say that he is keeping his promise only because he feels like it ("weil ich Lust dazu habe"), he privileges feeling, inwardness, a narcissistic version of faith, and thus makes a decidedly "Christian" gesture, even if "feeling" here takes on Romantic overtones of "impudence" (*Frechheit*), and so forth, which I read as a perpetuation of Protestant values. By mocking the moralism of Protestant Christianity, however, he cuts it so radically off from its Jewish predecessor that he ends up in a position that is no longer merely "Christian," but rather quasi-pagan, in a manner that "anticipates" or "prefigures" the Germanizing post-Romanticism of Wagner, even if in a more cosmopolitan and cerebral form.

10. This interpretation is complicated but by no means suspended by the fact that Schlegel's phrase on Lessing in "On Lessing," to the effect that Lessing was characterized by "unlimited contempt for the letter [*unbegrenzte Verachtung des Buchstaben*]" (II, 109), returns in his characterization of Dorothea as "someone so decidedly contemptuous of all writing and letteredness [*eine so entschiedene Verächterin alles Schreibens und Buchstabenwesens*]" (42). Schlegel's addressee seems to be at once Lessing and Dorothea: the one who despises the letter. But whereas he was (complicatedly) in favor of despising the letter in "On Lessing," he is now (qualifiedly) opposed to it, at least for a man such as himself, whose authorship he connects directly to his fascination with the letter.

11. For example, he claims to write not out of "Pflicht" but out of "Lust," which is to say not out of respect for the law but out of the desire that is akin to love. Further, writing is characterized as digging "the thoughts of God into the tables of nature," a decidedly spiritualizing, more specifically a phallogocentrically spiritualizing way of characterizing writing, even if it alludes to the Jewish Bible. Moreover, in the end of the passage Schlegel sets himself up as providing words for Dorothea's feelings, an external language for her inwardness, as if this language were a kind of fulfillment of the prefigurative silence of that inwardness. Here too, then, the positions of "letter" and "spirit" have been reversed, for "letter" comes to fulfill a "spirit" that anticipates it, but the fulfilling letter is the gift the Christian man offers to the Jewish woman.

12. If women have for Schlegel no relation to virtue other than religion, this suggests that they have, on the one hand, no relation to the law and that, in this sense, they are radically Christian. On the other hand, if women have no relation to the law, it is not only because they are outside the law but also because, given what Schlegel considers to be their earthbound materiality, they *are* the law, qua letter. However, the law (of the law) is spirit itself. Like the woman, in Schlegel, the Jew, who "is" the law, is excluded from the law (as law of the law), or from the content of the law, which is the spirit of Christian faith.

13. Although the Jewish letter has for Christianity a merely anticipatory function not only because of its materiality but also because of its abstractness, while the Christian spirit is figured as fulfillment not only for its spirituality but also for

its concreteness, still it would traditionally not be possible to identify the Jewish letter with philosophical spirituality because its abstraction is always marked as subspiritual, or its excessive spirituality always adds up to a lack of spirituality in the end.

14. This result accords remarkably well, moreover, with the impressions one receives of Schlegel's relationship with Dorothea as it proceeded. She appears to have occupied a position of extreme self-abnegation in order to have some sort of life with Schlegel, while he seems rather selfishly to have gone his own way, as if she hardly existed (or as if he contained her within himself), using her—for example, to copy his texts, that is, to function *as his letter*—for his own, "high" ends. See Chapter 5, on Dorothea's self-submission to Friedrich, as well as on her resistance to this position.

15. For example, Schlegel invites Veit at one point to deify him, while he immediately goes on to say that he will not reciprocate, since his proper object is not the beloved but the world-spirit or the universe (48–49).

16. The novel opens with a scene in which Julius contrasts his own highly inward spirituality, which is figured as fire: "A fine fire streamed through my veins" (7), with the social world outside, characterizing the latter as nothing less than "ash-gray figures devoid of movement" (7). The motif of "ash-gray figures" here communicates with the use of the figure of ashes to refer both to extinguished love and to the prejudices that tend to extinguish it in "Allegorie der Frechheit" (23). Julius argues that it is always possible to reenliven dead ashes—now figures for figures and hence for all figures of figures, including Jews—through love. By arguing for this possibility, he denies, or denegates, the reality of death, matter, and figurality, the reality of ashes.

17. F. Schlegel, *Lucinde*, 37. We receive confirmation here of what we saw in the "Conclusion" of Schlegel's essay "On Lessing": Schlegel's commitment to the fragmentary is ambivalent indeed.

18. He is initially drawn, moreover, to that fact that she was of a "similar sense and spirit" with him, while he later discovers more and more the "differences" (56) between them. But he recuperates these differences immediately in terms of the deeper sameness in which they are "grounded" (56).

19. Although she is a painter, and so associated with the traits or traces of the letter, Lucinde is a painter whose paintings breathe "the living breath of true air" (53), and so are incipiently inspirited even before she undergoes Julius's ostensibly perfecting influence. The excessively indeterminate outlines (53) of Lucinde's pictures, however, make it clear that, for all her spiritedness, she is less spiritual and a bit more bound up in natural materiality than Julius. This is the case even though the fact that she lacks schooling, as he says, makes her both natural (as opposed to artificial) and spiritual (in the sense of faithful, at some distance from the law of works). The result is the ambivalent situation in which, although she stands for, or is an example of, the feminine, Judaic letter, she is an example of that letter only

insofar as it has already developed toward the spirituality that is its destiny: natural, material feeling takes on some of the clarity of thought (even if the faithfulness of her feelings is still marked, in a salutary way, by the letter that gives it some degree of form), and she paints essentially out of "love": her work on the level of the traits of the (painted) letter is a work whose origin and end is in the faithful love of the spirit that is beyond all works.

20. Even before establishing his relationship with Lucinde, Julius is drawn into the materiality of language in that to persuade her to be with him he uses "rhetoric": "Beredsamkeit" (54) becomes the instrument of his persuasion of Lucinde to yield her materiality to his spiritual needs.

21. While Julius's works are said to possess the characteristic of *Anmut*—grace—which in Schiller takes on the canonical form of a harmonious interplay between inclination and duty, sensuality and ideality, letter and spirit, in the chapter on "Metamorphosen" the text goes beyond the ideal of *Anmut*: "Love is higher than grace" (60). Since *Liebe* is to be understood as an excess of spirituality beyond what mere *Anmut* offers, Schlegel's emphasis on spirit must be understood to be reasserting itself here. When, in "Two Letters" (discussed below), Julius declares that only real pregnancy can create a marriage, and not mere love, the excessive spirituality of love for love's sake tips over into its purely material opposite, reproductive power for reproductive power's sake.

22. When, in this phase, Julius gathers a group of extraordinary people around himself, "Lucinde bound and sustained the whole" (57), just as letter binds spirit, and when foreigners are allowed into their circle, Lucinde entertains them: the Jewish cosmopolitan is responsible for dealing with the foreigners and seeing that their difference becomes part of the harmonious unity of the group: "so that their grotesque universality and educated commonness at once amused the others, and neither stasis nor disharmony was excited in the spiritual music whose beauty consisted precisely in the harmonic manifoldness and alteration" (57).

23. One is tempted to find a trace of Schlegel's assimilation of Dorothea's femininity into his own masculinity when he says to her after their first kiss, "*herrliche Frau!*" which could be taken to mean not only glorious woman but also manlike woman, "Herr"-like Frau. Moreover, it may well be the case that the extraordinary feminine power that resides in Lucinde for Julius insofar as she is a mother (55) has to do with the fact that, as a mother, she has already combined herself significantly with, and has thus been marked by, the male spirit.

24. Julius introduces the "Dithyrambic Fantasy about the Most Beautiful Situation," parodying Leibnizian Enlightenment discourse, as an extension of our knowledge that this is, if not the best of all possible worlds, then at least the most beautiful. Two remarks on my own approach to the titular frame Schlegel gives this chapter: (1) despite Schlegel's parodic tone, which introduces a certain scepticism vis-à-vis the possibilities of rational knowledge of the objective world—there is still a cosmological dimension at play here. The most beautiful, most witty "situation"

realizes not only humanity but also worldliness, because it realizes the worldliness of humanity and the humanity of worldliness. The world, like humanity, is essentially a witty conjuncture or conjecture, a witty "situation." But since Schlegel makes the "Dithyrambic Fantasy" explicitly an "allegory of complete, whole humanity," I am focusing my analysis on the anthropological dimension. Nonetheless, the cosmotheological dimension of Schlegel's novel discussed below in terms of "Two Letters" is—and this is one of my more important points—also an overdetermining factor everywhere else in the novel, just as are the anthropological concerns of the novel. The question: What is it to be human? is everywhere more or less explicitly or implicitly at stake. And (2) if I am emphasizing the witty character of the situation in question, rather than its beautiful aspect, then this is because the notion of wit seems the more important concept for Schlegel both generally and here in particular. It is almost a witticism, indeed, for Schlegel to be calling the situation beautiful, rather than only witty. Schlegel's aesthetics is certainly not above all an aesthetics of the beautiful. Rather, he wants to mix the beautiful, the sublime, and the interestedly pleasurable together as only the concept of wit could justify: "to imitate and supplement the most beautiful chaos of sublime harmonies and interesting enjoyments" (9).

25. Cf. the reading of this scene that I proposed in an earlier essay on *Lucinde* and a certain number of fragments, "Writing (as) the Perverse Body in Friedrich Schlegel's *Lucinde*." This earlier reading contrasts sharply with the present one, having been the product of what now appears to me an underestimation of the idealist dimension of Schlegel's text.

26. Moreover, the expression of the desire to get beyond all language (and its tendency to repeat compulsively the persistent absence of what it represents), in order to let pure feeling express itself directly, arrives right on time in the first sentence of the next paragraph: "Words are flat and murky; also, I would have . . . to repeat always anew only the one inexhaustible feeling of our original harmony" (10).

27. F. Schlegel, *Lucinde*, 13. It is not possible to follow here the entirety of Julius's self-justification, since that would take us through the next chapter, "Charakteristik der kleinen Wilhelmine," where he compares his own indiscretions to those of a toddler unembarrassed about her nakedness, as well as into other chapters. The main structure of this self-defense, however, is everywhere the same. The child's innocent materiality is interpreted as spirituality insofar as spirituality is aligned with lawlessness, worklessness: faith.

28. The assimilation of writing to the externalization of the voice occurs also in "Allegorie der Frechheit." An internalized voice, apparently the voice of *Witz* (here overdetermined by *Fantasie*), appears personified in that chapter as Julius's guide through an allegorical dream. This guide is also a benevolent—and highly spiritualized (19)—father figure (23). The letter is spiritualized here in that it merely serves as a necessary vehicle for the presence of the spirit: "Cover up and bind the

spirit in the letter" (20). The letter becomes a dream of appropriate form, rather than the name for the necessity of nonappropriation.

29. Julius offers a similar formulation in the first of the "Two Letters" that precede "Eine Reflexion": "There should actually be only two classes of human beings, educators and the educated [*den bildenden und den gebildeten*], the masculine and the feminine, and instead of all artificial society a great marriage of these two classes and universal brotherhood of all individuals" (63).

30. Just as Schlegel did—linking in yet another way orality with spirituality—as he became ostentatiously more and more corpulent during his entire career, a development which he prophesied almost silently through his repeated use of the word "gefräßig" in the early texts such as "On Philosophy" (where he speaks, for example, of men as "the voracious sex [*das gefräßige Geschlecht*]" [46], and also of the necessity of the "voracious participation [*gefräßige Teilnahme*] in all of life" [49]), and which ended with the malicious rumors that circulated after his death: it was said that he had died choking on a piece of *fois gras.*

31. Like Julius in the novel's opening scene, on the inside looking out.

32. The relation between the psychological terms introduced here and the anthropological term *wit* can be stated briefly as follows: since wit by definition (for example in "Athenäum" fragment 366 on *Witz* as mechanical spirit between the organicism of identity and the mechanism of difference) mediates between identity and difference, and since contentment is the psychological equivalent of identity, while longing is the feeling of difference, contentment and longing can be determined as the twin moods of wit.

33. Cf. Eisler's informative introduction to *Lucinde* in *KA*, 5:XVII–LXIX, especially XXII–XXXV, in which Schlegel's attempt to synthesize sensuality with spirituality is contrasted by Eichner with the separation of sensuality and spiritual love in the eighteenth century in general. If it is true that *Lucinde* affirms the unity of mind and body, however, then it is no less true that it affirms this unity in the name of the mind, which is perhaps why the novel has been so scandalous, so irritating: one never really knows whether the novel is too spiritual or not spiritual enough.

34. The theme of the "proper" becomes more explicit as the theme of "property" in this chapter when Julius tells Lucinde she should go ahead and buy the country property they had been thinking of obtaining (62–63).

35. The term "beschneiden" appears also in "Idylle über den Müßiggang" as a term for the cutting back of wildly growing plants, this time with reference to *Lucinde* itself. Here too the sense of "beschneiden" as "to circumcise" must be taken into account, especially since he is in the process of describing the ostensibly spontaneous growth of the novel, as a work that is beyond all works, out of the spirit of laziness. Laziness functions here as a trope on faith that reinstates the privilege of faith over works, in Romantic terms, as the privilege of goalless spontaneity over purposive action. The naturally spiritual (non)work must not be

"trimmed" or "circumcised," because then it would become a work pure and simple, a work of artifice and a work of the letter: in short, a Jewish (or Catholic) work. "And freely as it [*Lucinde*] has sprouted forth, I thought, so should it grow and go wild luxuriously, and never do I want, out of a lowly love of order and parsimony, to cut back/circumcise the living fullness of superfluous leaves and tendrils" (26).

36. On the replacement of the patriarchal reign of the father by the fraternal reign of the brother in modernity, see MacCannell.

37. This effacement of writing is restated in the final paragraphs of the letter where the lovers' contact with each other through writing comes into question. When the two lovers are separated, they both claim that they "always inwardly . . . write" (68) to each other. Writing thus appears as a continuous and spontaneous process, rather than as the discontinuous and artificial event it naturally is. It appears further as totally absorbed into the inwardness of contemplative-amorous subjectivity, no longer as an inscription of the material body. Moreover, of Lucinde's letters, Julius says they are "not writing, but song" (68). Writing is perceived as voiced song here, thus is no more read at all as the silent writing it is, just as the letter disappears as letter when it enters into the literal truth in which, as opposed to figural representation, the spirit is supposed to be immediately present.

38. Moreover, the "Herrlichkeit" is also the man-like-ness, if we take the expression "literally," as I noted above with respect to the first word of love Julius speaks to Lucinde, "Herrliche Frau," for what he loves in her is the way she mirrors back to him a man.

39. On the motif of the foreign, see 63–64. Julius says she would not be hurt by the hurtful things he said in his last letter if she really loved him "without a reserve of foreignness" ("ohne einen Hinterhalt von Fremdem" [63]). This sort of logic, which prefigures the discourse of Wagner in such libretti as *Der fliegende Holländer*, is extended several lines further in the context of a pseudoaffirmation of misunderstandings as leading to the possibility that Lucinde, who is responsible for them even though they are situated *between* the two lovers and not *in* either one of them, might cast out their/her foreignness: "Misunderstandings are good, too, so that the most sacred thing can finally gain expression. The foreign element that now and then appears to exist between us, is not in us, in neither one of us. It is only between us and on the surface, and I hope that you will take this opportunity to drive it completely away from, and out of, you" (64). For Julius, then, dialogical unification is possible only insofar as *Lucinde* sheds the remainder of "foreignness" or difference *between* the interlocutors (for which he makes *her* responsible by this demand) so that she may disappear into Julius's native sameness.

40. This death brings back the memories of other lost babies and mothers within the text: the death of Lisette who had been pregnant with the young Julius's child (44), and Lucinde's loss of an earlier child (53).

41. Julius's imaginary experience of Lucinde's death is actually legible from the very first, in the words, "Farewell, . . . longing," cited above, in which he seems to be affirming the life of his wife and child, except that "longing" is the name of Lucinde, even if we don't know this for three more chapters, until "Sehnsucht und Ruhe."

42. The text of this epistle recalls two losses of literary-historical import close to Schlegel, Lessing's loss of his wife and child, and Novalis's loss of his bride, the former loss having preceded by little the composition of Lessing's *Nathan der Weise*, the latter having led in the opposite ideological direction, to the composition of the "Hymns to Night" and to the nightward, medievalizing turn Novalis registered in texts like "Christianity or Europe" and "Faith and Love, or the King and Queen." Schlegel's stereoscopic examination of ultimate loss and absence from the dual perspective of the progressive Enlightenment and the regressive counter-Enlightenment gives us in turn a glimpse of the tension in Schlegel's mind and work at this time, a tension which he will seek to alleviate by his conversion to Catholicism in 1808.

43. Julius's melancholy disparagement of works is stated also earlier on in the epistle: "The duty to live had triumphed, and I was once again in the tumult of life and people, of their impotent actions and flawed works, as well as my own" (70).

44. Lowenstein, 111–19 passim.

45. In the final chapter, "Dalliances of Fantasy," the mother-father-child triad is allegorized as a facultative triad of soul-understanding-fantasy. Here, soul is the spirituality of that which is open to the materiality of imagination (or simply matter spiritualized), while "understanding" takes on the sense of *Verstand*, rationalism as originally quasi-Judaic, mechanical, but here as concretized by virtue of the focus of its love on the soul of balance. In Lacanian terms, this triad would translate approximately into the triad, imaginary-symbolic-real. While the child, as child, real-izes the synthesis of the parents, soul and understanding, when the triad is in a harmonious relation, the mother-soul is envisioned, at the novel's close, as experiencing the presentation of meaning: "The man deifies the beloved, the mother the child, and all of them the eternal human being./Now the soul understands . . . what reveals itself meaningfully in flowers and stars through a secret writing of images [*Bilderschrift*]: the sacred sense of life as the beautiful language of nature. All things speak to her and everywhere she sees the dear spirit through the tender covering" (82). Writing becomes meaningful, life gives away its sense, and nature speaks a language that is beautiful and so combines supersensuous and sensuous sense. The forms of nature reveal their spiritual inwardness and the synthesis Schlegel desires is achieved. In this case, it is the mother, the soul, who is the site of the synthesis of the excessive spirituality of the father, pure understanding, with the excessive materiality or imaginariness of the child, fantasy, a synthesis that envelopes in its soft light the terms it brings together. The child, however, apparently remains both the proof of the parents' synthesis and the pos-

sibility-condition of the familial bliss whose receptive focus here is the mother-soul, no woman evidently becoming a mother without having a child. While this use of the family triangle explicates retrospectively the potential of the pregnancy in "Two Letters" to function as an allegory of the faculties, it does not imply that this allegorical function effaces the referential claims of the story, according to which only a real child ensures the union of the sexes on the level of nature. Schlegel's goal is precisely the synthesis of allegorical and historical or referential dimensions, the synthesis of figurality and literality.

46. Librett, "Figuralizing the Oriental, Literalizing the Jew."

CHAPTER 5

1. Dorothea Schlegel, *Florentin. Roman, Fragmente, Variationen.* In English, one can consult: Dorothea Mendelssohn Veit Schlegel, *Florentin: A Novel, Collected Writings*, vol. I. The notes for the continuation are in English as: *Camilla: A Novella, Collected Writings*, vol. II, Introd. Hans Eichner. Translations here, however, are my own, with references to the German edition given in parentheses.

2. By having Florentin save Schwarzenberg from what is, in the Jewish tradition, forbidden food, while figuring this forbidden food as female and angry, Veit condenses in what reads like a mildly sick joke the entire problematic of the translation of her own Judaism into the medium of a Christian discourse inimical to that very Judaism.

3. Most scholars see Veit more as borrowing from *Lucinde* and from Schlegel's thought than as answering with her own reflexions on what it would mean to read *Lucinde*, as I am suggesting. For example, see Touaillon, 557—77, especially 573, whose strikingly dismissive view—that Veit simply borrows the external trappings of Romanticism while lacking the spirit of romantic creativity, and so forth—follows along distressingly predictable lines the association of Jews with the dead, disfigurative letter. One small selection, "All of that is, however, more described than given form [*gestaltet*], and it does not come to a really lively rendering of the Romantic image of the woman" (568). For a much more sympathetic and also, despite its pathos-laden tone, critically astute and precise treatment of Veit, see Susman, 40—76, especially 55—58ff. Despite her capacity to appreciate the power and significance of Veit's person, however, including the dilemmas around which her conversions turned (64—65), even Susman finds it necessary to assert without any substantial argument that there is no common measure for *Florentin* and *Lucinde* because the latter is so much more ambitious. In the mode of *Quellenforschung*, Deibel, 38—39, 44 passim, makes of *Lucinde* one of the main sources that flowed into the (therefore relatively passive) production of *Florentin*.

4. Raich, I:194.

5. See the various combinations of admiration and impatience in Touaillon; Susman; Deibl; as well as the angry condemnation in Arendt, culminating in the

judgment: "She simply threw away her life on a momentary whim [*Sie hat ihr Leben an einen Augenblick einfach fortgeworfen*]," 40. Cf. the well-balanced and precisely nuanced account in the "Nachwort" by Weissberg to her edition of *Florentin* that I am citing here, 205–38, especially 215–24, 228.

6. As is argued by Hertz in her indispensable sociohistorical study, *Jewish High Society*, 172.

7. One way in which this consideration can be seen to manifest itself is in the fact that Veit's novel (i.e., her reading of Schlegel's novel) at once comes *after* and *before* Schlegel's novel: its composition and publication proceed upon that of *Lucinde*, but its plot, the story of a woman who *almost* loses interest in her "rightful" spouse and *almost* enters instead into an amorous and erotic relationship with an aesthetically sophisticated man who enchants her, a story that leaves hanging the question of whether or not this seduction will still come about after the text of Part I has broken off, precedes and anticipates (approximately) the events to which *Lucinde* refers, namely Dorothea Veit's decision to divorce Veit in order to be free for her relationship with Schlegel (or if one prefers, Lucinde's establishment of her bond with Julius). That what comes *after* comes *before* suggests that what *fulfills* (i.e., the *reading*) *prefigures* (i.e., is the text to be read).

8. The only other secondary literature of which I am aware that takes *Florentin* seriously as a subversive response to *Lucinde* is the excellent article by Helfer, "Dorothea Veit-Schlegel's *Florentin*." On the question of gender relations, I am in substantial agreement with Helfer, although I am not certain that I would see Veit-Schlegel as using mainly the device of parody, as Helfer suggests. Beyond this, our topics are differentiated by the fact that Helfer does not discuss either the questions of rhetoric or that of Judaism and Christianity in any detail.

9. D. Veit-Schlegel, *Florentin*, 23–25, 38, 41–42, 103–4.

10. When he introduces himself to Count Schwarzenberg at the outset, he supplies the latter with no paternal name or title and says he has no fatherland and will have none until he himself is called father by a child of his own.

11. This scene "prefigures" his appearance just in time (almost) to "save" Juliane from her marriage with Eduard, i.e., (not) to fulfill what prefigures himself.

12. Whose very title here—Prior—indicates his prefigurative status.

13. Veit's critique, in this novel, of the church's intervention in family life and its determination of *Bildung*, or education, there is both in agreement with her father's critique of all *Kirchenrecht*—all endowment of religion with earthly power—in *Jerusalem, or on Religious Power and Judaism* and an extension of that critique that in turn unsettles certain of its presuppositions. In Veit's text, it is not merely a matter of the critique of the mixing of church and state but also a critique of the mixing of church and *family*. Such a critique extends the notion of worldliness from the state to the family itself, from "public" to "private" world. The consequence of such an extension is to unsettle Mendelssohn's position even while extending it, for the domination of family by church was not considered illegiti-

mate in Mendelssohn's text. Indeed the entire notion of religion as rational spirituality in *Jerusalem* was a *private* notion. As a reading of *Jerusalem*, then, Veit's text can be seen as an extension and a critique at once, based on an understanding both that there is a sense in which the private is always already public and that it would be necessary still to establish, beyond this public aspect, what the purely private might be.

14. For further contortions to which it may be necessary for the reading of this scene to accommodate itself, see the section in Schlegel's "Über die Philosopie. An Dorothea" (*KA*, 8:42), which I discussed at length in Chapter 4, where while praising writing as the destiny of humanity (and more particularly of man), Schlegel suggests that even reading aloud can do no more than attempt not to ruin beautiful writing (42). He goes on to say that it will suffice for Dorothea if she keeps singing while reading more for herself, rather than letting others read to her. Florentin could be seen therefore as rebelling in Veit's place, in this scene, against Schlegel's warnings about keeping spirit in line with the letter, i.e., as figuring Veit's impatience with taking lessons in reading aloud from Schlegel, who himself has both usurped her (or her father's) place of mastery of the letter and retained control over the voice as spirit.

15. One example of the way in which the novel makes an explicit connection between Catholicism and rhetoric is the identification of the Catholic Church with "persuasion" (as opposed to "conviction") and "flattery." When Florentin turns out to be impervious to pure force and threats: "Then both my mother and the Prior applied every persuasive device, every flattery, in order to move me to decide freely to enter the monastery" (56).

16. In terms of the question of Jewish-German dialogue, what is perhaps most striking of all about *Florentin* as a novel written by Dorothea Veit is that it does not seem to present us with the slightest trace of literal Judaism—not a single literally Jewish character, not a single explicit mention of Jewish culture. But what would it mean, in the German secular literary-philosophical discourse of this period, for a Jewish figure *literally* to appear? In this discourse, the Jew figures the figural. How, then, are we to know when the figural has literally appeared? If the Jew as principle of figurality is there whenever a signifier presents itself as requiring the fulfillment of a signified or referent, then the Jew is swarmingly ubiquitous, but at the same time not delimitable as a literally finite phenemenon. This structure will become increasingly dangerous in the twentieth century when the theological attempt to literalize the figural under the figure of the Jew—an attempt that always allows for the transformation of the literally figural into the literally literal by way of conversion—gives way, under the pressure of secularization and assimilation, to the biologistic—which can only literally undo the Jew qua literalization of figurality by literally destroying the Jewish body of the letter, as the body of the Jewish letter.

17. For example, not unlike the Jews, he says that, while in Paris, he was

unhappy, "always to repeat the experience that I don't belong anywhere" (78), a line that doubtless applies thoroughly to Dorothea herself. Or for example on the night he arrives at the Schwarzenbergs', when, alone in his room, he reflects upon his position, Florentin realizes "that only he here was a foreigner [*ein Fremdling*], where it seemed to be a law to belong to each other, that he was alone, that in the wide world no being was related to him, no human existence linked to his own" (22). The world in which it is a law to belong to one another is strikingly exemplified, among the works of the generation that precedes the Romantics, by Schiller's ode "An die Freude."

18. Of course, Florentin is also a typical Romantic wanderer, but given Dorothea Veit's situation—already outside of her Jewish marriage, but not yet a Christian nor remarried—the context makes it unavoidable to read the Romantic wanderer *here* figurally, among other things, as a Jewish wanderer.

19. For the determination of "dissemination" alluded to here, see Derrida, *La dissémination*. A "Jew" such as Florentin—exiled from Judaism or from exile—could be read as a figure for a certain form of secularization (in this case embracing the notion of exile from origin as the "essence" of Judaism); or assimilation (the loss of Judaism as a second exile). It even evokes the Sabbatian notion of apostasy as condition of salvation that Gershom Scholem has so extensively and suggestively explored. See, for example, "Die Metamorphose des häretischen Messianismus der Sabbatianer in religiösen Nihilismus im 18. Jahrhundert," in *Judaica 3*, 198–217.

20. Needless to say, I am not focusing here on all of Florentin's literary precursors, who are legion, but only on certain particularly important ones who illuminate the text usefully from the perspective of the present study. Others, such as Jacobi's *Woldemar*, have been discussed in great detail in Deibel; Touaillon; and more recently in Weissberg.

21. Lessing, "Die Juden. Ein Lustspiel in einem Aufzuge. Verfertiget im Jahre 1749," in *Werke*, 249–89. It is not simply by chance, but rather based on the play of imaginary identifications, that Florentin, who tells his hosts nothing more about his name than "Florentin," suggests to the Count, when the Count is asking after his name in order to be able to introduce him to some other guests of the house, that he may call Florentin "Baron" ("If it is absolutely necessary to use more than my name," he said, "then add Baron: that indicates at least originally what I wanted to be, namely, a man" [34]).

22. Lessing, "Nathan der Weise," in *Werke*, vol. I, 593–735. Of course, as the outsider who desires, despite a certain ambivalence, inclusion in the group, Florentin is a close relative of Rousseau's Saint-Preux, Goethe's Werther, and other Romantic heroes of endless longing qua seducer-clowns. The ironic saviors in Lessing, such as the Jewish "Traveller" in *Die Juden* and the Tempelherr in "Nathan," are ethically "good" variations on this type. In the fact that Florentin seems to be possibly related to Clementina (e.g., as her son), there is a hint that Florentin cannot have/save Juliane because he is too closely related to her, as was

the Templar Knight to Recha. This implies further that, from one point of view, there can be no marital or erotic relation between Juliane and Florentin (nor therefore between the letter and spirit they marginally represent) not because the two are too radically *different* but because they are identical.

23. In Lessing's two plays, the two opposite reasons for a failed synthesis between the "savior" and the "saved" are played out: in the first case (i.e., *The Jews*), the man is too *far* from the woman, in the second case (i.e., *Nathan*), he is too close. In the first case the Jew is too far from the Christian, the figural too far from the literal to be translatable into it. In the second case the literal is so close to the figural that it would be a senseless repetition, and a forbidden senselessness, to combine the literal with itself. Neither does the figural figure the literal, then, nor does the literal figure itself.

24. Juliane even goes so far as to quote the motif of the salvation by an angel from *Nathan der Weise*, by whispering blushingly, in her first words to Florentin, "Unser guter Engel führte Sie auf diesen Weg!" (17).

25. That is, in the overdetermined tradition comprised by the Lessing plays and Florentin taken together (along with the "real-life" drama of Dorothea's life in which she plays Recha to Friedrich's Templar Knight, while Moses Mendelssohn posthumously gets to play himself), the roles of the saved (and of the potential rewards for having carried out the salvation) are divided between daughters and fathers, establishing (beginning at the latest with the composition of *Nathan der Weise*) homosocial indeterminacies on the levels of both gender and generation that parallel those on the level of religio-cultural identity.

26. See Hertz, 187–203.

27. The difficulty of knowing which one of Veit's names we should use—Brendel or Dorothea, Mendelssohn, Veit, or Schlegel, is an example of the problematic character of this structure. I have chosen for the most part not to use simply "Dorothea" here, due to the infantilizing sense of the gesture of using first names only for women (Caroline, Rahel, and so on), and I have been using "Veit" here for the most part insofar as that was her last name while she was composing the novel under discussion.

28. Despite differences of tilt, this determination of gender relations is very similar to the account of gender identity Friedrich Schlegel provides in "On Philosophy: To Dorothea," where women are defined as being naturally earthbound and therefore in need of philosophy to complete them as spirit, while men are defined as being naturally more spiritual and therefore in need of poetry to supplement them as letter. One can perhaps see the slight feminine tilt here, however, as a critical response to Friedrich's masculine bias as we have explored it in Chapter 4.

29. When Juliane tells the story (96–102) of a woman who has difficulty becoming pregnant and who prays to Mary for assistance, in a highly complicated scene to which I cannot do justice here, at least one of the suggestions of the story

is that there is always the danger of the absence of a sexual relation, one of whose phantasmatic ways of manifesting itself would be in sterility, the failure of masculine and feminine to connect in biological terms, the significance of which for the relationship between Dorothea and Friedrich Schlegel I have discussed at the end of Chapter 4.

30. Florentin makes his tornness between domestic "femininity" and worldly "masculinity" clear when he complains at one point to Eduard, "I am tempted to believe that I am actually destined for the limited life of the domestic sphere, because everything in me speaks for it, but an inimical fate always casts me far from the goal, like an evil daemon" (93).

31. In a complicated scene, Florentin falls asleep while in the middle of seducing a woman defined as desirability personified. This sudden loss of desire as well as consciousness is demonstrably caused by the doubling and displacement of the context of the "object" of desire, by her own doubling into material and spiritual versions of the self-same. In being caught between this sort of doubling, Florentin becomes just as disidentified with the position of desire as he is disidentified with the position of fulfillment. For philological considerations on the "influence" of texts by Rousseau, Goethe, and Wieland on this scene, see Deibel, 56; and Touaillon, 573.

32. The alternatives between whole and fragmentary work that Veit is facing can be stated in terms of literal and figural as follows: Is the novel "supposed" to be wrapped up at the end in a nice neat package? Or is it "supposed" to break off before it is finished, remaining a fragment, like a life lived until it is interrupted by death, still pointing toward a completion never attained? Is it "supposed" to be, that is, like a *literal*, proper use of language, properly related to itself as to its own self-contained property? Or is it "supposed," properly speaking, to remain, like a *figural*, improper use of language, ever distant from the meaning of what it says, and so forever pointing beyond itself to a meaning that is not its property and that it does not contain?

33. D. Veit-Schlegel, *Florentin*, 156–57.

34. The first understanding she cites is closer to the Enlightenment theory of the work; the second is closer to the Romantic theory. Her combination of the two here is thus one of the more important ways in which she manages to combine Enlightenment with Romanticism, or to remain on the border between the two, as several commentators on her work have suggested she does, although in rather different terms. See Thornton's "Enlightenment and Romanticism in the Work of Dorothea Schlegel," the most concerted effort in recent criticism to underscore the importance of certain Enlightenment motifs in Veit's work, especially the marked preference in Florentin for a *Humanitätsreligion* over Catholicism.

35. Despite the limitations of her traditional Jewish education, Veit will certainly have been familiar with the law positing that no project shall be completely finished until the restoration of the Temple in Jerusalem.

36. D. Veit-Schlegel, *Florentin*, 158.

37. One striking image in terms of which Veit argues for the unnecessariness of having a "satisfying ending" for a novel is the image of the sunset. Given that the sunset can be seen not only as an ending but also as an endless ending that promises to continue indefinitely (since the sun is always setting somewhere), so the novel does not need any ending that does not go on beginning forever. The sunset being strongly marked as a figure of melancholy fulfillment, it is clear that Veit means to argue through the figure that the fulfillment is a prefiguration, and therefore that both are something different from either one. Moreover, since Veit says to Schlegel, in the letter in which these argumentations are embedded, that she imagines him smiling over her silly "dithyramb," it seems clear also that this figure, the endless ending that is a beginning, *answers* to Schlegel's "Dithyrambic Fantasy about the Most Beautiful Situation" discussed above, the scene in which the gender difference is suspended through the mutual imitation of the two genders. "I had raised my eyes, and behold, the sun had gone down; across from me lay the beautiful mountains in the bluish, autumnal air [*Duft*] . . . and as I gazed on, still joyous and moved, and saw the white strands in the heaven form and again unform themselves in wondrous, light, transparent shapes . . . suddenly, from beyond the mountains, the silver shimmer of the moon peaked through, as if it were sent by the departing sun, in order to console us for the separation. Just think of this entire image! It was contentment, movement, and annunciation—promise of eternal presence, of new existence within the appearance of an ending. How you smile now over this dithyramb. . . . To make clear to you, what has become clear to me; namely, that a poem needs to have no more conclusive conclusion [*keinen schliesslicheren Schluss*] than a beautiful day" (158). Veit's use of the image of sunset here can in addition perhaps be understood as a trope on Herder's famous discussion of the sunset in *Älteste Urkunde des Menschengeschlechtes*, where the sunset is understood as the referential meaning of the fall from grace. The sunset in Veit's text would become by reference to Herder's text in turn an image of the fall. It is apparently fulfillment as fall into unfulfillment that is at the same time a prefigurative promise.

38. That Veit figures the unfinished text as naked doll here situates it midway between both models of the passage from idea to work. As a "doll," the toy is a fake, an imitation, and so the starting point is determined as figural; as a "naked" doll, the toy is the real thing, the literal. As figural starting point, it thus invokes the conventional model of composition Veit reverses with the supplement she adds. As literal starting point, it invokes the model she proposes, for which the beginning is the literal and the ending is the figural. Invoking both models at once, then, Veit is positing through the image of the doll that in each case, the crucial thing is for the passage from the beginning to the ending to occur as the interruption of the beginning. The beginning is, in each case, like the "nakedness" of a "doll," a moment split between naturalness and artificiality.

39. If Veit assumes the feminine position prescribed to her in the "Sehnsucht und Ruhe" section of *Lucinde*—the experience of contentment only in longing— by saying in the passage quoted above that "My reality and my satisfaction lie in longing and expectation," then here she seems to resist her inscription into that position by saying that "often [marriage] is where all suffering and all confusion just begin."

40. For example, Florentin seems to be Clementina's son, and his stepmother seems to be the friend of Clementina's about whom Juliane tells the story during the friends' excursion, but there is no resolution of these uncertain appearances into secured realities.

41. In terms of Kant's first antinomy in the *Critique of Pure Reason*, where he develops his critique of dogmatic rationalist metaphysics: Does the world have an end, or is it limitless in time and space? The finished novel here would represent implicitly the former alternative, whereas the unfinished novel would represent the latter, pointing as it does beyond itself to the inexhaustibility of its world, the non-presentability of its (infinite) totality. The fragmentary novel would be structured as the dialectical interplay without *Aufhebung* between the finished novel and the unfinished novel.

42. Cf. Freud, *Jenseits des Lustprinzips*.

43. After all, Florentin is at once both particularly intimate with others and entirely absent for them. His androgynous way of playing with the serious renders him always absent (through irony) in the very gestures by means of which he presents himself, and even more strangely, the converse, i.e., always present through the movement of his turning away. One example of this structure would be the way in which the *first person* narrative of Florentin's life and the *third person* narrative of the rest of the novel, in which that first-person narrative is embedded, remain in a suspended relation, especially since the worlds of Florentin's past and of the Schwarzenbergs' past remain suspended too. Florentin marries himself (his first person) to the world around him (the third person) by giving his autobiographical account to Juliane and Eduard, but by confessing ultimately that he does not know who he is, i.e., that he does not know what there would be to confess, he dies away from them in the same movement.

44. Of whom Veit writes in a posthumously published variant of the "Dedication" that he represents neither "the poet" nor "the poet's Ideal" (160) and that in this sense too the text is not merely a fiction but also a "true story": ". . . for this reason I must repeat my complaint and my regret that this story received the name, 'novel'! For, must not the hero of a good novel either represent the poet's personality or at least his or her ideal? And will one not seek in vain here for both of these things?" (160). The connection of the genre name *Roman* with the Roman Empire and in particular with the Roman Catholic Church would suggest one further reason why Veit, on her way from Judaism to Protestantism, might be having some difficulty here inscribing herself under the name of *Roman*.

CHAPTER 6

1. Friedrich Schlegel, "Lessings Gedanken und Meinungen," in *KA*, vol. 3, *Charakteristiken und Kritiken II (1802–1829)*, ed. Hans Eichner, 46–102.

2. On the level of psychobiography, Schlegel's Lessing anthology is published just as Schlegel is finally marrying Dorothea Veit under the authority of Protestant spirituality. In marrying Dorothea, he commits himself to a ritualism that partially Judaizes Protestantism, pulling it back within—or pushing it forward toward a renewal of—the realm of Catholic "works." From this angle, it is not so surprising that in Schlegel's introductions to the Lessing texts, the return to Catholicism has entered the picture as the paradoxically necessary consequence of a rigorous Protestantism, as a possible solution to the impossible dialectics of spirit and letter, even if the Schlegels are not yet quite on the brink of the leap into literal conversion. For a useful overview of Schlegel's development from the "Athenäum" years through those in which the Lessing anthology is edited, see Behler, *Zeitschriften der Brüder Schlegel*, 59–100.

3. F. Schlegel, "On the Character," *KA*, 3:87.

4. On polemic as a fundamental characteristic of early Christian religion, cf. Schleiermacher, "Über die Religion," 286–87.

5. F. Schlegel, "On the Character," *KA*, 3:86, 87. The terms of this distinction are curious. The opposition to which it alludes most closely in the theological discussions of the day is that between "positive" (or "revealed") and "natural" (or "rational") religion. By placing Protestantism in opposition to Catholicism as a "negative" against a "positive" religion, Schlegel puts Protestantism into the place of "natural" or "rational" religion (to which indeed it seems to have given rise in the course of a historical development of which Schlegel is one unsatisfied product). In accord with this trend, Schlegel redetermines such religion as "negative," implying that it is an antireligion, perhaps even a relentless secularization. On the other hand, his discussion of Protestantism otherwise emphasizes its radical religiosity. It is therefore evidently the immanent antireligiosity of religion, the immanent meaninglessness of meaning, with which Schlegel is here trying to come to terms.

6. Conversely, although this is—unfortunately—not equally Schlegel's concern, Jewish "legalism," textualism, and so forth, leads beyond the materiality of the letter to a high degree of cerebrality or theoreticism in its very attempt to maintain itself in proximity to the text itself.

7. Cf. *KA*, 2, "Lyceums Fragmente" 69, 155, on "negative sense," as that which arises when either spirit or letter is lacking.

8. F. Schlegel, "On the Character," *KA*, 3:87.

9. By going beyond all "dogma," Lessing's radicalized Protestantism (according to Schlegel's portrait here) coincides with the Judaism of the Mendelssohn of *Jerusalem*, where Judaism is defined as a revealed "law" without revealed "doctrine." The Neo-Catholic turn will provide an apparent home for this common excess beyond all dogmatism.

10. As one will have noted in the long passage cited in Chapter 3 on the two implicit tendencies of Lessing's *Nathan*, Schlegel has underlined there—against the suspicions of Jacobi and others who wanted to reduce Lessing's stance to mere pantheistic atheism—that the results of Lessing's critique of illiberalism in religion are not merely "negative" but "positive." While praising Lessing for having some "positive" notion of religion, Schlegel nonetheless criticizes him for going too far (or in the wrong manner) in this direction, i.e., for running the risk of dogmatism and for failing to recognize "the necessity of infinitely many religions" (*KA*, 2:123–24). According to a traditional schema, the "positivity" of religion is associated with the fixations of the letter, and Lessing is at once praised for having preserved or conserved some degree of positivity and gently criticized for having been too conservative in this regard, too much bound up with a unilateral literalism of the letter. While Schlegel's ambivalence about positivity in religion (or about the relationship between positivity and religion) will persist, his judgment of the appropriate degree and kind of positivity in religion will have shifted drastically by the time he writes "On the Character of the Protestants." Whereas Lessing was first thought to err by failing to see the proper positivity in an infinity of religions, Lessing's proper understanding of positivity is now situated in his having embraced the Catholic notion of the mediation of interpretation through the church community and its traditions.

11. F. Schlegel, "On the Character," *KA*, 3:88. It is important to note, both when we look back to Schlegel's dual affirmation of cynicism/pantheism and deism in the reading of *Nathan* he provided in "On Lessing" and when we look forward to the polemic *against* pantheism in *On the Language and Wisdom of the Indians* of 1808, that here pantheism, equated with "realism" (92–93), is seen as a first step in philosophy, like a prefiguring letter, that passes then to the doctrine of metempsychosis and ends in a new evangelism, a renewal of Christianity. Here, the letter of pantheism is *subordinate* in a way it was not in the earlier texts, but pantheism is not yet anathematized as it will be in the text on ancient Indian culture.

12. The identification with the religions of the letter is characterized in this passage as a "transitory crisis," which, Schlegel suggests, will lead to a decision for the religion of spirit. The fact that Schlegel elsewhere maintains, in a very prominent place—namely, in the "General Introduction" to *Lessing's Thoughts and Opinions*, called "On the Essence of Criticism" (51–60)—that Lessing is essentially and above all a critic (51ff.), implies that the "transitory crisis" is a permanent one. The critic, who operates between (the spirituality of) philosophy and (the materiality of) history (60), is indeed in a permanent state or space of crisis. Moreover, Schlegel remarks (52) on the great proximity between polemic and criticism. Polemic, in other words, is the mode of discourse caught, in critical condition, between spirit and letter, and that works against this condition, which it thereby endlessly perpetuates, as Schlegel both makes evident and denies. For a useful reading of the section, "On the Essence of Criticism," see Lacoue-Labarthe and Nancy, *L'absolu*

littéraire, 371–93. As already indicated above, Lacoue-Labarthe and Nancy focus above all on the early Romantic concern with the philosophy-poetry opposition, while they underemphasize the Romantics' concern with the theopolitical or religio-cultural—i.e., Jewish, Catholic, and Protestant—determinations of the spirit-letter opposition.

13. Huch (317–33, especially 330) sees Schlegel's move to Catholicism clearly as a kind of capitulation that is tantamount to intellectual suicide.

14. F. Schlegel, "On the Character," *KA*, 3:89.

15. For an unfolding of the linguistic and ontological implications of Schlegel's early reading of Fichte, see Werner Hamacher, "Der Satz der Gattung"; in English, "Position Exposed."

16. "On Philosophie: To Dorothea" (see Chapter 4 above) was, according to Schlegel's own account, the text through the writing of which he first discovered the monodialogical mode of writing that he employs again in the dedication to Fichte.

17. In the background to this discussion are at least two prominent debates in which Fichte had been engaged around the terms of letter and spirit. First, in the development of his own philosophy, Fichte repeatedly claimed to be following Kant's spirit, and not his letter; second, Fichte had broken with Schiller over their incapacity to sort out their difficulties concerning the relationship between letter and spirit. See "Über Geist und Buchstab in der Philosophie," in Fichte, *Fichtes Werke*, vol. VIII, 270–300. On the debate with Schiller, see Weissberg.

18. F. Schlegel, "To Fichte," *KA*, 3:46–47.

19. Indeed, by having called these productions "die freieren" Schlegel already claims that they are more spiritual than the systematic ones, since *spirit* and *freedom* are quasi-synonymous terms in this text. Cf. 46, 86, 88, 92 passim.

20. F. Schlegel, "To Fichte," *KA*, 3:47; emphasis added. Needless to say, by associating himself via Lessing with the task of "awakening" sleepy readers from their dogmatic "slumbers," Schlegel makes Lessing and himself play Hume to Fichte's Kant. The sleepers, it is quite clearly implied, slumber in the "dogmatism" of the letter.

21. When speaking of the style appropriate to scientific philosophy, moreover, Schlegel allows himself to say to Fichte that a terminology, "where the means are completely fixed, as otherwise only in dead languages" (48), is adequate to such a discourse. To say this, however, is tantamount to suggesting that systematic philosophy is a dead language, mere letter.

22. Schlegel will also write in "On the Character of the Protestants": "Further, the system of realism was for Lessing certainly more than mere system and letter" (93). Thus, he apparently uses "system" and "letter" interchangeably.

23. F. Schlegel, "To Fichte," *KA*, 3:51. For example, Schlegel mentions and defends Lessing's use of language taken from the "lively dialogical tone of real life" (48). Further, after speaking of the characteristics of a "dialogue [*Gespräch*]" (49),

he says, "Lessing's style possesses all of these characteristics in a quite eminent degree" (49). Moreover, he goes on to speak of "the lively, dramatic, dialectical, and dialogical spirit" of "Lessing's writings" (50). It is not surprising that Schlegel shifts here from speaking of "dialogue" as *form* to speaking of "dialogical spirit" as *content*, and then in the last section "On the Form of Philosophy" goes back to emphasizing that dialogue is a form, for the task of both dialogical form and polemical spirit is to *unite* form with content. For this reason, Schlegel's text drifts back and forth between characterizing dialogue, as well as polemic, as form and characterizing them as content. For this reason, too, both dialogue and polemic are to be collapsed into what he calls both "inner form" (as synthesis of—conventionally inner—content and—normally outer—form) and the apparent "formlessness" of Lessing's "form" (50).

24. Whose "dialogical" resonances with Fichte's own text we will not pursue here. See the discussion of "A Reflexion" from *Lucinde* in Chapter 4.

25. On the mutually constitutive mutual interference of the performative and constative-tropological dimensions of language, see the late works of de Man, for example, "The Resistance to Theory," in *Resistance to Theory*, especially 18–20.

26. Schlegel characterizes the dialogical "inner form" of Lessing's thought and expression also in terms of a "combination of thoughts that is quite peculiarly his own, whose surprising turns and configurations [*Wendungen und Konfigurationen*] are more perceptible than definable" (51). Lessing's dialogicity thus appears, on the one hand, as configurations and turnings—as a tropology or tropics, a rhetorical weave of material figures, language as letter—and, on the other hand, as "thoughts," as pure spirit. His "peculiar combination of thoughts," or what Schlegel also calls his "peculiar mode of connecting the particulars" (50), cannot quite be defined because it is beyond the definitional sphere of philosophy or science, i.e., because it is *between* philosophy/science and poetry/art, on the edge where letter and spirit overlap and interrupt each other's domains.

27. Ernst says, for example, "One thing is necessary: that not all statehood and humanity should disappear [*untergehe*], that old legal traditions [*altes Recht*], as well as old customs, honor, freedom, and princely dignity be to some degree maintained and brought about anew" (96). And Falk answers him a bit further on: "You regret the disappearance [*den Untergang*] of the state and of the constitution, while I would fear the dissolution of all religion, if this dissolution itself left any space for such a fear" (96).

28. His letter "On the Form of Philosophy" begins: "At a time when customs are degenerate [*entartet*], laws corrupted, when all concepts, classes, and relations are mixed, confused, and falsified, in a situation finally in which even in religion the memory of a divine origin has become a rare thing, there it is only through philosophy that the welfare of humanity can be reconstituted and maintained" (97).

29. By arguing that philosophy must now subserve the task of the rediscovery

of the original meaning of revelation, Schlegel is not only reversing Lessing but attempting to reconcile the opposition between Jacobi's antiphilosophical religiosity and Fichte's philosophy, which Jacobi had taken to constitute a human usurpation of revelation, a "nihilism."

30. See Lessing, *Werke*, "Ernst und Falk," 622ff. On the history of the relationship between Jews and Freemasonry in Europe, see Katz, *Jews and Freemasons*; and Katz, *Out of the Ghetto*, 44–47 passim.

31. On the spirit as flame some 150 years later within this tradition, in Heidegger, see Derrida, *De l'esprit*, 131ff.

32. F. Schlegel, "On the Form of Philosophy," *KA*, 3:99.

33. The fact that philosophy has for its object "the secret of all secrets" (99) and, thus, must reveal while concealing, is the reason for "the particular form of philosophy which, under all conditions and in all situations, is the enduring and authentically essential one: dialectical form. Not merely bound up with the imitation of dialogue, it takes place wherever a floating exchange of thoughts in a sequential connection takes place, that is, wherever philosophy takes place . . . and in every good philosophical dialogue there must be one who strives, desirous of knowledge, to unveil the secrets of the highest research, and one who in the possession of such secrets happily betrays them, always a bit further, through what he imparts, but when one believes he is about to do this completely and to express them completely, which he neither can nor may, then he suddenly breaks off, and excites our longing anew through the indefinite prospect he opens up onto the infinite" (99–100). The authoritarian character of Schlegel's notion of dialogue appears here in that it consists of a subject who is not only supposed to know but in fact possesses such knowledge as his property ("in possession of such secrets") and another subject desirous of knowledge.

CHAPTER 7

1. Karl Marx, "Zur Judenfrage," 244, 373. In English, "On the Jewish Question." I have altered the translation by Easton and Guddat where it seemed inaccurate. Page references given parenthetically in text, first to the English edition, and then (after a semicolon) to the German edition.

2. Manuel, 222–48.

3. F. Schlegel, *KA*, vol. 7 (1966), *Studien zur Geschichte*, c–ci; and vol. 21 (1995), *Fragmente zur Geschichte und Politik, zweiter Teil*, 100–101.

4. See *KA*, 7. Schlegel argues for the emancipation of the Jews in three articles of 1815–1816 (470–77), the first and longest of which is a positive review of a book by C. A. Buchholz, entitled "Documents concerning the improvement of the civil status of the Israelites [*Aktenstücke, die Verbesserung des bürgerlichen Zustandes der Israeliten betreffend*]." The pattern of argumentation that appears in the review, as the title of the book under discussion suggests, follows approximately the Enlightenment discourse of Dohm. What Buchholz, and through him, Schlegel, add to

the discussion are essentially two empirical facts: first, the Jews have fought for the German "Fatherland" in the struggle against the French invader. In this way, the Jews have proven that Judaism is not a political but a religious identity. (According to Ernst Behler in his Introduction to this volume [xcv], Schlegel's persuasion of the military serviceability of the Jews is strongly influenced by the fact that his stepson, Philipp Veit, fought valiantly in the wars of liberation.) Second, where they have had a chance, the Jews have moved from commerce into professions and manufacturing trades: thus, their "improvement" is possible. Interestingly, Schlegel reserves for those who deny this evidence the term "inimical sophistry" ("feindliche Sophistik," 472). Finally, Schlegel seems to have written in 1820 an article (477–82) on then recent linguistic research that led to the conclusion that the Native American tribes are in fact the ten lost tribes of Israel. (On the more general phenomenon of work in this direction, which supports the suggestion I have made in the Introduction that the Reformation puts the Jews in the position the Middle Ages had reserved for the pagans, see Manuel, 168–70.) While the authorship of the article remains to some extent in question (for Behler's comments on the inconclusive evidence in favor of Schlegel as author, see *KA*, 7:cxlii), the analogy Schlegel establishes, in *Über die Sprache und Weisheit der Indier*, between the ancient Indians and the Jews, receives here an amusing, phantasmatic confirmation. As the author of the article of 1820 remarks, the languages of the American Indians are like that of the Jews (Hebrew) in that they all make use of "well expressed metaphors and often allegory" (479). In this text, the Jewish American Indians Florentin went on to lead after the end of Dorothea Veit's novel, as we discussed in Chapter 5, turn out to be a "reality" after all!

5. Schlegel argues for the freedom of religion and the restoration of the rights of the Catholic Church in Germany, as well as for the importance of the Catholic Church for German unity (*KA*, 7:416), in several articles from 1814–1817 (414–17, 423–25, 430, 452–56, 463), allowing himself on occasion to support the notion that the church should be the "foundation" and "original principle" of the state ("Fundament . . . Urprinzip," 424–25). Indeed, Schlegel's partisanship for Rome was such that he became the object of some suspicion even in Metternich's Vienna (xcviiiff). Whenever either state or church is emancipated from the other, of course, it will tend to enslave that other. Thus, Schlegel's Neo-Catholic suggestion that the church should be freed from the state, which is occasionally phrased in terms of "enlightened government" (472), is also the first strategic step toward a reestablishment of the subordination of state to church which was the ego-ideal of the medieval European Subject. See also *KA*, 21:1–61, for Schlegel's fragments on history and politics from 1813.

6. Cf. Schopenhauer's discussion of the Indo-Christian wheel of "generation and birth," in *Parerga und Paralipomena*, 406–7. In English, *Parerga and Paralipomena*, 382.

7. The relatively "secular" character of this renewal of the Protestant "spirit" is

overdetermined also by the advances in modern science, technology, and industrialization across the nineteenth century.

8. While the French materialist Enlightenment already pushed relatively far in the direction of pagan atheism—hence, for example, Nietzsche's late admiration for figures of the French Enlightenment such as Voltaire—they did so in a more historically naïve or inexperienced and simple manner than the mid- to late-nineteenth-century figures. They reacted against the combined forces of church and absolute monarchy, and essentially against Judaism and Catholicism. In mid- to late-nineteenth-century Germany, in contrast, these traditional foes are overdetermined by Protestant orthodoxy and the bourgeoisie, as well as Neo-Judaic Enlightenment and Neo-Catholic Romantic ideologies.

9. This post-Romantic period—and so of course both Marx and Wagner in the analyses below—can further be characterized as "decadent" in the ironically negative sense in which Nietzsche uses the term in "Der Fall Wagner." In this context, a "decadent" is not merely someone who is on the decline or unnatural but principally someone who, while on the decline or tending away from nature, *claims to be the purely natural, the ascendant.* This decadence that denies decadence has two main extremes. One masquerades as, or tends to conflate itself with, Romanticism (Wagner), while the other tends to appear as Enlightenment (Marx). Each extreme, however, being historically *post*-Romantic, and so also *post*-Enlightenment, is inscribed structurally *between* Enlightenment and Romanticism, at the site of their pseudosublation in the double renewal of pagan Protestantism in the late nineteenth century.

10. For an analysis of the concepts of "left" and "right" in terms of their shaky foundations on insufficient grapplings with the undecidability of "necessity" as a modal concept, see Jeffrey S. Librett, "Interruptions of Necessity."

11. The self-emancipatory revolutionism of this humanism inscribes the latter in the structure of figural interpretation first of all by setting it up as the fulfillment of the—henceforth prefigural—escape of the ancient Hebrews from Egyptian bondage. As the realization of this Jewish figure, revolutionary humanism remains indebted to, and in this sense trapped within, or enslaved to, Judaism. In this way, Judaism becomes Egyptian. In fact one sees in the Young Hegelians, in such figures as Heine, an association of the Jews with Egyptians, characterizations of Judaism as "mummified," and so forth. The translation of the Blood Libel into the notion of Jewish capitalist Mammonism, traced very usefully in Rose, *Revolutionary Antisemitism*, 44–50 passim, reflects and overdetermines this structure.

12. On the complex development of this anticapitalist anti-Semitism in, around, and against the work of the post-Romantic generation, i.e., the Young Hegelians and Young Germany, many of whose leading lights—such as Börne, Heine, and Marx—were converted Jews, see Poliakov, 3:391–429; Rose, *Revolutionary Antisemitism*, 135–340; Gilman, *Jewish Self-Hatred*, on Börne, Heine, and Marx, 148–208.

13. While the diaspora Jews in Christian Europe, as merchants and money-lenders, had *from the beginning* been identified with money—that is, while they had always been pushed, by being excluded from other professions, to yield to this identification of both themselves and their prefigurative law with the universalizing tendency of money and the loan (for the prefiguration is always a loan)—these associations became *particularly* powerful as high capitalism developed.

14. On the gradual development of the racial dimension of Wagner's anti-Semitism under the influences of Darwinism and the cultural theories of Gobineau, see Rose, *Wagner*, 135–69. On racist anti-Semitism, above all in the form of bodily imagery, in Wagner's theoretical and operatic works, and even considerably prior to his encounters with Darwinism and Gobineau, see Weiner. For the development of racial anti-Semitism in Germany from the early nineteenth century through Wagner, see Poliakov, 3:380–457.

15. Marx writes much of the essay while on his honeymoon after his marriage to Jenny von Westphalen, the Christian beloved of his youth. See Murray Wolfson's useful contextualization of the essay against its biographical, political, and (among other things) Feuerbachian philosophical backgrounds, *Marx*, 74–103.

16. Peled, "From Theology to Sociology: Bruno Bauer and Karl Marx on the Question of Jewish Emancipation," argues that Marx is not an anti-Semite and that he supports Jewish emancipation. In order to defend this position, however, Peled must privilege what Marx has to say within the context of *political* emancipation—for it is only within *that* context, and thus quite provisionally, that Marx supports Jewish emancipation—while playing down what Marx says about *human* emancipation as emancipation of society and humanity *from* Judaism.

17. For a condensed survey of Hegel's views on the Jews, see Rotenstreich, *Recurring Pattern*, 48–75. For a more extended discussion of Judaism in various Hegelianisms, see Rotenstreich, *Jews and German Philosophy*, 73–172.

18. Hegel, *Philosophy of Right* (page references to English, then to German edition): "Thus technically it may have been right to refuse a grant of even civil rights to the Jews on the ground that they should be regarded as belonging not merely to a religious sect but to a foreign race. But the fierce outcry raised against the Jews, from that point of view and others, ignores the fact that they are, above all, human beings, and . . . that what civil rights rouse in their possessors is the feeling of oneself as counting in civil society as a person with rights, . . . [and from] this feeling of self-hood . . . the desired similarity in disposition and ways of thinking comes into being" (169n; 421). In contrast to Hegel's affirmation of Jewish emancipation, Marx's position is that, even if the Jews are to be freed within the political state, ultimately Judaism will have to be destroyed in order for humanity to constitute itself. Hegel tolerates the Jews because they are humans, while—in stark contrast—Marx makes the destruction of Judaism the condition of the possibility of any humanity whatsoever.

19. Hegel, *Philosophy of Right*, §270, 164–74; 415–31. This discussion of the

relations between state and religion begins with a critique of the grounding of state upon church that, according to a plausible suggestion made by Hegel's translator, T. M. Knox (365 n 11), alludes to "Friedrich Schlegel and other Romantics." Hegel sees that it is contradictory to maintain, on the one hand, that religion counsels us to be indifferent to the matters of this world, and on the other hand, that religion should be the guide of the state. For Hegel's arguments against the Romantic desire for a unity of church and state, see 173–74; 428. Hegel here associates the unity of church and state not only with medieval Europe but also with "oriental despotisms" (173; 428), in this way building problematically on the connection Schlegel had drawn between oriental and Catholic worlds, except that here if the oriental world "prefigures" Catholicism, then it prefigures that about Catholicism which is undesirable. For Hegel's other remarks against the Romantic Neo-Catholics in *Philosophy of Right*, see §141, Addition, 258–59; 290–91, where Hegel argues that the Neo-Catholics have converted because "they found their inner life worthless and grasped at something fixed, at a support, an authority, even if it was not the stability of thought which they caught" (258–59; 290).

20. "The state is mind on earth [*der Geist der in der Welt steht*]. . . . The state is the divine will as present spirit, which is unfolding itself into a real form and the organization of a world" (165, 166; 416, 417–18). Another place where Hegel's discussion of church-state relations alludes to Schlegel's work, and in this case, overlaps with Schlegel's attempt to move beyond Protestantism in the Lessing texts of 1804 (even if to a different end, namely, the end of the relegation of religion to civil society) is to be found in Hegel's remarks against the conflation of religiosity with the principle of *polemic* (167–68; 419–20). When religion renounces polemic, the state protects religion, going so far as to demand of its members that they have some religion, although what religion they then profess remains their private affair (168; 420–21).

21. Marx, "Jewish Question," 223; 352, and 242–43; 371–72.

22. Ibid., cf. 223, 232; 351–52, 361 passim.

23. Marx summarizes this as follows: "Man emancipates himself *politically* from religion by banning religion from public law into the sphere of private law" (227; 356).

24. According to Marx's account, not only is religion banished by secular politics to civil society but also civil society becomes henceforth essentially the place of religion; civil society is not just the place within which religion is situated, but civil society is as such religious, and religion is the religion of civil society.

25. The concept of fulfillment, accomplishment, or literal realization of the prefiguration is expressed by Marx in some cases in terms of "Vollendung," or "completion," as where he asserts (228; 357) that the secular state realizes or "completes" the "figural expression" [*überschwenglicher Ausdruck*] of humanity constituted by Christianity.

26. In the political state, religion "is no longer the essence of *community*, but

rather the essence of *difference*. It has become the expression of the *separation* of the human being from the *community* [Gemeinwesen]" (227; 356). The fact that civil society as principle of difference occupies, in Marx's understanding of Bauer's Hegelianism, the prefigurative position traditionally assigned to the Jews is indicated, among other ways, by Marx's use of the term "exile" to refer to the condition of religion in civil society with respect to the state: religion, he says, "has been tossed among numerous private interests and exiled [*exiliert*] from the community as community" (227; 356).

27. In terms of the interplay between letter and spirit, Marx argues that the secular state is true to the spirit as well as the letter of the Christian Gospel, whereas the Christian state can be true only to its spirit and not to its letter. This means in turn that the Christian state can be true only to the letter of the Gospel and not to its spirit, because the meaning of "the letter" is difference, while that of "the spirit" is identity, and because the separation of spirit from letter is, qua separation, an act of allegiance to the letter rather than the spirit (230; 359). In transgressing the spirit of letter-spirit unity, or of orthodox Lutheran literalism, the Christian state is always quasi-Jewish, in the sense of quasi-Catholic. To this limited degree, Marx goes on to agree with Hegel's critique of Schlegel's political theology (231; 360).

28. See Heidegger, "Die onto-theologische Verfassung der Metaphysik," in *Identität und Differenz*, 31–67.

29. For Marx, accordingly, the separation of civil society and state that Bauer envisions makes of the isolated atom of civil society the highest being, or God: "Political democracy is Christian in that it regards man—not merely one but every man—as the *sovereign* Being, the highest Being" (231; 360).

30. As we pass from religion to political emancipation, so we then pass from political emancipation to human emancipation. The homology between these two passages is suggested by the following, even if the order of the corresponding terms is inverted here: "The question of the *relation of political emancipation to religion* becomes for us the question of the *relation of political emancipation to human emancipation*" (223; 352).

31. For a comparative reading of the reception of Mendelssohn in Heine and Marx, see Prawer. Prawer shows (424–28) how Marx drastically overestimates Mendelssohn's anti-Spinozism, and so risks confusing Mendelssohn with Jacobi himself.

32. See F. Schlegel, *KA*, vol. 14, *Vorlesungen über Universalgeschichte* (1805–1806), ed. Jean-Jacques Anstett, especially 151–57, 165–74, 211–17, 253–56.

33. While I cannot broach here a detailed analysis of the very complex matter of Marx's reception of the Romantics, for a perspicacious reading of the Romantic poetry Marx wrote at the beginning of his career, a reading which sees the young Marx as attempting to subjectivize the objective (which I would translate as "attempting to spiritualize the letter"), see Wessell. On the importance of Roman-

tic philosophy of nature, and so of Schelling (no doubt the most "pagan" of the early Romantics, and one whose career lasts well into the nineteenth century), for the young Marx, see Frank; and Röder.

34. The Introduction to "Toward a Critique of Hegel's Philosophy of Right," written in the same phase of Marx's career and also published in the *Deutsch-Französischen Jahrbücher*, displays in a number of ways the same incompleteness as "On the Jewish Question" with respect to the overcoming of theology. While a more detailed reading would be worthwhile, I can signal here the following: (1) the text begins with the thesis, "The critique of religion is the presupposition of all critique" (249; 378), which implies, although Marx doesn't seem to notice this (for in the context he has just claimed that "For Germany the critique of religion is essentially finished" [250; 378]), that the critique of religion endlessly precedes itself and is never complete; (2) Marx claims here that man makes religion, not religion man (250; 378), and so he replaces God with man, consequently overlooking the fact that discourse—e.g., religion as discourse—indeed contributes to what "man" is and becomes, that is, overlooking the discursive inscription of the "human"; (3) Marx defines "religion" here as "the self-consciousness and self-feeling of the human who either has not yet gained or already lost himself again" (251; 378), whereas if the human is not simply self-attainable, if there is no absolute propriety of the human, as the "present" study evidently presupposes, then there is no end, in Marx's terms, to "religion."

35. The notion that such a synthesis could occur in an anticipatory form on the level of a *materialist-empiricist* dialectic (i.e., no dialectic at all, since dialectics would in principle have to go beyond the choice between idealism and materialism) begs the question of the relation between materialism-empiricism and idealism-rationalism, a question which is raised implicitly by such passages as the following: "Where the political state has achieved its true development, man leads a double life—a heavenly and an earthly life, life in the *political community* [politischen Gemeinwesen], in which he counts for himself as a *communal being/political community* [Gemeinwesen], and life in *civil society* [bürgerlichen Gesellschaft], in which he is active as a *private person* . . .—not only in thought, in consciousness, but in *reality*, in *life*" (355). Here too, the privilege of "reality" is problematic, but it occurs in the context of a "not only in thought, in consciousness, but also in reality" that provides a balance perhaps even beyond what Marx intends. Whereas Marx here raises this question "figuratively," by positing as his telos the unification of the "heavenly" realm of (secular) politics and the "earthly" realm of (still-religious) civil society, that is, by positing as (currently) undecidable the relationship between the ideality of reason and the materiality of the empirically given, Marx simply *decides* this question on the level of his own methodological ideology, dogmatically and thus ineffectively, in favor of the material-empirical.

36. On the relation between Marx and Spinoza, see Yovel, 78–103.

37. For a persuasive reading of Marx's anti-Semitism in the context of his work

with and against Bauer, Hess, and others, and in the biographical light of his having been converted as a child, see Gilman, *Jewish Self-Hatred*, 188–208; and on Marx's attempt and failure to avoid both the material and concrete language designated as Jewish, and the abstraction that is at the same time attributed to Jewish language, see especially 195–98. For a reading of Marx that works toward a deconstruction of the opposition between idealism (or spirit) and materialism (or letter) in his text, see Derrida, *Spectres de Marx*.

38. Cf. the ludicrously credulous but nonetheless useful rapprochement of Luther and Marx operated by Jürgen Mahrenholz, "Erwägungen zum Luther- und Marx-Jahr 1983," and for strikingly explicit indications of the way in which the early Marx wants to appropriate Luther for pagan or naturalistic purposes, see Marx, "Luther as Arbiter Between Strauss and Feuerbach." Here, Marx quotes Luther in support of Feuerbach, as opposed to Strauss. Luther is for Marx "a very good authority, an authority greater, infinitely, than all Protestant dogmas altogether, because with Luther religion was *immediate truth*, was *Nature*, so to speak" (94), and in turn Feuerbach is the "antichrist" who has revealed "the essence of Christianity in its true, unveiled form" (95).

39. In his indignation about the sphere of economics replacing that of religion, Marx registers unwittingly his continuing devotion, despite all "materialism," to the purity of the "religious" discourse, its unequivocal separation from and domination over the sphere of the "economic."

40. The motif of the "body" is important here, as well, in the term "Leibeigenen," evocative as it is of associations of the Jews with the body, and it returns a few pages later when Marx contrasts the Christians' "egoism of eternal bliss" [*Seligkeitsegoismus*] with the Jews' "body-egoism" [*Leibesegoismus*] (248; 377).

41. Marx, "Jewish Question," 245; 374. The link between letter and death is made manifest here by the fact that the Jews, along with the pagan polytheism they embody, are associated with faeces by way of the obsessional law.

42. Wolfson, 79–82, traces the interplay of polytheistic and Protestant motifs in Feuerbach, Marx's predecessor; and Carlebach, 169, characterizes Marx's early work in terms of a synthesis of "heathen" and Christian spirituality in the wake of Feuerbach, but of course neither approaches the question in terms of the historiography of Judaeo-Christian religiocultural identities as determined by figural interpretation.

43. Marx, "Jewish Question," 246; 375. The passage that immediately precedes this quotation defines the "chimerical nationality" of the Jew as one of "the merchant . . . the monied man" (246; 375). So Marx is sliding here from the characterization of the worldly God of the Jews in terms of money to the characterization of this God in terms of "law," a slide which, since money and law share the trait of abstract materiality, feels smooth within the context of an anticapitalist revision of the Christian condemnation of Jewish law.

44. Cf. de Fontenay.

CHAPTER 8

1. Wagner, "Das Judenthum in der Musik," in *Gesammelte Schriften und Dichtungen*, vol. 5, 85–108. In English, "Judaism in Music," in Wagner, *Judaism in Music and Other Essays*, 75–122. Quote on 81; 87. The English edition prints together with the text of the essay the appended explanations (to which we will have occasion to refer below), which Wagner printed elsewhere in his collected works (*Gesammelte Schriften und Dichtungen*, vol. 8, 299–323), in accordance with chronological order of composition, although they appeared together with the essay in the 1869 edition. Page references given parenthetically in text, first the English, then the German edition.

2. See, for example, Adorno, *Versuch über Wagner*; Rose, *Wagner*, which treats the essay in various contexts; Weiner, *Richard Wagner*, which treats anti-Semitic corporeal iconography in Wagner's musical materials; Poliakov, vol. 3, which places Wagner's essay within the context of German nineteenth-century racialist nationalism; Katz, *The Darker Side*, which usefully places the essay in the context of Wagner's career, despite the fact that, as Rose points out, Katz naïvely and mistakenly assumes that very little of Wagner's anti-Semitism can be found in his artworks themselves. For recent critical work on Wagner in general from a sociohistorical point of view, see Grimm and Hermand. On the Wagner circle from the standpoints of Friedrich Nietzsche and his sister, see Peters. Susan Bernstein, "Journalism and German Identity: Heine, Wagner, and Adorno," analyzes and compares constructions of German identity in these three writers in terms of the rise of journalism seen as an unsettling excess of semiosis.

3. Three notable exceptions would be Bernstein; Lacoue-Labarthe and Nancy, *Le mythe nazi*; and David J. Levin, whose illuminating analysis of narrative in Wagner shares much with my analysis of the temporal letter there, although without thematizing typology or the theopolitics of aesthetics directly.

4. Cf. Lacoue-Labarthe's excellent work on the imitation of the originality of the Greeks he situates at the unstable foundation of German modernism, in *Le sujet de la philosophie* and *L'imitation des Modernes*. Lacoue-Labarthe underestimates, however, the modern German concern with, and anxiety over, the originality of the Jews in the Pauline Judaeo-Christian structure.

5. Wagner, *Judaism*, 79; 85.

6. Wagner, *Judaism*, 80, n 1. The German source is here Richard Wagner ("K. Freigedank"), "Das Judenthum in der Musik" in *Neue Zeitschrift für Musik*, 1.

7. On Wagner's Aryan Christianity, as articulated in the "Wibelungen" essay and under Schopenhauer's influence, see Rose, *Wagner*, 89–101, 141–69. For Schopenhauer's position on the Jews, and responses to Schopenhauer, see Rotenstreich, *Jews and German Philosophy*, 173–99. While Schlegel's Neo-Catholic orientalism construes the ancient Indian East as a pagan anticipation of the Jewish anticipation of the Christian fulfillment, Schopenhauer's Neo-Protestant (even if atheist) neopaganism makes Brahmanism and Buddhism the pagan fulfillment

avant la lettre of a (quasi-Catholic) Christianity that appears thus as a belated figuration of that fulfillment. On Schopenhauer's view, Christianity has been led astray from its own Aryan pessimistic truth by the nefariously optimistic influence of Judaism. See Schopenhauer, *Parerga und Paralipomena*, 214–55 ("Zur Ethik"), and 343–419 ("Zur Religion"); in English, *Parerga and Paralipomena*, 201–39 ("On Ethics"), and 324–94 ("On Religion"). For Hegel, Judaism was too pessimistic because it (sublimely) separated God from the world; for Schopenhauer, Judaism is too optimistic because it makes the world into a place of potentially fulfilled desires. On Aryanizing orientalism in Schopenhauer and Wagner, see Suneson and Schwab, 427–34, 438–48.

8. Wagner, *Judaism*, 80; 86.

9. On Wagner's later disappointment with what he saw as the philo-Semitism of Bismarck's Germany, see Rose, *Wagner*, 142, 152, 159 passim.

10. Wagner, *Judaism*, 80; 86.

11. While Wagner's irrationalism is more than readily legible in his insistence on the self-legitimating character of prejudiced affect (the *reductio ad absurdum* of Hans-Georg Gadamer *avant la lettre*), this irrationalism should not blind one to Wagner's claim to represent at the same time a kind of higher "reason" or "rationality," and even rationalism or idealism (81; 87).

12. While Wagner appeals repeatedly to the "Europeans" (for example, 83, 84; 88, 90), no doubt because his career ambitions are of European scope, he implicitly narrows his audience to a Germanic one not only by praising only German composers and poets but also by allowing himself a number of typically counterrevolutionary and German-nationalist anti-French remarks (referring to the "war of liberation [*Befreiungskampfe*]" [82; 88] from the Jews and polemicizing against Meyerbeer by saying "he writes operas for Paris" [97; 104]. The stereotype of French formalism overdetermines here that of Jewish formalism. For an exemplary discussion of the layering in Wagner's nationalism, see Peter U. Hohendahl, "Reworking History: Wagner's German Myth of Nuremberg," in Grimm and Hermand, 39–60. Hohendahl problematizes in particular the Nazis' attempt to establish Wagner as their "prefiguration" (48, 58).

13. For a succinct summary of the Geyer question and indications of the literature on the subject, see Weiner, *Richard Wagner*, 3–4, 355.

14. "Der Jude, der bekanntlich einen Gott ganz für sich hat, fällt uns im gemeinen Leben zunächst durch seine äußere Erscheinung auf" (88). ("The Jew—*who, as everyone knows, has a God all to himself*—in ordinary life strikes us primarily by his outward appearance" [82–83; emphasis added].)

15. While in the Introduction I have operated a rapprochement between symbolism and realism insofar as they share a common, empiricist-realist ontorhetoric, an important difference remains: symbolism tends to idealize the literal material of representation, i.e., the image, whereas realism tends to realize the literal material of the represented, reality itself. Wagner's literalist symbolism is materialist in its

pagan-secularizing-sensualist traits (drawn in part from Young Germany), while it is idealist in its Neo-Protestant tendency toward the spiritualizing overcoming of the material dimensions of Neo-Catholic Romanticism.

16. Of course Wagner is struggling also against the opposite of what he says here: for similarly, and conversely, the Christian discourse that borrows the figures of the Jews in order to literalize them is bound sooner or later to confront the fact that it speaks the language of the Jews, the language of the other. Wagner thus blames the Jews for the Pauline construction of Christianity. In a similar, but slightly different move, Fichte had blamed Paul—because he was a Jew, and because he made Christianity dependent on Judaism—for the Judaization of Christianity. In this way, Fichte broached the tradition of "Aryan Christianity." On Fichte's nationalist anti-Semitism and its continuation by the work of his student, Jakob Fries, see Poliakov, 3:180–82, 300–301, 380–98 passim; Rose, *Revolutionary Antisemitism in Germany*, 117–34; and Martyn. These nationalist anti-Semites provide the transition from the Catholicizing Romantics to the pagan "secular religion of human redemption" (Rose, *Revolutionary Antisemitism*, 131) that has come to full flower and gone to seed in figures such as Marx and Wagner. On the twentieth-century legacy of Fichte insofar as he was seen to prefigure German fascism by many of the German fascists themselves, see Sluga, 29–52.

17. Wagner, *Judaism*, 84; 90.

18. Wagner, *Judaism*, 85; 91. The physical obtrusiveness of the Jew's speech is particularly distressing to Wagner because it is an obtrusiveness of the (material) *form* of speech, rather than its (spiritual) *content* (85; 91). In this light it appears questionable, almost "Jewish," when Wagner says that he will next "consider *how* it grew possible to the Jew to become a musician" (87; 93).

19. On the importance of the notion that the Jew is without feelings to German anti-Semitism of the nineteenth and early twentieth centuries, see Mosse, *Germans and Jews*, 34–60.

20. Wagner, *Judaism*, 86; 91.

21. In the case of his reference to the Jews as thinkers, Wagner alludes to Schlegel's famous "Athenäum" fragment 80, "The historian is a prophet facing backwards," by saying "the Thinker is the backward-looking poet; but the true Poet is the foretelling Prophet" (88; 94). This trope transforms Schlegel's reflection on the structure of the future-anterior in historiography into an attack on reflexivity itself, in this case that of the Jews, in order to install the anti-self-conscious German poet as the supplement of the Judaic prophet.

22. In the analysis of the example of Mendelssohn, Wagner ties this formalism directly to the theme of figurality versus feeling: "Nothing beyond our more or less amusement-craving Phantasy was roused through the presentment, stringing-together and entanglement of the most elegant, the smoothest and most polished figures [*glättesten und kunstfertigsten Figuren*]—as in the kaleidoscope's changeful play of form and colour—but never where those figures [*Figuren*] were meant to

take the shape [*Gestalt*] of deep and stalwart feelings of the human heart" (94; 101). Wagner goes on in this context to link Mendelssohn to Bach as formalist (again, concerned with not the "what" but the "how" [95; 102]), contrasting both to Beethoven, who had ostensibly exceeded formalism in the direction of pure expression, and linking this formalism to the Egyptian sphinx (a dim memory of Hegel's aesthetics), while he links the classical expressiveness of Mozart and especially Beethoven to Greek statues (95; 102–3).

23. Wagner's extension of this discussion of musical aesthetics to literary aesthetics, carried out with reference to Heinrich Heine, works in terms of the following analogy: formalism is to music as lying is to poetry. Accordingly, for Wagner Heine could become a German poet only "when our poetry became a lie" (99; 107). As the Jew can only imitate musical forms, so the Jew can tell the truth about only lies, but not the truth itself. Thus Heine was able "to bare . . . that lie, that bottomless aridity [*bodenlose Nüchternheit*] and jesuitical hypocrisy [*jesuitische Heuchelei*]of our Versifying [*Dichterei*], which still would give itself the airs of true poesis" (100; 107), but not to become a true poet himself.

24. Wagner, *Judaism*, 93; 99–100. The notion that the polar opposites of German and Jew coincide in uncanny ways in Wagner's text is supported by the fact that in the appendix, written in 1869, Wagner characterizes (117–18; 328) the typical weakness of the Germans, which allows them to be taken advantage of by the Jews, as their "inertia" ("Trägheit"), so that the force of death, in the form of inertia, is characterized first as Jewish and then as the peculiar internal weakness of the Germans.

25. It is curious that Wagner situates the Jews in the position of *death*, which in the German post-Kantian tradition means *disorganization*, whereas—especially in the appendix written in 1869—he views the Jews, in a classically paranoid manner, as being more *organized* than their German opponents. The Jews are thus defined as the principle of hyperorganization, which is at once the principle of disorganization. The Jews are more dead and deadly than others because they are more alive than others, more alive because they are more dead. Perhaps the connection between paranoia and German fascist anti-Semitism—interestingly studied by Canetti and others, most recently Eric L. Santner is to be situated here.

26. Wagner, *Judaism*, 99; 105–7. The worms in this passage recall the worms mentioned in Moses Mendelssohn's *Letters on Sentiments* (*JubA*, 1:46), where in 1755 they already represented the dissecting function of rationality qua Jewish sophistry in the mind of the anti-Semitic Christian empiricist, Euphranor, one of the two interlocutors in the text.

27. On this honorable tradition of gastronomic Judaeo-phobia (i.e., the theory of Jewish molochism) from Daumer to Feuerbach, and on the continuation of this tradition in Wagner's fearful desire for blood, see Poliakov, 3: 410–16, 448–57.

28. On the figure of Ahasuerus, or the "wandering Jew," see Rose, *Revolutionary Antisemitism*, 23–43 passim; and Körte and Stockhammer. For Nietzsche's cri-

tique of Wagner as denying the necessarily "Judaic" character of the modern artist (and thus of course also of himself) as wandering Jew, see "Der Fall Wagner," in Nietzsche, *Kritische Studienausgabe*, 6:18. The text of *The Case of Wagner* can be read as a direct answer to, and in a sense also parody of, Wagner's *Judaism in Music*, insofar as Nietzsche makes Wagner responsible for the ruination or decadence of current music taste in the same way as Wagner had tried to make the Jews responsible. Interestingly, as S. Levy notes in his polemical critique of Wagner's anti-Semitism, *Das Judentum in der Musik: eine kritisch-historische Betrachtung*, Bizet, with ironically enthusiastic praise of whom Nietzsche begins his essay, was "a Spanish half-Jew" (28). For an excellent analysis of Nietzsche's development from an early anti-Semitism to the later critique thereof, see Kofman. On Nietzsche's complex relationship with Wagner, see Hollinrake; Wapnewski; Zumbini; and Santaniello, 9–20. On the sense in which Nietzsche's later critique of Wagner's anti-Semitism illuminates Nietzsche's "modernism," see my Postscript below.

29. Wagner, *Judaism*, 100; 108.

30. Wagner, *Judaism*, 100 n; in German, "Das Judenthum in der Musik," *Neue Zeitschrift für Musik*, 112.

31. As Rose repeatedly points out (*Revolutionary Antisemitism*, xvii, 123ff. passim; *Wagner*, 3, 5, 76, 86, 99, 152 passim), there is often some ambiguity as to whether the destruction of the Jews is meant figurally or literally, whether their destruction as a cultural entity or as a race is intended. But as Rose does not consider, this ambiguity derives from the structural—and not simply historical, or contingently "contextual"—impossibility of distinguishing without remainder between the figural and the literal. Further, because the Jews stand, in this (Judaeo) Christian tradition, for the figural—in the sense of that which is taken to threaten at all times to render uncertain the very distinction between itself and its other (i.e., between the figural and the literal)—the discourse that proposes the destruction of the Jews proposes thereby the destruction of the unknown cause of its own uncertainty about what it means by destruction and about what it means to destroy. The temptation to undertake the literalization of this destruction is tremendous, however, since the urge to destruction in this case regards the figural itself (in the literal form of the Jews) as the very thing that it needs to destroy in order to come into being as what it is.

POSTSCRIPT

1. On the question of the extent to which the common German "people" carried out the Holocaust, see most recently Goldhagen, *Hitler's Willing Executioners*, and the extremely lively and often bitter discussion that has ensued upon its publication, as recorded for example in Shandley, ed., *Unwilling Germans?*; and Heil and Erb, eds., *Geschichtswissenschaft und Öffentlichkeit: der Streit um Daniel J. Goldhagen*. In Shandley, the various contributions by Norbert Frei (35–40), Christopher Browning (55–74), Hans-Ulrich Wehler (93–104), Götz Aly (167–

74), and Klaus Theweleit (211–16) strike me as particularly appropriate, useful, and measured, even when emphatic. See also the collection of responses to the recent traveling exhibition, "War of Annihilation—Crimes of the German Army [*Vernichtungskrieg—Verbrechen der Wehrmacht*], 1941–1944," organized by the Institute for Social Research of Jan Philipp Reemtsma and published in Prantl, *Wehrmachtsverbrechen*. Despite the many weaknesses of Goldhagen's work, chiefly the capitulation to the desire for monocausal explanation of the Holocaust and an essentialist treatment of "the Germans," his interests in a general anti-Semitism and the role of "ordinary" Germans are legitimate. As the chapters above make sufficiently clear, however, in accordance with my field and training, in retracing the development of German anti-Semitism, I view it more as discourse than as a national psychology, and I place much stronger emphasis than he on the rhetoric-philosophy, letter-spirit opposition, and so forth. On the specific, important, and very difficult historical question of the identity of the perpetrators of the Holocaust, see further Hilberg; for Hilberg's critical response to Goldhagen, see Heil and Erb (27–38); and on the history of the international historiography of the Holocaust, see Dawidowicz.

2. See Mosse, "The Secularization of Jewish Theology," in *Masses and Man*, 249–62; Tal; and Meyer, "Reform Jewish Thinkers and Their German Intellectual Context." In this very useful summary of the positions of Salomon Ludwig Steinheim (1789–1866), Salomon Formstecher (1808–1889), and Samuel Hirsch (1815–1889), Meyer emphasizes the self-assertiveness of these thinkers with respect to the nineteenth-century philosophical languages into which, or in response to which, they nonetheless try to translate Jewish thought for their contemporaries. The price paid by Meyer's optimistic emphasis, of course, is a momentary underestimation of the hopelessness or impossibility of the enterprise of (resistance to) translation undertaken by these thinkers. What is perhaps most striking about Steinheim, Formstecher, and Hirsch, from the perspective of the present study, alongside their continuing partial adherence to Enlightenment paradigms, is the prominence in each of their philosophies of the concern with the *pagan*, alongside the Christian and Jewish, a concern which bears witness to the presence, by the mid- to late nineteenth century, and in the wake of Neo-Catholic Romanticism, of *paganism* as a force to be reckoned with.

3. On the *Kulturkampf*, I am interpreting essentially the account given in Tal, 81–120 passim.

4. If the liberal Protestants were under pressure to prove that Christianity in fact superceded Judaism, then this was in part because historical studies of the New Testament had situated those elements of Christian theology that were more accessible to modern reason in the earliest Christian writings, which precede the intervention of the pagan elements taken up by the medieval Church but which also suggest, by their proximity to Judaism in historical terms, that if Christianity is to escape the paganism of Catholicism it must become Jewish. Thus, liberal Protes-

tants are struggling in the late nineteenth century against the Enlightenment over-coming of the Reformation, but they are doing so in the wake of Romantic Neo-Catholicism. From this point of view, while they are clearly on top of the situation in the Second Empire, they are in danger, on the one hand, of collapsing back into an identity with such Romanticism and, on the other hand, of falling forward into the Neo-Judaic modernism that, as we will see in a moment, is already announced in the late nineteenth century. See Tal, 200–20.

5. See Mosse, "German Socialists and the Jewish Question in the Weimar Republic," in *Masses and Man*, 284–316; and "Left-Wing Intellectuals in the Weimar Republic," in *Germans and Jews*, 171–228. For a perspective that diverges from Mosse's, see Jacobs, *On Socialists and "the Jewish Question" After Marx*; and for an explicit critique of Mosse, "Marxism and Anti-Semitism: Kautsky's Perspective." Jacobs's critique remains remarkably naïve, though, insofar as it sees, in Kautsky's desire to do away with every trace of Judaism through assimilation, nothing that would not be reconcilable with a perfectly friendly attitude toward the Jews.

6. On the strangely spiritualized Germanic nationalism that formed the Nazis' discourse, see Mosse, "The Mystical Origins of National Socialism," in *Masses and Man*, 197–213. On the interplay between Christian and anti-Christian anti-Semitism in the years prior to World War I, see Tal, 223–89. On the ways in which some German Jews assumed the proto-Nazi discourses, see Mosse, "The Influence of the Volkish Idea on German Jewry," in *Germans and Jews*, 77–115.

7. It is no doubt important to note in passing—given the focus of the foregoing chapters on the complexities affecting dialogicity—the profound debt that Martin Buber's "dialogical" thought owes to these Volkish currents, and the fact that Scholem, in this context, calls for a return to Jewish tradition, as against the Volkish aspects of the youth movement ideology, an intervention which seems, under the circumstances, to have been relatively reasonable.

8. On the complex development of German racist "science," in its application to the notion of the linguistically faulty Jews, and the various forms of resistance to this development, from Wagner on, in such diverse figures as Wilhelm Marr (for example in his pamphlet tellingly entitled, *The Conquest of the Jews over the Germans*, of 1879), Eugen Dühring, Heinrich von Treischke, Theodor Billroth, Friedrich Ratzel, Thomas Frey, Moritz Lazarus, Adolf Bartels, Otto Hauser, Fritz Mauthner, Karl Kraus, Otto Weininger, Adolf Hitler, and Sigmund Freud, a list that includes both some of the more glaring instances of racist anti-Semitism and some of the more glaring instances of the *internalization* of such anti-Semitism by Jews who were subject to it from morning til night, see Gilman, *Jewish Self-Hatred*, 209–308.

9. I have examined the internalization of anti-Semitic motifs in the Zionist texts of Leo Pinsker, Theodor Herzl, and Martin Buber, although not in any of the Marxist Zionists, in "Schizotechnotheology in Some Zionist Texts." It is moreover

sadly obvious that the externalized bad Semite in Israel at times still returns as the Arab (or Sephardic Jew) on whom exclusionary violence must then be practiced, and not only from the most manifestly right-wing perspectives in Israel.

10. For literary discourse per se, this implies that Marxist literary currents are premodernist when considered in terms of the rhetorical history of Judaeo-Christian discourse. The same, of course, would go for all Volkish literature, including the Volkish aspects of expressionism that emerge in people like Gottfried Benn. Both extreme right- and extreme left-wing literatures would comprise different kinds of "realism," insofar as they are linked to the subjective and objective naturalisms of national spirit and class position respectively, for the "real" (as a figure of necessity) is that on which they each attempt to base themselves. This would not exclude the possibility of mixed forms, of course, and clearly there is little that one could characterize as "purely" Marxist or Wagnerite/Volkish literature. The mixtures that one can graph in different writers, however, would—at least this is my hypothesis—be best "understood" in terms of the rhetorical historiography of Judaeo-Christian discourse I am tracing here.

11. On the eternal return in Nietzsche, see Klossowski; and Derrida, "Otobiographies: The Teaching of Nietzsche and the Politics of the Proper Name." In the latter essay, which forms the background of Derrida's remarks (in his "exchange" with Gadamer) on Heidegger's all-too-philosophical misappropriation of Nietzsche as thinker of the totality of Being, the "moment" of the eternal return is figured as a "moment" of signature (14 passim). In signature, the "spirit" or "life" of the thinker detaches itself from the "work" or "letter" of the thought, or the letter of the person detaches itself from the spirit of the work. Either way, on this border, which cannot be determined, and which thus endlessly repeats and displaces itself, the link and distinction are to be "situated" between the Christian and the Jewish moments. The eternal return as that of the signature is thus in Derrida the site of the Jewish-Christian "dialogue," neither writing nor speech, but the speech of writing and the writing of speech. In this sense, Derrida de-emphasizes, when he countersigns Nietzsche's signature, the "Judaic" character of modernist neo-Enlightenment, reading modernism on the edge where it is always about to become its forever deferred postmodern other.

12. On the right-wing use of the distinction between culture and civilization, see Mosse, "Culture, Civilization, and German Anti-Semitism," in *Germans and Jews*, 34–61.

13. Franz Rosenzweig's major work, *Der Stern der Erlösung*, and also his popularizing text, *Das Büchlein vom gesunden und kranken Menschenverstand*, are excellent examples of modernist antiphilosophy as quasi-seamlessly articulated with Judaism and, at the same time, with Enlightenment. The very title of the latter book alludes to Mendelssohn's use of the term "common understanding," his defense of rationality as compatible with faith, against Jacobi's counter-Enlightenment attempt to oppose rationality to faith.

14. On death as sacrifice for the Volk in pre-Nazi and Nazi thinking, see Mosse, "Death, Time, and History: Volkish Utopia and its Transcendence" and "The Jews and the German War Experience, 1914–1918," in *Masses and Man*, 69–86 and 263–83.

15. See the excellent account of this question in Kofman. My discussion of the relation between especially the later Nietzsche's thought and a certain notion of Judaism as exiled from (super)natural salvation should not be confused, of course, with any of the very naïve, post-Romantic, early Viennese Jewish readings of Nietzsche which, focusing on the early Nietzsche and the Dionysian principle, in particular, tended to identify the Jewish people with that principle. On the history of these readings and certain more critical voices that responded to them as they appeared, see the informative articles by Mattenklott, "Nietzsche dans les revues culturelles juives de langue allemande, 1900–1938," and Jacques Le Rider, "Les intellectuelles juifs viennois et Nietzsche. Autour de Sigmund Freud," in Bourel and Le Rider, eds., *De Sils-Maria à Jerusalem*, 93–109 and 181–201, respectively. For the most recent in-depth treatment of this theme, stressing Nietzsche's ambivalence, see Mandel, *Nietzsche and the Jews*.

16. "Who taught us, if not Wagner, that . . . even the wandering Jew is redeemed, *settles down*, when he marries? . . . What happens to the 'wandering Jew' ['*ewigen Juden*'] whom a woman bows down to and stabilizes? He simply stops wandering [*ewig zu sein*]; he marries, he is no longer of any interest.—Translated into reality: the danger of the artists, the geniuses—and it is they who are the 'wandering Jews'—lies in woman: the women who bow down to them are their ruination," "Der Fall Wagner," in *Kritische Studienausgabe*, vol. 6, 17, 18 (and in *The Birth of Tragedy and the Case of Wagner*," 160–61). Granting the distastefulness of Nietzsche's misogyny, which turns against the woman in the moment when the figure of the Jew is affirmed, as if someone must always be there to take sacrificial responsibility for nonassimilable materiality, the point of the passage for our specific purposes here is that the artist is posited as "Jew," while the artist's temptation is the desire to yield to narcissism, to the adoption of an imaginary and fulfilling-fulfilled identity that would attempt to put an end to drift. Further, astonishingly, Nietzsche parodically and subversively imitates in "The Case of Wagner" the argumentational *form* of Wagner's "Judaism in Music." As Wagner shows first why the Jews don't belong in music and then nonetheless shows what role they have played in the music of the present, Nietzsche explicitly shows first why Wagner does not belong in the history of music, then goes on to show the significance Wagner has had for that history. This parallel could hardly be by chance.

17. Gay, *A Godless Jew*; Yerushalmi, *Freud's Moses*; Derrida, *Mal d'Archive*; Lemérer, *Les deux Moïse de Freud*; Balmès, *Le nom, la loi, la voix. Freud et Moïse*; Rabinovitch, *Écritures du meurtre. Freud et Moïse*.

18. Freud, *Der Mann Moses*, 568, 564.

19. Freud, *Der Mann Moses*, 579. Through the word "Rausch," Freud attributes

to Jewish morality, which as morality is on the side of Apollo, what Nietzsche had made most characteristic of the Dionysian spirit in *The Birth of Tragedy*, thus situating tragedy, through the combination of intoxication and ethics, in Jewish culture itself, all along its development. Freud thus confirms and develops further those moments in Nietzsche where the Jewish takes on positive connotations, such as the passage on the artist as "Wandering Jew" in *The Case of Wagner*. Moreover, in the same context, Freud supplements but does not deny the partial truth of Nietzsche's account of the Jewish affirmation of law (as it appears in *The Antichrist*, for example), which sees in the Jewish law the expression of the need of the Jews to confirm their chosenness after exile by means of the confirmation of their own guilt. Freud adds to the motives Nietzsche supplies—which Freud qualifies, without naming Nietzsche, as "superficial" (579)—the ostensibly deeper origin of the sense of guilt in the murder of the *Urvater*. In these two ways, Freud grants the Jews a tragic dignity in Nietzschean terms, as fusion of Dionysos ("Rausch") and Apollo ("moralischer Askese," primitive guilt), but beyond what Nietzsche himself explicitly allows. Freud may seem more aggressively anti-Nietzschean where he reduces the *Übermensch* to the barbaric *Urvater*, as he does more than once in the late texts. But I would suggest that this polemic concerns the 1920s–1930s reactionary use of Nietzsche more than Nietzsche himself, for it is at least possible to read the *Übermensch* as the one who affirms eternal return and so affirms repetitive anticipation in the letter, while in turn this position is traditionally "Judaic" and "non-Christian."

20. The proximity of this position to that of Mendelssohn in *Jerusalem* as well as to that of the early Schlegel already allows us to see one sense in which Freud's discourse may be regarded as leaning anticipatorily toward a supplementary renewal of Neo-Catholicism, as we will see below, even as the Romantics' Neo-Catholic drama virtually repeats itself anticipatorily around him in the aesthetic decadence of the years leading up to the publication of the *Interpretation of Dreams*.

21. On extreme right-wing post-Nietzschean Catholics who build selectively on Nietzsche's works, see the excellent article by Richard Faber, "Rome contre la Judée, La Judée contre Rome. Critique du Nietzschéisme Noir," in Bourel and Le Rider, *De Sils-Maria à Jérusalem*, 247–60. On the link between antimodernism and anti-Semitism in the Austrian Catholic parties between the wars, see Pauley, 150–73. On the sense in which early Romantic thinking prefigures certain aspects of Nietzschean modernism, see Seyhan. While Seyhan's excellent study rightly demonstrates that the early Romantics broach the critique of presence, my own more historizing and negative discussion of them has been concerned to apply to them one of the principal lessons Seyhan draws from their work beyond their nascent thematization of radical temporality: the importance of the attempt to "understand why certain models, analogies, and heuristic fictions are valorized at certain periods while others are discredited" (158).

22. On the case of Hofmannsthal, see Gilman, *Smart Jews*, 132–37.

23. Perhaps, indeed, one has to understand the later pseudo-Catholic moment in Wagner's trajectory in this way, and Nietzsche's late critique of Wagner as an attempt to demystify not only the pagan-Protestant mixture, but also the precociously antimodernist pseudo-Catholic addition to this mixture.

24. Freud, *Der Mann Moses*, 581.

25. Moreover, as Yerushalmi recounts (27ff.), the object of one of Freud's greatest anxieties concerning the publication of *Moses and Monotheism* is the danger that Wilhelm Schmidt, a prominent Viennese priest and scholar who is also an opponent both of psychoanalysis and of the Nazis, will act to have psychoanalysis banned in Vienna. Freud's psychoanalysis depends on the good graces of Catholicism, which it aspires to supplement, for protection from the Nazis. In this sense, too, the very basis of psychoanalysis, the ground of its possibility, that to which it owes its most profound debts, is perilously close to becoming identifiable as the Catholic Church itself. In *Mal d'Archive*, Derrida emphasizes both through the content and the form of his own text the motif of prefigurative repetition in his discussion of Freud and historicity. By insisting on the undecidability of inside and outside, of messianicity and spirit (he writes of a "messianicité spectrale" that "travaille le concept d'archive" [60]), he argues for a Freud who is neither Jewish (or of the outside and messianic expectation) nor proto-Christian (of the inside and the interiorized past of a salvation). Thus, Derrida attempts to push the contemporary reading of Freud off the merry-go-round of positive religion, whereas my own reading, which shares that desire, is more concerned to show the multiple and contradictory ways in which Freud tends to situate himself, or to allow of situation, always ideologically and within the history of ideology, on the merry-go-round.

26. If there were a (displaced) repetition of the Christian critique of Judaism in the postmodernist critique of modernism, it would perhaps be located in the critique of formalist and innovationist aspects of the modernist canon (or "dead letter"), as viewed by those postmodernists in various domains who emphasize historicism, as in postmodern architecture, for example, as well as in the critical modalities of new historicism, cultural studies, and postcolonial criticism. The complexity of the question exceeds, however, the present context.

27. Traverso, 144, 156, is here quoting the historian Michael Schneider. For a much more extensive, detailed, and perhaps also measured treatment of this encounter than Traverso provides, see Herf, *Divided Memory*.

28. Traverso, 154, is alluding here to Saul Friedländer's position on the generations born during and after the war.

29. Two excellent essays on the historians' debate that emphasize with reference to Freudian concepts the sense in which the desire for "normalization" has to do with a refusal of the working-through that is essential to mourning over traumatic loss, are those by Dominick LaCapra, "Representing the Holocaust: Reflections on

the Historians' Debate"; and Eric L. Santner, "History beyond the Pleasure Principle: Some Thoughts on the Representation of Trauma," in Friedländer, ed., *Probing the Limits of Representation*, 108–27 and 143–54, respectively. Neither LaCapra nor Santner focuses on the connection between repetition and modernism per se, however, and when in the same collection Hayden White ("Historical Emplotment and the Problem of Truth," 37–53) argues, interestingly, that the Holocaust can only be represented in a modernist mode, he omits consideration of the sense in which the twentieth-century totalitarianisms belong to the age of modernism mainly, or even only, as the *refusal* to participate in that age.

30. Walser, 17.

31. The combination of echoes of anti-Semitic discourse and absence of explicit anti-Semitic material in Walser's discourse accounts perhaps for the fact that Ignatz Bubis, the leading spokesperson for the Jewish community in Germany, at first characterized Walser discourse as anti-Semitic, and then recanted, under the pressure of a public opinion that he certainly does not control, and perhaps also of his own incapacity to explain to himself exactly how the echoes of anti-Semitism in Walser's discourse were to be situated.

32. In the French Jewish context, Alain Finkielkraut has made an important contribution to the working-through and displacement of a Holocaust-determined Jewish identity in *The Imaginary Jew*.

Works Cited

Adorno, Theodor. *In Search of Wagner*. Trans. Rodney Livingstone. Trowbridge and Esher, Eng.: NLB, 1981.

——. *Versuch über Wagner*. Frankfurt am Main: Suhrkamp, 1952.

Allison, Henry. *Lessing and the Enlightenment: His Philosophy of Religion and its Relation to Eighteenth-Century Thought*. Ann Arbor: University of Michigan Press, 1966.

——. "Lessing's Spinozistic Exercises." In *Lessing Yearbook Supplement: Humanität und Dialog*, 223–33. Detroit: Wayne State University Press, 1982.

Altmann, Alexander. *Die trostvolle Aufklärung. Studien zur Metaphysik und politischen Theorie Moses Mendelssohns*. Stuttgart: Friedrich Frommann Verlag, 1982.

——. *Essays in Jewish Intellectual History*. Hanover and London: University Press of New England, 1981.

——. "Gewissensfreiheit und Toleranz—eine begriffsgeschichtliche Untersuchung." *Mendelssohn Studien: Beiträge zur neueren deutschen Kultur- und Wirtschaftsgeschichte* 4 (1979): 9–46.

——. *Moses Mendelssohn: A Biographical Study*. University: University of Alabama Press, 1973.

——. "Moses Mendelssohn über Naturrecht und Naturzustand." In *"Ich handle mit Vernunft,"* ed. Norbert Hinske, 164–91. Hamburg: F. Meiner Verlag, 1981.

Arendt, Hannah. *Rahel Varnhagen, Lebensgeschichte einer deutschen Jüdin aus der Romantik*. 1959; reprint, München and Zürich: R. Piper, 1981.

Arkush, Allan. *Moses Mendelssohn and the Enlightenment*. Albany: State University of New York Press, 1994.

Auerbach, Erich. "Figura." In *Gesammelte Aufsätze zur romanischen Philologie*, 55–92. Bern and München: Francke, 1967.

——. "Figura." In *Scenes from the Drama of European Literature*, trans. Ralph Manheim, 11–78. Minneapolis: University of Minnesota Press, 1984.

Baeck, Leo. "Besitzt das alte Judentum Dogmen?" *MGWJ* 70 (1926): 225–36.

——. *Judaism and Christianity*. Trans. Walter Kaufmann. Philadelphia: The Jewish Publication Society of America, 1958.

Bahti, Timothy. *Allegories of History*. Baltimore: Johns Hopkins University Press, 1992.

Balmès, François. *Le nom, la loi, la voix. Freud et Moïse: écritures du père 2*. Ramonville Saint-Agne, France: Erès, 1998.

Bamberger, Fritz. "Mendelssohns Begriff vom Judentum." *Korrespondenzblatt des Vereins zur Gründung und Erhaltung einer Akademie für die Wissenschaft des Judentums* 10 (1929): 4–19.

Behler, Ernst. *Die Zeitschriften der Brüder Schlegel. Ein Beitrag zur Geschichte der deutschen Romantik*. Darmstadt: Wissenschaftliche Buchgesellschaft, 1983.

———. "Friedrich Schlegels Theorie des Verstehens: Hermeneutik oder Dekonstruktion." In *Die Aktualität der Frühromantik*, ed. Ernst Behler and Jochen Hörisch, 141–60. Paderborn: Ferdinand Schöningh, 1987.

Beiser, Frederick. *The Fate of Reason: German Philosophy from Kant to Fichte*. Cambridge: Harvard University Press, 1987.

Benjamin, Walter. *Der Begriff der Kunstkritik in der deutschen Romantik, Gesammelte Schriften*, I, 1. Ed. Rolf Tiedemann and Hermann Schweppenhäuser. Frankfurt am Main: Suhrkamp, 1980.

———. *Der Ursprung des deutschen Trauerspiels, Gesammelte Schriften*, I. Ed. Rolf Tiedemann and Hermann Schweppenhäuser. Frankfurt am Main: Suhrkamp, 1963.

Berghahn, Klaus L., ed. *The German-Jewish Dialogue Reconsidered: A Symposium in Honor of George L. Mosse*. New York: Peter Lang, 1996.

Bergman, Shmuel Hugo. *Dialogical Philosophy from Kierkegaard to Buber*. Trans. Arnold Gerstein. Albany: State University of New York, 1991.

Bernstein, Susan. "Journalism and German Identity: Communiqués from Heine, Wagner, and Adorno." *New German Critique* 66 (fall 1995): 65–93.

Biale, David. *Power and Powerlessness in Jewish History*. New York: Schocken, 1986.

Blanchot, Maurice. *The Infinite Conversation*. Trans. and foreword by Susan Hanson. Minneapolis: University of Minnesota Press, 1993.

Bolz, Norbert. "Der aufgegebene Gott." In *Die Aktualität der Frühromantik*, ed. Ernst Behler and Jochen Hörisch. Paderborn: Ferdinand Schöningh, 1987.

Bourel, Dominique, and Jacques Le Rider, eds. *De Sils-Maria à Jerusalem. Nietzsche et le Judaïsme, les intellectuels juifs et Nietzsche*. Paris: Les Éditions du Cerf, 1991.

Boyarin, Daniel. *A Radical Jew: Paul and the Politics of Identity*. Berkeley and Los Angeles: University of California Press, 1994.

Breuer, Edward. "Politics, Tradition, History: Rabbinic Judaism and the Eighteenth-Century Struggle for Civil Equality." *Harvard Theological Review* 85, no. 3 (1992): 357–83.

———. "Rabbinic Law and Spirituality in Mendelssohn's *Jerusalem*." *The Jewish Quarterly Review* 86, nos. 3–4 (January-April 1996): 299–321.

Buber, Martin. *Ich und Du.* 1923; reprint, Heidelberg: Verlag Lambert Schneider, 1983.

Buber, Martin, and Franz Rosenzweig. *Scripture and Translation.* Ed. and trans. Lawrence Rosenwald and Everett Fox. Bloomington: Indiana University Press, 1994.

Carlebach, Julius. *Karl Marx and the Radical Critique of Judaism.* London: Routledge and Kegan Paul, 1978.

Cassirer, Ernst. "Die Idee der Religion bei Lessing und Mendelssohn." *Bulletin des Leo Baeck Instituts* 84 (1989): 5–22.

Conley, Thomas M. *Rhetoric in the European Tradition.* Chicago and London: University of Chicago Press, 1990.

Damrosch, David. "Auerbach in Exile." *Comparative Literature* 47, no. 2 (spring 1995): 97–117.

Dawidowicz, Lucy S. *The Holocaust and the Historians.* Cambridge: Harvard University Press, 1981.

Deibel, Franz. *Dorothea Schlegel als Schriftstellerin im Zusammenhang mit der romantischen Schule.* Berlin: Mayer und Müller, 1905.

de Man, Paul. *Aesthetic Ideology.* Ed. Andrzej Warminski. Minneapolis: University of Minnesota Press, 1996.

———. *Allegories of Reading: Figural Language in Rousseau, Nietzsche, Rilke, and Proust.* New Haven, Conn.: Yale University Press, 1979.

———. *Blindness and Insight: Essays in the Rhetoric of Contemporary Criticism.* Minneapolis: University of Minnesota Press, 1983.

———. *The Resistance to Theory.* Ed. Wlad Godzich. Minneapolis: University of Minnesota Press, 1986.

———. *The Rhetoric of Romanticism.* New York: Columbia University Press, 1984.

Derrida, Jacques. *Adieu, à Emmanuel Levinas.* Paris: Galilée, 1997.

———. *De la grammatologie.* Paris: Éditions de Minuit, 1967.

———. *De l'esprit: Heidegger et la question.* Paris: Galilée, 1987.

———. "Foi et savoir: les deux sources de la «religion» aux limites de la simple raison." In *La religion,* ed. Jacques Derrida and Gianni Vattimo, 9–86. Paris: Seuil, 1996.

———. *Glas.* Paris: Galilée, 1974.

———. "Interpretations at War: Kant, the Jew, the German." *New Literary History* 22 (1991): 39–95.

———. *La dissémination.* Paris: Éditions du Seuil, 1972.

———. *La vérité en peinture.* Paris: Flammarion, 1978.

———. *L'écriture et la différence.* Paris: Éditions du Seuil, 1967.

———. *Le monolinguisme de l'autre, ou la prothèse d'origine.* Paris: Galilée, 1996.

———. *Mal d'Archive.* Paris: Galilée, 1995.

———. *Of Grammatology.* Trans. G. C. Spivak. Baltimore: Johns Hopkins University Press, 1974.

———. *Psyche: inventions de l'autre*. Paris: Galilée, 1987.

———. *Schibboleth, pour Paul Celan*. Paris: Galilée, 1986.

———. *Specters of Marx: The State of Debt, the Work of Mourning, and the New International*. Trans. Peggy Kamuf. New York and London: Routledge, 1994.

———. *Spectres de Marx: l' État de la dette, le travail du deuil, et la nouvelle internationale*. Paris: Éditions Galilée, 1993.

———. *The Ear of the Other: Otobiography, Transference, Translation*. Ed. Christie V. McDonald; trans. Avital Ronell. New York: Schocken, 1985.

———. "Un ver à soie." In *Voiles*, by Jacques Derrida and Hélène Cixous. Paris: Galilée, 1998.

Derrida, Jacques, and Geoffrey Bennington. *Jacques Derrida*. Paris: Éditions du Seuil, 1991.

Derrida, Jacques et al. *Moscou aller-retour*. Paris: de l'Aube, 1995.

Dohm, Christian Konrad Wilhelm von. *Über die bürgerliche Verbesserung der Juden. 2 Teile in einem Band. Im Anhang Franz Reuß' "Christian Wilhelm Dohms Schrift 'Über die bürgerliche Verbesserung der Juden' und deren Einwirkung auf die gebildeten Stände Deutschlands. Eine kultur- und literaturgeschichtliche Studie."* 1781–1783, and 1891; reprint, Hildesheim and New York: Georg Olms Verlag, 1973.

Eichner, Hans. *Friedrich Schlegel*. New York: Twayne, 1970.

Fenves, Peter D. *A Peculiar Fate: Metaphysics and World-History in Kant*. Ithaca, N.Y.: Cornell University Press, 1991.

———. "The Renunciation of Progress in Mendelssohn's *Jerusalem*." Unpublished paper.

Fichte, Johann Gottlieb. *Fichte Werke*. Ed. Immanuel Hermann Fichte. 11 vols. Berlin: Walter de Gruyter and Co., 1971.

Finkielkraut, Alain. *The Imaginary Jew*. Trans. Kevin O'Neill and David Suchoff. Lincoln: University of Nebraska Press, 1994.

Fishbane, Michael. *The Garments of Torah: Essays in Biblical Hermeneutics*. Bloomington: Indiana University Press, 1989.

Fletcher, Angus. *Allegory: The Theory of a Symbolic Mode*. Ithaca, N.Y.: Cornell University Press, 1964.

Fontenay, Élisabeth de. *Les figures juives de Marx*. Paris: Éditions Galilée, 1973.

Foucault, Michel. *Power/Knowledge: Selected Interviews and Other Writings (1972–1977)*. Ed. Colin Gordon; trans. Colin Gordon, Leo Marshall, John Mepham, and Kate Soper. New York: Pantheon, 1980.

Frank, Manfred. *Der unendliche Mangel an Sein: Schellings Hegelkritik und die Anfänge der Marxschen Dialektik*. Frankfurt am Main: Suhrkamp, 1975.

Freud, Sigmund. *Jenseits des Lustprinzips, Studienausgabe*. Vol. III, 215–73. Frankfurt am Main: Fischer, 1982.

———. *Der Mann Moses und die monotheistische Religion: drei Abhandlungen, Studienausgabe*. Vol. IX, 455–584. Frankfurt am Main: Fischer, 1982.

Friedländer, Saul, ed. *Probing the Limits of Representation: Nazism and the "Final Solution."* Cambridge: Harvard University Press, 1992.

Friedrichsmeyer, Sara. *The Androgyne in Early German Romanticism.* New York: Peter Lang, 1983.

Gasché, Rodolphe. "Ideality in Fragmentation." Foreword to Friedrich Schlegel, *Philosophical Fragments,* trans. P. Firchow, vii–xxxii. Minneapolis: University of Minnesota Press, 1991.

Gay, Peter. *A Godless Jew: Freud, Atheism, and the Making of Psychoanalysis.* New Haven, Conn.: Yale University Press, 1987.

Geiger, Ludwig. "Dorothea Veit-Schlegel." *Deutsche Rundschau* 160 (1914): 119–34.

Gilman, Sander L. *Difference and Pathology: Stereotypes of Sexuality, Race, and Madness.* Ithaca, N.Y.: Cornell University Press, 1985.

———. *The Case of Sigmund Freud: Medicine and Identity at the Fin de Siècle.* Baltimore and London: Johns Hopkins University Press, 1993.

———. "'Hebrew and Jew': Moses Mendelssohn and the Sense of Jewish Identity." In *Lessing Yearbook Supplement: Humanität und Dialog,* 67–82. Detroit: Wayne State University Press, 1982.

———. *Jewish Self-Hatred: Anti-Semitism and the Hidden Language of the Jews.* Baltimore and London: Johns Hopkins University Press, 1986.

———. *The Jew's Body.* New York and London: Routledge, 1991.

———. *Smart Jews: The Construction of the Image of Jewish Superior Intelligence.* Lincoln: University of Nebraska Press, 1996.

Goldhagen, Daniel Jonah. *Hitler's Willing Executioners: Ordinary Germans and the Holocaust.* New York: Alfred A. Knopf, 1996.

Grab, Walter. *Der deutsche Weg der Judenemanzipation, 1789–1938.* München: Piper, 1991.

Graff, Gil. *Separation of Church and State: Dina de Malkhuta Dina in Jewish Law, 1750–1848.* University: University of Alabama Press, 1985.

Green, Geoffrey. *Literary Criticism and the Structure of History: Erich Auerbach and Leo Spitzer.* Lincoln: University of Nebraska Press, 1982.

Grimm, Reinhold, and Jost Hermand, eds. *Re-Reading Wagner.* Madison: University of Wisconsin Press, 1993.

Guttmann, Julius. "Die Normierung des Glaubensinhalts im Judentum." *MGWJ* 71 (1927): 241–55.

———. "Mendelssohns *Jerusalem* und Spinozas *Theologisch-Politischer Traktat.*" In *Achtundvierzigster Bericht der Hochschule für die Wissenschaft des Judentums,* 31–67. Berlin: n.p., 1931.

Habermas, Jürgen. *Philosophisch-politische Profile.* Frankfurt am Main: Suhrkamp Verlag, 1971.

———. *Philosophical-Political Profiles.* Trans. Frederick G. Lawrence. Cambridge: MIT Press, 1983.

Hamacher, Werner. "Der Satz der Gattung: Friedrich Schlegels poetologische

Umsetzung von Fichtes unbedingtem Grundsatz." *Modern Language Notes* 95 (1980): 1155–80.

———. *Pleroma—zu Genesis und Struktur einer dialektischen Hermeneutik bei Hegel.* In *Der Geist des Christentums*, by G. W. F. Hegel; ed. W. Hamacher. Frankfurt am Main: Ullstein, 1978.

———. "Position Exposed: Friedrich Schlegel's Poetological Transposition of Fichte's Absolute Proposition." In *Premises: Essays on Philosophy and Literature from Kant to Celan*, by Werner Hamacher; trans. Peter Fenves, 222–60. Cambridge: Harvard University Press, 1996.

Hammacher, Klaus. *Die Philosophie Friedrich Heinrich Jacobis.* München: Wilhelm Fink Verlag, 1969.

———. "Über Friedrich Heinrich Jacobis Beziehungen zu Lessing im Zusammenhang mit dem Streit um Spinoza." In *Lessing und der Kreis seiner Freunde*, ed. Günter Schulz, 51–74. Heidelberg: Verlag Lambert Schneider, 1985.

Hardenberg, Friedrich von (Novalis). *Schriften.* Ed. Paul Kluckhohn and Richard Samuel. 4 vols. Stuttgart: W. Kohlhammer Verlag, 1960.

Hazard, Paul. *La crise de la conscience européenne, 1680–1715.* Paris: Fayard, 1961.

Hegel, G. W. F. *Grundlinien der Philosophie des Rechts, oder Naturrecht and Staatswissenschaft im Grundriße. Werke in zwanzig Bänden.* Vol. 7, ed. Eva Moldenhauer and Karl Markus Michel. Frankfurt am Main: Suhrkamp Verlag, 1970.

———. *Philosophy of Right.* Trans. and ed. T. M. Knox. London: Oxford University Press, 1967.

Heidegger, Martin. *Identität und Differenz.* Pfullingen: Günther Neske, 1957.

Heil, Johannes, and Rainer Erb, eds. *Geschichtswissenschaft und Öffentlichkeit: der Streit um Daniel J. Goldhagen.* Frankfurt am Main: Fischer, 1998.

Heine, Heinrich. *Zur Geschichte der Religion und Philosophie in Deutschland.* In *Heines Werke in fünf Bänden*, vol. 5, ed. Helmut Holtzhauer. Berlin and Weimar: Aufbau Verlag, 1981.

Heinemann, Isaak. "Scientific Allegorization during the Jewish Middle Ages." In *Studies in Jewish Thought: an Anthology of German Jewish Scholarship*, ed. Alfred Jospe, 247–69. Detroit: Wayne State University Press, 1981.

Helfer, Martha B. "Dorothea Veit-Schlegel's *Florentin*: Constructing a Feminist Romantic Aesthetic." *The German Quarterly* 69, no. 2 (spring 1996): 144–60.

Herder, Johann Gottfried. *Schriften zum Alten Testament.* Ed. Rudolf Smend, vol. 5 of *Werke in zehn Bänden*, ed. Günter Arnold et al. Frankfurt am Main: Deutsche Klassiker Verlag, 1993.

Herf, Jeffrey. *Divided Memory: The Nazi Past in the Two Germanies.* Cambridge: Harvard University Press, 1997.

Hertz, Deborah. *Jewish High Society in Old Regime Berlin.* New Haven, Conn., and London: Yale University Press, 1988.

Herz, Henriette. *Berliner Salon. Erinnerungen und Portraits.* Ed. Ulrich Janetzki. Frankfurt am Main and Berlin: Ullstein, 1984.

Hilberg, Raul. *Perpetrators, Victims, Bystanders: The Jewish Catastrophe 1933–1945.* New York: HarperCollins, 1992.

Holborn, Hajo. *A History of Modern Germany, vol. II: 1648–1840.* Princeton, N.J.: Princeton University Press, 1982.

Hollinrake, Roger. *Nietzsche, Wagner, and the Philosophy of Pessimism.* London: George Allen and Unwin Ltd., 1982.

Huch, Ricarda. *Die Romantik: Blütezeit, Ausbreitung, und Verfall.* Tübingen: Rainer Wunderlich Verlag Herman Leins, 1951.

Jacobi, Friedrich Heinrich. "Über die Lehre des Spinoza, in Briefen an den Herrn Moses Mendelssohn." Breslau: Gottl. Löwe, 1785; reprinted in *Die Hauptschriften zum Pantheismusstreit zwischen Jacobi und Mendelssohn,* ed. Heinrich Scholz, 45–282. Berlin: Reuther and Reichard, 1916.

Jacobs, Jack. "Marxism and Anti-Semitism: Kautsky's Perspective." *International Review of Social History,* 30, no. 3 (1985): 400–30.

———. *On Socialists and "the Jewish Question" after Marx.* New York: New York University Press, 1992.

Kampmann, Wanda. *Deutsche und Juden: die Geschichte der Juden in Deutschland vom Mittelalter bis zum Beginn des Ersten Weltkrieges.* Frankfurt am Main: Fischer, 1979.

Kant, Immanuel. *Werkausgabe.* Ed. Wilhelm Weischedel. Frankfurt am Main: Suhrkamp, 1977.

Katz, Jacob. *Jews and Freemasons in Europe 1723–1939.* Cambridge: Harvard University Press, 1970.

———. *Out of the Ghetto: The Social Background of Jewish Emancipation, 1770–1870.* New York: Schocken, 1973.

———. *The Darker Side of Genius: Richard Wagner's Anti-Semitism.* Hanover and London: University Press of New England, 1986.

Kellner, Menachem. *Dogma in Medieval Jewish Thought: From Maimonides to Abravanel.* Oxford: Oxford University Press, 1986.

Klossowski, Pierre. *Nietzsche et le cercle vicieux.* Paris: Mercure de France, 1969.

Körner, Josef. "Mendelsohns Töchter." *Preussische Jahrbücher* 214 (1928): 167–82.

Körte, Mona, and Robert Stockhammer, eds. *Ahasvers Spur: Dichtungen und Dokumente vom "Ewigen Juden".* Leipzig: Reclam Verlag Leipzig, 1995.

Kofman, Sarah. *Le mépris des Juifs. Nietzsche, les Juifs, l'antisémitisme.* Paris: Galilée, 1994.

Krüger, Johanna. *Friedrich Schlegels Bekehrung zu Lessing.* Weimar: Alexander Duncker Verlag, 1913.

Lacan, Jacques. *Écrits.* Paris: Éditions du Seuil, 1966.

Lacoue-Labarthe, Philippe. "L'avortement de la littérature." In *Du féminin,* ed. Mireille Calle, 3–19. Québec: Les éditions le griffon d'argile, 1992.

———. *Le sujet de la philosophie (Typographies 1)*. Paris: Aubier-Flammarion, 1979.

———. *L'imitation des Modernes (Typographies 2)*. Paris: Éditions Galilée, 1986.

———. *Typography: Mimesis, Philosophy, Politics*. Ed. Christopher Fynsk. Cambridge: Harvard University Press, 1989.

Lacoue-Labarthe, Philippe, and Jean-Luc Nancy, eds. *L'absolu littéraire: théorie de la littérature du romantisme allemand*. Paris: Éditions du Seuil, 1978.

———. *Le mythe nazi*. La Tour d'Aigues: Éditions de l'Aube, 1991.

———. *The Literary Absolute: The Theory of Literature in German Romanticism*. Trans. Philip Barnard and Cheryl Lester. Albany: State University of New York Press, 1988.

Lemérer, Brigitte. *Les deux Moïse de Freud (1914–1939). Freud et Moïse: écritures du père I*. Ramonville Saint-Agne, France: Erès, 1998.

Lessing, Gotthold Ephraim. *Nathan the Wise: A Dramatic Poem in Five Acts*. Trans. Bayard Quincy Morgan. New York: Frederick Ungar, 1955.

———. *Werke in drei Bänden*. Ed. Herbert G. Göpfert. 3 vols. München and Wien: Carl Hanser Verlag, 1982.

Levin, David J. *Richard Wagner, Fritz Lang, and the Nibelungen: The Dramaturgy of Disavowal*. Princeton: Princeton University Press, 1998.

Lévinas, Emmanuel. *Autrement qu'être ou au-delà de l'essence*. The Hague: Martinus Nijhoff, 1974.

———. *Noms Propres*. Paris: Fata Morgana, 1976.

———. *The Levinas Reader*. Ed. Seán Hand. Oxford: Basil Blackwell, 1989.

———. *Totalité et infini, Essai sur l' extériorité*. The Hague: Martinus Nijhoff, 1961.

Levy, S. *Das Judentum in der Musik: eine kritisch-historische Betrachtung*. Erfurt: Gutenberg-Druckerei Stolzenberg and Co., 1930.

Librett, Jeffrey S. "Can a Jew Have Feelings?—the Aesthetics of Cultural Suicide in Moses Mendelssohn's *Letters on Sentiments*." In *The Spirit of Poesy: Essays in Honor of Géza von Molnár*, ed. Richard Block and Peter Fenves. Evanston, Ill.: Northwestern University Press, 1998.

———. "Figuralizing the Oriental, Literalizing the Jew: On the Attempted Assimilation of Letter to Spirit in Friedrich Schlegel's *Über die Sprache und Weisheit der Indier*." *The German Quarterly* 69, no. 3 (summer 1996): 260–76.

———. "Humanist Antiformalism as a Theopolitics of Race: F. H. Jacobi on Friend and Enemy." *Eighteenth Century Studies* 32, no. 2 (1998–1999): 233–45.

———. "Interruptions of Necessity: Being Between Meaning and Power in Jean-Luc Nancy." In *On Jean-Luc Nancy*, ed. Darren Sheppard, Simon Sparks, and Colin Thomas, 103–39. London: Routledge, 1997.

———. "Schizotechnotheology in Some Zionist Texts: Melanie Klein and Martin Heidegger in the Promised Land." *The American Journal of Semiotics* X, nos. 3–4 (1993): 27–80.

———. "Vom Spiegelbild zur Unterschrift: Paul de Mans Ideologiebegriff und

Schillers Dramen." In *Asthetik und Rhetorik: Lektüren zu Paul de Man*, ed. Karl Heinz Bohrer, 206–52. Frankfurt am Main: Suhrkamp, 1993.

———. "Writing (as) the Perverse Body in Friedrich Schlegel's *Lucinde*." In *Thinking Bodies*, ed. Juliet Flower MacCannell and Laura Zakarin, 132–40. Stanford, Calif.: Stanford University Press, 1994.

Liepert, Anita. "Der Spinozismus Lessings (1729–1781)." *Deutsche Zeitschrift für Philosophie* 27 (1979): 59–70.

Lowenstein, Steven M. *The Berlin Jewish Community: Enlightenment, Family, and Crisis, 1770–1830*. Oxford: Oxford University Press, 1994.

Luther, Martin. "Ein Sendbrief an den Pabst Leo X: Von der Freiheit eines Christenmenschen (1520)." In *Luthers Werke in Auswahl*, ed. Otto Clemen and Albert Leitzmann, vol. II, 1–28. Berlin: Walter de Gruyter, 1967.

Lyotard, Jean-François. "Lessons in Paganism." In *The Lyotard Reader*, ed. Andrew Benjamin, 122–54. Oxford: Basil Blackwell, 1989.

MacCannell, Juliet Flower. *The Regime of the Brother: After the Patriarchy*. London and New York: Routledge, 1991.

Mahrenholz, Jürgen. "Erwägungen zum Luther- und Marx-Jahr 1983." *Deutsche Studien* 20, no. 80 (December 1982): 395–414.

Mandel, Siegfried. *Nietzsche and the Jews: Exaltation and Denigration*. Amherst, N.Y.: Prometheus Books, 1998.

Manuel, Frank E. *The Broken Staff: Judaism through Christian Eyes*. Cambridge: Harvard University Press, 1992.

Martyn, David. "Borrowed Fatherland: Nationalism and Language Purism in Fichte's *Addresses to the German Nation*." *The Germanic Review* 72 (fall 1997): 303–26.

Marx, Karl. "Luther as Arbiter Between Strauss and Feuerbach." In *Writings of the Young Marx on Philosophy and Society*, trans. and ed. Lloyd B. Easton and Kurt H. Guddat, 93–95. New York: Anchor Books, 1967.

———. "On the Jewish Question." In *Writings of the Young Marx on Philosophy and Society*, trans. and ed. Lloyd D. Easton and Kurt H. Guddat, 216–48. New York: Anchor Books, 1967.

———. "Zur Judenfrage." In *Werke*, by Karl Marx und Friedrich Engels, vol. 1, 347–78. Berlin: Dietz Verlag, 1970.

Mendelssohn, Moses. *Gesammelte Schriften, Jubiläumsausgabe*. Ed. Alexander Altmann et al. Stuttgart: Friedrich Frommann Verlag, 1971–.

———. *Jerusalem, or on Religious Power and Judaism*. Trans. Allan Arkush; Intro. and commentary by A. Altmann. Hanover and London: University Press of New England, 1983.

Menninghaus, Winfried. *Unendliche Verdopplung: die Frühromantische Grundlegung der Kunsttheorie im Begriff absoluter Selbstreflexion*. Frankfurt am Main: Suhrkamp, 1987.

Meyer, Michael A., ed., *German-Jewish History in Modern Times*. Vol. 1 of *Tradition and Enlightenment, 1600–1780*. New York: Columbia University Press, 1996.

———. "Reform Jewish Thinkers and Their German Intellectual Context." In *The Jewish Response to German Culture*, by Jehuda Reinharz and Walter Schatzberg, 64–84. Hanover, N.H.: University Press of New England, 1985.

Michelfelder, Diane P., and Richard E. Palmer. *Dialogue and Deconstruction: The Gadamer-Derrida Encounter*. Albany: State University of New York Press, 1989.

Morgan, Michael L. "Liberalism in Mendelssohn's Jerusalem." *History of Political Thought* 10, no. 2 (summer 1989): 281–94.

———. "Mendelssohn's Defense of Reason in *Jerusalem*." *Judaism* 38 (1989): 449–59.

Mosse, George L. *Germans and Jews: The Right, the Left, and the Search for a "Third Force" in Pre-Nazi Germany*. New York: Howard Fertig, 1970.

———. *Masses and Man: Nationalist and Fascist Perceptions of Reality*. New York: Howard Fertig, 1980.

Newmark, Kevin. "L'absolu littéraire: Friedrich Schlegel and the Myth of Irony." *MLN* 107 (1992): 905–30.

Nietzsche, Friedrich. *Kritische Studienausgabe*. Ed. Giorgio Colli and Mazzino Montinari. München: Deutscher Taschenbuch Verlag, 1988.

———. *The Birth of Tragedy* and *The Case of Wagner*. Trans. Walter Kaufmann. New York: Random House, 1967.

———. *The Antichrist* and *Twilight of the Idols*. Trans. R. J. Hollingsdale. Harmondsworth, Eng., and Baltimore: Penguin, 1968.

Norris, Christopher. *Spinoza and the Origins of Modern Critical Theory*. Oxford: Basil Blackwell, 1991.

Nüsse, Heinrich. *Die Sprachtheorie Friedrich Schlegels*. Heidelberg: Carl Winter Universitätsverlag, 1962.

Oberman, Heiko A. *Wurzeln des Antisemitismus*. Berlin: Severin und Seidler, 1981.

———. *The Roots of Antisemitism in the Age of Renaissance and Reformation*. Trans. James I. Porter. Philadelphia: Fortress Press, 1984.

Patzold, Detlef. "Spinoza-Bilder in der deutschen Aufklärung." *Wissenschaftliche Zeitschrift. Gesellschaftswissenschaftliche Reihe* 37 (1988): 518–26.

Pauley, Bruce F. *From Prejudice to Persecution: A History of Austrian Anti-Semitism*. Chapel Hill and London: University of North Carolina Press, 1992.

Peled, Yoav. "From Theology to Sociology: Bruno Bauer and Karl Marx on the Question of Jewish Emancipation." *History of Political Thought* XIII, no. 3 (autumn 1992): 463–86.

Peters, H. F. *Zarathustra's Sister: The Case of Elisabeth and Friedrich Nietzsche*. New York: Marcus Wiener, 1977.

Poliakov, Léon. *The History of Anti-Semitism*. 3 vols. Trans. Miriam Kochan. New York: Vanguard Press, 1975.

Prantl, Heribert, ed. *Wehrmachtsverbrechen: eine deutsche Kontroverse.* Hamburg: Hoffmann and Campe Verlag, 1997.

Prawer, Siegbert S. "Moses Mendelssohn zwischen Heine und Marx: ein Kapitel deutsch-jüdischer Wirkungsgeschichte." In *Moses Mendelssohn und die Kreise seiner Wirksamkeit,* ed. Michael Albrecht, Eva J. Engel, and Norbert Hinske, 411–30. Tübingen: Max Niemeyer, 1994.

Rabinovitch, Solal. *Écritures du meurtre. Freud et Moïse: écritures du père 3.* Ramonville Saint-Agne, France: Erès, 1998.

Raich, J. M., ed. *Dorothea von Schlegel, geb. Mendelssohn und deren Söhne Johannes und Philipp Veit. Briefwechsel im Auftrage der Familie Veit herausgegeben.* 2 vols., I, 194. Mainz: Franz Kirchheim, 1881.

Ravid, Benjamin. "'How Profitable the Nation of the Jewes Are': The *Humble Addresses* of Menasseh Ben Israel and the *Discorso* of Simone Luzzatto." In *Mystics, Philosophers, and Politicians: Essays in Jewish Intellectual History in Honor of Alexander Altmann,* ed. J. Reinharz et al., 159–80. Durham, N.C.: Duke University Press, 1982.

Röder, Petra. "Von der Frühromantik zum jungen Marx. Rückwärtsgekehrte Prophetie eines qualitativen Naturbegriffs." In *Romantische Utopie, Utopische Romantik,* ed. Gisela Dischner and Richard Faber, 149–73. Hildesheim: Gerstenberg, 1979.

Roetzel, Lisa C. "Introductory Essay: Feminizing Philosophy." In *Theory as Practice: A Critical Anthology of Early German Romantic Writings,* ed. Jochen Schulte-Sasse et al., 361–81. Minneapolis: University of Minnesota Press, 1997.

Rose, Paul Lawrence. *Revolutionary Antisemitism in Germany from Kant to Wagner.* Princeton, N.J.: Princeton University Press, 1990.

———. *Wagner: Race and Revolution.* New Haven, Conn., and London: Yale University Press, 1992.

Rosenzweig, Franz. *Das Büchlein vom gesunden und kranken Menschenverstand.* Düsseldorf: J. Melzer, 1964.

———. *Der Stern der Erlösung.* Frankfurt am Main: Suhrkamp Verlag, 1976.

Rotenstreich, Nathan. *Jews and German Philosophy: The Polemics of Emancipation.* New York: Schocken, 1984.

———. *The Recurring Pattern: Studies in Anti-Judaism in Modern Thought.* London: Weidenfeld and Nicolson Ltd., 1963.

Santaniello, Weaver. *Nietzsche, God, and the Jews: His Critique of Judeo-Christianity in Relation to the Nazi Myth.* Albany: State University of New York Press, 1994.

Santner, Eric L. *My Own Private Germany: Daniel Paul Schreber's Secret History of Modernity.* Princeton, N.J.: Princeton University Press, 1996.

Schlegel, Dorothea. *Camilla: A Novella, Collected Writings in Eleven Volumes.* Vol. II, Introd. Hans Eichner; trans. Edwina Lawler. Lewiston, N.Y.: Edwin Mellen Press, 1990.

———. *Florentin: A Novel, Collected Writings in Eleven Volumes.* Vol. I, translated, annotated, and introduced by Edwina Lawler and Ruth Richardson. Lewiston, N.Y.: Edwin Mellen Press, 1988.

———. *Florentin. Roman, Fragmente, Variationen.* Ed. and with an Afterword by Liliane Weissberg. Frankfurt am Main and Berlin: Ullstein, 1986.

Schlegel, Friedrich. *Kritische Friedrich Schlegel Ausgabe.* Ed. Ernst Behler, Jean-Jacques Anstett, and Hans Eichner. München and Paderborn: Verlag Ferdinand Schöningh, 1960.

Schleiermacher, Friedrich Daniel Ernst. "Über die Religion. Reden an die Gebildeten unter ihren Verächtern." *Kritische Gesamtausgabe,* ed. Hermann Fischer et al., vol. I, 12, ed. Günter Meckenstock. Berlin and New York: Walter de Gruyter, 1995.

Schmidt, Gilya Gerda. *Martin Buber's Formative Years: From German Culture to Jewish Renewal, 1897–1909.* Tuscaloosa: University of Alabama Press, 1995.

Schmitt, Carl. *Römischer Katholizismus und politische Form.* Stuttgart: Ernst Klett Verlag, 1984.

Scholem, Gershom. *Judaica 1.* Frankfurt am Main: Suhrkamp, 1963.

———. *Judaica 2.* Frankfurt am Main: Suhrkamp, 1970.

———. *Judaica 3: Studien zur jüdischen Mystik.* Frankfurt am Main: Suhrkamp, 1970.

———. *On Jews and Judaism in Crisis: Selected Essays.* Ed. Werner J. Dannhauser. New York: Schocken, 1976.

———. *The Messianic Idea in Judaism.* New York: Schocken, 1971.

———. *Zur Kabbala und ihrer Symbolik.* Frankfurt am Main: Suhrkamp, 1973.

Schopenhauer, Arthur. *Parerga und Paralipomena: kleine philosophische Schriften.* In *Sämtliche Werke,* vol. 6, ed. Arthur Hübscher. Wiesbaden, Germany: Brockhaus, 1972.

———. *Parerga and Paralipomena: Short Philosophical Essays.* Trans. E. F. J. Payne. Oxford: Clarendon Press, 1974.

Schwab, Raymond. *The Oriental Renaissance: Europe's Rediscovery of India and the East, 1680–1880.* Trans. Gene Patterson-Black and Victor Reinking. New York: Columbia University Press, 1984.

Seyhan, Azade. *Representation and Its Discontents: The Critical Legacy of German Romanticism.* Berkeley and Los Angeles: University of California Press, 1992.

Shandley, Robert R., ed. *Unwilling Germans? The Goldhagen Debate.* Trans. Jeremiah Riemer. Minneapolis and London: University of Minnesota Press, 1998.

Shell, Marc. *Children of the Earth: Literature, Politics, and Nationhood.* New York and Oxford: Oxford University Press, 1993.

Sluga, Hans. *Heidegger's Crisis: Philosophy and the Politics of Nazi Germany.* Cambridge: Harvard University Press, 1993.

Snow, Dale Evarts. "F. H. Jacobi and the Development of German Idealism." *Journal of the History of Philosophy* 25 (1987): 397–415.

Sorkin, David. *Moses Mendelssohn and the Religious Enlightenment.* Berkeley and Los Angeles: University of California Press, 1996.

———. *The Transformation of German Jewry, 1780–1840.* Oxford: Oxford University Press, 1987.

Strohschneider-Kohrs, Ingrid. "Lessings letzter Brief an Moses Mendelssohn. Text und Kontext." In *Disiecta Membra. Studien. Karlfried Gründer zum 60. Geburtstag,* ed. Odo Marquard, 53–65. Basel: Schwabe, 1989.

———. "Lessing und Mendelssohn im Dialog des letzten Lebensjahrzehnts. 1770–1781." *Deutsche Vierteljahrschrift für Literaturwissenschaft und Geistesgeschichte* 3 (1987): 419–40.

Suneson, Carl. *Richard Wagner und die indische Geisteswelt.* Trans. from Swedish by Gert Kreutzer. Leiden: E. J. Brill, 1989.

Susman, Margarete. *Frauen der Romantik.* 1929; reprint, Köln: Melzer, 1960.

Tal, Uriel. *Christians and Jews in Germany: Religion, Politics, and Ideology in the Second Reich, 1870–1914.* Trans. Noah Jonathan Jacobs. Ithaca, N.Y., and London: Cornell University Press, 1975.

Talmage, Frank. "Apples of Gold: The Inner Meaning of Sacred Texts in Medieval Judaism." In *Jewish Spirituality from the Bible through the Middle Ages,* ed. Arthur Green, 313–55. New York: Crossroad, 1986.

Taubes, Jacob. *Die Politische Theologie des Paulus.* Ed. Aleida Assmann and Jan Assmann. München: Wilhelm Fink Verlag, 1993.

Thornton, Karin Stuebben. "Enlightenment and Romanticism in the Work of Dorothea Schlegel." *The German Quarterly* 39 (1966): 162–73.

Touaillon, Christine. *Der deutsche Frauenroman des 18. Jahrhunderts.* Vienna and Leipzig: Wilhelm Braumüller, 1919.

Traverso, Enzo. *The Jews and Germany: From the "Judeo-German Symbiosis" to the Memory of Auschwitz.* Trans. Daniel Weissbort. Lincoln and London: University of Nebraska Press, 1995.

Wagner, Richard. "Das Judenthum in der Musik." In *Gesammelte Schriften und Dichtungen,* vol. 5, 85–108. Leipzig: E. W. Fritsch, 1872.

———. "Das Judenthum in der Musik." In *Neue Zeitschrift für Musik* 33, nos. 19–20 (1850): 101–12.

———. *Gesammelte Schriften und Dichtungen.* Vol. 8. Leipzig: E. W. Fritzsch, 1873.

———. *Judaism in Music and Other Essays.* Trans. William Ashton Ellis. Lincoln: University of Nebraska Press, 1995.

Walser, Martin. *Erfahrungen beim Verfassen einer Sonntagsrede. Friedenspreis des Deutschen Buchhandels 1998.* Frankfurt am Main: Suhrkamp, 1998.

Walzel, Oskar. *German Romanticism.* Trans. Alma Elise Lussky, 91–102. New York: Frederick Ungar, 1965.

Wapnewski, P. "Nietzsche und Wagner. Stationen einer Beziehung." *Nietzsche-Studien* 18 (1989): 401–23.

Weil, Kari. *Androgyny and the Denial of Difference.* Charlottesville: University of Virginia Press, 1992.

Weiner, Marc A. *Richard Wagner and the Anti-Semitic Imagination.* Lincoln and London: University of Nebraska Press, 1995.

Weissberg, Liliane. *Geistersprache: philosophischer und literarischer Diskurs im späten achtzehnten Jahrhundert.* Würzburg: Königshausen und Neumann Verlag, 1990.

Wessell, Leonard P., Jr. "Marx's Romantic Poetry and the Crisis of Romantic Lyricism." *Studies in Romanticism* 16 (fall 1977): 509–34.

Wiener, Max. "Jüdische Frömmigkeit und religiöses Dogma." *Monatsschrift für Geschichte und Wissenschaft des Judentums* 67 (1923): 153–67.

Wolfson, Murray. *Marx: Economist, Philosopher, Jew: Steps in the Development of a Doctrine.* New York: St. Martin's Press, 1982.

Yerushalmi, Yosef Hayim. *Freud's Moses: Judaism Terminable and Interminable.* New Haven, Conn.: Yale University Press, 1991.

Yovel, Yirmiyahu. *Spinoza and Other Heretics: The Adventures of Immanence.* Princeton, N.J.: Princeton University Press, 1989.

———. *Spinoza and Other Heretics: The Marrano of Reason.* Princeton, N.J.: Princeton University Press, 1989.

Zac, Sylvain. *Spinoza en Allemagne: Mendelssohn, Lessing, et Jacobi.* Paris: Méridiens Klincksieck, 1989.

Zammito, John H. *The Genesis of Kant's Critique of Judgment.* Chicago: University of Chicago Press, 1992.

Zumbini, M. Ferrari. "Nietzsche in Bayreuth: Nietzsches Herausforderung, die Wagnerianer und die Gegenoffensive." *Nietzsche-Studien* 19 (1990): 246–91.

Index

In this index an "f" after a number indicates a separate reference on the next page, and an "ff" indicates separate references on the next two pages. A continuous discussion over two or more pages is indicated by a span of page numbers, e.g., "57–59." *Passim* is used for a cluster of references in close but not consecutive sequence.

Cultural Memory | in the Present